TYPOLOGICAL STUDIES IN LANGUAGE (TSL)

A companion series to the journal "STUDIES IN LANGUAGE"

Honorary Editor: Joseph H. Greenberg
General Editor: T. Givón

Volumes in this series will be functionally and typologically oriented, covering specific topics in language by collecting together data from a wide variety of languages and language typologies. The orientation of the volumes will be substantive rather than formal, with the aim of investigating universals of human language via as broadly defined a data base as possible, leaning toward cross-linguistic, diachronic, developmental and live-discourse data. The series is, in spirit as well as in fact, a continuation of the tradition initiated by C. Li *(Word Order and Word Order Change, Subject and Topic, Mechanisms for Syntactic Change)* and continued by T. Givón *(Discourse and Syntax)* and P. Hopper *(Tense and Aspect: Between Semantics and Pragmatics).*

Volume 3

T. Givón (ed.)

TOPIC CONTINUITY IN DISCOURSE:
A QUANTITATIVE CROSS-LANGUAGE STUDY

TOPIC CONTINUITY IN DISCOURSE:
A QUANTITATIVE CROSS-LANGUAGE STUDY

edited by

T. GIVÓN
Linguistics Department
University of Oregon, Eugene
and
Ute Language Program
Southern Ute Tribe
Ignacio, Colorado

JOHN BENJAMINS PUBLISHING COMPANY
Amsterdam/Philadelphia

1983

TABLE OF CONTENTS

TOPIC CONTINUITY IN DISCOURSE: AN INTRODUCTION

T. GIVÓN
Linguistic Department
University of Oregon, Eugene

and

Ute Language Program
Southern Ute Tribe
Ignacio, Colorado

TABLE OF CONTENTS

1. The 'topic' strand: Micro traditions

The intuition, expressed under whatever terminology, which lead to shifting the attention of the linguist from the purely structural notion of 'subject' toward the more discourse-functional notion of 'topic', or under some other guises 'theme', may be traced back to a number of sources, among which I find myself disinclined to apportion historical primacy. The sources most of us who became involved with the renascent 'topic movement' in the early nineteen seventies tended — and still tend — to cite more often were either the Prague School (cf. Firbas, 1966a, 1966b), the Firthian tradition (cf. Halliday, 1967) or Bolinger (1952, 1954). In one form or another, the various strands of this tradition tended to divide sentences ('clauses') into two distinct components, one of them the 'focus' ('rheme', 'comment', 'new information'), the other the 'topic' ('theme', 'old information'). And it was the second, the topic, which all early practitioners would then link to discourse structure, communicative intent, communicative dynamism, functional sentence perspective etc., in ways that tended to be often both vague and mysterious.[1]

In the early 1970's, when a number of us became involved in studying the phenomena of 'topic' and 'subject' (cf. Hawkinson and Hyman, 1974, Li,(ed.) 1976, *inter alia*), we tended to incorporate uncritically our predecessors' view of 'topic' as an *atomic, discrete* entity, a single constituent of the clause. When we worried about the relation between 'topic' and 'subject', in one way or another we gravitated toward viewing the subject as *grammaticalized topic* (cf. Givón, 1976a), And some of us went further and proposed typologies, whence 'topic prominent languages' exhibited paucity in such grammaticalization, while 'subject prominent language' displayed richer grammaticalization of 'topic'; which soon turned out to mean *morphologization* (cf. Li and Thompson, 1975). But already then, there was a range of rather recalcitrant data which suggested that, at least at the functional level, 'topic' was not an atomic, discrete antity. One could consider, for example, the commonplace phenomena of R- and L-dislocation, as in:

(1) a. *L-dislocation*: *John, we* saw *him* yesterday
  b. *R-dislocation*: *We* saw *him* yesterday, *John*
  c. *Simplex*: *We* saw *John* yesterday

In both (1a,b) above, the conventional wisdom went, 'John' is the topic. But then, what was the status of the subject 'we'? Obviously, the clause could have more than one 'topic', one grammaticalized as 'subject', the other of a different status yet to be elucidated.

The problem is further compounded when the dislocated constituent is coreferential with the grammatical subject, as in:

(2) a. *L-dislocation*: *John, he* came yesterday
    b. *R-dislocation*: *He* came yesterday, *John*

Here the same argument is both 'topic' and 'subject'. Is it carrying a *double function*? What function? how defined?

Just as disturbing were the data concerning dative-shifting ('promotion to direct object'), when it became clear (cf. Givón, 1975, 1979, Ch. 4, further expanded in Givón, 1981a; see also Shir, 1979) that the direct object is also, in some clear way demonstrable by both syntactic and discourse-pragmatic tests, a 'topic' case in the sentence, albeit perhaps a *secondary grammaticalized topic*, as against the *primary* one, the subject. So that in sentences such as:

(3) a. *John* gave *the book* to *Mary*
    b. *John* gave *Mary the book*

there existed actually three different 'topics', perhaps hierarchized by *degree*. But degree of what? Importance? Topicality?

The data pertaining to the relation between 'topic', 'definite NP', 'pronoun', 'agreement' and 'zero anaphora' were not intially considered overly damaging to the concept of topic as a functional *prime*. Eventually, however, their import was bound to sink in. Consider, for example, the various expressions of the subject-topic NP in the following:

(4) a. ...(he came in) and $\emptyset$ sat down... (zero anaphora)
    b. ...(he came in;) *he* then sat down... (unstressed pronoun)
    c. ...(she came in;) then *hé* joined her... (stressed pronoun)
    d. ...(the woman came in;) then *the man* joined her... (definite NP)
    e. ...*now the man, he* never joined... (L-dislocated NP)

In each example in (4), the italicized NP is subject, topic and definite. In each, however, it seems to perform a different discourse function. But how defined? And how related to 'topic' or 'topicality'?

Several things had then become evident, and received less than consistent expression in some of my own earlier excursions into the subject:

(a) We were dealing with a non-discrete entity of 'topicality', or at best a multi-point scale (cf. Givón, 1975, 1976a, 1976b); or perhaps

(b) We were dealing with a functional dimension – or a number of dimensions – for which the notion 'topicality' was rapidly losing explanatory power.

Experimenting with labels of greater functional (and hopefully psychological) import, I toyed briefly with 'degree of presuppositionality' (Givón, 1978, 1979 ch. 2), which translated itself rather naturally via 'degree of backgroundiness' into degree of *predictability* and thus *continuity* of topic NP's. And those in turn translate, at least eventually when all the empirical dust is raised and then allowed to settle, into a performance dimension of *topic accessibility* (cf. Givón 1978, 1979 Ch. 2). This is, in brief, one strand of the antecedence of this volume. Like other myopic views of a tapestry yet to be completed, it remains to some extent parochial.[2]

2. The 'paragraph' strand: Macro traditions

The *clause* ('sentence') is the basic information processing unit in human discourse. A word may have 'meaning', but only the proposition – grammaticalized as clause – carries information. Human discourse, further, is *multipropositional*. Within it, chains of clauses are combined into larger thematic units which one may call *thematic paragraphs* (cf., under various terminological guises, Longacre 1976, 1979, Hinds 1979, Chafe 1979, *inter alia*). These may further combine into larger yet discourse units (such as 'paragraphs', 'sections', 'chapters', 'parts' or 'stories'). The thematic paragraph is the most immediately relevant level of discourse within which one can begin to discuss the complex process of *continuity in discourse*.

There are, broadly, three major aspects of discourse continuity which are displayed in or mediated through the thematic paragraph, and which in turn receive structural/grammatical/syntactic expression within the clause. These three continuities thus bridge the gap between the *macro* and *micro* organizational levels of language.

(a) Thematic continuity
(b) Action continuity
(c) Topics/participants continuity

While this volume deals primarily with the most concrete of the three, (c), the three are nontheless deeply interconnected within the thematic paragraph.

Thematic continuity is the overall matrix for all other continuities in the discourse. It is the hardest to specify, yet it is clearly and demonstrably there. Statistically, it coincides with topic and action continuity to quite an extent within the thematic paragraph. The thematic paragraph is *by definition* about the same theme. Most *commonly* it also preserves topic and action continuity. However, topics/participants may change within the discourse without *necessarily* changing either action continuity or theme continuity. And action continuity may change without *necessarily* changing thematic continuity. One is perhaps justified in viewing the three as an *implicational hirarchy* (or 'inclusion set'):

(5)   THEME > ACTION > TOPICS/PARTICIPANTS

Finally, since the 'theme' is the most nebulous, *macro*-oriented entity out of the three, it is only to be expected that its structural expression in the 'grammar' is the most weakly coded.[3] Thematic continuity is most commonly coded — if at all — via conjunction or clause-subordination particles in the SVO or VSO typology (of, say, English), or via verb-final or clause-chain final suffixes in the strict SOV typology (of, say, Japanese or the New Guinea Highlands).

Action continuity pertains primarily to *temporal sequentiality* within thematic paragraph, but also to temporal *adjacency* therein. Most commonly, within a thematic paragraph actions are given primarily in the natural sequential order in which they actually occured, and most commonly there is small if any temporal gap — or pause — between one action and the next.[4] In the grammar/ syntax, which is primarily (though not exclusively) a clause-level coding instrument, action continuity receives its expression strongly and universally via the tense-aspect-modality sub-system most commonly attached to the verbal word (cf. Hopper, 1979, Givón, 1977, 1982a, 1983, ch. 8).

The functional domain of topic/participant continuity is the main concern of this volume. It is linked to the thematic paragraph in a statistically significant but not absolute fashion: Within the thematic paragraph it is most common for one topic to be the continuity marker, the *leitmotif*, so that it is the participant *most crucially involved* in the action sequence running through the paragraph; it is the participant most closely associated with the higher-level 'theme' of the paragraph; and finally, it is the participant most likely to be coded as the *primary topic* — or *grammatical subject* — of the vast majorty of sequentially-ordered clauses/sentences comprising the thematic paragraph. It is thus, obviously, the most *continuous* of all the topics mentioned in the various clauses in the paragraph. The grammatical sub-system which codes clause-level topics, or the structural correlates of the *functional domain* of topic identification, topic maintenance and topic continuity in discourse, are the main focus of the various studies in this volume.

3. *Major topic functions within the thematic paragraph*

If the thematic paragraph is indeed a chain of equi-topic clauses, i.e. a string of clauses whose *main/primary* topic remains the same, then one could perceive an initial division of main topics into three major types according to their position within the paragraph. One would, further, expect the grammar/syntax to code these three main functions in some fashion. The three are:

(a) *Chain initial topic*:
    (i) Characteristically a newly-introduced, newly-changed or newly-returned topic; thus
    (ii) Characteristically a *discontinuous* topic in terms of the *preceding* discourse context; but
    (iii) Potentially — if an important topic — a rather *persistent* topic in terms of the *succeeding* discourse context.

(b) *Chain medial topic*:
    (i) Characteristically a *continuing/continuous* topic in terms of the preceding discourse context; and also
    (ii) Characteristically *persistent* — but *not maximally* so — in terms of the *succeeding* discourse context, even when an important topic.

(c) *Chain final topic*:
    (i) Characteristically a *continuing/continuous* topic in terms of the preceding discourse context; but
    (ii) Characteristically a *non-persistent* topic in terms of the *succeeding* discourse context, even if an important topic.

As we shall see further below, these general, indeed almost *a priori* consideration, are intimately involved in the kind of predictions one may make concerning the discourse behavior of various topic-marking devices, as well as the type of measurements one may devise to identify them.

4. *The discourse file: Topic availability to the hearer*

Linguists traditionally deal with the binary distinction between definite and indefinite, with the former marking topics which the speaker assumes the hearer can identify uniquely, is familiar with, are within his file (or *register*) and thus *available* for quick retrieval. On the other hand, indefinites are presumably topics introduced by the speaker for the first time, with which the hearer is not familiar, which therefore are not available to the hearer readily in his file, and for which he thus has to open the initial *file.*

In terms of the topic functions within the thematic paragraph, section 3. above, one may say that paragraph-medial (b) and paragraph-final (c) topics must both be *definite*. But paragraph initial topics may be either *definite* (already identified to the hearer at some prior time, by whatever means) or *indefinite.* If the discourse file has psychological reality as an internal filing system, it is legitimate to ask whether it is a *permanent* file — long term memory — or a *temporary* file — short term memory, or perhaps a *double* filing system involving both. When the structural/syntactic/morphological coding system of a language codes strongly the definite/indefinite distinction, that constitutes one type of evidence supporting the existence of a permanent file. On the other hand, when the coding system of the language treats in the same fashion indefinite topics introduced for the first time and definite topics brought back into the discourse register after a considerable gap of absence, that constitutes some evidence for the register being a short-term, *temporary* file, where a gap of absence of a certain length precipitates *erasure* from the file. As we shall see throughout this volume, languages present syntactic and discourse evidence in support of *both* filing systems.

There is enough cross-language evidence, further, to suggest that some important topics are in the file permanently, and are thus always available to speakers/hearers as part of their *generic* firmament. These are most typically unique important features of the universe, such as the sun, the moon, the world etc. They are also inalienably possessed body parts ('my head') or kinship terms ('my mother'). And they are most typically names ('Johnny'). What one observes about these permanently-filed topics and their discourse behavior is that they are *much less predictable* than other definite topics in terms of their position within the thematic paragraph. They thus often constitute exceptions to the text measurements that reveal the rules which govern the discourse distribution of topics that are not filed as permanently and as uniquely.

5. *Factors affecting topic availability*

The discourse measurements performed in the various studies in this volume are derived from certain assumptions concerning what may reasonably affect the *degree of difficulty* that speakers/hearers may experience in *identifying* a topic in discourse, i.e. in filing it appropriately in their internal register, so that predications or new information transmitted about those topics would in turn be *addressed* correctly. The major factors are listed as follows:

(a)   *Length of absence from the register*: If a topic is indefinite and thus introduced for the first time, it is *maximally difficult* to process, by definition, since a new file has to be opened for it. If a topic is definite and returns to the register after a long gap of absence, it is still difficult to process. The shorter is the gap of absence, the easier is topic identification; so that a topic that was there in the preceding clause is by definition *easiest* to identify and file correctly.

(b)   *Potential interference from other topics*: If no other topics are present in the immediately preceding discourse environment, i.e. the short-term eresable file, topic identification is *easiest*. The more other topics are present in the immediate register, the more *difficult* is the task of correct identification and filing of a topic, especially if those other topics qualify semantically (in terms of their 'selectional restrictions') for the *role* within the clause which the topic in question occupies.

(c)   *Availability of semantic information*: Especially when other topics clutter the immediate register and may thus create potential interference and difficulties in topic identification, the availability of so-called 'redundant' semantic information within the clause in question may play an important role in facilitationg topic identification. This information comes primarily from the *predicate* of the clause, less so from verb-phrase *adverbials* (in particularly of manner), less so from other *topics/participants* of the clause. This information concerns *generic probabilities* that a particular topic could participate in the clause in the specific semantic/grammatical role in question (i.e. as subject, agent, patient, recipient etc.).

(d)   *Availability of thematic information*: Much like generic semantic information about permanent likelihoods, thematic information available from the preceding discourse could help in topic identification — especially when other topics in the register may potentially interfere. Such information establishes *specific probabilities* — for this story, in this chapter, in this section or in this thematic paragraph — as to the topic identification within a particular clause and in a particular role. It also establishes, for particular discourses, some ranking

of *importance* of the various topics/ participants, and thus affects their behavior
in terms of the *permanent file*, at least as pertaining to the particular discourse.

The discourse measurements developed in this study are based at least in part
on the four factors outlined above. In particular, we have attempted to assess
the more concrete and more readily measurable factors (a) and (b). The fact
that it is not yet possible to quantify rigorously factors (c) and (d) in spite of
their undeniable importance creates a certain degree of *indeterminancy* in the
results, so that correlations between grammatical devices and particular measurements appear to be *less than categorial.* They are nevertheless dramatic, with
residues that are important but not devastating. The role of semantic and
thematic information in topic identification is going to remain an imponderable
for a while, toghether with the more elusive role of personality and memory of
speakers and hearers, their specific life experience and the more subtle assumptions they make about each other and their respective abilities to identify
referents specifically as well as in general. That our correlations are as strong as
they are merely suggests that over large bodies of texts of rather diverse types,
the role of the less obvious factors affecting the grammar of topic identification
is less than dominant, while the role of the more easily measurable factors is in
some sense decisive.[5]

6. *Discourse measurements of topic continuity*

So far I have talked primarily in terms of topic availability or identification.
The approach pursued in this volume is to some extent speaker-hearer neutral,
but nevertheless is couched in terms of assumptions that the speaker makes
about topic-availability to the hearer. The transition from "availability" or
"identifiability" to the more neutral "continuity" is motivated by certain assumptions concerning gestalt psychology:

(6) a.   "What is continuing is more predictable"
     b.   "What is predictable is easier to process"
           or conversely
     c.   "What is discontinuous or disruptive is less predictable"
     d.   "What is less predictable, hence surprising, is harder to process"

Since our measurements are performed on *texts* rather than on speakers or
hearers, assumptions such as (6) are fundamental in a certain chain of reasoning
and empirical justification. The text itself does not reveal the assumptions

made by speakers or hearers as to topic identifiability in a direct way, nor does it reveal the ease or difficulty they experience in processing and filing topics in discourse. The text reveals, however, two types of information which in this study we have endeavored to correlate:

(i)   The grammatical, 'purely linguistic' devices used by the speaker to code various topics/participants in the discourse; and
(ii) The exact position of those topics in the discourse, in terms of thematic paragraph structure, distance from last previous appearance, the clustering with potential other interfering topics, persistence in subsequent discourse context.

Hopefully, once stable, strong and cross-linguistically viable correlations are established between these two types of information available to the linguist in his/her capacities of grammarian and discourse analyst, one may proceed to the obvious next step, that of correlating the grammatical and discourse-distribution data with *psycho-linguistic* experimentation and measurement.

In the following sub-sections I will describe briefly the three main discourse measurements to which texts were subjected in this study. Previous works attempting to treat these topics cross-linguistically were either devoid of quantification or did not attempt to impose the same methodology across the sample of languages and topics (see eg. Hinds, ed., 1978 or Givón, ed., 1979, *inter alia*). This study is thus quite an extent unique, although it clearly draws on inspired guesses, intuitions and insights gained from previous and less rigorous work.

6.1. *Referential distance ('look-back')*

This measurement assesses the gap between the previous occurence in the discourse of a referent/topic and its current occurence in a clause, where it is marked by a particular grammatical *coding device*. The gap is thus expressed in terms of *number of clauses to the left*. The minimal value that can be assigned is thus *1 clause*, which is maximally continuous. Since it is impossible to deal adequately with infinity, and since there are grounds for suspecting that the erasable, *short-term* file is the crucial psychological correlate of this measurement,[6] one must impose a maximal integer on topics whose referential gap exceeds certain range. In this study I have chosen to impose that arbitrary upper bounds at *20 clauses* to the left. When a topic does not appear within that range, the value of 20 is automatically assigned and scanning discontinued. This means that *referential indefinite* topics are assigned this maximal value by definition.

'Presence in the register' at some preceeding point is not necessarily overt, but may also be represented by a *zero anaphore*, provided the topic/referent is indeed a *semantic argument* of the predicate of the clause.

6.2. *Potential interference ('ambiguity')*

This measurement assesses the disruptive effect which other referents within the immediately preceding register may have on topic availability or identification within a clause. In order to minimize an obvious correlation with referential distance,[7] the "immediately preceding register" was defined arbitrarily as *between 1 and 5 clause to the left,* most commonly *3 clauses* to the left in the studies in this volume. This is based on the assumption that if a topic has already occupied a dominant/continuous position and umambiguous identification within the last 3 clauses in the register, the presence of other, potentially-interfering topics further away in the preceding register does not interfere as significantly with the task of topic identification.[8]

This measurement was further mitigated by the factor of semantic compatibility with the predicate of the relevant clause: An interfering topic was counted only if it was just as *semantically compatible* (most commonly in terms of animacy, humanity, agentivity or semantic plausibility as object or subject) with the predicate of the clause as the topic under consideration. This measurement thus combines an assessment of both factor (b) and (c) in section 5., above, although (c) is probably less dominant.

If no potentially interfering referent was found within the relevant distance, the value of 1 was assigned. If one or more referents were found within the relevant distance, the value of 1 was assigned. Only in some of the studies, higher values — commonly not exceeding 3 — were assigned.

6.3. *Persistence ('decay')*

The first two measurements outlined above relate in an obvious fashion to our postulated 'continuity' and 'identifiability'. Both involve the *preceding* discourse context; both would hopefully correlate, in some fashion, to the hearer's task of identifying referents and filing them in the register. Our third measure, that of topic persistence in *subsequent* discourse, is of a different kind. Most directly it is a reflection of the topic's *importance* in the discourse, and thus a measure of the *speaker's* topical intent. We will accept as self-evident, by definition, the assumption that:

(7) "More important discourse topics appear more frequently in the register,
i.e. they have a higher probability of persisting longer in the register after
a relevant measuring point".

Assumption (7) also justifies, at least in part, treating topics that are highly
continuous in terms of low referential distance as *potentially* important discourse topics. But as will be shown shortly, this correlation is not as strong.

In this study, we measure persistence in terms of the number of clauses to
the right — i.e. in subsequent discourse from the measured clause — in which the
topic/participant continues an *uninterrupted presence* as a *semantic argument*
of the clause, an argument of whatever *role* and marked by whatever *grammatical
means*. The minimal value that can be assigned is thus *zero*, signifying an argument that *decays immediately*, i.e. of the *lowest* persistence. There is no
maximal value assigned *by definition* in this case.

As one could guess following the discussion of thematic paragraphs and equi-
topic chains in section 3. above, there is a partially predictable relation between
our measures of referential distance (6.1.) and persistence (6.3.). This relation,
as pertaining to topics of relatively *high importance* in the discourse, may be
given as in (8) below:

(8)

topic position within paragraph	referential distance	persistence
initial	high (low continuity)	high (high continuity)
medial	low (high continuity)	medium (medium continuity)
final	low (high continuity)	low (low continuity)

7. *The grammatical coding of topic continuity*

7.1. *Preliminaries: Functional domains and syntactic coding*

In the approach to the study of human language pursued here, it is a fundamental assumption that there exists a systematic correlation between message
and code. That the correlation is never perfect is a fact that those of us endeav-
oring to study the use of language in communication — rather than its structural

properties in the artificial medium of isolated 'sentences' — have had to learn to live with, appreciate and slowly come to understand. The syntactic coding of discourse function, which is the bulk of the functional correlates to syntax[9] — is imperfect but geared for a certain efficiency of processing, whereby the loss accruing in the cause of efficient processing is to a large extent offset by the omnipresence of the discourse context, refering particularly to:

(a)   *Generically shared* knowledge coded in the culturally shared lexicon and known semantic likelihoods;

(b)   *Specifically shared* knowledge of the *particular discourse*, what was said earlier and various inferences thereof including verbal or non-verbal feedback;

(c)   *Specifically shared* knowledge of the particular *speaker and hearer*, what they know or tend to assume about each other, their respective knowledge, motivation and propensities, *not* excluding possible telepathy, however unlikely on general grounds.

Context thus plays a crucial role in allowing syntax to be an efficient processing device while retaining — when one ignores context — a less-than-perfect correlation between code and message (for further discussion see Givón, 1979, Ch. 5, 1982b).

As can be easily gathered from the preceding section, the area of topic identification in discourse is a complex *functional domain* rather than a simple 'function'. This is indeed typical of syntactic coding in general (cf. Givón, 1981b, 1983). If the complex functional domain under scrutiny here is provisionally termed "*degree* of topic accessibility", then it is clear that at least in some respect we are dealing here with a *scalar*, graded continuum. Such functional domains are quite common in language, both in the message realms of lexicon, propositional semantics and discourse pragmatics (see discussion in Givón, 1980a, in reference to the semantics of verb complementation). Along a scalar functional domain, different languages may use varying number of *coding points*, i.e. syntactic devices — comprising of word-order, morphology, intonation or their possible combinations. Some language may either *over-code* or *under-code* the entire domain or sub-segments of it. This possibility may be schematically represented as in:

(9) *coding points:*

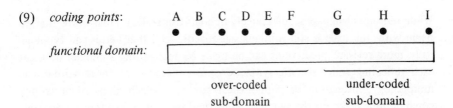

To the extent that there exists any language-internal and cross-language predictability as to what coding devices ('syntactic constructions') are more likely to code what relative portions of the scalar domain, the coding points in (9) must represent an *implicational hierarchy.* One may not predict the coding *density* in any particular language, nor whether a particular language will *actually have* a particular coding device, nor even the *exact* functional point on the scale (or exact boundaries of a sub-section) to be coded by a particular device. One could, however, predict with extreme accuracy that within any particular language the *relative order* of the coding points along the scale would be maintained. And thus that if a certain device X codes a certain functional point (or sub-section) of the domain, a certain device Y could only code a higher point on the domain, but never a lower point. This is indeed one of the most stable results demonstrated by this cross-language study.

7.2. Scales in the coding of topic accessibility

In earlier discussions of the syntactic coding of topic accessibility, I was inclined to take for granted that indeed we deal here ultimately with a single though complex scale, thus ranking the most common grammatical devices involved — cross-linguistically — in coding this domain along the following scale (cf. for example Givón, 1978, 1979, 1981b, 1982c):

(10) *most continuous/accessible topic*

zero anaphora
unstressed/bound pronouns or grammatical agreement
stressed/independent pronouns
R-dislocated DEF-NP's
neutral-ordered DEF-NP's
L-dislocated DEF-NP's
Y-moved NP's ('contrastive topicalization')
cleft/focus constructions
referential indefinite NP's

most discontinuous/inaccessible topic

While our cross-language studies largely upholds this scale, it is clear now that, to begin with, the scale is still too language-specific, and that better and typologically more relevant predictions can be made by recognizing a number of scales each reflecting some specific syntactic *coding means* — be those word-order, morphology, intonation or phonological size[10] — which alone or in various combinations make up the syntactic constructions that code our scalar domain. The discerning reader should detect by now the rather ambitious goal we have set ourselves: To define, in a preliminary but cross-linguistically stable fashion, the basic principles of *iconicity* underlying the syntactic coding of the topic identification domain.

7.2.1. *The scale of phonological size*

As is transparent from the overall scale in (10) above, the following sub-scale exists in the grammar of topic identification:

(11)   *more continuous/accessible topics*

     zero anaphora
     unstressed/bound pronouns ('agreement')
     stressed/independent pronouns
     full NP's

more discontinuous/inaccessible topics

The inconicity principle underlying this scale must be simple:

(12)   "The more disruptive, surprising, discontinuous or hard to process a topic is, the more *coding material* must be assigned to it"

In turn, this may translate into a relatively sane psychological and indeed motor-behavior principle:[11]

(13)   "Expend only as much energy on a task as is required for its performance"

The coding scale in (11) is only one expression of our phonological size scale. Another involves *stress*, and may be given in the following three sub-hierarchies:

(14)   a.   stressed pronouns > unstressed pronouns
     b.   cleft/focus NP's > non-focus NP's
     c.   Y-moved NP's > non-Y-moved NP's

In each case in (14), the more heavily stressed device to the left is used to code more discontinuous/inaccessible topics than the device to the right. And stress is merely one type of phonological material.

Finally, at least some studies in this volume[12] demonstrate that NP's modified by restrictive modifiers code more discontinuous/less accessible topics than unmodified NP's. This must be a reflection of the phonological size scale, since obviously a modification increases the size of the NP.

7.2.2. The word-order scale

The gross overall scale in (10) presents already one prediction concerning the use of word-order to code topic continuity, i.e. the relative position of R-dislocation vs. L-dislocation. These two devices pertain to languages with *rigid word-order*, such as English (SVO) or Japanese (SOV). They are further found only in the informal, unplanned colloquial register of such languages (cf. Keenan, 1977, Givón, 1979, ch. 5). The specific scalar prediction in such languages is thus:

(15) R-dislocation > neutral word-order > L-dislocation

whereby the left-most on the scale codes more continuous topics, the right-most more discontinous ones. This scale is corroborated by the results reported here for colloquial English (Givón, in this volume) as well as by the results obtained in Givón (1982d) for Pidgin English spoken by Philippine (VO) and Korean (VO/OV)/ speakers in Hawaii. In addition, in languages with pragmatically-controlled flexible word-order, such as Spanish (SV/VS), Biblical Hebrew (SV/VS) or Ute (SV/VS, OV/VO), in this volume, a clearly related scale is evident:

(16) a.   VS > SV
      b.   VO > OV

The scales in (15) and (16) are quite transparently one and the same, and may be given as pertaining to the relative position of the topic vs. the comment, following Givón (1982d), as:

(17)   COMMENT-TOPIC > TOPIC-COMMENT

again with the left-most element in each implicational scale coding more continuous topics, the right-most less continuous ones.

In order to demonstrate beyond a shadow of doubt the fundamental sameness of the word-order scales (15), (16) and (17), I would like to cite the numerical results pertaining to *referential distance* taken from several studies in this volume as well as from Givón (1982d). The results are presented in Table I, below.

While the numerical values are not always the same, the relative ranking is amazingly consistent, with *topic-comment* orders in each case showing higher average referential distance values than *comment-topic* orders.

Finally, following Givón (1982d), it is possible to integrate the size universals in section 7.2.1. with the word-order universals in this section into a single implication scale:

(18)   COMMENT > COMMENT-TOPIC > TOPIC-COMMENT > TOPIC
         (zero topic)   (zero comment)

One may then go on to suggest that the most obvious topics receive their coding as *zero*, the least obvious topics receive their coding as *topic repetition* (zero comment), and the *comment-topic* and *topic-comment* orders are merely the intermediate-/coding points between those two extremes. The whole scale thus abides by one simple psychological principle:

(19) "Attend first to the most urgent task"

When the topic is most obvious, making the comments is surely a more urgent task. When the topic is less obvious, establishing it is more urgent. In Pidgins and spoken registers (see Givón, 1982d as well as Givón's Spoken English paper, in this volume), when the topic is least available, thus most problematic, topic repetition is the preferred coding device.

The last comment to be added here is that both Y-movement (contrastive topicalization) and cleft-focus can be considered instances of more discontinuous/surprising topic constructions where the topic is placed to the left of the comment. Most commonly the source of the surprise/disruption here is either referential distance or the presence of other referents, as well as some element of *counter expectation*.

7.2.3. *The scale of roles and animacy*
     To many of us (cf. Hawkinson and Hyman, 1974, Givón, 1976a, *inter*

TABLE I: Correlation between Referential Distance
and Word-Order
[definite NP's]

	AVERAGE REFERENTIAL DISTANCE		
DATA SOURCE (i) Dislocations	TOPIC-COMMENT L-DISLOCATION SV or OV	NEUTRAL ORDER (IF ANY)	COMMENT-TOPIC R-DISLOCATION VS or VO
Philippino-English Pidgin (Givón, 1982d) [subject NP only]	16.20	8.00	1.00
Korean-English Pidgin (Givón, 1982d) [object NP only]	15.8	(11.86/8.23)	1.00
Spoken English (Givón, in this volume) [subject NP only]	15.35	10.15	1.00
(ii) Variation (a) Object			
Korean-English Pidgin (Givón, 1982d)	11.86	/	8.23
Ute (Givón, in this volume)	9.67	/	4.46
(b) Subject Ute (Givón, in This volume)	13.31	/	1.48
Spanish-English Pidgin (Givón, 1982d)	13.00	/	3.42

Spoken Spanish
(Bentivoglio, in
this volume
  unmodified NP:
  modified NP:
	
	3.41
	9.24
		
		/
		/
			
			1.00
			7.53

Biblical Hebrew (Fox, in this volume)	8.47	/	4.83

alia) the hierarchy of the case-roles was our first acquaintance with the scalar concept of topicality. The semantic or grammatical case-roles, pending on one's orientation at the time, seemed to exhibit different propensities for becoming the 'topics' of clauses. The semantically based case-role hierarchy may be given as:

(19) AGT > DAT/BEN > ACC > OTHERS

Almost all languages[13] have a grammaticalized subject case-role, singled out by word-order, morphology, intonation or their combination(s). Most though perhaps not all languages have some grammatical manifestations of a *direct-object*, which I have argued elsewhere (Givón, 1979, Ch. 4 and more comprehensively in Givón, 1981a) is a "secondly topic" of clauses, with the subject then being the "primary topic". In most languages the coding of the direct object involves word-order, with the more topical direct object most commonly *preceding* all other objects. In a sub-set of languages, such word-order coding is also accompanied by a morphological coding, most commonly assigning the *morphologically-unmarked* form of the *accusative* to "promoted" direct object (which are semantically not accusative), but occasionally (cf. Nez Perce, see Rude, 1982) also by assigning *marked* accusative morphology to "promoted" direct objects. If one recognizes the direct object as a secondary topic, then the case-role hierarchy may be also expressed as a hierarchy of *grammatical* cases:

(20)   SUBJ > DO > OTHERS

This hierarchy does not contradict the semantic-role hierarchy in (19), but rather incorporates it, given the following universal tendencies of human discourse:

(a) Agents tend to be made the clausal *subjects* in discourse; and
(b) When dative/benefactive objects are present, they tend to be promoted either obligatorily or in high frequency to *direct object* (see discussion in Givón, 1981a).

One strand running through all the papers in this study is a massive substantiation and amplification of both topic hierarchies, at least so far as the higher topicality of *subjects* and *human/animate/agents* is concerned. Unfortunately, the sample of languages involved does not allow us as comprehensive a treatment of the topicality status of the direct object, except in one paper (Cooreman, Chamorro) and there somewhat indirectly. What is shown there is that the *anti-passive* construction in Chamorro, which typically *demotes* accusatives from their DO status, also renders them of the *lowest* topicality, in terms of two of our continuity measures, referential distance and persistence. Further quantitative support of the same type may also be found in Rude (forthcoming), where a similar treatment is given to various grammatical constructions in Nez Perce. The cumulative effect of all these quantified studies is to demonstrate explicitly what exactly one means by the higher topicality of subjects vs. objects and direct objects vs. all other objects.

7.3. *Topicality and passive vs. active*

Two studies in this volume, Fox (Biblical Hebrew) and Cooreman (Chamorro) deal with the topicality of passives vs. active. In general, in languages where the passive is really a passive (rather than an incipient Ergative, see discussion in Givón, 1981b as well as text-studies in Hopper and Thompson, 1982 and Fox, 1982), the text frequency of passives is much much lower than that of actives, somewhere between 5-20 percent of all main, affirmative, declarative clauses (for text counts in English ses Givón, 1979, Ch. 2 and for Biblical Hebrew, Fox, in this volume). This by itself tags the passive as a *discontinuous* device in discourse, by virtue of its rarity. In addition, our measures also show that the subjects of passives tend to be more discontinuous than the subjects of active. To some extent, however, this is a function of *text-rarity* of passives.

Cooreman's study of Chamorro (in this volume), takes a somewhat different direction, showing that the topicality of non-agent — by our measurements — is much higher when they are subjects (of the passive) than when they are objets (of the middle-voice or Ergative constructions). And it is the lowest, as indicated above, when they appear in the anti-passive.

While the passive is a complex, multi-dimentional functional domain (Givón, 1981b), it is clear that one of its dimensions overlaps, to quite an extent, with our domain of topic continuity and topic identification.

7.4. *Topic continuity and main vs. subordinate clauses*

The conventional wisdom in many discourse studies (see eg. Givón, 1977, 1979, Ch. 2, Hopper, 1979, *inter alia*) used to be that main clauses carry the bulk of sequentially-ordered new information in discourse, and various subordinate clauses may carry discontinuous, non-sequential background information. While this is certainly true in some language types (cf. Biblical Hebrew, Givón,

1977), it is hardly the whole story. And in fact, one type of so-called subordinate clause, *non-finite* or *participial* ones, tend to be used — often in long *clause chains* — as a typical subject/topic continuity device. Some examples may be brought from English to illustrate this potential:

(21) *Purpose clauses:* I did it *to attract attention*
(22) *Participials:* a. *Having finished*, he left
b. *Working hard and fast*, he managed to plug the hole

One may argue that these examples are 'localized' and 'grammaticalized', but the total predictability of the identity of the subject, which not accidentally is marked by *zero*, is clearly an example of the coding of high topical continuity. Further, one could show that the devices in (22) could easily render English a true clause-chaining language. Thus consider:

(23) *Working* hard and not *getting* anywhere, trying again and again, *marshalling* all her ingenuity and internal resources yet *finding* the going rougher and rougher and *getting* progressively more frustrated, she finally conceded the obvious and gave up.
(24) *Having seen* the product and *having decided* to cancel the order, but *having* then *had* a change of heart, he took the day off.

While clause-chaining is a stylistic option in English (as well as in Amharic, see Gasser, in this volume), in some languages it is the main — perhaps only — expressive vehicle in continuous discourse. In languages such as English or Amharic, where other stylistic venues are open, non-finite clause-chaining usually involves obligatory *equi-subject* (equi-topic) conditions. In languages with no other stylistic alternative, while at the text-frequency level equi-subject predominates inside clause-chains, special provisions are made for switch-subject — switch reference — within such chains. As an example, consider the following passage from Chuave (Thurman, 1978):

(25) a. . . .meina i ne-*ro*
money get eat-SS
'. . . (I) took the money
b. ena tekoi u-*re*
then again come-SS
then (I) came back

c.   iki moi-i-*koro*,
house be-I-DS
and I stayed home,

d.   tekoi u boi-n-*goro*,
again call out-he-DS
so then he sent for me again,

e.   inako de-*ro*
return leave-SS
and so (I) came back

f   fu-i-*goro*
go-I-DS
and I went there

g.   tokoi numba lin-lin numba-i naro-∅-m-e.
again number one-one number-that give-PAST-he-DECLAR
and again he made me foreman (of the work-line)'.

Of the entire passage above, only the final clause (25g) is finite in the sense of being marked for tense-aspect-modality and speech-act value. The SS (same subject) and DS (different subject) markers are obligatory in the non-finite chain which precedes, and they are *anticipatory* — alerting the hearer to subject change in the *following* clause. Two other characteristics of these markers are of interest. First, the SS marker is phonologically *smaller* than the DS marker. In some related languages (cf. Haiman, 1980) the SS is *zero* and the DS a phonologically-realized suffix. Further, in each case where the DS suffix is used above, the subject — about to be changed — is marked overtly with a pronoun. But when the SS suffix is used the subject — more predictable — is marked by *zero*. These, I believe, are fairly transparent reflections of our phonological size iconicity principle (12), above.

7.5. *Referential-indefinite NP's and existential-presentative devices*

As suggested earlier, referential-indefinite NP's, being introduced into the discourse for the first time, should be considered maximally surprising/disruptive/discontinuous, at least as far as their continuity vis-a-vis the *preceding* discourse context is concerned. In addition, however, one could study them instructively as to their *persistence* properties, which would then indicate their potential topical/thematic importance in the subsequent discourse. Grammatical devices may then be categorized according to whether they are used to introduce into the register important, persistent topics or unimportant and fast-decaying ones. Some of the studies in the volume have clear bearing on this. For example, Fox (Biblical Hebrew) shows that if one introduces a referential indefinite argument into the register at the *accusative object* position, it decays much faster than if one introduces it as an indefinite-referential *subject*, typically with the SV word-order. Human indefinite subjects persist on the average *2.90 clauses* after first being introduced, while human indefinite direct objects persist on the average only *0.83 clauses* after entry into the register.

In other languages (cf. Hetzron, 1971, but see also Givón, 1978 for further discussion) it is not the SV but rather the VS word order that tends to be a *presentative* device, introducing important topics into the register in *subject* position. Such languages tend to be *rigid word-order* languages, most commonly SVO, such as English or Mandarin (see Li and Thompson, 1975), where the post-verbal order is used to introduce indefinites into the register. In languages with flexible, pragmatically controlled wordorder, such as Ute (for both subject and object) and Biblical Hebrew (for the subject only), the word-order principles outlined earlier above (section 7.2.2.) holds, and the *pre*-verbal position is used to introduce idefinite into the register.

Another theme that often runs through the grammatical coding of referential-indefinites is the use of morphological means normally reserved for marking logically *non-referential* NP's for coding referential NP's of *lesser importance* as they enter the register. I have identified this device elsewhere for languages using the numeral 'one' to mark referential-indefinites as well as languages using other devices to affect the same contrast (Givón, 1978, 1981c). As an example consider the following from Israeli Hebrew:[14]

(26) a.   . . . az atsárti ba-xanút ve-kaníti itón-*xad* ve-hitxálti
             so I-stopped at-the-store and-I-bought paper-*one* and-I-started
      '. . . so stopped by the store and I bought *this one paper* and I began
             li-kró *oto* ve-hayá *sham* maamár-xad norá meanyén *ve-ha-itón
             kulo*. . .
             to-read *it* and-was *there* article-one very interesting *and-the-
             paper all-of-it*
             to read *it* and *it* had a very interesting article and *the entire
             paper*. . .'

      b.   . . . az atsárti ba-xnút ve-kaníti itón-∅ ve-haláxti ha-báyta
             so I-stopped at-the-store and-I-bought *paper* and-I-went home
      '. . . so I stopped by the store and go a paper and I went home

ve-axálti másheu ve-axár-kax haláxti lishón. . .
and-I-ate something and-after-that I-went to-sleep
and I ate something and then I went to sleep. . .'

In both (26a) and (26b) 'paper' is logically referential. However, in (26a) it turns out to be an important, persistent topic in the discourse, and it is marked by the numeral 'one'. In (26b), however, the actual referential identity of the apper is only incidental; it decays rapidly, it retains no import in the discourse, the speaker merely did some 'paper-buying'. So in spite of being logically refe-iential[15], 'paper' appears with no morphological marking.

7.6. *Topic continuity and definite-marking morphology*

While most of the studies in this volume largely skirt around this complex issue, one must point out that in many language various "topic marking particles", be they prefixal as in Lahu (Matisoff, 1975) and Lisu (Li and Thompson, 1976) or suffixal as in Korean, (Hwang, 1982) or Japanese (Hinds, in this volume), play various role in the grammatical coding of topic continuity, in terms of referential distance, persistence, emphatic contrast (in the presence of other referents) etc. Similarly, in English (Linde, 1979), Dutch (Kirsner, 1979), Persian (Mahootian, 1979) and many others (Givón, 1978) demonstrative articles/pronouns assume similar functions, often developing into definite and indefinite articles of various kinds.

7.7. *The use of restrictive modifiers*

Restrictive modifiers, such as adjectives and relative clauses, very clearly are involved in the grammar of topic continuity, and at least one study in this volume (Bentivoglio, colloquial Spanish) documents their behavior in terms of both our referential distance and potential interference measurements (see section 7.2.1. as well as Table I, above).

8. *The studies in this volume*

Without casting the fine details in cement, we have attempted to follow the same quantitative methodology and the same general approach in all the studies in this volume. While the selection of particular languages to be studied was not by itself completely systematic, we have attempted to insure a reasonable typological balance in the areas of the grammar that count most heavily in the coding of topic continuity: Word-order typology and morpho-tactics. In this section I will briefly survey the studies included in this volume, touching upon what seems to be the salient typological variables involved in the grammatical coding of topic continuity.

8.1. *Japanese*: This is a study of a rigid SOV languages with suffixal case-marking, post-nominal topic-marking particles (-ga, -wa) and a relative paucity of clitic-pronoun/verb-agreement morphology, and thus an extensive use of zero anaphora, with independent pronouns being largely contrastive. The possibility of clause-chaining is present but not fully investigated here, remaining a stylistic option in Japanese.

8.2. *Amharic*: Equally rigid as an SOV language, Amharic has the rich pronominal/agreement morphology of Semitic. It has a mix of prefixal and suffixal case-marking morphology, excluding the subject and indefinite direct object. It also exhibits a number of topic-marking suffixes which are clearly not of Semitic origin. Finally, clause-chaining is a stylistic option that is well documented here.

8.3. *Ute*: An ex-SOV Uto-Aztecan language with complete word-order flexibility controlled by the pragmatics of topic-continuity, Ute exhibits suffixal cas-marking that interacts, for subject and direct object, with the noun-gender suffixes and the grammar of referentiality. Clitic pronouns/agreement are optional for both subject and direct object, but are much more extensively used for objects. Further, their position is not fixed on the verb (though statistically the verbs in discourse carry most clitics), but rather they cliticize on the first word in the clause. Zero anaphora in predominant for subjects, less so for objects. Various topic-marking particles, including demonstratives, are used but not studied here.

8.4. *Biblical Hebrew*: This ancient Semitic language is rigidly VO but shows a pragmatically-controlled VS/SV variation. Subject agreement/clitic pronoun is obligatory, but not for direct objects. Independent pronouns are contrastive for subjects of verbal forms but could be also anaphoric for subjects of non-verbal predicates as well as for direct objects. Zero anaphora is a minor phenomenon, for objects only.

8.5. *Colloquial Spanish*: Typologically very close to Biblical Hebrew, except that it is already gravitating toward rigidification of SVO. As a result, while some VS/SV variation controlled by topic-continuity pragmatics is exhibited, its extent is smaller that in BH. And the 'presentative' VS word-order — totally absent from BH — is already evident here.

8.6. *Written English*: A rigid SVO language, with unstressed pronouns used anaphorically, in effect like clitics, but also a stylistic option of zero anaphora, primarily for subjects. The same pronouns when stressed are used contrastively. Clause-chaining is a stylistic option but probably of limited currency.

8.7. *Colloquial English*: The same typological characteristics as above. However, the colloquial variety exhibits the use of L- and R-dislocation as well as topic repetition and hesitation as topic-marking devices sensitive to the discourse-pragmatics of topic continuity/predictability.

8.8. *Hausa*: A rigid SVO Chadic language, with an extensive agreement/pronominal morphology roughly of the BH or Spanish type. The use of zero anaphora is thus attested but limited to objects, and even there not statistically extensive.

8.9. *Chamorro*: A fairly rigid V-first language that nevertheless allows highly contrastive/discontinuous NP's — primarily subjects — to be moved pre-verbally (thus an SVO variant), a situation that is fairly characteristic of the V-first languages of the Austronesian family. Further, it is an old Ergative language, with the ERG/ABS contrast manifested primarily on the verb-agreement (clitic pronouns) paradigm. This study is divided into two:
(I) A study paralleling the rest of the papers in this volume; and
(II) A study, using only the measures of referential distance and persistence, documenting the behaviour of the five constructions which can code transitive sentences in Chamorro,
   (a)   Agentless passive
   (b)   Agented passive
   (c)   Middle-voice active
   (d)   Ergative active
   (e)   Anti-passive active

in terms of the topic-continuity properties — hence topicality — of the subject and direct object of clauses. The results are exciting both methodologically and substantively, allowing for the first time a rigorous, discourse-based definition of a mature 'surface' Ergative language. Novel uses of the messurement methodology developed in this volume are thus revealed.

   The major typological hole in this collection, so far as the goals of its editor

are concerned, is the absence of a study of a language with a clear "promo-
tional" direct object case that is *pragmatic* rather than purely semantic (i.e.
'accusative') (Givón, 1981a). Indirectly the Chamorro study, part II, bears on
this area, since the anti-passive may be considered as "demotion" of the direct
object (most commonly also its total deletion from the surface text). We hope
to supplement this with an ongoing study of Nez-Perce, which has both the
"promotion" and "demotion" phenomena (Rude, 1982, Rude, forthcoming).

9. *Typological predictions in the grammar of topic continuity*

In this section I will outline the kind of typological predictions that one
could project out of the studies in this volume taken together. While many of
the details are yet to be worked out, a number of solid correlations seem to be
emerging. I will deal with them in order.

9.1. *Zero anaphora, pronouns and agreement*

In terms of the functional domain of topic continuity, as defined most
firmly by our measurements of *referential distance* and *potential interference*,
one could identify three major coding points covering this section of the continuum of topic accessibility. They may be defined functionally with both no-
tional labels as well as our measurements, with point A being the most continuous, point B intermedaite and point C the least continuous:

(27)

	A	B	C
overall continuity:	highest	intermediate	lowest
topic continuity:	high	high	low
theme continuity:	high	intermediate	low
ave. ref. distance:	1.00	1.00-1.20	1.70-2.00
ave. interference:[16]	1.00	1.00	close to 2.00

In terms of how individual languages code these three semi-discrete sections of
the continuum, one observes the following generalizations:
(a)   All languages code point C — the most discontinuous of the three — with
      stressed independent pronouns. They are used either contrastively or as
      topic switchers.
(b)   In languages with *obligatory verb agreement* — most commonly pertaining
      to the subject — (cf. Biblical Hebrew, Amharic, Hausa, Spanish) — those
      clitic pronouns/agreement will code both points A and B.

(c) In languages such as English or Ute, where *unstressed/clitic pronouns*[17] are not obligatory, a three way division tends to be observed for the coding of *subjects*:

  (i) Stressed/independent pronouns code point C
  (ii) Unstressed/clitic pronouns code point B
  (iii) Zero anaphora codes point A

However, there is probably a strong quantitative difference between Ute and English in terms of the relative frequency of zero anaphora vs. unstressed pronouns: In Ute subjects are coded in discourse primarily by *zero anaphora*, while in English probably primarily by *unstressed pronouns.*[18]

For *objects* the situation is different, so that in both Ute and English the coding distribution is:

  (i) Stressed/independent pronouns code point C
  (ii) Unstressed/clitic pronouns code both points B and A

(d) Given the generalizations in (c) above, one could make a *markedness prediction* concerning the *coding density* of subjects, direct objects and obliques: "A language may never have more coding points on the topic continuity functional domain to code a case-role that is *lower* on the topicality hierarchy". In other words, subjects may exhibit more coding points than DO's, and DO's more than obliques, but not vice versa. This is a reflection of the old notion of *functional load.*

(e) Languages without unstressed pronouns – such as Japanese, Korean and Mandarin (cf. Li and Thompson, 1979) – will exhibit the following coding distribution:

  (i) Stressed pronouns code point C
  (ii) Zero anaphora codes points B and A

(f) Non-finite forms of verbal clauses, either with or without *genitive subject* ('agreement'), will on the whole code point A, much like zero anaphora. However, this is relevant only for *subject* topics, a restriction that again relfects the markedness prediction give in (d) above.

9.2. *Word-order variation and dislocations*

The use of word-order devices to code topic continuity obviously pertains to a much more *discontinuous* section of the topic continuity scale, involving either independent pronouns or full NP's, both already highly discontinuous devices. Typologically, one could divide languages into two separate groups here.

9.2.1. *Languages with rigid word-order*
　　　This category will include, of the languages studied in this volume:
　　　　　SVO: English, Hausa
　　　　　SOV: Japanese, Amharic
　　　　　VSO: Chamorro
For all these languages, Y-movement and dislocations are attested, at least to some extent, although they are most clearly attested in SVO languages. The *neutral* word-order has an overall continuity value somewhere between the two extremes of pre-verbal ordering (L-dislocation, Y-movement) and post-verbal ordering (R-dislocation). The three specialized ('marked') devices may be described via the same parameters as in (27) above.

(28)

	R-dislocation	*Y-movement*	*L-dislocation*
overall continuity:	high	low	low
topic continuity:	high	low	low
theme continuity:	high	high	low
ave. ref. distance:	1.00-2.00	2.00-3.00	above 15.00
ave. interference:	1.00-1.50	2.00	1.50-1.75

The three devices may thus be characterized as:

(i)　*Y-movement*: Relatively *localized* in terms of ref. distance, with the discontinuity/surprise due primarily to *contrast* with other referents in the immediately-preceding discourse environment, thus exhibiting high potential interference;

(ii)　*L-dislocation*: Used to return topics back into the register over long gaps of absence, thus high ref. distance, and also consequently fairly high potential interference values; often associated with *major thematic breaks* in discourse structure, i.e. typically a *paragraph-initial* device.

(iii)　*R-dislocation*: This is the 'hegde strategy', Hyman's (1975) 'afterthought topic', with topic-discontinuity a bit higher than that characteristic of unstressed/clitic pronouns, and probably due more to *potential interference* than to ref. distance.

In addition, some more specific predictions can be made concerning the likely distribution of these three word-order devices:

(a)　*SVO language* tend to exhibit all three devices, in addition to cleft which is also a pre-verbal movement and highly contrastive;

(b)   *SOV languages* tend to exhibit primarily R-dislocation as a distinct 'move-ment rule', since the neutral position of nominal topics is pre-verbal. The cleft-focus position quite often is fixed *immediately preceding the verb*. Y-movement is most commonly handled by *stress* with or without added topic-marking *morphology*. The function covered elsewhere by L-dislocation is most commonly handled by topic-marking *morphology*;

(c)   *VSO languages* most commonly allow left-movement (pre-verbal ordering) only for highly *contrastive* functions such as cleft-focus, L-dislocation and Y-movement. The functions performed elsewhere by R and L-dis-location are most commonly handled by either topic/case-marking *mor-phology*, including passivization (cf. Philippine languages), but may also involve word-order changes *on the right* of the verb

9.2.2. *Languages with pragmatically-flexible word-order*

The three languages in our sample which display pragmatically-controlled word-order — Ute, Biblical Hebrew and Spanish — are hierarchized in terms of the scope of this phenomenon, with Ute displaying complete flexibility of both subject and object position, Biblical Hebrew complete flexibility of only the subject position (and rigid VO for the object), and Spanish a much more restric-ted flexibility of only the subject, which is on its way to becoming — at least in colloquial Spanish — a rigidly held pre-verbal element (i.e. SVO). This hier-archy, which is probably a *diachronic* cline[19], is another reflection of the markedness prediction given in section 9.1. above, whereby a particular prag-matic device has a wider scope of application for the *main* topic — subject — than for the secondary topic.

In a language with pragmatically-controlled word-order flexibility, the pre-verbal position of NP's covers a wide range of *discontinuity*, including what in a strict SVO language would be L-dislocation and Y-movement (with the latter distinguished most commonly by stress). While the post-verbal position covers an equally wide range, including probably both the 'neutral' word-order (cf. the proportionately high frequency of the VS word-order in both Ute and Biblical Hebrew) and R-dislocation. One may thus say that a pragmatically-flexible language is *undercoded* in the functional domain of topic continuity, at least as far as the use of word-order is concerned, as compared to (at least) a rigid SVO language. This relationship may be schematically expressed as:

(29)   *rigid SVO*: L-disloc. Y-movement neutral w.o. R-dislocation

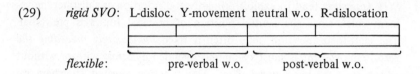

        flexible: pre-verbal w.o.   post-verbal w.o.

It is quite likely, however, that the coding slack is picked up in a flexible word-order language by various topic-marking, definitizing and indefinitizing morphemes.

9.3. *Indefinites and existential-presentative constructions*

As both Ute and Biblical Hebrew demonstrate, the pre-verbal position of the topic (SV in both, OV in Ute) is used in a flexible word-order language not only to code discontinuous definite topics, but also to mark *referential indefinite* topics. On the other hand, Spanish, which is gravitating toward rigidification of SVO, already employs the so-called *existential-presentative* VS word order to introduce indefinite *subjects* into the register for the first time. This is a typical case of "markedness reversal",·and may be summarized schematically (excluding V-first languages) as:

(30)   rigid word-order   flexible word-order

	rigid word-order	flexible word-order
neutral/ unmarked/ continuous	SV	VS
indefinite subject	VS	SV

In V-first languages an existential-presentative construction with the verb 'be' may be used, but at least in some of them (Philippines) the subject must then be fronted, a grammatical operation that is reserved for the *most discontinuous* topics, such as Y-movement and cleft. Thus, consider the following from Bikol:[20]

(31) a.   *DEF-subject*: nag-gadán 'ang-laláke ning-kandíng
                           AGT-kill   TOP-man   ACC-goat
                           'The man killed a goat'

b. *INDEF-subject*: marái 'ang-laláke na nag-gadán   ning-kandíng
                     be   TOP-man   SUB AGT-kill ACC-goat

$\left\{\begin{array}{l}\text{'There's a man who killed a goat'}\\\text{'A man killed a goat'}\end{array}\right\}$

One may of course argue that (31b) represents two separate sentences, the first one with the verb 'be' being the "presentative" sentence, the second being a relative clause. While historically that may be true, the argument may hinge on pure terminology. Within the presentative "sentence" itself, indeed one observes a VS word-order, characteristic of rigid word-order SVO and SOV languages. However, the verb *marái* 'be' is completely *neutralized* in terms of verb morphology (see predictions to this effect in Givón, 1976a), so that one may just as easily call it an "indefinite subject morpheme". Further, semantically the verb 'kill' in (31b) still carries the bulk of the predicate information. And with respect to that verb, the indefinite subject *is* placed at a pre-verbal position. One may thus conclude that in V-first languages, where the order VS is the *neutral* order for highly *continuous* definite subjects, the same relative word-order contrast is observed as for flexible word-order languages in (30). Which obviously makes sense in terms of *coding differentiation.*

9.4. *Topic continuity and morphology*

At this point it is probably premature to make typological prediction concerning the exact role of various morphological sub-systems in the marking of topic continuity in discourse. Many such sub-systems obviously interact in intricate ways with word-order, intonation and our quantity universals in coding this rich functional domain. I have surveyed many of them elsewhere (Givón, 1978), and at this point one might simply list the main categories that tend to be involved cross-linguistically:

(a) Definite and indefinite articles
(b) Demonstratives/deictics
(c) Case-markers and other "topic markers"[21]
(d) The verb 'be'/'exist' or some similar lexeme[22]

NOTES

1) 'Vague' and 'mysterious' are neither synonymous nor necessarily linked in a causal fashion. Under a more charitable reading of 'vague', hereby adopted, one would interpret

it to mean 'not fully specified', or 'leaving some details that are not yet well understood out of the description'. Under this more charitable reading, then, 'vagueness' is simply the common scientific practice of handing one's readers a blank check, with the tacit understanding – or at least hope – that future research will fill in the detail.

2) The luxury of sharp, elevated perspective is seldom enjoyed by those engaged at the outlying regions of the tapestry, for which context is yet to be specified.

3) It is of course somewhat transparent that we are dealing here with another instance of the most general *iconic* expression in grammar, this time mandating that the most *macro,* hardest-to-define levels of expression receive the least overt structural coding at the lowest, clause level. While the more *micro,* more concrete levels – action and topic/participant, in that order – receive increasingly more detailed clause-level coding. One could add to this the ontological observation that in Pidgins and child language, the earliest grammatical coding sub-system discernible involves topic-identification, while the other two lag considerably behind (see Givón, 1979, Ch. 5, 7, as well as 1982b).

4) One may thus arrive at a concept of 'unities' startlingly akin to the classical Greek Theater's: Unity of *time, place and action,* to which one may add, given our somewhat expanded perspective in epistemology if not in art, the unities of *theme* and *topics/participants.* Most commonly, one finds tighter unities (or 'contiguities') in all five *within* the thematic paragraph than one finds *across* thematic paragraph boundaries. And this may easily develop into a heuristic test for thematic paragraphs as well as higher discourse units (see eg. Givón's Ute contribution, in this volume).

5) Ultimately, anything goes that does the job in human communication, including telepathy. The relatively predominant (and thus demonstrable) role of more measurable factors such as referential distance and potential interferance once again points to human language as a *routinized* system of communication, where high-probability (though not absolute!) predictions can be made, and where a *rough but efficient* processing system – grammar – has indeed evolved.

6) There are gounds for suspecting that the value *20 clauses* is actually over-estimated. Our cross-language study shows that, characteristically, the average values for the most *discontinuous* definite-topic devices, i.e. those used to return a topic into the register after a relatively long gap of absence, is around 15-17 clauses. This value is already itself *biased upward* by the arbitrarily assigned 20 clause value. Further, in a number of languages studied here and elsewhere, the very same grammatical device – involving either word-order or morphology or both, is used to mark *both* definite topics returning into the register after a long gap of absence, as well as indefinites introduced for the first time. This is as strong a suggestion as one can obtain from 'purely linguistic' data that speakers/hearers tend to assign the *same degree of processing difficulty* to those two types of discontinuity. To the extent that this suggestion pans out, one is justified in using the average referential distance values of definites returning into the register after a long absence as (i) a rough estimation of the maximal length of the pertinent discourse register, and thus (ii) the arbitrarily assigned referential distance value of referential-indefinites.

7) If the relevant value were stretched further, say to our maximal assigned value of 20 clauses, then automatically topics with a high referential distance would show – all other things being equal – more interfering topics in the preceding register, since more clauses allow more arguments/referents, at least potentially.

8) This is again a rough guess about the nature of immediate memory/recall, assuming that there is a certain *decay effect* associated with referential distance of topics/referents. Eventually such an assumption requires experimental psycho-linguistic support.

9) The other major functional correlate being that of *propositional semantics*, involving the specification of the predicate type, hence action/event/state type, including most obviously the semantic role-function of the various case-arguments vis-a-vis the predicate. For a extensive discussion, see Givón (1983).

10) As in the lexicon, a correlation exists in syntax between the phonological size of a coding device and some *functional size* along a scalar dimension – provided such a dimenson indeed exists. This will be demonstrated repeatedly below. I first broke the topic identification coding scale into this and other sub-scales in Givón (1982d).

11) This is *not*, as Haiman (1982, ms) would have it, purely an *economy principle*, although clearly there is some element of the law of energy conservation – and thus of inertia – in it. It reflects the need to *jar the mind* and *attract the attention* of hearers when their attention is focused elsewhere. The inertia of heares during the processing of discourse is not due to the mind's being asleep or sluggish, but rather it's being engaged elsewhere. Breaking that inertia requires more effort than going along with it.

12) See in particular Bentivoglio's paper on Spanish (in this volume).

13) An argument may be raied that Ergative languages don't really have a uniformly well-marked subject (cf. Anderson, 1976), but there are counter arguments to this analysis (cf. Givón, 1980b). In a different vein, Li and Thompson (1976) have argued that some language are 'topic prominent' rather than 'subject prominent'. The argument, however, is based only on case-marking morphology or grammatical agreement, and does not take into account actual text distribution of the 'subjects' or 'topics' in discourse.

14) Other languages where the numeral 'one' functions similarly are Creoles (Bickerton, 1975), Turkish, Sherpa, Persian, Neo-Armaic, older versions of German, English, Spanish and French, Mandarin Chinese and probably many others. Ute makes use of object suffixes and their removal (via object incorporation into the verb) to affect a similar discourse-pragmatic contrast. Bemba achieves the same end via the use of the prefixintial vowel of nouns. For details see Givón (1978).

15) For further discussion of the pragmatics of referentiality, see Givón (1982b).

16) On the scale of 1.00 to 2.00, with 1.00 denoting no interference, and 2.00 denoting interference by one or more referents in the immediately preceding discourse environment.

17) In English the writing system obscures the stress difference between stressed and unstressed pronouns, but a field linguist would easily identify the English unstressed pronouns as clitics. In Ute the independent pronouns have extra phonological material in addition to stress.

18) The frequency differences merely point out the slight artificiality of cutting the continuum into only three sections. There is a good reason to believe, cf. the frequencies, that in English unstressed pronouns code portions of point A as well. The frequency of zero vs. clitic subject pronouns in Ute (Givón, in this volume) is 321 vs. 42 or roughly *8 to 1*. In English the relation is reversed, with (colloquial English, Givón, in this volume) 117 zeros to 423 pronouns (mostly unstressed), or roughly a ratio of *1 to 3* in favor of the pronouns.

19) Late Biblical Hebrew lost its flexibility and became a rigid SVO language just like Spanish is currently doing (Givón, 1977). French, currently a fairly rigid SVO language,

has probably undergone a similar change, as has also Portuguese (Naro, in personal communication). There are also grounds for suspecting that Middle English had a wide range of VS/SV flexibility, currently reflected only in frozen constructions.

20) Bikol is a rigid V-first language of the Philippines, closely related to Tagalog. The data is from my own field notes, originally due to Manuel Factora (in personal communication).

21) Cf. Japanese, Korean or Amharic. But one must consider the case-marking status of *subjects* and *direct objects* in general (cf. Givón, 1981a) as part of the grammar of topic continuity, seeing that subjects tend to be the more continuous ('primary') topics, while direct objects tend to be less continuous ('secondary') topics, though obviously more continuous than obliques.

22) Cf. the Bikol data in (31) above. Any bona fide locative verb, such as 'be', 'stand', 'sit' 'stay', 'lie down' etc., may historically become the grammaticalized existential-presentative marker. Less common are 'appear', 'remain', 'be left', 'be put there', 'enter' etc. All these verbs may be characterized as either verbs of "being there" or of "entering into the scene". See further discussion in Givón (1976a).

REFERENCES

Anderson, S. (1976) "On the notion of 'subject' in Ergative languages", in C. Li (1976, ed.)

Bickerton, D. (1975) "Creolization, linguistic universals, natural semantax and the brain", U. of Hawaii, Honolulu (ms)

Bolinger, D. (1952) "Linear modification". in his *Forms of English*, Cambridge: Harvard University Press [1965]

————— (1954) "Meaningful word order in Spanish", *Boletin de Filología*, Universidad de Chile, vol. 8

Chafe, W. (1976) "Givenness, contrastiveness, definiteness, subjects, topics and point of view", in C.Li (1976, ed,)

Chafe, W. (1979) "The flow of thought and the flow of language", in T. Givón (1979, ed.)

Firbas, J. (1966a) "Non-thematic subjects in contemporary English", *Traveaux Linguistiques de Prague*, 2

————— (1966b) "On defining the theme in functional sentence analysis", *Traveaux Linguistiques de Prague*, 1

Fox, B. (1982) "Clause linking and focus affixes in Old Javanese", UCLA (ms)

Givón, T. (1975) "Promotion, accessibility and case-marking: Toward understanding grammar", *Working Papers in Language Universals*, vol. 19, Stanford University

————— (1976a) "Topic, pronoun and grammatical agreement", in C. Li (1976, Ed.—

————— (1976b) "On the VS word-order in Israeli Hebrew: Pragmatics and typological change", in P. Cole (ed.) *Studies in Modern Hebrew Syntax and Semantics*, Amsterdam: North Holland

————— (1977) "The drift from VSO to SVO in Biblical Hebrew: The pragmatics of tense-aspect", in C. Li (ed.) *Mechanisms for Syntactic Change*, Austin: University of Texas Press

————— (1978) "Difiniteness and referentiality", in J. Greenberg (ed.) *Universals of Human Language*, vo. 4, *Syntax*, Stanford: Stanford University Press

————— (1979) *On Understanding Grammar*, NY: Academic Press

————— (1979 ed.) *Discourse and Syntax, Syntax and Semantics*, vol. 12, NY: Academic Press

————— (1980a) "The binding hierarchy and the typology of complements", *Studies in Language,* 4.3

————— (1980b) "The drift away from ergativity in Sherpa", *Folia Linguistica Historica,* 1.1

————— (1981a) "Direct object and dative shifting: Semantic and pragmatic case", in F. Plank (ed.) *Objects*, NY: Academic Press (in press)

————— (1981b) "Typology and functional domains", *Studies in Language*

————— (1981c) "On the development of the numeral 'one' as an indefinite marker", *Folia Linguistica Historica,* 1.2

————— (1982a) "Tense-aspect-modality: The Creole prototype and beyond", in P. Hopper (ed.) *Tense and Aspect: Between Semantics and Pragmatics, Typological Studies in Language*, vol. 1, Amsterdam: J. Benjamins

————— (1982b) "Logic vs. pragmatics, with human language as the referee: Toward an empirically viable epistemology", *J. of Pragmatics*, 6.2

————— (1982c) "Topic continuity in discourse: The functional domain of switch-reference", in J. Haiman and P. Munro (eds) *Switch Reference, Typological Studies in Language*, vol. 2, Amsterdam: J. Benjamins (in press)

————— (1982d) "Universals of discourse structure and second language acquisition", in W.Rutherford (ed.) *Language Universals and Second Language Acquisition, Typological Studies in Language*, vol. 5, Amsterdam: J. Benjamins (in press)

————— (1983) *Syntax: A Functional-Typological Introduction,* (in preparation)

Haiman, J. (1980) *Hua Grammar*, Amsterdam: J. Benjamins

————— (1982, MS) *Iconicity in Language*, Cambridge: Cambridge University Press (in press)

Halliday, M.A.K. (1967) "Notes on fransitivity and thema in English", *J. of Linguistics*, 3

Hawkinson, A. and L. Hyman (1974) "Natural topic hierarchies in Shona", *Studies in African Linguistics*, 5

Hetzron, R. (1971) "Presentative function and presentative movement", *Studies in African Linguistics, supplement* 2

Hinds, J. (1978, ed.) *Anaphora in Discourse*, Edmonton: Linguistic Research

—————(1979) "properties of discourse structure", in T. Givón (1979 ed.)

Hopper, P. (1979) "Aspect and foregrounding in discourse", in T. Givón (ed., 1979)

————— and S. Thompson (1982) untitled paper read at the *Conference on Language Universals and Second Language Acquisition*, University of Southern California, February 1982 (ms)

Hwang, M. (1982) "Topic continuity and discontinuity in Korean narrative", UCLA (ms)

Hyman, L. (1975) "The change from SOV to SVO: Evidence from Niger-Congo", in C. Li (ed.) *Word Order and Word Order Change*, Austin: University of Texas Press

Keenan, Elinor (1977) "Why look at planned and unplanned discourse?" in E. Keenan and T. Bennett (eds) *Discourse Across Time and Space*, SCOPIL vol. 5, Los Angeles: University of Southern California

Kirsner, R. (1979) "Deixis in discourse: An explanatory quantitative study in Modern Dutch demonstrative adjectives", in T. Givón (1979, ed.)

Li, C. (1976, ed.) *Subject and Topic*, NY: Academic Press

————— and S. Thompson (1975) "The semantic function of word-order in Mandarin Chinese", in C. Li (ed.) *Word Order and Word Order Change*, Austin: University of Texas Press

————— (1976) "Subject and topic: A new typology for language", in C. Li (1976, Ed.)

————— (1979) "Pronouns in Mandarin Chinese discourse", in T. Givón (ed., (1979, Ed.)

Linde, C. (1979) *"Syntax & Semantics*, vol.12, *Ac Press"*, in T. Givón (1979, Ed.)

Longacre, R. (1976) *Anatomy of Speech Notions*,

————— (1979) "The paragraph as a grammatical unit", in T. Givón (ed., 1979)

Mahootian, S. (1979) "Given/new and definite/indefinite in Farsi", U. of Oregon, Eugene (ms)

Matisoff, J. (1975) *Lahu Grammar*, Berkeley: U.C. Press

Rude, N. (1982) "promotion and topicality of Nez Perce Objects", *BLS*, vol. 8,

Berkely: University of California

————— (forthcoming) *Studies in Nez Perce Grammar and Discourse*, PhD Dissertation, University of Oregon, Eugene (ms)

Shir, N. (1979) "Discourse constraints on dative movement", in T. Givón (ed.) *Discourse and Syntax, Syntax and Semantics*, vol. 12, NY: Academic Press.

Thurman, R. (1978) *Interclausal Relations in Chuave*, MA Thesis, UCLA (ms)

TOPIC CONTINUITY IN JAPANESE[1]

JOHN HINDS
Center for English as a Second Language
Penn State University
University Park, Pennsylvania

TABLE OF CONTENTS

1.0 *Introduction*

In this chapter I investigate the ways in which referential items in general, and topics in particular, are continued or discontinued in Japanese conversational interaction. The primary means of indicating continued reference in Japanese is through ellipsis, although pronominal forms also play a role. Parameters discussed by Givón 1983 and in the introduction to this volume are especially important in assessing continuity in a variety of discourse types.

These parameters introduced by Givón provide a significant improvement over earlier attempts to plot topic progression. One of the earliest attempts at plotting topic progressions is advanced by Daneš 1970, working in the framework of the Prague School. Daneš discussed five basic types of topic progression in discourse, each a variation of the concept of communicative dynamism, where thematic elements typically precede rhematic elements. In this formulation, sentences are divided into themes and rhemes, and a text progresses, for example, as a first rheme becomes a succeeding theme, or as a first theme is followed by a succession of different rhemes.

As a descriptive statement, there is little to be said about this approach – it is correct as far as it goes. As an explanatory statement, however, there are difficulties. Despite extensive psychological evidence that there are optimal organizing frameworks in discourse [see for example McKoon 1979], the statements of the Prague School provide no means to predict which progression is more marked than others.

Givón 1983 has given an account of topic progression in discourse which provides such a prediction. He claims that discourse is built of clause-level units which (a) comprise the same theme, and (b) tend to repeat the same participant/topic continuity. In this view, topic continuity, those instances in which the same topic extends over numerous clauses, is the unmarked form. Topic change is the marked form.[2]

Givón 1983 further claims that there is a scale of crosslinguistic coding devices which may be used to indicate topic continuity in discourse, and these are presented in the Introduction to this volume. This scale provides a point of departure for the discussion of topic continuity in Japanese conversational interaction. Two specific grammatical features of Japanese must first be mentioned.

1.1 *Word Order*

Japanese has a basic SOV word order, although variations occur with impunity. In addition to "scramblings" which occur in preverbal position, items may be freely "postposed" (right-dislocated) to the position following the verb. Postposing typically requires a special intonation contour, although this is not a strict requirement [details may be found in Hinds 1982, chapter 7, Shibamoto 1982.[3]

1.2 *Case Relationships*

Postpositional particles are one way to indicate case relationships. A major activity in Japanese linguistic studies has been the investigation of particle alternations and distributions [see Kuno 1973, Kuroda 1978, Tonoike 1975-76]. In addition to particles which mark basic case relationships, there is a set of special particles which function to subdue or highlight themes [Martin 1975]. Of interest is the fact that these special particles may obliterate particles which indicate case relationships. Included in this special set are *wa* and *nara* 'topic marking particles', and *mo* 'too', *sae* 'even', and *dake* 'only'. Examples follow.[4]

(1) a. dare ga sushi o tabemashita ka?
        who SM sushi OM ate-polite   QU
        Who ate the sushi?

    b. minako-san wa fumiko-san ni hon o   agemashita.
                Ms TM   Ms IO book OM gave-polite
        Minako gave Fumiko the book.

    c. asoko ni hon ga arimasu   ne.
        there LC book SM exist-polite EM
        There's a book over there, isn't there.

    d. yoshi-kun wa   tookyoo kara oosaka made jibun no
               Mr TM Tokyo   SR Osaka GL   self   LK
            jitensha de ikimashita yo.
            bicycle IN went-polite EM
        Yoshi went from Tokyo to Osaka by his own bike,
            you know.

    e. sensei mo biiru dake nomimasu ne.
        teacher too beer only drink-polite EM
        The teacher drinks only beer too, doesn't he.

In Hinds 1983 I have demonstrated that there are actually five possible means to indicate case relationships in Japanese. These are (a) the use of postpositional particles, (b) word order, (c) "selectional" restrictions, (d) a saliency principle, and (e) "world knowledge". The presence of any one of these is enough to indicate case relationships, although in conversational interaction there is usually a measure of redundancy.

2.0 *Grammatical devices investigated*

In this section, I introduce and illustrate the grammatical devices which play a role in topic continuity. All devices occur with each case relationship.

2.1 *Ellipsis (Zero anaphora)*

It has been show (Clancy 1980, Hinds 1978, 1983, 1982, Shibamoto 1980, 1982) that ellipsis is the unmarked form of topic continuity. The pervasiveness of this phenomenon in Japanese conversational interaction cannot be overstated. In fact, one way to understand the importance of ellipsis in Japanese is through a consideration of the frequency of its occurrence.

2.1.1 *Ellipsis of Subject*

Martin 1975:185 cited statistics to show that grammatical subjects, for example, may be ellipted as much as 74% of the time in normal conversational interaction, and as much as 37% of the time in expository styles such as news broadcasts. Shibamoto 1982 demonstrates a difference between rates of ellipsis for males and females, with males ellipting subject noun phrases in multiparty conversational interaction approximately 61% of the time, and females approximately 73% of the time. Hinds 1982 supports these statistics and shows that noun phrases in all case relationships, postpositional particles, and even main verbals may be ellipted with considerable frequency. It is also shown there that ellipsis may be used to introduce a noun phrase into the disourse if certain conditions are met. Thus, it is quite common for participants in a conversation to make reference to themselves without any overt noun phrases.[5]

H5.   doko de umaremashita?
        where at was-born
        Where were *you* born?
W6.   ano-ne, anoo, ehime-ken no oomishima tte iu   chitcha-na
        uh   uh   Ehime   LK Omishima QT say small
          shima de umaremashita.
          island at was-born
        Uh, let's see, *I* was born on a small island in Ehime
        Prefecture called Omishima.

It is also important to note that, unlike many other languages which allow ellipsis in subject position, Japanese has no marking on the verb to provide any clues to the identity of the ellipted subject.[6] The following example, decontextualized, could refer to the actions of a first, second, or third person subject, singular or plural.

W9.   mm, soko wa umareta dake de,
                 there TP was-born only copula
           No, *I* was only born there, and then

This example actually referred to the actions of the speaker, but in other contexts, the one who was born there could be the addressee, or some other person.

2.1.2 *Ellipsis of Object*

In contrast to the situation described by Givón for Ute, object ellipsis also occurs with considerable frequency in Japanese conversational interaction. Shibamoto 1980, for instance, reports that the objects of verbal predicates are ellipted as often as 67% of the time. Either animate or inanimate objects may be ellipted, as the following examples demonstrate.

A135.   nonde-ru to omou n   da kedo.
           taking   QT think nom cop but
           I think she was taking *them*, but,
A71.   tada, onna-no-ko wa ippen dekiru to
           just   girl   TM once make   when
           I think that once a girl gets pregnant [makes *a baby*]
A72.   sodatetaku-natchau n   ja-nai ka.
           want-to-raise   nom neg-tag QU
           she wants to have *the baby*.

2.2 *Stressed/independent Pronouns*

In present day Japanese, there is little, if anything, to differentiate "pronouns" from nouns syntactically (despite the claims of Hinds 1971), although there are clearcut distributional differences (see below). There are a large number of pronominal elements available to speakers, and a representative list of singular forms is indicated in the following chart. See Hinds 1978:138ff for a discussion of plurality.

I	MALE	boku
		ore
	FEMALE	atashi
		atakushi
	SEX-NEUTRAL	watashi
		watakushi
II	SEX-NEUTRAL	anata
		kimi
		anta
		omae
III	MALE	kare
	FEMALE	kanojo
	INANIMATE	kore 'this'
		sore 'that'
		are 'that over there'

Historically, all of these forms are derived from nouns, and they function syntactically as nouns do in the present day language. For example, it is relatively common for these pronominal forms to have modifiers or determiners preceding them. Thus, the following examples all have determiners modifying the head nouns. A80 and A81 have pronouns as head nouns, while A10 and A67 have nouns.

A10.   da-kedo ne, da-kedo, boku wa, boku wa, *sono onna-no-ko*
         but   EM but   I   TM I   TM that girl
         baka da to omotte   nee.
         fool cop QT think-and EM
         But, uh, but, I, I think that girl's stupid, and

A67.   un, sore ne, da-kara, ippen *sono banii no yatsu* wa shikago
         un that EM so   once that Bunny LK guy   TM Chicago
         ni ai   ni itte, ne, biru ni ai   ni itte,
         to meet to go-and EM Bill to meet to go-and
         Um, about that, one time that Bunny went to Chicago to
         see him, to see Bill, and

A80.   da-kedo, ima, *sono kanojo* mo   ne, nanka, kookai, kono-mae
        but   now   that she   too   EM uh   regret   recently
        tegami ni kaite   kite   ne, yappari,   kookai
        letter in write-and come-and EM expectedly regret
        shite ne.
        do-and EM
        But, now, that girl too, uh, she regrets, she wrote in a
        letter recently that she regrets, and
A81.   *sono kanojo,* atama ii   n   da yo, sugoku.
        that she   head good nom cop EM very
        That girl is smart, you know, very.

The forms *kare* and *kanojo*, used currently as third person pronouns, owe
some part of their frequency of usage to influences from western languages and
the requirement there that all sentences have an expressed subject. The use of
these forms is further complicated in that they also mean 'boyfriend' and 'girl-
friend', respectively (see Hinds 1975 for a complete discussion). Data adduced
later will provide some of the feel for these observations – traditional narratives
never employ the forms *kare* and *kanojo*, while participants in normal conversational interaction use them in accordance with their own perceptions of good
usage.

2.3 Right-dislocated definite NP (Postposed NP)

Subsequent discussion does not include reference to right-dislocated NP
(postposed NP), and so a brief explication of this phenomenon is offered here.
Considerable effort has been spent in attempting to describe the characteristics
of postposed constructions in Japanese (the most recent being Hinds 1982,
chapter 7). It is an important construction since it appears to figure in typological word order change, creating either verb medial or verb initial typologies
from verb final (see Givón this volume for additional comments).

The existence of this phenomenon has never been questioned. Peng 1977
claims, for instance, that postposing occurs in 9.2% of all conversational utterances. Shibamoto 1982 finds that females postpose elements 12.7% of the time,
while males postpose 5% of the time. Clancy 1980:167, while not citing percentages, states:

> Another device, which appears to function at least partly to clarify
> cases of elliptical switch reference, is the use of a postposed sub-
> ject . . .

The data base examined in this study, however, simply does not have enough instances of postposing to warrant detailed discussion or conjecture. There are no instances of postposing in the narrative Momotaro, understandable since this is a planned rather than spontaneous performance. In all, 567 clauses in three interactions have been examined, and only 5 postposed constructions (0.9%) were found. Of these, three involved reference to the speaker herself, and two others were at transition points, or boundaries, in the conversation.

2.4 Scrambling

Another device which deserves mention, but which will not receive detailed examination is "scrambling", the mutation of the basic SOV word order. Again, although this phenomenon has been insightfully discussed in the literature [Shibamoto 1980, 1982], the total percentage of scrambling in the current data base does not make it worth pursuing. Of 567 clauses, 8 (1.4%) evidenced a scrambled word order.

2.5 Postpositional particles

2.5.1 Subject/Topic Marking Particles

In this section I discuss a number of issues in the realm of highlighting, focussing on the contrast between noun phrases marked by *wa* and noun phrases marked by *ga*. I attempt to do this without becoming embroiled in terminological and theoretical matters which surround this issue, and which have little to do with how noun phrases marked by these particles function in topic continuance.

The clearest statement on the difference in meaning for noun phrases marked by these two particles comes from pedagogical grammars of Japanese. Alfonso 1966:973, for instance, states what he terms a 'fundamental rule' for the distinction between these two particles.

> Use WA when you introduce a topic or when the topic IS KNOWN ALREADY and you want to direct the other's attention to what FOLLOWS.[8]
>
> Use GA to mark the subject when WHAT FOLLOWS is already known and you want to draw attention to the SUBJECT ITSELF.

This contrast is illustrated in Jorden 1954:43 with the following types of examples.

(2)   kore ga   akai desu.
           this SM red cop
           THIS is red (tells which one is red).
(3)   kore wa   akai desu.
           this TM red cop
           This is RED (tells what color this is).

The distinction is frequently spoken of in terms of *wa* and *ga* [Kuno 1973], although the distinction is more properly considered a distinction between *wa* and particles which do not 'subdue' [Martin 1975]. I shall continue to speak of the difference between *wa* and *ga* since, as Martin 1975:59 has pointed out, 'both ellipsis and thematization appear to be more common for subjects than for objects'.

In isolated sentences, many subjects may be marked by either *wa* or *ga*, and both versions are judged grammatical —astute judges will discern a difference in focus. When a preference is shown in an isolated sentence, judges generally prefer the initial noun phrase to be marked by *wa*, undoubtedly because there are fewer shared assumptions to be made.

There are two types of constructions which distribute these particles in a less random manner, even in isolation. The first of these occur when a question word is involved. A WH-question word in Japanese never allows *wa* to follow it, whereas *ga* is quite common.

(4)   dare ga(*wa) koobe ni ikimashita ka?
           who SM   Kobe to went   QP
           Who went to Kobe?
(5)   nani ga (*wa) arimasu ka?
           what SM   be   QP
           What do you have?

Conversely, a question word in the rhematic portion of the sentence exerts a strong influence for the subject noun phrase to be marked by *wa*.

(6)   kore wa(? ga) nan   desu ka?
           this TM   what cop QP
           What is this?
(7)   ginkoo ni itta hito   wa(? ga) dare desu ka?
           bank   to went person TM   who cop QP
           Who is the person who went to the bank?

The second construction involves subordination. Kuno 1973:56 claims that the distinction between *ga* and *wa* is neutralized in subordinate clauses.

(8)   taroo ga(*wa) suki na ko   wa akiko desu.
          Taro SM   like LK girl TM Akiko cop
          The girl who Taro likes is Akiko.

There are complications involving what has been termed the 'contrastive' use of the particle *wa*, but Kuno's analysis has generally been accepted.

In a specific context, of course, the distribution of *ga* and *wa* is less free, although even here there is considerable latitude for individual variation and intentions. Examine, for example, line 58 in Appendix A. Despite the fact that this line has a rigid preceding and following context, either *ga* or *wa* is acceptable to all speakers.

A third possibility for marking a subject or topic is to ellipt the particle altogether. Kuno 1973 has claimed that all such instances are cases of ellipted *wa*, but this position is challenged by Martin 1975 and Hinds 1982.

The ellipsis of particles indicates a more relaxed way of speaking [see Hinds 1976, chapter 5], and so does does not occur at all in the semi-memorized folktale *Momotaro*. The ellipsis of such particles is illustrated by the following examples.

A75.   da-kedo, chotto kodomo kawaisoo da na.
         but   just   child pitiful   cop EM
         But it's the child I feel sorry for.
A88.   kodomo tsumi ga nai n   da kara,
         child sin   SM bot bom cop since
         since the child is without sin,

2.5.2 *Object Marking Particles*

There are a number of ways the second of two noun phrase arguments for two place predicates may be marked. The most common ways are with the particles *o, ni,* and *ga*. These are illustrated in the following.

H120.   soo, [NN] imiron   o   yaru-to-shitara
         so   semantics OM   try-do-if
         So, if you try to do semantics,

H169.   a, dare ga suki?
             a who SM like
             Uh, who do you like?
W88.   ma, tokidoki nihonjin ni au keredomo,
             well sometimes Japanese to meet but
             Well, sometimes I met some Japanese, but

There are generalizations which can be made about the verbal categories which require different object particles. Typically, nonstative verbals require *o*, stative verbals require *ga*, and verbals of interaction require *ni*. There are major exceptions to these generalizations, however [see Hinds 1982 for an organizing schema].

The potential ambiguity caused by *ga* marking both "subjects" and "objects" of stative verbals is compounded by the frequency with which these arguments may be ellipted entirely. It is not too difficult to imagine a context in which H169 *dare ga suki?* could mean "Who likes [someone we've been talking about]? "

Additionally, the "object" of a verbal can be marked by the topic marker *wa* or the highlighting particle *mo* 'also', as well as by a number of other particles which obscure case relationships. The role of the other types of indicators of case relationships mentioned in 1.2 above come into play in these situations.

A final possibility is that, identical to subjects, objects may not be marked by a particle at all. Again, speech containing this option is considered less formal. This is illustrated in the following.

H36.   anoo, itsumo nani-go   tsukatte-masu?
             uh   always what-language using
             Uh, what language do you use?
W111.   gimon kanjiru keredomo,
             doubt feel   but
             I have some doubts, but

2.6 *Summary of grammatical devices examined*

The following chart indicates precisely which grammatical constructions are analyzed quantitatively.

SUBJECT/TOPIC
Noun Phrase ga
Noun Phrase wa/mo
Noun phrase ∅ (NO OVERT PARTICLE)
Pronoun ga
Pronoun wa/mo
Pronoun ∅
Ellipsis (Zero Anaphora)
DIRECT OBJECT
Noun Phrase o/ni/ga
Noun phrase ∅
Pronoun o/ni/ga
Pronoun ∅
Ellipsis

The major division is between subject/topic and direct object. Within each of these categories, the role of full noun phrase, pronoun, and ellipsis is examined, as is the type of particle used to mark each of these items.

3.0 *Description of methodology*
3.1 *Texts*

As has been mentioned previously, three texts have been analyzed in quantitative terms. The first is a stylized retelling of the folktale *Momotaro*. The second is a semi-structured interview involving two females, and the third is a relaxed conversation between two males. Segments of each have been presented as Appendices A, B, and C.

In preparation for analysis, I have divided each text into clause length utterances. In the actual analysis I have eliminated "backchannel" expressions such as *nn* 'Oh', *soo ne* 'Right'. Additionally, in the folktale *Momotaro* I have not analyzed any of the quoted material, nor have I counted the ellipted indirect object of the verb *iu* 'say'. Finally, for the female interaction I have included only the first 169 utterances in the quantitative analysis.

Any examples taken from the folktale *Momotaro* are preceded by numbers without prefixes or parens. Any data cited from the conversation between two male speakers are preceded by the letters A or B, indicating which participant is speaking. Examples from the interview are preceded either by W or H. In the event examples are constructed or taken from another sourcce, the example is predeced by a number in parens, as in (1).

3.2 *Measurements*

Continuity/discontinuity has been discussed by Givŏn [Introduction] according to three separate measurements, two of which will be considered here.

(a) Distance – The distance from the present mention of a noun phrase by a particular device and the last clause where the same referent was a semantic argument of that clause, in numbers of clauses.

(b) Decay – The number of clauses to the right from the locus of study that the same referent remains an argument of the predication.

In studying *distance*, all tokens of a specific noun phrase are assigned a value of 1 to 20, with 1 representing maximum continuity and 20 maximum discontinuity. That is, the lower the number, the closer the token is to its referent. Initial introduction of a noun phrase receives maximum value of 20.

In studying *decay*, the presence of a noun phrase in a clause which "goes nowhere", which is not referred to in the succeeding clause, is assigned a value of 0. The number of clause in which a noun phrase is continued to be referred to without interruption is then N-1. A continued reference to a noun phrase for seven consecutive clauses thus receives a score of 6. For this measure, the higher the score, the greater the continuity.

4.0 *Numerical Results of Measurements*
4.1 *Topic Continuity Properties of Subjects/Topics*
4.1.1 *Distance*

The three sets of data examined here provide slightly different results with respect to distance scores. Each data set will be examined separately, and in 4.1.4 all scores will be computed.

4.1.1.1 *Momotaro*

Results for *Momotaro* are presented in Tables I and II, animate noun phrases and inanimate noun phrases, respectively. As was pointed out earlier, pronouns are never used in narratives of this type, and the ellipsis of particles is uncommon. There are no examples of particle ellipsis in this narrative.

TABLE I

Momotaro (animate noun phrase)

category	N	Average referential distance by number of clauses
NP-ga	14	11.4
NP-wa	39	4.0
Ellipsis	48	1.1
NP-o	48	5.3
NP-ni	32	4.6

TABLE II
Momotaro (inanimate noun phrases)

category	N	Average referential distance by number of clauses
NP-ga	2	10.5
NP-wa	0	–
Ellipsis 2	2	1.0
NP-o	19	14.4
NP-ni	4	20.0

The figures for both animate and inanimate noun phrases indicate that the greatest continuity is achieved by ellipsis, and that noun phrases marked by *wa* show more continuity than noun phrases marked by *ga*. This coincides with the claims made in Hinds and Hinds 1979, for instance, where it was stated that NP *ga* is used to introduce new noun phrases into a story, and noun phrase *wa* is used to highlight that noun phrase. A three-tiered system is established for animate topics, then, in which the sequence NP-*ga* – NP-*wa* – ellipsis indicates a progression from least continuity to most.

4.1.1.2 *Female conversational interaction*

Because this conversational interaction is less stylized, particles have been ellipted frequently, and pronouns appear with some regularity. Results for this interaction are presented in Tables III and IV. Ellipsis again is shown to be the most effective device for achieving continuity for either animate or inanimate topics.[9]

TABLE III
INTERVIEW BETWEEN FEMALES (animate noun phrases)

category	N	Average distance
NP-ga	2	20.0
NP-wa/mo	6	13.7
NP-∅	3	7.3
PRO-ga	–	–
PRO-wa/mo	2	8.5
PRO-∅	1	20.0
Ellipsis (topic/sbj)	83	1.6
NP-o/ga/ni	3	7.3
PRO-o/ga/ni	–	–
NP-∅	–	–
PRO-∅	–	–
Ellipsis	1	1.0
NP-ni	1	20.0
Ellipsis (ni)	–	–
NP-to	–	–
PRO-to	–	–
Ellipsis (to)	–	–

TABLE IV

INTERVIEW BETWEEN FEMALES (inanimate noun phrases)

category	N	Average distance
NP-ga	7	12.3
NP-wa/mo	7	14.7
NP-∅	4	10.8
PRO-ga	2	1.0
PRO-wa/mo	1	1.0
PRO-∅	–	–
Ellipsis (topic/sbj)	16	1.7
NP-o/ga/ni	3	13.7
PRO-o/go/ni	3	7.3
NP-∅	22	8.9
PRO-∅	2	1.0
Ellipsis	8	1.3
NP-ni	–	–
Ellipsis (ni)	–	–
NP-to	–	–
PRO-to	–	–
Ellipsis (to)	–	–

As Table III demonstrates, there are not enough instances of animate beings in nonsubject/topic position to make any generalizations. Inanimate objects, however, show that ellipsis achieves most continuity, and that pronouns are intermediate between ellipsis and full noun phrases.

Tables V and VI collapse categories from this conversational interaction. In Table V, noun phrase topics/subjects have been combined to compare with pronominal topics/subjects, regardless of which particle is used to mark them. Table VI displays the data from the perspective of particle marking, collapsing pronouns and noun phrase categories.

TABLE V
TOPIC/SUBJECT

category	N	Average distance
NP	11	13.1
PRO	3	12.3
Ellipsis	83	1.6

TABLE VI
PARTICLE CHOICE

category	N	Average distance
N/PR-ga	2	20.0
N/PR-wa/mo	8	12.4
N/PR-∅	4	10.5
Ellipsis	83	1.6

Detailed discussion of these figures will be postponed until figures from the male conversational interaction are presented. Informally collapsing the figures on inanimates, it is clear that the expected progression of "overt particle – no particle – ellipsis" corresponds to a scale of most discontinuity to most continuity.

4.1.1.3 *Male conversational interaction*

A third category beyond animate and inanimate is introduced here. This is the role of "participant" in the conversation. In defense of this proliferation of categories, I offer the following three points. First, most instances of participant reference are coded as if the participants are participants – how they think about something, what they believe is the case.[10] Some instances of participant reference, however, describe actions of the participants as if these participants were characters in the story being narrated. This is the case in A109 through A117 in which A describes the travails of Bill, Tom, and himself. Note in particular that the use of *boku* 'I' in A109 introduces *boku* into the story as a character. A shift in perspective has occurred, and this is the reason for the occurrence of *boku* in A109, despite its previous overt appearance in A108, in which A was offering a comment on the actions of Bill and the girl [see Hinds

1982].

Second, in Japanese, it is difficult to draw a line between instances of participant ellipsis and nonspecification. For narrative texts, the way ellipsis, as opposed to nonspecification, is recognized is that ellipsis occurs when a 'case frame' is not overtly filled [see Minsky 1975, Hinds 1980, 1982].

In the case of verbals denoting internal states, however, it is not clear that a case frame analysis is efficacious. Examine, for instance, A72 in which the verbal *kawaisoo da* 'is pitiful' occurs. From the perspective of case frames, no first person referent is present. From the perspective of the meaning involved in the statement, there is as much personal involvement as there is in A52 in which the verbal *omou* 'think' appears. The case frame for *omou* calls for a first person pronoun to be specified. Similarly, the fact that *kiita* 'heard' in A44 requires a first person pronoun based on its case frame does not make it any more personalized' than A1 in which *rashii* 'seems' occurs. As a final contrast of this type, consider A15 in which the force of 'I think' is conveyed through the particle sequence *ka naa*, and A43 in which the same force is conveyed through *to omou* (notice also A50 in which both *ka na* and *to omotte* combine to convey the same force).

The third point is the infrequent usage of first and second person pronouns in Japanese conversational interaction, and the possibility that their appearance may be for cosmetic reasons more than anything else. This is obviously related to the notion of rhetorical underlining [see Longacre 1976].

Tables VI, VII, and VIII present this information.

TABLE VI
MALE CONVERSATION (animate noun phrases)

category	N	Average distance
NP-ga	7	6.7
NP-wa/mo	6	6.9
NP-∅	11	10.8
PRO-ga	7	2.7
PRO-wa/mo	6	7.0
PRO-∅	7	4.9.
Ellipsis (topic/sbj)	83	2.7
NP-o/ga/ni	–	–
PRO-o/ga/ni	1	1.0
NP-∅	9	7.7
PRO-∅	–	–
Ellipsis	–	–
NP-ni	1	13.0
Ellipsis (ni)	7	2.14
NP-to	–	–
PRO-to	–	–
Ellipsis (to)	2	3.5

TABLE VII
MALE CONVERSATION (inanimate noun phrases)

category	N	Average distance
NP-ga	4	20.0
NP-wa/mo	2	11.0
NP-∅	10	12.6
PRO-ga	–	–
PRO-wa/mo	4	10.8
PRO-∅	1	2.0
Ellipsis (topic&sbj)	16	5.1
NP-o/ga/ni	6	1.0
PRO-o/ga/ni	1	1.0
NP-∅	9	17.8
PRO-∅	–	–
Ellipsis	8	3.6
NP-ni	3	7.7
Ellipsis (ni)	–	–
NP-to	–	–
PRO-to	–	–
Ellipsis (to)	–	–

TABLE VIII
MALE CONVERSATION (participants)

category	N	Average distance
NP-ga	–	–
NP-wa/mo	–	–
NP-∅	–	–
PRO-ga	–	–
PRO-wa/mo	2	7.5
PRO-∅	2	8.5
Ellipsis (topic/sbj)	17	9.4
NP-o/ga/ni	–	–
PRO-o/ga/ni	–	–
NP-∅	–	–
PRO-∅	–	–
Ellipsis	–	–
NP-ni	–	–
Ellipsis (ni)	–	–
NP-to	–	–
PRO-to	–	–
Ellipsis (to)	–	–

Note in particular the clear difference in the use of ellipsis in Table VIII and every other table presented so far. This is because the insertion of opinions appear sporadically, and this necessitates assigning such ellipted expressions a value of 20 [see again Bentivoglio this volume].

Collapsing the tables for topic/subject and for particle choice for animates creates tables IX and X.

TABLE IX
TOPIC/SUBJECT (animates)

category	N	Average distance
NP	24	8.6
PRO	20	4.8
Ellipsis	83	2.7

TABLE X
PARTICLE CHOICE (animate)

category	N	Average distance
N/PR-ga	14	4.7
N/PR-wa/mo	12	6.9
N/PR-∅	18	8.5
Ellipsis	83	2.7

4.1.1.4 *Generalizations about distance*

Tables XI and XII present the complete picture with respect to animate reference in terms of noun phrase type and particle type.

TABLE IX
TOPIC/SUBJECT (all interactions, animate)

category	N	Average distance
NP	88	7.8
PRO	23	5.8
Ellipsis	214	1.9

TABLE XII
PARTICLE CHOICE (all interactions, animate)

category	N	Average distance
N/PR-ga	30	9.5
N/PR-wa/mo	59	5.8
N/PR-∅	22	8.9
Ellipsis	214	1.9

What Tables XI and XII indicate quite clearly is that there is a progression for topics in which ellipsis demonstrates most continuity, a full noun phrase least, with independent pronouns falling midway between. Moreover, a noun phrase marked by *wa* falls into an intermediate position between noun phrases marked by *ga* and ellipsis.

4.1.2 *Decay*

This measurement offers a fairly clear picture of the extent to which noun phrases introduced by various grammatical devices are continued to be referred to in succeeding interaction. The higher the average, the more continuous referent to that item is made. That is, the higher the average, the more continuity is shown.

Table XIII displays averages for grammatical devices in animate subject/topic position for all three data sets.

TABLE XIII
DECAY OF SUBJECT/TOPIC (animate)

	Momotaro		Females		Males		TOTALS	
	N	Average	N	Average	N	Average	N	Average
NP ga	12	1.2	6	1.0	19	0.3	37	0.6
NP wa	33	1.1	3	1.3	7	0.7	43	1.1
NP ∅	–	–	1	15.0	10	0.5	11	1.8
Pr ga	–	–	–	–	4	0.5	4	0.5
Pr wa	–	–	2	2.5	4	3.3	6	3.0
Pr ∅	–	–	1	1.0	2	0.5	3	0.7
∅	–	–	11	4.4	17	1.6	28	2.7

The result which stands out most clearly is that ellipsis again indicates the highest degree of continuity. Other results are not as clear. Tables XIV and XV, however, present collapsed categories, and these are instructive. In XIV, noun, pronouns, and ellipsis are grouped together, regardless of particle choice. In XV, particle choice is displayed regardless of whether a full noun phrase or a pronoun precedes.

TABLE XIV
DECAY (animate)

	N	Average
Nouns	81	1.1
Pronouns	13	1.7
Elipsis	28	2.7

TABLE XV
DECAY (animate)

	N	Average
-ga	31	0.8
-wa	49	1.3
-∅	14	1.6
Ellipsis	28	2.7

Both tables indicate the predicted direction of hierarchical organization. Data on inanimates are scanty, and so are presented in table XVI without comment.

TABLE XVI
DECAY (inanimate)

	N	Average
-ga	7	0.3
-wa	6	1.8
-∅	2	0
Ellipsis	2	0

4.2   *Topic Continuity Properties of Direct Objects*
4.2.1 *Distance*

Tables XVII and XVIII summarize the effect of distance for direct objects.

TABLE XVII
DIRECT OBJECT (inanimate)

	N	Average
NP-prt	11	15.3
pro-prt	5	4.8
NP-∅	31	11.5
pro-∅	2	1.0
Ellipsis	16	2.4

TABLE XVIII
DIRECT OBJECT (animate)

	N	Average
NP-prt	16	5.2
pro-prt	1	1.0
NP-∅	9	7.7
pro-∅	–	–
Ellipsis	6	2.7

The major tendencies which may be seen for direct objects is that ellipsis has a lower average than fully specified noun phrases. Table XIX shows the results of collapsing categories without respect to overt or ellipted particles for inanimate direct objects.

TABLE XIX
DISTANCE FOR DIRECT OBJECTS (inanimate)

	N	Average
Nouns	42	12.5
Pronouns	7	3.7
Ellipsis	16	2.4

4.2.2 *Decay*

Tables XX and XXI list inanimate and animate direct object decay scores, respectively.

TABLE XX
DECAY OF DIRECT OBJECT (inanimate)

	Momotaro		Females		Males		TOTALS	
	N	Average	N	Average	N	Average	N	Average
NP o	18	0.3	3	1.3	6	0.8	27	0.4
NP ga	–	–	5	0.2	2	0.0	7	0.1
NP ∅	–	–	10	1.7	20	0.3	30	0.8
NP ni	3	0.0	–	–	2	0.0	5	0.0
NP wa	–	–	2	1.0	3	0.0	3	0.4
∅	–	–	1	0.0	–	–	1	0.0

TABLE XXI
DECAY OF DIRECT OBJECT (animate)

	Momotaro		Females		Males		TOTALS	
	N	Average	N	Average	N	Average	N	Average
NP o	9	0.0	—	—	—	—	9	0.0
NP ga	—	—	1	3.0	—	—	1	3.0
NP ∅	—	—	1	0.0	7	0.3	8	0.3
NP ni	2	0.0	1	0.0	1	0.0	4	0.0
NP wa	—	—	—	—	—	—	—	—
∅	—	—	—	—	—	—	—	—

What is clear is that inanimates are more apt to be direct objects than animates, and that both inanimate direct objects and animate direct objects show a lower degree of continuity with respect to decay than do subjects/topics.

4.3 Topic Continuity Properties if Indirect Objects
The total number of indirect objects measure in the three sets of data examined is 8. This figure is too small to make any generalizations.

5.0 Discussion
5.1 Distance
Results of this study in general have confirmed Givón's topic continuity hierarchy. What is most pertinent with respect to the literature on Japanese, is that the category "pronoun" is shown to have an intermediate functional status between ellipsis and full nouns. This is best seen in Figure 1 where the referential distance of both animate and inanimate referents is plotted for subject/topic position. As is also expected, inanimate referents have a higher average distance, indicating that they demonstrate less continuity than animate referents.

In Figure 2 this difference between animate and inanimate is shown to hold when particle choice is measured. Here there is a general tendency to progress from ellipsis, which shows the highest degree of continuity, to noun phrases marked by *ga,* which shows the highest degree of discontinuity. This finding supports research which claims that referents may be introduced into discourse with the particle *ga,* and then subsequently be marked by *wa,* or be ellipted [see Hinds and Hinds 1979, Clancy 1980 for comments].

Figure 1
Referential distance of subject/topic

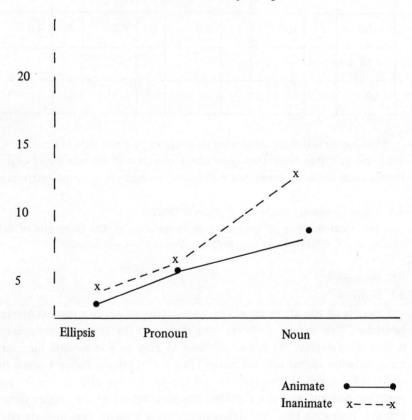

Figure 2
Referential distance of subject/topic

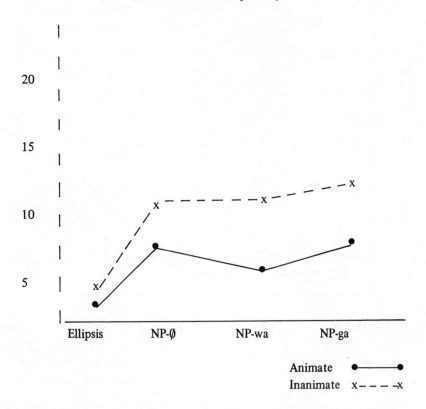

Animate ●────●
Inanimate x────x

Figures 3 and 4 represent aimate and inanimate distance for direct objects. Again there is a general trend to progress from ellipsis through pronouns to full nouns for both inanimate and animate referents. Here, inanimate shows a higher degree of continuity, consistent with the fact that direct objects typically refer to inanimate rather than animate noun phrases [Figure 3]. Figure 4 presents contradictory results in that inanimate nouns are more discontinuous than animate nouns. A larger data base must be examined to determine exactly what is going on.

Figure 3
Referential distance of direct object

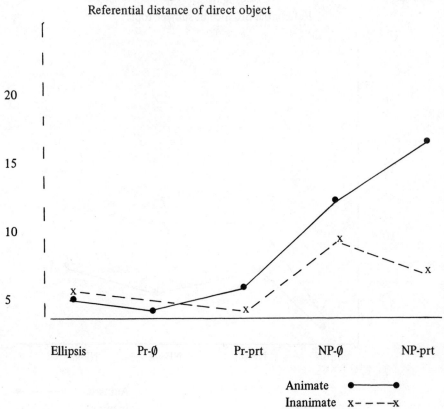

Figure 4
Referential distance of direct object

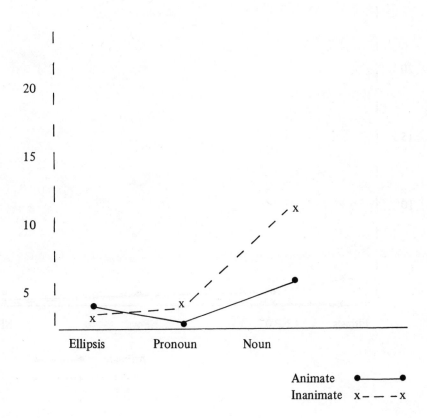

5.2 *Decay*

For decay, there is again a tendency for ellipsis to exhibit a greater degree of continuity while noun phrases marked by *ga* exhibit a greater degree of discontinuity [Figure 5]. Figure 6 represents in graph form information on the decay of direct object, although there is not a large enough data base to make any statements with assurance.

Figure 5
Decay of subject/topic

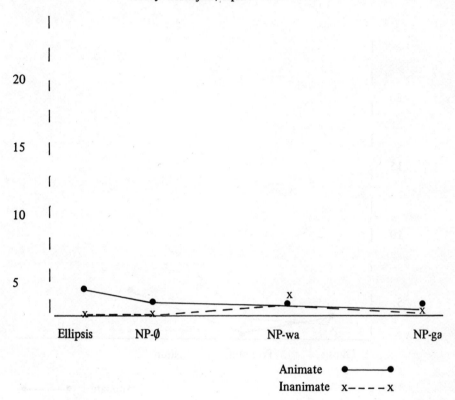

Figure 6
Decay of Direct Object

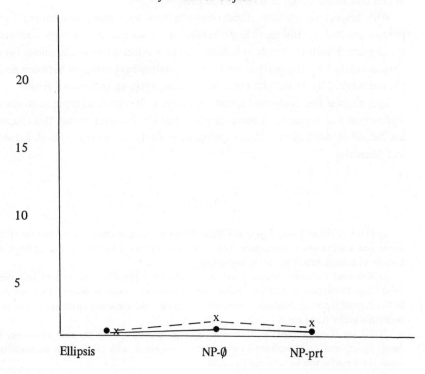

6.0 Conclusion

This chapter has demonstrated, as have the other chapters in this collection, that the quantitative study of topic continuity is a viable and fruitful area for investigation. In many ways, this study has served to confirm expectations. Earlier studies of my own and other researchers in Japanese discourse analysis have stated that ellipsis is the unmarked form of topic continuation, and this has now been demonstrated conclusively through the application of two measures developed by Givón − distance and decay.

One finding which is particularly noteworthy is that the category "pronoun" emerges as a functionally relevant entity. Prior studies [Hinds 1971, 1975] have stressed the uniqueness of this category in syntactic and semantic terms, but there has always been the suspicion that pronouns do not show sufficient differences from noun to warrant establishing a separate category. The fact that pronouns fall into an intermediate position between full noun phrases and ellipsis with respect to the measures developed by Givón demonstrates that they do in fact constitute a unique grammatical category.

With respect to particle choice, expectations were again vindicated. Noun phrases marked by the particle *ga* exhibit the least amount of topic continuity, consistent with their role as indicator of new information in discourse. Noun phrases marked by the particle *wa* form an intermediate category between noun phrases marked by *ga* and ellipted noun phrases, again an anticipated result.

This chapter has uncovered specific findings with respect to topic continuity/discontinuity in Japanese. A more significant result, however, is that this chapter has helped to demonstrate that a quantitative study of this type is both feasible and desirable.

NOTES

1) I wish to thank Talmy Givón and Wako Hinds for reading a preliminary version of this paper and making useful comments. This work was supported in part by a grant from the College of Liberal Arts, Penn State University.

2) Reported dialogue, discussed below, constitutes a possible exception to this statement since the nature of dialogue is that speakers alternate turns at speech. Each speaker, in the case of reported dialogue, constitutes the topic, and topic discontinuity rather than topic continuity is the norm.

3) To say that grammatical devices occur with impunity, or to say that items may be freely "postposed" says nothing of the relative frequency with which such permutations occur. This matter will be returned to below.

4) Abbreviations used are: SM – subject particle; EM – emphatic particle; OM – object particle; LC – locative particle; QU – question particle; SR – source particle; TM – topic particle; IN – instrumental particle; – IO – indirect object particle; GL – goal particle

5) Data are marked to indicate whether they are taken from analyzed sources, or whether they are constructed. The conventions are explained in section 3.1. of this chapter.

6) The honorific system (*keigo*) may contribute to the understanding of some instances of ellipted subjects.

8) In Hinds 1982, this apparently dichotomous nature of the particle *wa* is discussed with respect to written expository styles. There I show that the pragmatic function of *wa* in those instances in which newly introduced information is so marked is to signal the addressee to treat the new information as if it were known information.

9) The number of inanimate pronouns is too low to constitute a serious counterargument to this claim.

10) This is reflected in the analysis by Bentivoglio [this volume] in which she states: "From my analysis thus far it seems clear that such interference (e.g. the insertion of *yo creo* 'I believe', *pienso* 'I think', etc) does not break the reference of a given topic.

REFERENCES

Alfonso, Anthony. 1966. Japanese Language Patterns. Tokyo: Sophia University Press.

Bentivoglio, Paola. 1983. Continuity and discontinuity in discourse: A study on Latin-American spoken Spanish. This volume.

Clancy, Patricia. 1980. Referential choice in English and Japanese narrative discourse. The Pear Stories. Edited by Wallace Chafe. Ablex Publishing Corporation: Norwood.

Daneš, František. 1970. One instance of Prague School methodology: Functional analysis of utterance and text. Method and Theory in Linguistics. Edited by Paul Garvin. Mouton Publishers: The Hague.

Givón. 1979. On Understanding Grammar. Academic Press: NY.

Givón. 1983. Topic continuation in discourse: The functional domain of switch reference. Switch Reference: Typological Studies in Language, Vol. 2. Edited by J. Haiman and P. Munro. J. Benjamins: Amsterdam.

Givón. 1983. Topic continuity and word-order pragmatics in Ute. This volume.

Grimes, Joseph. 1975. The Thread of Discourse. Mouton Publishers: The Hague.

Hinds, John. 1971. Personal pronouns in Japanese. Glossa 5:145-55.

Hinds, John. 1975. Third person pronouns in Japanese. Language in Japanese Society. Edited by Fred C. C. Peng. Tokyo University Press: Tokyo.

Hinds, John. 1976. Aspects of Japanese Discourse Structure. Kaitakusha: Tokyo

Hinds, John. 1978. Anaphora in Japanese conversation. Anaphora in Discourse. Edited by John Hinds. Linguistic Research, Inc.: Alberta.

Hinds, John. 1983. Case marking in Japanese. Linguistics [to appear]

Hinds, John. 1981. Case marking in Japanese. Paper presented at the LSA Winter Meeting: New York City.

Hinds, John. 1982. Ellipsis in Japanese Discourse. Linguistic Research, Inc.: Alberta.

Hinds, John and Wako Hinds. 1979. Participant identification in Japanese narrative discourse. Explorations in Linguistics: Papers in Honor of Kazuko Inoue. Edited by G. Bedell, E. Kobayashi, M. Muraki. Kenkyusha: Tokyo.

Ikeda, Takashi. 1975. Classical Japanese Grammar Illustrated with Texts. The Toho Gakkai: Tokyo.

Inoue, Kazuko. 1976. Henkei Bumpoo to Nihongo. Taishukan: Tokyo.

Inoue, Kazuko. 1978. Nihongo no Bumpoo Kisoku. Taishukan: Tokyo.

Kitagawa, Chisato. 1982. Topic constructions in Japanese. Lingua [To appear]
Kuno, Susumu. 1973. The Structure of the Japanese Language. MIT Press:
    Cambridge, MA.
Kuroda, S.-Y. 1978. Case marking, canonical sentence patterns, and counter
    equi in Japanese (A preliminary survey). Problems in Japanese Syntax and
    Semantics. Edited by John Hinds and Irwin Howard. Kaitakusha: Tokyo.
Longacre, Robert. 1976. An Anatomy of Speech Notions. Peter de Ridder
    Press: Lisse.
Martin, Samuel. 1975. A Reference Grammar of Japanese. Yale University Press:
    New Haven, CT.
Peng, Fred C. C. 1977. Josei Gengo no Chiikisa, Nendaisa to Kojinsa: Toshika
    ni yoru Ikkoosatsu. Language and Context. Bunka Hyoron: Tokyo.
Shibamoto, Janet. 1980. Language use and linguistic theory: Sexrelated varia-
    tion in Japanese syntax. Unpublished Ph. D. Dissertation: University of
    California at Davis.
Shibamoto, Janet. 1982. Subject ellipsis and topic in Japanese. Unpublished
    paper: UC/Davis.
Shibatani, Masayoshi. 1977. Grammatical relations and surface cases. Language
    53:789-809.
Tonoike, Shigeo. 1975-76. The case ordering hypothesis. Papers in Japanese
    Linguistics 4:191-208.

APPENDIX A
First 20 clauses of Momotaro

1   mukashi mukashi aru tokoro ni ojiisan   to
         old   old   one place in old-man and
             obaasan   ga   sunde-imashita.
             old-lady SM   lived
         Once upon a time, there was an old man and
             an old lady.
2   ojiisan   wa yama   e shibakari ni ikimashita.
         old-man TM mountain to wood-get to went
         The old man went to the mountain to gather wood.
3.   obaasan   wa kawa   e sentaku   ni ikimashita.
         old-lady TM river to laundry   to went
         The old lady went to the river to do the laundry.

4.   obaasan   ga   kawa de sentaku o   · shite-iru to
           old-lady SM   river   at laundry OM doing   when
           While the old lady was doing the laundry at the river,

5   kami-no-hoo kara ooki-na ooki-na momo ga   nagarete-kimashita.
           upstream   from big   big   peach SM came-floating
           a great big peach came floating down from upstream.

6   "donburakokko-sukkokko donburakokko-sukkokko" to
           bobbing   bobbing   QT
             nagarete-kimashita.
             came-floating
           It came bobbing down the stream.

7   obaasan wa   sore o   mite
           old-lady TM   that OM see-and
           The old lady looked at that, and

8   "maa ooki-na momo da   koto.
           oh   big   peach COP fact
             uchi e kaette   ojiisan ni misete-agenakucha" to iimashita.
             home to return-and old-man to must-show   QT said
           said, "Oh what a big peach. I'll take it home and
             show it to my husband."

9   sore-de   sono obaasan wa "yoisho-yoisho" to   sono ooki-na
           with-that that old-lady TM oomph   QT that big
             momo o   motte-kaerimashita.
             peach OM carried-home
           With that, the old lady picked up the big peach and carried
             it home.

10   uchi ni   kaeru   to
           home to   return   when
           When she got home,

11   ojiisan wa me   o   maruku-shite
           old-man TM eye   OM make-round-and
           The old man's eyes widened,

12   "oo ooki-na taihen-na momo da.
           oh big   great   peach COP
             kore o   watte-tabechaoo" to   iimashita.
             this OM split-eat   QT said
           and he said, "Oh, what a fantastic, large peach.
             Let's split it open and eat it."

13   obaasan ga hoochoo o   motte-kite
        old-lady SM knife   OM bring-and
        The old lady brought a knife, and

14   sono momo o   kiroo-to-suru to
        that peach OM try-to-cut   when
        when she tried to cut up the peach,

15   potto momo ga warete
        plop peach SM split-and
        the peach split open by itself, and

16   sono naka kara wa ooki-na kawaii otoko-no-ko ga
        that middle from TM big   cut   boy   SM
             dete-Kimashita.
             came-out
        a big cute boy came out from the inside.

17   momo kara umareta node
        peach from was-born since
        Since he was born from a peach,

18   ojiisan to obaasan wa kono kodomo o   momotaroo to-iu
        old-man and old-lady TM this child   OM Momotaro called
             namae ni suru koto ni shimashita.
             name to do   fact to did
        The old man and the old lady decided to call this child Momotaroo.

19   momotaroo wa sukusuku-to ookiku-natte
        Momotaro   TM quickly   became-big-and
        Momotaro grew up very rapidly, and

20   aru hi onigashima ni onitaiji ni iku koto ni shimashita.
        one day Onigashima to ogre-fight to go fact to did
        one day he decided to go to Onigashima to fight the ogres.

APPENDIX B
27 clauses of male-male interaction

A38.   aa,a, soo na no?
        ah ah so LK nom
        Oh. Oh, really?

B39 un, taigai soo yo.
     un generally so EM
     Right, that's generally the case.

B40. mukashi wa ne, furui koro wa, anoo, otoko ga ne, aa,
     old   TM EM old time TM uh male SM EM ah
     onna no hoo ga, are da, dare-tomo tsukiatte-inakatta
     female LK side SM that cop no-one not-associated
     tte koto o shoomei shinai-to-dame yo. .
     QT fact OM prove must-do   EM
     In the old days, a long time ago, the male, uh, the female
     you know, had to prove that she hadn't been with anyone.

B41. da-kedo sa, ima wa sa, otoko no hoo ga kanojo no
     but   EM now TM EM male LK side SM female LK
     hoo ga hoka-no otoko to tsukiatte-ta tte koto o
     side SM other male and associated QT fact OM
     shoomei shinai-to-dame yo.
     prove must-do   EM
     But, nowadays, the male has to prove that the female
      has been with another male.

A42. aa, kibishiku natte-ru wake ne?
     ah strict became reason EM
     Oh, it's really gotten tougher.

B43. un, onna no hoo ga tsuyoku natte-ru wake.
     un female LK side SM strong became reason
     Yeah, women have become much stronger.

A44. aa, soo ka.
     ah so QU
     Oh really.

A45. da-kedo, kanojo wa hoka-no otoko to tsukiatte-ta to omou
     but she TM other male and associated QT think
     ga ne.
     but EM
     But, I think she was going with some other guys.

A46. tada ne, kon-mae nanka kiita hanashi de-wa,
     just EM before something heard story according-TM
     Anyway, I heard from someone,

A47.   sono biru ga ne, sono saiban kanojo ga yaru tte itte-ru
        that Bill SM EM that court she   SM do QT saying
        n   de
        nom cop-and
        that ever since Bill found out that she is going to take him to court,

A48.   nanka   sugoku shoosoo shichatte sa.
        something very   agitated   do-and   EM
        he's been very agitated.

B49.   un.
        un
        Yes.

A50.   nanka   sugoku yasete
        something very   become thin-and
        Well, he lost a lot of weight, and

A51.   nanka   kenkoo mo, nanka   are da tte iu kara.
        something health too something that cop QT say since
        they say his health has deteriorated too.

A52.   sore-de ne, boku mo yappari   biru no kodomo ka-na
        and   EM I   too of-course Bill LK child   wonder
        to omotte.
        QT think-and
        And of course that made me wonder whether it's his child.

A53.   jibun no kodomo ja-nakattara ne,
        self LK child   if-not   EM
        I think that if it wasn't his child,

A54.   sonna-ni yoo-suru-ni ki-ni-yandari   suru koto
        that   in-short   worry-representative do   fact
        nai to omou n   da ne.
        neg QT think nom cop EM
        he wouldn't be so worried.

B55.   un, sorya, wakannai   yo.
        un that-TM don't-know EM
        Yeah, I'm not sure about that.

B56.   datte, jibun no kodomo ja-nai no-ni
        but   self LK child   not   even-if
        But, even if it's not your own child,

B57. saiban kakerareru   to   omottara
      court hold-passive QT   think-if
      if you think wou'll be taken to court

B58. yokei iya   ja-nai.
      over   bad   neg-tag
      it'd be terrible.

A59. un, yoku wakannai   kedo
      un well don't-know, but
      Yeah, well I don't know, but

A60. fukuzatsu   ni   natte-kita.
      complicated to   become-came
      it's gotten complicated.

A61. da-kara, boku wa, da-kara, dotchi no shoonin   ni   mo
      so   I   TM   so   which LK   witness   as   too
         denai   koto ni shite-aru kedo sa.
         appear-not fact to be-done   but EM
      So, I decided not to be a witness for either of them.

A62. maa, mukoo kara tanomi ni konai   kedo.
      well there   from request to come-not but
      They haven't asked me, though.

A63. daitai,   moo   honoruru kichatte-ru kara ne,
      generally already Honolulu came   since EM
      Anyway, I've been here in Honolulu so

A64. wakannai.
      don't-know
      I don't really know what's been happening.

APPENDIX C
20 clauses of female interaction

H1.   wako san, toshi wa ikutsu   desu ka?
      Wako Ms age   TM how-many cop QU
      Wako, how old are you?

W2.   toshi? he he.
      age   ha ha
      How Old?

W3.   nijuushichi.
          27
          I'm 27.
H4.   nijuushichi?
          27
          Twenty-seven?
W5.   nn.
          un
          Yes.
H6.   doko   de   umaremashita?
          where at   was-born
          Where were you born?
W7.   ano-ne, anoo, ehime-ken no oomishima tte iu chitcha-na
          uh   uh   Ehime   LK Omishima   QT say small
              shima de   umaremashita.
              island at   was-born
          Uh, let's see, I was born on a small island in Ehime
              Prefecture called Omishima.
H8.   a   soo?
          o   so
          Oh really?
H9.   anoo, soko   de sodatta no?
          uh   there at grew-up QU
          Uh, did you grow up there?
W10.   mm, soko   wa umareta dake   de [NN],
          mm there TM was-born only   cop-and
          Un-uh, I was only born there, and
W11.   sugu, anoo, hyoogo-ken no takarazuka-shi tte iu   toko
          soon   uh   Hyogo   LK Takarazuka   QT say place
              ni utsurimashita.
              to moved
          soon, uh, I moved to a place in Hyogo Prefecture called
              Takarazuka City.
H12.   a   soo?
          o   so
          Oh really?

H13.   sore-kara   amerika ni kita wake?
           and-then   America to came reason
           And then you came to America?

W14.   soo.
           so
           Yes.

W15.   kookoo   made da   kara,
           high-school until   cop since
           Since I was there until high school,

W16.   soko ni ite,
           there LC be-and
           I was there, and

W17.   sono ato, a,   amerika ni kite,
           that after uh America to come-and
           after that I came to America, and

W18.   daigaku sotsugyoo shita.
           college graduate   did
           graduated from college.

H19.   amerika- amerika e kita no   wa itsu desu ka?
           America- America to came nom TM when cop QU
           When was it that you came to America?

W20.   un-to ne,   dakara, kookoo sotsugyoo shita toki dakara
           uh   EM so   h.s.   graduate   did time so
           juuhassai no toki.
           18   LK time
         Uh, let's see, well, it was when I graduated from
           high school, so it was when I was 18.

TOPIC CONTINUITY IN WRITTEN AMHARIC NARRATIVE

MICHAEL GASSER
Interdepartmental Program in Applied Linguistics
University of California, Los Angeles

TABLE OF CONTENTS

1. *Introduction*

This paper examines the relative topic continuity of a number of constructions in written Amharic narrative. Topic arguments persist with varying degrees of continuity in discourse, and it is this continuity which is quantifiable and basic rather than the notion of topic itself. In narrative, relatively continuous topics are the norm, and each language makes use of various grammatical devices to signal degrees of discontinuity. While each of these devices also serves other functions, it should be possible to arrange them on a scale of topic continuity/discontinuity by establishing their average values for measurements which reflect continuity.

For each occurrence of an argument in text, three measurements were made:

1) LOOKBACK, the distance back (in number of clauses) to the last mention of the referent of the argument

2) POTENTIAL AMBIGUITY, a measure of competition from previous arguments for the identification of the referent of the argument in question, obtained by first replacing the device used for the argument by the most continuous possible device (in Amharic, normally verb agreement) and then identifying mentions of referents in the preceding five clauses which could replace that of the argument (a value of 2 assigned when there are competing referents and 1 when there are not)

3) DECAY, the number of successive clauses after the argument which contain further mentions of its referent.

The three measurements are illustrated for *abbatu* 'his father' in clause (d) of the following portion of text:

(1) (a) birhanu y-abbat-u-n   dăbdabbe kăft-o,
          Birhanu of-father-his-ACC   letter   open(CONVB)-he
          'When Birhanu opened his father's letter,

     (b) s-iy-anăbb,
          when-he-read(NON-PAST)
          and read (it),

     (c) dănăggăt'-ă.
          be=shocked(PAST)-he
          he was shocked.

     (d) *abbat-u*   l-i-măt'a   năbbăr.
          father-his   that-he-come(NON-PAST)   be (PAST)
          His father was coming.

(e)   almaz-in-inna   lij-očč-u-n   s-iy-ay-aččäw
       Almaz-ACC-and   child-PL-the-ACC   when-he-see(NON-PAST)-them
       When he saw Almaz and the children,

(f)   min yi-l   yi-hun?
       what he-say(NON-PAST)   it-become(JUS)
       What would he say?

(g)   birhanu däbdabbe-u-n   at'f-o,
       Birhanu letter-the-ACC   fold(CONVB)-he
       Birhanu folded the letter,

(h)   quč'č' bil-o,
       sit(CONVB)-he
       sat down,

(i)   m-assälasäl   jämmär-ä.
       INF-think=over   start(PAST)-he
       and started to think (things) over.'

The last reference to the father is in clause (a), so the LOOKBACK value is 3.
With *abbatu* left out in (d), either Birhanu or the father could conceivably be the
subject of the verb *limät'a näbbär*; hence the POTENTIAL AMBIGUITY is 2.
Since the father is referred to again in (e) and (f) but not in (g), the DECAY is 2.

LOOKBACK and POTENTIAL AMBIGUITY, taken together, provide a relatively direct measure of topic accessibility, the difficulty which the listener/
reader faces in identifying the referent of an argument. Since topic continuity
reflects the speaker/writer's assessment of topic accessiblity, it is these two
measurements which will be generally referred to in discussion of the continuity
of constructions. DECAY, on the other hand, measures what happens to an argument in following clauses, and it is therefore not as indicative of the continui-
ty/discontinuity marked by a device as the other measurements are. However,
it can be useful in comparing the continuity of constructions with similar LOOK-
BACK and POTENTIAL AMBIGUITY values, and it will be interesting to determine whether there is a correlation between topic expectedness, as measured
by LOOKBACK and POTENTIAL AMBIGUITY, and topic persistence, as
measured by DECAY.

The text used for the counts was Girmaččäw Täklä Hawaryat's *Ar'aya*, a
popular novel dealing primarily with the challenges faced by Ethiopian society
in the 1930's and 40's. The story line follows closely the actions of the central
character and thus maintains a relatively high degree of participant continuity.

2. The SOV Syntax, Clause Types and Paragraph Structure of Amharic

Amharic is an SOV language, and this order is adhered to quite strictly in the written language.

Sentences always end in main clauses, which have the full range of tense possibilities and also convey sentence mood. In narration, main clauses are usually in the past tense (traditionally called the "perfect"). Non-punctual (habitual or progressive) events are coded in the past continuous tense ("short imperfect" + auxiliary *năbbăr*), and anterior (preceding the main line of the narrative) events or states are marked by the past perfect tense ("converb" + auxiliary *năbbăr*). A main clause may also precede the final clause in a sentence. In such a case the two clauses are always in the same tense, and the verb of the first clause usually has the suffixed conjunction *-nna* 'and.'

The great majority of non-final clauses, however, are subordinate. Subordinate clauses are of the following types:

1) *adverbial clauses*

The specific semantic value ('when,' 'while,' 'after,' 'because,' 'if,' etc.) is signaled by a conjunction or prepositon prefixed either to a tensed verb form, or, much less frequently, to an infinitive.

2) *subject and verb complement clauses*

These have either an infinitive with no conjunction or a tensed verb form with the prefixed conjunction *indă-* 'that.'

3) *converb clauses*

The "converb" (also referred to as the "gerundive") is a non-tensed form which is marked for the person, number and gender of the subject like tensed verbs. It signals a "tight" relationship with the following clause, usually one involving close sequentiality. Converb clauses correspond roughly to English participial phrases but are much more frequent.

Relative clauses may also be embedded in any main or subordinate clause but they will not concern us in this study. (Relative clauses were not treated as "clauses" in the LOOK-BACK, DECAY and POTENTIAL AMBIGUITY counts, and counts were not made for arguments in relative clauses.)

Converb and temporal adverbial clauses are essentially tenseless (the tense used in temporal clauses is governed by the choice of conjunction and has no particular semantic significance) while reason adverbial clauses and subject/verb complement clauses take tense. Thus these latter types may, in addition to main-line events and states, also code anterior events and states.

Amharic narrative makes frequent use of sentences consisting of a series, potentially very long, of subordinate clauses followed by a single main clause.

The subordinate clauses in these "clause chains" are, at least in comparison to the final main clause, topical/presupposed rather than assertive, but as in other clause-chaining languages (see Givón, 1982), the subordinate clauses may also stand in topic-comment relations to one another. There is thus the possibility of a hierarchy of topicality among the clauses of a single sentence. The following is an example of a sentence with a relatively long chain of clauses and several embedded topic-comment relationships:

(2) (a) innắ-ar'aya . . .iyyắ-tắzắwawwắr-u,   *temporal adverbial*
          PL-Ar'aya   while-travel(PAST)-they
          'Ar'aya and the others, traveling around,

     (b) t'ắlat   ind-a-y-at'ắq-aččắw,   *purpose adverbial*
          enemy   that-NEG-he-attack(NON-PAST)-them
          in order not to be attacked by the enemy,

     (c) s-it't'ắbabbắq-u,   *temporal adverbial*
          when-they-be=careful(NON-PAST)-they
          being careful,

     (d) s-i-ččal-aččắw,   *temporal adverbial*
          when-they-be=possible(NON-PAST)-them
          whenever they could,

     (e) yắ-dingắt   adắga   iyyắ-t'al-u,   *temporal adverbial*
          of-surprise danger   while-throw(PAST)-they
          carrying out surprise attacks on them,

     (f) s-iy-asčắggir-u-t,   *temporal adverbial*
          when-they-give=trouble(NON-PAST)-they-him
          and giving them trouble,

     (g) bizu gize kắ-sắnắbbắt-u   bắhwala, *temporal adverbial*
          much time from-spend(PAST)-they   after
          after spending a long time (doing this),

     (h) . . . and qắn bắ-bulga . . . sắfr-ắw,   *converb*
              one day at-Bulga   camp(CONVB)-they
          one day, (Ar'aya and the others) having camped in Bulga,

     (i) t'ắlat   bắ-t'ắqwami   tắ-mắrt-o,   *converb*
          enemy   by-spy   PASS-lead(CONVB)-he
          the enemy, led by a spy,

     (j) bizu t'or   yiz-o,   *converb*
          much weapon carry(CONVB)-he
          with many weapons

(k)   măt't'-a-bbaččăw.   *main*
       come(PAST)-he-them(ADVRS)
       attacked them.'

(Girmaččăw, 1939 E.C., p. 323)

The clauses in this sentence are related topically in the following ways (an
"→" indicates a topic-comment relation):

$$
\left.\begin{array}{l} \text{(a)} \\ \text{(b)} \end{array}\right\} \rightarrow \text{(c)} \\ \text{(d)} \quad \rightarrow \text{(e)} \rightarrow \text{(f)} \left.\begin{array}{l} \\ \\ \\ \end{array}\right\} \rightarrow \text{(g)} \rightarrow \text{(h)} \rightarrow \left.\begin{array}{l} \text{(i)} \\ \text{(j)} \end{array}\right\} \rightarrow \text{(k)}.
$$

Infinitive clauses differ from others in having no marking for tense or obligatory subject agreement on the verb. The person, number and gender of the
subject may be copied on the infinitive in the form of a possessive suffix, or
there may be no subject marking on the verb at all. Infinitives with no subject
marking and no overt NP subject constitute the only possibility of ZERO-
ANAPHORA in Amharic. ZERO-ANAPHORA seems to occur only with the
relatively infrequent *adverbial* infinitive clauses; infinitives in verb-complement
clauses normally take the possessive subject marker. The following illustrate
adverbial and verb-complement infinitive clauses.

(3)   (a)   . . .   kă-nnat-u   gara wădă dirre dawa-nna
                       with-mother-his with to   Dire Dawa-and
              ' . . . traveling to Dire Dawa and to Harar with
              wădă harăr-im   bă-mă-mmălalăs   *temporal adverbial*
              to   Harar-also in-INF-travel   (ZERO-ANAPHORA)
              his mother,
       (b)   fărănj̆-očč-in   tămălkit-o   năbbăr.   *main*
              foreigner-PL-ACC see(CONBV)-he
              he had seen foreigners.'

(Girmaččăw, 1939 E.C., pp. 16-17)

(4)   (a)   săwiyyă-w abbat-wa   mă-hon-u-n   *verb-complement*
              man-the   father-her   INF- be-his-Acc
              'That the man was her father
       (b)   al-awwăq-ăčč-im.   *main*
              NEG-know(PAST)she-NEG
              she didn't know.'

3. Some Other Features of Amharic Grammar

3.1. Case and Verb Agreement

Agreement with the person, the number, and, for second and third person singular, the gender of the subject is obligatory on all verbs except infinitives. The markings consist of prefixes and suffixes in the non-past and jussive/imperative and suffixes in the past and converb. These are given, for all but the jussive/imperative, in Tables 1, 2 and 3.

Amharic has two sets of non-subject case markings. The *adnominal* markers, consisting of prepositions, postpositions or combinations thereof, are attached to NPs. The other set, which agree in person, number and gender with the argument, are suffixed to verbs; these will be referred to as OBJECT AGREEMENT particles. The case of an unstressed pronominalized object is indicated by OBJECT AGREEMENT. The case of a full noun phrase or of a stressed pronoun is usually signaled by an adnominal marker and may also be indicated on the verb with OBJECT AGREEMENT.

There are three categories of OBJECT AGREEMENT, one DIRECT, also called "plain," and two INDIRECT, also called "prepositional." The two sets of INDIRECT markers are derived historically from the prepositions (and ad-

Table 1. SUBJECT AGREEMENT: Past Tense

		Singular	Plural
1		qắt't'ắr-*ku* '*I* hired'	qắt't'ắr-*n*
2	m.	qắt't'ắr-*k*	qắt't'ắr-*aččihu*
	f.	qắt't'ắr-*š*	
3	m.	qắt't'ắr-*ä*	[1] qắt't'ắr-*u*
	f.	qắt't'ắr-*äčč*	

1) 3rd pers.pl. forms are also used for 2nd and 3rd pers. singl. *polite*.

Table 2. SUBJECT AGREEMENT: Non-Past Tense ("Short" Form[2])

		Singular	Plural
1		*i*-qắt' (i)r 'I hire/will hire'	*inni*-qắt' (i)r
2	m.	*ti*-qắt' (i)r	*ti*-qắt'r-*u*
	f.	*ti*-qắt'r-*i*	
3	m.	*yi*-qắt' (i)r	[1] *yi*-qắt'r-*u*
	f.	*ti*-qắt' (i)r	

Table 3. SUBJECT AGREEMENT: Converb

		Singular	Plural
1		qắt'irr-*e* 'I having hired'	qắt'r-*ăn*
2	m.	qắt'r-*ăh*	qắt'r-*ăččihu*
	f.	qắt'r-*ăš*	
3	m.	qắt'r-*o*	[1] qắt'r-*ăw*
	f.	qắt'r-*a*	

1) 3rd pers.pl. forms are also used for 2nd and 3rd pers. singl. *polite.*

2) In main clauses, the non-past also takes a conjugated suffix derived from the verb of existence *allă.*

nominal case markers) *lă-* and *bă-*; they will be referred to here as *b* and *l* OB-JECT AGREEMENT. The OBJECT AGREEMENT markers are given in Tables 4, 5 and 6.

There are more case markers in the adnominal set (at least five), and these do not always match the OBJECT AGREEMENT markers in neat, one-to-one relationships. The possible combination of markers from the two sets and the semantic nuances each combination conveys have been worked out in detail

Table 4. DIRECT OBJECT AGREEMENT: Past Tense, 3rd Person
Singular Masculine Subject

		Singular	Plural
1	m.	qắt't'ắr-ắ-*ňň* 'he hired *me*'	qắt't'ắr-ắ-*n*
2.	m.	qắt't'ắr-ắ-*h*	qắt't'ắr-∅-*aččɨhu*
	f.	qắt't'ắr-ắ-*š*	
	pol.	qắt't'ắr-∅ -*wot*	
3	m.	qắt't'ắr-ắ-*w*	[1] qắt't'ắr-∅-*aččắw*
	f.	qắt't'ắr-∅-*at*	

1) 3rd pers. pl. forms are also used for 3rd pers. singl. *polite*.

Table 5.1 OBJECT AGREEMENT: Past Tense, 3rd Person
Singular Masculine Subject

		Singular	Plural
1		qắt't'ắr-ắ-*lliňň* 'he hired *for me*'	qắt't'ắr-ắ-*llin*
2	m.	qắt't'ắr-ắ-*llih*	qắt't'ắr-ắ-*llaččihu*
	f.	qắt't'ắr-ắ-*lliš*	
	pol.	qắt't'ắr-ắ-*llwot*	
3	m.	qắt't'ắr-ắ-*llắt*	[1] qắt't'ắr-ắ-*llaččắw*
	f.	qắt't'ắr-ắ-*llat*	

Table 6. b OBJECT AGREEMENT: Past Tense, 3rd Person
Singular Masculine Subject

		Singular	Plural
1		qắt't'ắr-ắ-*bbiňň* 'he hired *to my detriment*'	qắt't'ắr-ắ-*bbin*
2	m.	qắt't'ắr-ắ-*bbih*	qắt't'ắr-ắ-*bbaččihu*
	f.	qắt't'ắr-ắ-*bbiš*	
	pol.	qắt't'ắr-ắ-*bbwot*	
3	m.	qắt't'ắr-ắ-*bbắt*	[1] qắt't'ắr-ắ-*bbaččắw*
	f.	qắt't'ắr-ắ-*bbat*	

1) 3rd pers. pl. forms are also used for 3rd pers. singl. *polite.*

by Hetzron (1970). Only the most common combinations, namely, those occurring in the portions of the text considered, are dealt with in this paper. These are outlined in Table 7. The cases are illustrated in the following:

ACCUSATIVE

(5)   *sim-un -n*   qăyyăr-ă-*w*.
q   *name-his-Acc*   change(PAST)-he-*him/it*
         'He changed *his name*.'

DATIVE

(6)   *lä-girma*   hullu-n-im   năggăr-ă-*w*.
         to/for-Girma   all-ACC-also   tell(PAST)-he-*him*
         'He told *Girma* everything.'

(7)   *lä-girma*   gănzăb-u-n   măllăs-ă-*llät*.
         to/for-Girma   money-the-ACC   return(PAST)-he-*him*
         'He returned the money *to Girma*.'

(8)   *girma*   bărrăd-ă-*w*.
         Girma   be=cold(PAST)-he/it-*him*
         '*Girma* is cold.'

BENEFACTIVE

(9)   *lä-girma*   bărr-u-n   kăffăt-ă-*llät*.
         to/for-Girma   door-the-ACC   open(PAST)-he-*him(BEN)*
         'He opened the door *for Girma*.'

ADVERSATIVE

(10)   *hizb-u*   tilliq siqay   dărrăs-ă-*bbăt*.
         people-the   great suffering   arrive(PAST)-he/it-*him/it(ADVRS)*
         'Great suffering befell *the people*.'

NECESSITATIVE

(11)   *girma*   mă-nnăsat   năbbăr-ă-*bbăt*.
         Girma   INF-get=up   exist(PAST)-he/it-*him(NEC)*
         '*Girma* had to get up.'

POSSESSOR

(12)   *girma*   bet   năbbăr-ă-*w*.
         Girma   house   exist(PAST)-he/it-*him*
         '*Girma* had a house.'

Table 7. Case Marking in Amharic

Case	Adnominal Marker	Object Agreement
ACCUSATIVE	NP-*n* on all definite, some generic NPs ∅ for all indefinite-referential NPs	DIRECT
DATIVE 1) with certain verbs, e.g., *sät't'ä* 'give,' *näggärä* 'tell'	*lä*-NP	DIRECT
2) with other verbs, e.g., *gälläs'ä,* 'explain,' *mälläsä* 'return, answer'	*lä*-NP	l
3) with impersonal verbs, e.g., *bärrädä* 'be cold,' *rabä* 'hunger'	[1] ∅	DIRECT
BENEFACTIVE	*lä*-NP	l
ADVERSATIVE, NECESSITATIVE	[1] ∅	b
POSSESSOR	[1] ∅	DIRECT
INSTRUMENTAL	*bä*-NP	b
AGENTIVE (in PASSIVE)	*bä*-NP	not possible
LOCATIVE, ABLATIVE, GOAL	*i-*, *kä-*, *bä-*, *wädä-*, etc. NP (+ *lay,* *ga,* etc.)	b

1) For the purposes of this paper, these subjects which take OBJECT VERB AGREE-MENT are considered to be objects.

The cases not exemplified are not dealt with in this paper.

As noted above, when an argument is pronominalized and unstressed, the case is marked only with an AGREEMENT. This is illustrated in the following example for an ACCUSATIVE object:

(13) (a)   azeb zămăd-u   silă-năbbăr-ăčč,
          Azeb relative-his because-be (PAST)-she
          'Because Azeb was his relative,
     (b)   qăt't'ăr-*φ-at.*
          hire(PAST)-he-*her*
          he hired *her.*'

Even without the adnominal marker, the case is usually clear in such cases from the form of the AGREEMENT and from the context.

For overt NPs, the occurrence of AGREEMENT on the verb in addition to the adnominal case marking is governed by the following rules:

   1) Regardless of how many non-subject arguments a clause has, the verb may take at most one OBJECT AGREEMENT particle (see (6), (7) and (9) above).

   2) Only definite non-subjects may take verb AGREEMENT.

Definite and indefinite accusative objects are illustrated in the following:

(14) (a)   girma   *bet-u-n*   găzza-φ.
          Girma *house-the-ACC* buy(PAST)-he
          'Girma bought *the house.*'
     (b)   girma   *bet-u-n*   găzza-φ-w.
          Girma *house-the-ACC* buy(PAST)-he-*him/it*
          Girma bought *the house.*'
     (c)   girma   *bet*   găzza-φ.
          Girma *house*   buy(PAST)-he
          'Girma bought *a house.*'
     (d) *girma   *bet*   găzza-φ-w.

For definite overt non-subjects, there is therefore the choice between the adnominal case marking alone or the adnominal case marker plus an OBJECT AGREEMENT particle. Since the case relationship is generally clear from the adnominal marker, the OBJECT AGREEMENT, when present, is largely redundant and is sometimes referred to as a *resumptive pronoun.* Getatchew (1970) and Hetzron (1971) have demonstrated that resumptive pronouns have a "topic-alizing" and "presentative" function. Thus, following (14b) above, one expects further reference to the "house" whereas there is no such expectation for (14a).

3.2. *Independent Pronouns*

Table 8 gives the INDEPENDENT (stressed) PRONOUNS. Note that these takes the normal adnominal case markers. Note also that the INDEPENDENT PRONOUN system makes only one distinction not made in the SUBJECT/OBJECT AGREEMENT markers: the third person plural. (The distinction between second person singular polite and third person plural is made with the OBJECT AGREEMENT particles as well as the INDEPENDENT PRONOUNS but not with the SUBJECT AGREEMENT particles.)

Table 8. Independent Pronouns

| | | | SUBJECT | OBJECT | | |
				ACCUSATIVE	DATIVE-BENEFACTIVE	AGENTIVE-LOCATIVE
Sing.	1		ine	ine-n	lă-ne	bă-ne
	2	m.	antă	antă-n	l-antă	b-antă
		f.	anči	anči-n	l-anči	b-anči
		pol.	irswo	irswo-n	lă-rswo	bă-rswo
	3	m.	issu	issu-n	lă-ssu	bă-ssu
		f.	isswa	isswa-n	lă-sswa	bă-sswa
		pol.	issaččăw	issaččă-n	lă-ssaččăw	bă-ssaččăw
PL.	1		iňňa	iňňa-n	lă-ňňa	bă-ňňa
	2		innantă	innantă-n	lă-nnantă	bă-nnantă
	3		innăssu	innăssu-n	lă-nnăssu	bă-nnăssu

3.3. *Definiteness and Indefiniteness*

Definite nouns, other than names, which are not modified by possessives or demonstratives are marked with the definite suffix *-u* (masculine), *-wa* (feminine) (see (5), (7), (9) and (14)). This suffix appears either on the noun itself or on a modifying adjective or relative clause verb. In relative clauses it takes the form of the direct object agreement particle. Further examples of the definite suffix:

(15)   tıllıq-*u*   zaf   wăyra   năw.
        large-*the*   tree   olive   be (NON-PAST)
        '*The* large tree is an olive.'

(16)   yă-qorrăt'-n-*ăw*   zaf   wăyra   năw.
        REL-cut (PAST)-we-*the*   tree   olive   be (NON-PAST)
        '*The* tree which we cut down is an olive.'

There is no indefinite article; however, singular indefinite-referential NPs are frequently preceded by *and* 'one' to distinguish them from indefinite-non-referential (generic) NPs. This distinction is illustrated in the following:

(17) (a)   măs'haf ı-făllıg-allăhu.
           book   I-look=for (NON-PAST) - I(MC)
           'I'm looking for a book.' (any book or particular book)

     (b)   *and* măs'haf ı-făllıg-allăhu.
           one book   I-look=for (NON-PAST) - I (MC)
           'I'm looking for a (particular) book.'

Recall that definite object NPs are further distinguished from indefinite object NPs in two ways: the -n suffix is obligatory on definite ACCUSATIVE objects, but not possible on indefinite-referential objects; and definite objects, but not indefinite objects, may take verb agreement.

3.4. *Passive*

Passive in Amharic is marked by the verb prefix *tă-*. (When *tă-* follows a SUBJECT AGREEMENT prefix, it assimilates to the stem-initial consonant and is realized as gemination on this consonant.) Passive occurs with and without the agent expressed. (b) and (c) below illustrate the passive.

(18) (a)   and lij   măskot-u-n   săbbăr-ă.
            one child window-the-ACC break(PAST)-he
            'A child broke the window.'
     (b)   măskot-u   b-and   lij   tă-săbbăr-ă.
            window-the AG-one child PASS-break(PAST)-he/it
            'The window was broken by a child.'
     (c)   măskot-u   tă-săbbăr-ă.
            window-the PASS-break(PAST)-he/it
            'The window was broken.'

One function of passive is to mark topic discontinuity. In the following
example, passive and an indefinite-referential NP, another discontinuous device,
coincide with the introduction of a new participant, who in fact becomes the
main protagonist of the novel.

(19) (a)   siddist yahil   lij-ŏčč   kă-higg   mist-ăččăw
            six   amount child-PL from-law   wife-his(POL)
            'He sired six children by his legal wife,
            wăld-ăw,
            bear/sire(CONVB)-he(POL)
     (b)   hullum   s-i-mot-u-bbaččăw,
            all   when-they-die(NON-PAST)-they-him(POL,ADVRS)
            and all of them died,
     (c)   măč'ărrășa băstă-rjinna   and wănd   lij
            end   toward-old=age   one male child
            but finally in his old age a son was born,
            tă-wăld-o,
            PASS-bear/sire(CONVB)-he
     (d)   sim-u-n-im   ar'aya   bil-ăw-t   năbbăr.
            name-his-ACC-TOP Ar'aya say(CONVB)-they-him COP(PAST)
            and they named him Ar'aya.

Note that the active form of the verb in the passive clause, wăllădă 'bear, sire',
has appeared in clause (a), again with an indefinite-referential patient. The
passive and indefinite referential *subject* mark clause (c) as the more discontinuous.

3.5. *Topic Markers*

Amharic has two topic-shift markers, *-ss* and *-m*. *-ss*, which points to a strong contrast between the element marked and a preceding or following element, appears only in the conversations in the text and hence was not included in the counts.

-m, on the other hand, occurs frequently in narration as well as in conversation. It may be suffixed to a member of any word class, including an indefinite NP, and an NP in any case. *-m* marks either a similarity or a mild contrast between the element it stands on and a preceding element. It says, in effect, "I've been talking about X; now I'm going to talk about Y (marked with *-m*), and what I say about Y will not contrast strongly with what I have said about X." *-m* is "contrastive" in the sense that it marks a topic shift.

It often translates as 'also,' as in the following:

(20) (a) girma   abɨyot-u-n   yɨ-dǎggɨf
          Girma   revolution-the-ACC he-suport(NON-PAST)
          'Girma supported the revolution.
          nǎbbǎr.
          be (PAST)
     (b) ihɨt-u-*m*   bǎt'am   tǎramaǰ   nǎbbǎr-ǎčč.
          sister-his-*m* very   progressive be (PAST)-she
          His sister was *also* very progressive.'

Here the sister is compared to Girma. With less similarity between the compared or contrasted elements, the particle's function as a topic-shift marker is even clearer. The following passage from a description of a dream in *Ar'aya* (pp. 198-199) contains a number of instances of this usage:

(21) (a) madam   dǎbon   fuwa   ɨǰ̌ǰ̌-wa-n   zǎrgɨt-a
          Madame Dǎbon   Fuwa   hand-her-ACC   stretch(CONVB)-she
          'Madame Dǎbon Fuwa, stretching out her hand,
     (b) "na! wǎdǎ-ne,   ar'aya   lɨǰ̌-e!"
          come to-me   Ar'aya   son-my
          "Come to me, Ar'aya, my son!"
     (c) ɨyy-al-ǎčč
          while-say PAST)-she
          she said

(d) wắdắ issu ti-mắt'a   žắmmắr.
     to   him   she-come(NON-PAST) begin(PAST)
     and began to come toward him.

(e) issu-*m*, ya-mắžắmmắriya-w diniggat'e
     he-*m*   of-beginning-the   surprise
     After his initial surprise passed,
     k-allắf-ắ-llắt   bắhwala,
     from-pass(PAST)-it-him(BEN)

(f) "aye!   irswo   nắwot?
     oh   you(POL)   be(NON-PAST,you,POL)
     "Oh! Is it you?

(g) al-awwắq-hu-wot-im   nắbbắr,"
     NEG-know(PAST)-I-you(POL)-NEG   be(PAST)
     I didn't recognize you,"

(h) iyy-al-ắ,
     while-say (PAST)-he
     he said,

(i) wắdắ isswa tắmắllắs-ắ.
     to   her   return(PAST)-he
     and he returned to her.

(j) isswa-*m* hazắn   bắ-mm-i-ssắmma-bbắt
     she-*m*   sadness by-REL-it-be=heard(NON-PAST)-him/it(LOC)
     In a voice filled with sadness she spoke
     dims'   indih   si-tt-il,
     voice   like=this when-she-say(NON-PAST)

(k) t'ắyyắq-ắčč-iw.
     ask(PAST)-she-him
     and asked him,

(l) "ar'aya, min   hon-k-ibbiňň?
     Ar'aya, what become(PAST)-you-me(ADVRS)
     "Ar'aya, what happened to you?

(m) min nắw   sắwinnắt-ih hullu indih
     what be(NON-PAST)   body-your   all   like=this
     Why has your body all changed?"
     tắ-lắwwắt'-ắ?" '
     PASS-change(PAST)-he/it

(n)   ar'aya-*m*   bǎ-zziya gize sǎwɨnnǎt-u-n   tǎmǎlkɨt-o,
        Ar'aya-*m*   at-that time body-his-ACC look(CONVB)-he
        Then Ar'aya looked at his body,

(o)   iwnǎt-*im*   tǎ-lǎwwɨt'-wal. . . .
        truth-*m*   PASS-change(CONVB)-he/it(PR=PF)
        and it really had changed. . . .

(p)   bǎ-zziya-*m* gize bǎ-zuriya-w   s-i-yastǎwɨl,
        at-that-*m*   time in-surrounding-the   when-he-look(NON-PAST)
        Then when he looked around him,

(q)   bɨzu   sǎw   tǎsǎbsɨb-o,
        much   person   gather(CONVB)-he
        that many people had gathered

(r)   ɨndǎmm-i-mmǎlǎkkǎt-ǎw
        that-he-watch(NON-PAST)-him
        and were watching him

(s)   ayy-ǎ.
        see(PAST)-he
        he saw.

(t)   madam dǎbon fuwa-*m*   dɨnɨggat'e-w-ɨn   b-ayy-ǎčč
        Madame Dǎbon Fuwa-*m*   surprise-his-ACC at-see(PAST)-she
        Madame Dǎbon Fuwa, when she saw his surprise,
        gize,
        time

(u)   tǎt'ǎgg-ačč-ɨw-ɨnna
        approach (PAST) -she-him-and
        approached him,

(v)   tikǎša-w-ɨn   yaz-ǎčč-ɨw,
        shoulder-his-ACC   hold(PAST)-she-him
        held his shoulder,

(w)   ras-u-n-ɨm   dabbǎs-ǎčč-ɨw.
        head-his-ACC-m   stroke(PAST)-she-him
        and stroked his head.'

The -*m*'s on the names and pronouns referring to the two characters here clearly
indicate the shifts in subject/topic. The -*m* on *iwnǎt* in clause (o) compares what
Ar'aya sees to be the case with what Madame Dǎbon Fuwa has just asserted.
The -*m* on *bǎzziya* in clause (q) contrasts that moment with the time before it.

Topic shifts may also be signaled by the words *dǎgmo* 'also,' comparable to
-*m*, and *gin* 'but,' comparable to -*ss*.

4. *The Use of Topic-Continuity Devices in Amharic*

LOOKBACK, DECAY and POTENTIAL AMBIGUITY were counted for occurrences of the following devices:

1) ZERO-ANAPHORA:
Ø subjects in infinitive adverbial clauses, subject not marked as possessive on infinitive

2) VERB AGREEMENT:
SUBJECT or OBJECT AGREEMENT on a verb, including possessive marking of "subject" on infinitives, no overt subject

3) INDEPENDENT PRONOUNS

4) DEFINITE NP SUBJECTS:
verb agreement obligatory

5) DEFINITE NP OBJECTS with and without OBJECT AGREEMENT

6) INDEFINITE-REFERENTIAL NPs:
verb agreement obligatory for subjects, no object agreement

7) PASSIVE SUBJECTS

8) NP SUBJECTS with -*m* (contrasted with NP subjects without -*m*)

9) ADVERBIAL, CONVERB and SUBJECT/VERB-COMPLEMENT SUBORDINATE CLAUSES and MAIN CLAUSES.

Devices 1) to 8) are ordered here in terms of their continuity properties; discussion of the ordering is given in section 6.

For each device HUMAN and NON-HUMAN arguments were distinguished.

5. *Results of Counts*

5.1. *ZERO-ANAPHORA*

Results for ZERO-ANAPHORA are given in Table 9. In each cell of this, and of the succeeding tables, the figure in the upper left corner is the mean value for the measure, and the figure in the lower right corner is the number of tokens counted. Means based on fewer than 10 tokens are enclosed in parentheses.

Note the very low LOOKBACK and POTENTIAL AMBIGUITY values (1 is the minimum possible for both) for this highly continuous device and also the high DECAY value, indicating persistence.

5.2. *VERB AGREEMENT*

Results for VERB AGREEMENT are given in Table 9.

The POTENTIAL AMBIGUITY and DECAY figures here show this to be a slightly less continuous device used for less persistent participants than

ZERO-ANAPHORA. We also see higher continuity/persistence for SUBJECTS and DATIVE/BENEFACTIVE/ADVERSATIVE-NECESSATIVE OBJECTS than for ACCUSATIVE OBJECTS.

Table 9. Continuity Measures for ZERO-ANAPHORA
and VERB AGREEMENT

		ZERO ANAPH SUBJ	VERB AGREEMENT		
			SUB	ACC	DAT/BEN ADV/NEC
LOOKBACK	HUMAN	1.1 28	1.1 333	2.0 50	1.2 91
LOOKBACK	NON-HUMAN	(1.0) 1	1.4 28	(1.2) 4	(1.0) 2
DECAY	HUMAN HUMAN	3.9 28	2.6 333	2.1 50	2.3 91
DECAY	NON-HUMAN	(1.0) 1	1.5 28	(0.8) 4	(2.0) 2
POTENTIAL AMBIGUITY	HUMAN	1.11 28	1.15 333	1.22 50	1.36 91
POTENTIAL AMBIGUITY	NON-HUMAN	(1.0) 1	1.25 28	(1.5) 4	(1.0) 2

Table 10 gives a more detailed breakdown for HUMAN NON-ACCUSATIVE OBJECTS. For each type the adnominal case marker and OBJECT AGREEMENT are given. What stands out here are the high DECAY figures for POSSESSOR and DIRECT OBJECT AGREEMENT DATIVE, the high POTENTIAL AMBIGUITY counts for the two categories of DATIVE with adnominal *lǎ-*, and the low POTENTIAL AMBIGUITY value for BENEFACTIVE.

Table 10. Human Non-Accusative Objects (VERB AGREEMENT)

	POSSESSOR Ø, DO	DATIVE Ø, DO	DATIVE lä, DO	DATIVE lä, 1 OB	BEN lä, 1 OB	ADV/NEC Ø, b OB

LOOKBACK	1.0
	    13
		1.3
		    30
			1.1
			    19
				1.1
				    14
					1.1
					    19
						(1.4)
						    9

DECAY	3.5
	    13
		1.19
		    30
			2.7
			    19
				1.6
				    14
					1.9
					    19
						(2.8)
						    9

POTENTIAL
AMBIGUITY
	1.31
	    13
		1.33
		    30
			1.47
			    19
				1.50
				    14
					1.16
					    19
						(1.44)
						    9

5.3. *INDEPENDENT PRONOUNS*

Result for HUMAN INDEPENDENT PRONOUNS are shown in Table 11. There were too few NON-HUMAN INDEPENDENT PRONOUNS to warrant inclusion here.

The LOOKBACK and POTENTIAL AMBIGUITY figures for PRONOUN SUBJECTS indicate slightly greater discontinuity than for SUBJECT VERB AGREEMENT.

5.4. *DEFINITE NP SUBJECTS*

Results for DEFINITE NP SUBJECTS are given in Table 12.

Here we see a further increase in discontinuity. The LOOKBACK and DECAY figures also point to greater continuity and persistence for HUMAN than for NON-HUMAN arguments.

5.5 *DEFINITE NP OBJECTS With and Without OBJECT AGREEMENT*

Results for DEFINITE NP OBJECTS are shown in Table 12.

Note that alll NON-ACCUSATIVE DEFINITE OBJECTS counted had VERB AGREEMENT. ACCUSATIVE OBJECTS with and without OBJECT AGREEMENT are seen to differ mainly in their DECAY values, with greater persistence for those with AGREEMENT.

Table 11. Continuity Measures for
INDEPENDENT PRONOUNS (Human)

	SUB	ACC	DAT, BEN, ADV/NEC
LOOKBACK	1.2 31	(1.8) 6	(4.0) 3
DECAY	2.2 31	(1.3) 6	(0.0) 3
POTENTIAL AMBIGUITY	1.29 31	(1.5) 6	(1.0) 3

Table 12. Continuity Measures for DEFINITE NP'S

		SUB	ACC w/ V AGR	ACC w/o V AGR	DAT, BEN, ADV/NEC
LOOKBACK	HUMAN	9.6 125	12.2 23	11.8 19	8.6 18
LOOKBACK	NON-HUMAN	14.5 103	12.5 17	15.8 126	(7.7) 3
DECAY	HUMAN	2.5 125	1.7 23	0.6 19	1.6 18
DECAY	NON-HUMAN	0.5 103	0.4 17	0.1 126	(0.7) 3
POTENTIAL AMBIGUITY	HUMAN	1.40 125	1.13 23	1.47 19	1.50 18
POTENTIAL AMBIGUITY	NON-HUMAN	1.37 103	1.29 17	1.35 126	(1.67) 3

Comparing the LOOKBACK figures for DEFINITE NP SUBJECTS and ACCU-
SATIVE OBJECTS, we again see evidence for the greater discontinuity of AC-
CUSATIVES.

5.6. *REFERENTIAL-INDEFINITE NPs*

Results for INDEFINITE-REFERENTIAL NPs are given in Table 13.
POTENTIAL AMBIGUITY was not counted because more continuous devices
such as VERB AGREEMENT are in any case ruled out for arguments being
introduced for the first time, and competition from other arguments is thus
irrelevant to the selection of this device over others. No NON-ACCUSATIVE
INDEFINITE-REFERENTIAL OBJECTS were found in the text.

Here we note the very high LOOKBACK counts (maximum of 20). In fact,
one might expect averages of 20.0 for arguments which are introduced for the
first time; they are slightly lower because in some cases the class of the argument has been mentioned previously and in this case the LOOKBACK value is
the distance back to that mention. Note also the high DECAY value for HUMAN
SUBJECTS, an indication that these are relatively persistent arguments.

Table 13. Continuity Measures for
INDEFINITE-REFERENTIAL NPs

		SUB	ACC
LOOKBACK	HUMAN	17.7 22	18.3 11
	NON-HUMAN	19.1 47	19.3 49
DECAY	HUMAN	2.6 22	0.8 11
	NON-HUMAN	0.5 47	0.2 49

5.7. *PASSIVE SUBJECTS*

Results for PASSIVE SUBJECTS are shown in Table 14.

For the most part, the numbers of tokens here are too small to warrant any immediate conclusions. One point that does come out in the figures for VERB AGREEMENT and DEFINITE NP HUMAN arguments is the higher DECAY value for PASSIVE SUBJECTS than for ACTIVE SUBJECTS.

Table 14. Continuity Measures for PASSIVE SUBJECTS

		V AGR	PERS PRON	DEF NP	INDEF-REF NP	TOTAL
LOOKBACK	HUMAN	1.0 13	(1.0) 1	10.4 14	(20.0) 2	6.6 30
	NON-HUMAN	(5.0) 5	0	16.0 16	(20.0) 8	14.0 29
DECAY	HUMAN	1.5 13	(8.0) 1	2.0 14	(0.5) 2	1.9 30
	NON-HUMAN	(2.8) 5	0	0.3 16	(0.2) 8	0.7 29
POTENTIAL AMBIGUITY	HUMAN	1.08 13	(1.0) 1	1.50 14		1.29 29
	NON-HUMAN	(1.25) 5	0	1.31 16		1.29 21

5.8. *DEFINITE SUBJECTS NP with -m*

Table 15 compares results for HUMAN DEFINITE NP SUBJECTS with an without the topic-shift marker *-m*.

There are clear differences for all three measures. Here the LOOKBACK and POTENTIAL AMBIGUITY figures seem to contradict one another; however, this pattern of results is not surprising given the use of -*m* as a contrastive device. The reasoning behind this is discussed in 6.1.

5.9 *SUBORDINATE and MAIN CLAUSES*

Table 16 compares the LOOKBACK and DECAY figures for HUMAN SUBJECTS indicated with VERB AGREEMENT in MAIN CLAUSES and the three major types of SUBORDINATE CLAUSES. All of the clause types have comparable LOOKBACK values while the DECAY values vary, with MAIN CLAUSES having a more rapid DECAY rate than SUBORDINATE CLAUSES and CONVERB CLAUSES having a slightly slower DECAY rate than other SUBORDINATE CLAUSES.

Table 17 gives the mean values for the measures across all construction types for SUBJECTS and ACCUSATIVE OBJECTS in MAIN CLAUSES, CONVERB and ADVERBIAL CLAUSES combined, and VERB-COMPLEMENT CLAUSES. The pattern of results is somewhat complicated, with the difference in the clause types depending heavily on whether the arguments considered are HUMAN or NON-HUMAN and SUBJECT or ACCUSATIVE. For example, for HUMAN SUBJECTS, MAIN CLAUSES clearly have the highest LOOKBACK value whereas for HUMAN ACCUSATIVE OBJECTS, CONVERB and ADVERBIAL CLAUSES have the highest value.

Table 15. Continuity Measures for DEFINITE NP'S
(Human, Subjects) With and Without -*m*

	DEF NP -*m*-	DEF NP -*m*
LOOKBACK	6.2 36	10.9 89
DECAY	3.4 36	2.1 89
POTENTIAL AMBIGUITY	1.53 36	1.31 89

Table 16. Continuity Measures by Clause Type
(VERB AGREEMENT, Human Subjects)

	MAIN	CON-VERB	ADVERB-IAL	SUB/V-COMP
LOOKBACK	1.2 80	1.2 31	1.1 42	1.3 28
DECAY	1.8 80	2.9 31	·2.6 42	2.5 28

Table 17. Continuity Measures by Clause Type
(All Constructions)

		SUBJECT			ACCUSATIVE		
		MAIN CLAUSES	ADV, CONVB CLAUSES	VERB COMP CLAUSES	MAIN CLAUSES	ADV, CONVB CLAUSES	VERB COMP CLAUSES
LOOKBACK	HUMAN	5.9 134	2.3 261	2.5 67	5.6 45	9.8 64	5.4 11
LOOKBACK	NON-HUMAN	13.6 120	11.5 66	18.4 24	15.6 70	16.0 128	17.2 16
DECAY	HUMAN	2.4 134	2.9 261	2.4 67	1.7 45	1.3 64	1.0 11
DECAY	NON-HUMAN	0.9 120	0.2 66	0.1 24	0.2 70	0.2 128	0.1 16
POTENTIAL AMBIGUITY	HUMAN	1.34 129	1.14 256	1.11 64	1.27 41	1.28 47	1.09 11
POTENTIAL AMBIGUITY	NON-HUMAN	1.38 65	1.32 55	1.20 10	1.28 40	1.38 95	1.33 12

Table 18. Continuity Measures for Sentence-Medial Converb and Adverbial Clauses
(All Constructions, Human Subjects)

LOOKBACK	1.54 54
DECAY	2.56 54
POTENTIAL AMBIGUITY	1.22 54

The values of the three measures for sentence-medial CONVERB and AD-VERBIAL CLAUSES were also counted. These results are given in Table 18. Note especially the low LOOKBACK figure for these clauses, indicative of high continuity.

5.10. *Frequency of Construction Types*

Table 19 shows the number of tokens in the various categories occurring in 571 clauses. (Relative frequencies in other tables are not valid because the number of clauses looked at varied with the category of construction.) GENERIC (INDEFINITE-NON-REFERENTIAL) NPs are included for comparison.

Here we see the general tendency for more continuous devices to occur more frequently. The notable exception is the INDEPENDENT PRONOUNS. The skewed distributions of HUMAN vs. NON-HUMAN arguments and of the different cases is also striking. Note in particular the interaction between the presence/absence of OBJECT AGREEMENT with ACCUSATIVE DEFINITE NPs and the HUMAN/NON-HUMANNESS of the referent.

Table 20 gives mean clauses per paragraph of the clause types considered. The relatively large proportion of subordinate clauses which we see here is typical of clause-chaining languages.

6. *Discussion and Evaluation*

6.1. *LOOKBACK*

Figure 1 summarizes the LOOKBACK values for the various constructions

Table 19. Total Occurrence of Construction Types (571 Clauses)

		SUB	ACC w/ V AGR	ACC w/o V AGR	DAT	BEN	ADV-NEC
VB AGR	HUMAN	324	29	–	29	3	2
	NON-HUMAN	7	1	–	1	0	0
IND PRON	HUMAN	3	1	1	0	0	0
	NON-HUMAN	1	0	0	0	0	0
DEF NPs	HUMAN	88	20	17	2	0	0
	NON-HUMAN	58	10	91	0	0	0
DEF NP+-m	HUMAN	21	2	3	0	0	0
	NON-HUMAN	3	1	1	0	0	0
INDEF-REF NPs	HUMAN	11	0	6	0	0	0
	NON-HUMAN	27	0	30	0	0	0
GEN NPs	HUMAN	0	0	3	0	0	0
	NON-HUMAN	8	0	10	0	0	0
PASS SUB	HUMAN	16					
	NON-HUMAN	11					

Table 20. Mean Number of Clauses Per Paragraph (50 Paragraphs)

Main Clauses	2.96	35.5%
Subordinate Clauses	5.38	64.5%
Adverbial	3.10	37.1%
Converb	1.72	20.6%
Sub/V-Complement	0.56	6.7%
Total	8.34	100.0%

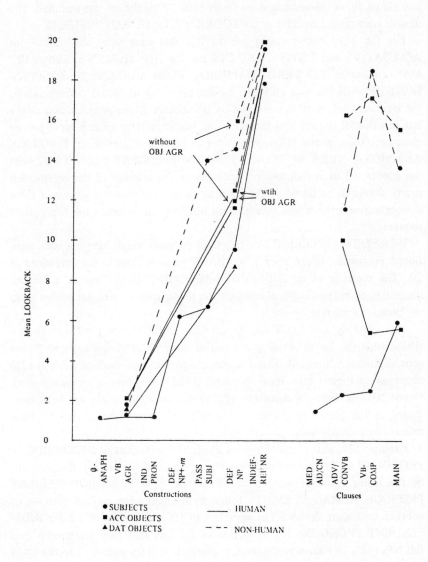

Figure 1. Mean LOOKBACK for all Construction and Clause Types

and clause types. Means based on fewer than 10 tokens are not included. The devices are arranged in order of the LOOKBACK for HUMAN SUBJECTS.

For the seven constructions, we see that this same order also obtains for ACCUSATIVE and DATIVE OBJECTS and for NON-HUMAN as well as HUMAN arguments. For ZERO-ANAPHORA, VERB AGREEMENT, INDEPENDENT PRONOUNS, and DEFINITE NPs, the order of course corresponds to the increasing information conveyed by the devices. As the distance back to the last mention of the referent increases, the reader must be given a more precise characterization of the referent in order to be able to identify it. For ZERO-ANAPHORA, VERB AGREEMENT and INDEPENDENT PRONOUNS, what the counts tell us is that the last mention of the referent of the argument is nearly always to be found in the previous clause. The presence of one of these devices instructs the reader that he need not look far to locate the appropriate referent.

INDEFINITE-REFERENTIAL NPs have referents which have not been mentioned previously; hence their LOOKBACK value is close to the maximum of 20. The presence of an INDEFINITE-REFERENTIAL NP signals a marked discontinuity in the discourse and tells the reader that he need not bother looking back for a referent.

The relatively low LOOKBACK value for DEFINITE NPs with -*m* is consistent with the use of -*m* as a contrastive device. Contrastive topic shifts are generally made within a localized context; reported conversations, such as (21) above, are a typical case. What -*m* marks is the *resumption* of a recently mentioned NP as a topic. In clause (n) of (21), for example, *Ar'aya* has been mentioned in the preceding clause. In clause (t) *Madame Dâbon Fuwa* has been referred to 9 clauses back.

Example (21) also provides a good illustration of the use of INDEPENDENT PRONOUNS for contrastive purposes (clauses (e) and (j)). In fact, this seems to be the major disourse function of this device. (74% of the INDEPENDENT PRONOUN HUMAN SUBJECTS found in the text were marked with -*m* or another topic-shift device.) The very low LOOKBACK value of 1.2 for INDEPENDENT PRONOUNS is a reflection of the fact that they are chosen over full NPs (with -*m*) when relatively few clauses have been given over to the other topic. Compare this value to the 6.2 obtained for DEFINITE NPs with -*m*.

For PASSIVE SUBJECTS we must bear in mind that the value given for HUMAN arguments, 6.6, is the average for all construction types, e.g., VERB AGREEMENT, DEFINITE NPs. Comparing this value with the average LOOKBACK for all ACTIVE HUMAN SUBJECTS, 3.4, we see a significantly higher level of unexpectedness/discontinuity associated with PASSIVE SUBJECTS. Considering only DEFINITE NP SUBJECTS, we find the same ordering (9.6 for ACTIVE, 10.4 for PASSIVE) though the magnitude of the difference is a good deal smaller. On the other hand, there is no corresponding difference for ACTIVE and PASSIVE SUBJECTS marked with VERB AGREEMENT. This seeming discrepancy may be explained as follows: The use of SUBJECT VERB AGREEMENT alone, whether in ACTIVE or PASSIVE voice, is not really possible for relatively unexpected arguments; therefore, when PASSIVE appears without SUBJECT VERB AGREEMENT, it is more likely an instance of another of the functions of PASSIVE, for example, agent suppression (see Givón, 1979), than of topic discontinuity. In this regard, note the relative infrequency of this combination of devices; 45% of total HUMAN PASSIVE SUBJECTS but 76% of total HUMAN ACTIVE SUBJECTS have VERB-AGREEMENT alone. For NON-HUMAN SUBJECTS the LOOKBACK values for ACTIVE and PASSIVE are comparable (for all constructions, 13.5 and 14.0 respectively). What this seems to point to is that NON-HUMAN OBJECTS are promoted to SUBJECT position as a means of suppressing the agent rather than signaling topic discontinuity.

Consider now the LOOKBACK for DEFINITE NP ACCUSATIVES with and without OBJECT AGREEMENT. For HUMAN arguments the values are very close, while the difference is quite large for NON-HUMAN arguments. Recalling that OBJECT AGREEMENT tends to occur with relatively topical arguments, we find here what we would expect for NON-HUMAN ACCUSATIVE OBJECTS. As a signal of relative continuity of OBJECTS, OBJECT AGREEMENT, which occurs with most HUMAN ACCUSATIVES and nearly all (HUMAN) DATIVES, may be significant only for NON-HUMAN ACCUSATIVES, for which it is a relatively marked device, occurring in only about 11% of the cases.

From the figures for all of the constructions, we note that ACCUSATIVE OBJECTS are more surprising/discontinuous and DATIVE-BENEFACTIVE-AD-VERSATIVE-NECESSATIVE OBJECTS slightly less surprising/discontinuous than SUBJECTS. This means that for a given distance back to the last mention of an argument, the writer tends to select a more discontinuous device for a DATIVE OBJECT and a more continuous device for an ACCUSATIVE OBJECT than he does for a SUBJECT. This could be due to the writer's sensitivity to the norms for the continuity of the three categories or to differences among the categories in the average number of potential confusers in preceding clauses. As the POTENTIAL AMBIGUITY figures reveal (see 6.2), the latter alternative is a plausible explanation.

The greater discontinuity associated with NON-HUMAN arguments is also clear from the graph. This is a reflection of the fact that people tend to talk about people (see Givón, 1976); on the average a, reader must look back further to find the referent of a DEFINITE NON-HUMAN argument than that of a DEFINITE HUMAN argument. Seen from the writer's perspective, for a given LOOKBACK value, a more discontinuous device is normally chosen for HUMAN than for NON-HUMAN arguments. Again this may be a reflection of greater competition for the identity of the referents of HUMAN arguments. The PO-TENTIAL AMBIGUITY counts, however, do not give a clear picture in this regard.

Consider now the clause types. We expect relatively great discontinuity to occur at the beginnings of sentences, especially at the beginnings of paragraphs, and in sentence-final (MAIN) clauses, which are always assertive and more like-ly to contain new/surprising information than other clauses. (70% of INDEFINI-TE-REFERENTIAL NP SUBJECTS, for example, appear in MAIN CLAUSES.) Thus it is sentence-MEDIAL SUBORDINATE CLAUSES which have the lowest LOOKBACK value. HUMAN SUBJECTS in MAIN CLAUSES are characterized by relatively high discontinuity for the reason mentioned above and also because the subjects of sentence-final clauses often appear in sentence-initial position. In this position, of course, one expects higher discontinuity than in any succeed-ing SUBORDINATE CLAUSES, which in most cases have the same initial NP as SUBJECT, but marked only with SUBJECT VERB AGREEMENT. Since HUMAN arguments are relatively topical, we can expect them to occur as MAIN CLAUSE SUBJECTS at the head of relatively long chains of SUBOR-DINATE CLAUSES. NON-HUMAN arguments are less likely to appear as sub-jects/topics of long chains; hence NON-HUMAN MAIN CLAUSE SUBJECTS do not show much greater discontinuity than NON-HUMAN SUBORDINATE SUBJECTS.

The OBJECTS of the final clauses in clause chains, on the other hand, seldom appear in sentence-initial position, so MAIN CLAUSE ACCUSATIVE OBJECTS do not have the same tendency to higher discontinuity than SUBORDINATE CLAUSE ACCUSATIVE OBJECTS as we saw with SUBJECTS. Why MAIN CLAUSE OBJECTS should display significantly higher *continuity* than SUB-ORDINATE CLAUSE OBJECTS is not clear. Also difficult to account for is the unusual behavior of VERB-COMPLEMENT SUBJECTS and OBJECTS.

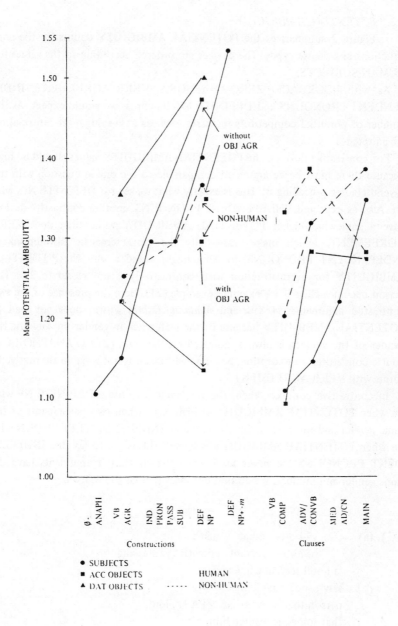

Figure 2. Mean POTENTIAL AMBIGUITY for all Construction and Clause Types

6.2. *POTENTIAL AMBIGUITY*

Figure 2 summarizes the POTENTIAL AMBIGUITY counts for the constructions and clause types. The devices are ordered according to the values for HUMAN SUBJECTS.

As with LOOKBACK, ZERO-ANAPHORA, VERB AGREEMENT, INDEPENDENT PRONOUNS and DEFINITE NPs line up as we would expect. As the number of potential competitors increases, devices conveying more information are adopted.

For contrastive devices, the POTENTIAL AMBIGUITY values should be high because there must be an argument comparable to the one in question with the several clauses preceding it. This is exactly what we see for DEFINITE NPs with *-m.* Also as expected, INDEPENDENT PRONOUNS, another contrastive device, have a somewhat higher POTENTIAL AMBIGUITY value than does VERB AGREEMENT, which makes essentially the same semantic distinctions as INDEPENDENT PRONOUNS do. One might wonder why the POTENTIAL AMBIGUITY for a construction used contrastively is not closer to 2.0. The reason becomes clear if we examine example (21). Here the presence of the two contrasted arguments, *Ar'aya* and *Madame Däbon Fuwa*, does not lead to POTENTIAL AMBIGUITY because of the difference in gender: in Amharic the gender of the subject is always indicated on the verb. (ZERO-ANAPHORA of course constitutes an exception, but in most cases it is not a viable alternative to forms with VERB AGREEMENT.)

In contrastive contexts, then, the tendency is to use a DEFINITE NP with *-m* when POTENTIAL AMBIGUITY is high, e.g., when two participants of the same gender and number are involved, and an INDEPENDENT PRONOUN with *-m* when POTENTIAL AMBIGUITY is lower. This is not to say that INDEPENDENT PRONOUNS are never used when the contrasted arguments have the same gender and number. We do find instances such as the following:

(22) (a)   ... yä-hotel aškär   mät't'a-nna
             of-hotel servant come(PAST,he)-and
             'a hotel servant came and

    (b)   säw   indämm-i-fällig-äw
            person that-he-want(NON-PAST)-him
            that someone wanted him

(c)   năggăr-ă-w.
       tell(PAST)-he-him
       he told him.
(d)   *issu-m* kă-ingida   marăfiya   bet   wărd-o,
       he-*m* from-guest   resting   room   come=down(CONVB)-he
       He (Ar'aya) came down from the lounge and
(e)   tăgănaňň-ă.
       meet(PAST)-he
       met (the person).'

Here the use of the INDEPENDENT PRONOUN, as well as the topic shift marker -*m*, tells us that the subject of clauses (d) and (e) is not the "hotel servant" but rather the "him" which is the object of clauses (b) and (c). It is cases such as this which account for the difference in the POTENTIAL AMBIGUITY of INDEPENDENT PRONOUNS and VERB AGREEMENT.

For PASSIVE SUBJECTS, a discontinuous device, we expect relatively high POTENTIAL AMBIGUITY figures, and this is what we find when we compare ACTIVE and PASSIVE HUMAN SUBJECTS for the same constructions. The values for all construction types are 1.20 for ACTIVE and 1.29 for PASSIVE; for DEFINITE NPs the values are 1.40 and 1.50 respectively. As with LOOK-BACK, these differences do not hold for VERB AGREEMENT or for NON-HUMAN SUBJECTS.

ACCUSATIVE OBJECTS with and without OBJECT AGREEMENT vary on this measure; for HUMAN OBJECTS the difference is striking. The greater POTENTIAL AMBIGUITY for the less topical OBJECTS without AGREE-MENT reflects the fact that there are more likely to be other, more topical, competing arguments in the clauses preceding them. A HUMAN OBJECT with AGREEMENT is relatively topical and may be the only HUMAN argument within several clauses.

For DATIVE-BENEFACTIVE-ADVERSATIVE-NECESSITATIVE OBJECTS vs. SUBJECTS and ACCUSATIVE OBJECTS, we find the opposite pattern here from that with LOOKBACK. The high POTENTIAL AMBIGUITY figures for DATIVE-BENEFACTIVE-ADVERSATIVE-NECESSITATIVE are understandable if we consider that predicates with DATIVE OBJECTS often have HUMAN SUBJECTS. In Amharic this is nearly always true for DATIVE OBJECTS with the adnominal marker *lă-*. In Table 10 we see that it is these which have the highest POTENTIAL AMBIGUITY. We expect other DATIVES (second column in Table 10) to have a somewhat lower value because these are actually the

DATIVE SUBJECTS of impersonal verbs.

We do not find the same difference between HUMAN and NON-HUMAN arguments here as we did with the LOOKBACK counts. There is no real reason to expect that there would be more arguments of one type or another to present competition. If POTENTIAL AMBIGUITY took into account the case/syntactic role of potential confusers, we might see a difference, however. Listeners/ readers are sensitive to case/syntactic role in assigning a referent to an argument. This is especially true for subjects; listeners/readers expect the subject of a clause to be co-referential with the subject of the preceding clause unless they are led to believe otherwise through the presence of a discontinuous device. Because subjects tend to be HUMAN, on the average we would expect more competition for the identity of HUMAN than for that of NON-HUMAN SUBJECTS.

For clause types it is somewhat difficult to make predictions regarding POTENTIAL AMBIGUITY. We might expect it to correlate with LOOKBACK, and up to a point it does: MAIN CLAUSES show higher POTENTIAL AMBIGUITY (lower continuity) for SUBJECTS and lower POTENTIAL AMBIGUITY for ACCUSATIVE OBJECTS than do SUBORDINATE CLAUSES. Within the SUBORDINATE types, however, the pattern of results: differs MEDIAL CLAUSES have relatively high vlaues and VERB-COMPLEMENT CLAUSES are consistently lowest.

6.3. *DECAY*

Figure 3 summarizes the counts for DECAY. The devices are arranged in order of decreasing values (faster DECAY rates) for HUMAN SUBJECTS.

We must be careful not to interpret the DECAY figures of the most continuous devices as a direct measure of topic persistence. For ZERO-ANAPHORA and VERB AGREEMENT SUBJECTS, the argument in question has nearly always appeared in the previous clause (LOOKBACK close to 1.0) and, more often than not, in one or more clauses immediately preceding that. Thus the DECAY values of 3.9 and 2.6 for these two devices are really indicative of topic chains of at least 6 and 5 clauses respectively, including the clause with the device itself. For other devices, the counts are more meaningful. INDEFINITE-REFERENTIAL NPs, for example, appear at the beginning of topic chains, so the value of 2.6 for HUMAN SUBJECTS can be interpreted directly as indicating an average topic chain of 3.6 clauses.

With this in mind, we can see, first of all, that the results for the more continuous, non-contrastive devices, ZERO-ANAPHORA, VERB AGREEMENT and DEFINITE NPs, correlate nicely with the LOOKBACK and POTENTIAL

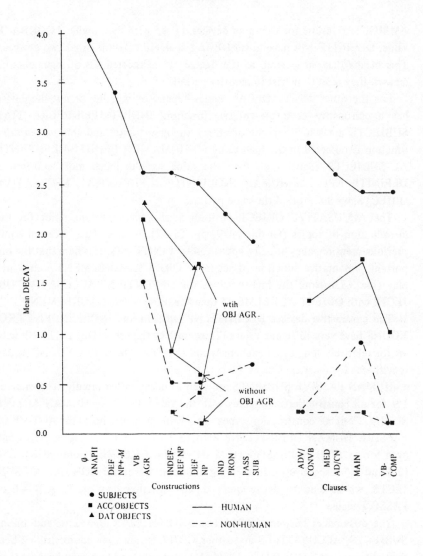

Figure 3. Mean DECAY for all Construction and Clause Types

AMBIGUITY results for the same devices. (Even with their higher LOOKBACK value, DEFINITE NPs have lower DECAY than either of the other two devices.) This means that, in general, as the degree of unexpectedness of arguments increases, they tend to persist for shorter periods.

For the other devices, DECAY values depend on whether or not the device haa a contrastive or a presentative function. INDEFINITE-REFERENTIAL SUBJECTS are a major point of entrry for new topics, and this *presentative* function is reflected in the high value for HUMAN INDEFINITE-REFERENTIAL SUBJECTS, higher even than the value for the much more continuous DEFINITE NPs. For HUMAN INDEFINITE-REFERENTIAL ACCUSATIVE OBJECTS, we do not find the same pattern.

The ACCUSATIVE OBJECT position is also an important point for the introduction of topics (Givón, 1979, pp. 51-52). If these have received some previous mention, they usually appear as DEFINITE NPs. It is here that the important presentative function of recursive OBJECT AGREEMENT comes into play (see 3.1.). Note the higher values for DEFINITE NP ACCUSATIVE OBJECTS with OBJECT AGREEMENT than for those without AGREEMENT.

The contrastive devices DEFINITE NP with *-m* and INDEPENDENT PRONOUNS have very different values. These reflect the use of DEFINITE NP with *-m* for relatively long topic exchanges and INDEPENDENT PRONOUNS (usually with *-m*) for short exchanges.

HUMAN PASSIVE SUBJECTS are seen to decay rather rapidly. The value of 1.9 for all constructions compares with the value of 2.7 for HUMAN ACTIVE SUBJECTS of all construction types. This difference also holds for ACTIVE vs. PASSIVE HUMAN DEFINITE NP SUBJECTS (2.5 and 2.0 respectively) and even for ACTIVE vs. PASSIVE HUMAN VERB-AGREEMENT-only SUBJECTS (2.6 and 1.5 respectively). It does not obtain, however, for NON-HUMAN SUBJECTS, which tend to decay quite rapidly whether they are in ACTIVE or PASSIVE clauses.

The differences between HUMAN and NON-HUMAN arguments and among SUBJECTS, ACCUSATIVES and other OBJECTS are even more striking here than they are for LOOKBACK. HUMAN arguments tend to persist because they are of greater import to people than NON-HUMAN arguments. This agrees with what we have seen for LOOKBACK and is also evident in other data. Recall, for example, the differences in the relative frequencies of HUMAN and NON-HUMAN arguments for the various construction types (Table 19); NON-HUMAN arguments are greatly underrepresented in the VERB AGREEMENT category but constitute the majority of instances of DEFINITE, INDEFINITE-

REFERENTIAL and GENERIC NPs.

SUBJECTS persist, on the average, much longer than ACCUSATIVE OBJECTS and somewhat longer than other OBJECTS. This is, of course, what we expect; topics tend to be SUBJECTS (Givón, 1976). The faster DECAY rate for ACCUSATIVE than for DATIVE-BENEFACTIVE-ADVERSATIVE-NECESSITATIVE OBJECTS is, at least in part, due to the fact that the latter category is overwhelmingly HUMAN while the former is usually NON-HUMAN (see Table 19). Note that the various types of NON-ACCUSATIVE OBJECTS considered differ to a surprising extent in their DECAY values (Table 10). The very high persistence of POSSESSORS would seem to be related to the relative lack of topical competition from the other argument in the clause, the normally NON-HUMAN, POSSESSED argument. We would expect faster DECAY from the DATIVE OBJECT of a verb such as *give*, which has a usually HUMAN SUBJECT with a good chance of remaining topical. For this argument to hold, however, DATIVE OBJECTS of impersonal verbs (second column in Table 10) should show a DECAY rate comparable to that for POSSESSORS. Their low value, as well as the difference between the values for the other two types of DATIVES, presents something of a puzzle.

For clause types, there are two factors which favor lower DECAY values for MAIN CLAUSES. First, sentences, and hence all paragraphs, end in MAIN CLAUSES, and DECAY was not counted beyond paragraph boundaries. Second, as we have already noted, sentence boundaries, even within paragraphs, are points of relative discontinuity in a clause-chaining language such as Amharic. Sentence-medial MAIN CLAUSES are not frequent enough to compensate for these factors, but there is another important factor which, from the results, apparently almost does. This is the tendency, which we have already discussed, for the subjets of MAIN CLAUSES to appear at the heads of sentences, even when a number of SUBORDINATE CLAUSES intervene. These SUBORDINATE CLAUSES nearly always contain references to the MAIN CLAUSE SUBJECT, and they were counted in the DECAY for such SUBJECTS. These clause chains with MAIN CLAUSE SUBJECTS in initial position are frequent enough to bring the DECAY value for HUMAN MAIN CLAUSE SUBJECTS to within 0.5 of that for HUMAN CONVERB-ADVERBIAL CLAUSE SUBJECTS. For NON-HUMAN SUBJECTS, which are much more often full NPs, MAIN CLAUSES show a higher value.

The relatively slow DECAY for MAIN CLAUSE HUMAN ACCUSATIVE OBJECTS is puzzling. It may be due to the placement of MAIN CLAUSE *OBJECTS* at the head of chains of several clauses, but this does not seem to occur often enough to account for the results.

Among the SUBORDINATE CLAUSE types, we expect CONVERB CLAU-
SES, because of their close link to the following clause, to show relatively
high DECAY values. As the data in Table 16 indicate, their DECAY is higher,
though not a great deal higher, than that for ADVERBIAL CLAUSES. The
slightly lower value for MEDIAL than for TOTAL CONVERB-ADVERBIAL
CLAUSES is understandable when we consider that sentence-initial clauses are
more likely to be followed by other SUBORDINATE, relatively topical,
CLAUSES than are MEDIAL CLAUSES.

7. *Summary*

The LOOKBACK, POTENTIAL AMBIGUITY and DECAY counts have
provided empirical evidence for the following hierarchy of topic-continuity
devices[1]:
ZERO-ANAPHORA < VERB AGREEMENT < INDEPENDENT PRO-
NOUNS < DEFINITE NP SUBJECTS and DATIVE OBJECTS < DEFINITE
NP ACCUSATIVE OBJECTS with OBJECT AGREEMENT < DEFINITE NP
ACCUSATIVE OBJECTS without OBJECT AGREEMENT < (HUMAN)
PASSIVE SUBJECTS < DEFINITE NPs with -*m* < INDEFINITE-REFER-
ENTIAL NPs.
In addition, the results indicate, or are at least consistent with, the following:
1) the contrastive topic-shift function of INDEPENDENT PRONOUNS and
   -*m*
2) the persistence of DEFINITE NP OBJECTS with OBJECT AGREEMENT
3) the relative discontinuity associated with MAIN CLAUSE vs. SUBOR-
   DINATE CLAUSE SUBJECTS
4) the high continuity associated with sentence-MEDIAL SUBORDINATE
   CLAUSES
5) the higher continuity of HUMAN than NON-HUMAN arguments
6) the correlation between topic continuity/expectedness and topic persistence for the more continuous devices.

---

1) This list is not a complete one; Amharic has other devices for indicating relative
discontinuity, for example, CLEFT and PSEUDO-CLEFT constructions, though these are
infrequent in written discourse.

REFERENCES

Getatchew Haile (1970). "The suffix pronoun in Amharic", In C.-W. Kim and H. Stahlke (Eds.), *Papers in African Linguistics.* Edmonton: Linguistic Research, Inc.

Girmaččäw Täklä Hawaryat (1939 Eth.Cal.). *Ar'aya.* Addis Abeba: Berhanenna Selam.

Givón, T. (1976). "Topic, pronoun and grammatical agreement", In C. Li (Ed.), *Subject and Topic.* New York: Academic Press.

Givón, T. (1979). *On Understanding Grammar.* New York: Academic Press.

Givón, T. (1982), "Tense-aspect-modality: the Creole prototype and beyond", In P. Hopper (ed.), *Tense and Aspect: Between Semantics and Pragmatics, Typological Studies in Language*, vol. 1, Amsterdam: Benjamins.

Hetzron, R. (1970). "Toward an Amharic case grammar", *Studies in African Linguistics 1*(3).

Hetzron, R. (1971). Presentative function and presentative movement. *Proceedings of the 2nd Conference on African Linguistics*, Studies in African Linguistics, Supplement 2.

TOPIC CONTINUITY AND WORD-ORDER PRAGMATICS IN UTE

T. GIVÓN
Linguistics Department
University of Oregon, Eugene

and

Ute Language Program
Southern Ute Tribe
Ignacio, Colorado

TABLE OF CONTENTS

1. *Introduction: Ute and the Ute texts*[1]

Many aspects of the study of topic continuity in Ute duplicate closely the findings reported for other languages in this volume, particularly in regard to the relative valuation of zero anaphora, clitic pronouns, independent pronouns and full definite NP's. Typologically, Ute is a mature SOV language with a high degree of pragmatically-controlled word-order flexibility. This pertains not only to the position of the subject, where Ute exhibits a variation rather similar to that found in Early Biblical Hebrew (see Fox, this volume), but also to the position of the object. The language is thus perched at an ideal point, in terms of word-oreder drift, for studying the pragmatic motivation for word-order change from SOV.

The texts used in this study are taken out of a collection of Ute Traditional Narrarives[2] recorded from elders of the Southern Ute Tribe in Ignacio, Colorado. Verbatim transcripts of the texts were used, so that they represent essentially oral materials. The stories are of entertainment and instructional nature, with the main characters being animals that stand for various, well known human archetypes within traditional Ute culture. The main line of the story tends to be well known to the audience, so that the difference between definite and indefinite NP's is more or less meaningless so far as major participants are concerned. The audience's interest thus hinges more on the embellishments and added texture and characterizations supplied by individual story tellers, than on the main plot-line per se. Much of the referential system, particularly in the use of deictic particles (demonstratives, articles), relies on that familiarity as well as on the face-to-face story-telling situation, in terms of gestures, spatial organization via pointing, facial expressions, audience feedback etc. For this reason, a number of the linguistic features of Ute cannot be fruitfully and exhaustively investigated via these texts, and will require a more complete video account in order to understand their use.

2. *The grammatical devices investigated*

2.1. *Subject marking devices*

2.1.1. *Zero anaphora*

Numerically this is the most common subject expression in Ute narrative. As examples consider the following:[3]

(1)   . . .x-'urá   'uwás puí-av   túpuna-pugá,
            then   he   eye-OWN   pull-out-REM
           '. . . then he pulled out his own eye,

'u-má-tugwá-ax̂   tȳrávi-pȳgá,
there-LOC-toward-it   throw-REM-∅
threw it in there,
'u-rúx   múkwi-pȳgá,
there-to   stick-head-REM-∅
and stuck his head under there,
'úu-pa-taa-s   taví-pȳgá. . .
there-DIR-EMPH-CONJ   fall-REM-∅
and it dropped back there (into his eyesocket). . .'

2.1.2. *Clitic pronouns/grammatical agreement*

The same set of clitic pronouns in Ute is used to refer to either the subject, the direct object or the possessor('genitive'). While most commonly in connected narrative these pronouns appear suffixed on the verbal word, they may appear suffixed on other words as well, including adverbs, conjunctions, subjects or objects. The general Uto-Aztecan rule of "second position clitics" does not apply in Ute in an absolute, mechanical fashion, though it may have in the past.[4] But one may nevertheless find instances of that usage in text. Thus consider first the following example of the clitic pronoun as verb suffix:[5]

(2)   . . . 'uwá-vaa-cugwá-pȳgá-amȳ –
             him-LOC-approach-REM-*they*
             '. . . so they approached him –
             'úuuuniguni-'urá –
             lo-be
             and lo! –
             'uwá-vaa-cugwá-pȳgá-amȳ. . .
             him-LOC-approach-REM-*they*. . .'
             they approached him. . .'

In the example above, the independent pronoun 'him' is actually incorporated into the verb, since the verb/postposition -*cugwá/cux* is morphologically 'defective' and cannot any more stand on its own without an object. The subject pronoun 'they' is thus suffixed to the verbal word which is also the first word in the clause in both instances. As an example of a subject pronoun cliticizing as suffix to a non-verbal clause-initial word, consider:[6]

(3)   . . . má-ra-taani- amu̧   'uní-pu̧gá. . .
              that-KIND-OBJ-*they* do-REM
              '. . .so they brought him that type. . .'

2.1.3. *Independent pronouns in the VS word-order*
        Independent subject pronouns, like subject NPs, exhibit word-order
flexibility in Ute. As an example of their post-verbal position, consider:[7]

(4)   . . . 'ú-vwaa-n-'urá   'aví-na-pu̧gá   'uwás. . .
              there-LOC-be   lie-HABIT-REM   he
              '. . . he was lying there for quite a while. . .'

In both the preverbal and post-verbal position, the independent subject pronoun
is often either preceded or followed by the topic-marking particle *'urá* 'be'. In
this study I did not attempt to distinguish pronouns (or NP's) which appear
with it from those which appear without it. As an example of the use of *'urá*
with a pronoun, consider:[8]

(5)   . . . "'úvwaya-ĝa"   máy-pu̧gá   'urá-'uwás. . .
              "alright"   say-REM   be-he
              '. . ."alright" he said. . ."

2.1.4. *Independent pronouns in the SV word-order*
        As an example of this pre-verbal position of the independent subject
pronoun, consider:[9]

(6)   . . . x-'urá   'uwás   pu̧i-av   túpu̧na-pu̧gá. . .
              then-be   he   eye-OWN   pull-out-REM
              '. . .so he pulled out his eye. . .'

The pre-verbal independent pronoun may also be accompanied by the particle
'urá 'be', most commonly as suffix, as in:[10]

(7)   . . . naná-nakwá-tu̧-s   'uwás-'urá   'uní-pu̧gá. . .
              each-one-NOM-CONJ   he-be   do-REM
              '. . .he did the same with each (eye). . .'

2.1.5.   *Definite NP's in the VS word-order*

The definite subject NP in Ute may appear by itself or with either demonstratives/articles or the indepenent pronoun functioning as article, or occasionally both. In this study I have not attempted to differentiate between the use of definite NP's with and without those extra markers in the VS word-order, and thus lumped the numerical results together. The subject noun itself is morphologically marked in Ute by the *silencing* of the final vowel, normally the suffix vowel (for further detail, see Givón, 1981). As an example of an unmodified definite subject NP, consider:[11]

(8)   . . . "nʉ́-aa"   máy-pʉgá   kucú-pukú-raa-*ci*
          "I-Q"   say-REM   cow-domestic-DIM-SUBJ
          '. . ."who, me?" said the small buffalo-cow. . .'

In counting subject constructions in the VS word-order, I have not attempted to distinguish between those that come without a pause or with a pause intervening between the verb and the subject NP. This is so because the pauses in that position are extremely common and of varying duration. Also, in general, the delivery style of most old story-tellers involves such pauses between almost all constituents within the clause, so that their discourse-functional is somewhat hard to assess.[12]

More commonly, definite subject NP's in the VS word-order appear with demonstrative articles, as in:[13]

(9)   . . . 'u-'úni-*ci*-'urá   'urá-vaac*i*   'ú   yʉʉpʉ-*ci*. . .
          RED-do-NOM-be   be-BCKGR   that   porcupine
          '. . . he used to behave like that, porcupine did. . .'

Less commonly, the definite subject NP may appear post-verbally with an independent pronoun, a device that may also be considered an 'afterthought'[14]. Thus consider:[15]

(10)   . . . na'áyh-pʉgá   'uwás   Sináwav*i*. . .
          angry-REM   he   Sináwav*i*
          '. . . so he became very angry, Sináwavi did. . .'

2.1.6.   *Definite NP's in the SV word-order*

The pre-verbal definite subject NP may be a noun or name, as in:[16]

(11)   ... Sináwaví 'urá-pugá...
            Sináwaví be-REM
            '... It was Sináwaví...'

Or it may be modified by a possessive pronoun, as in:[17]

(12)   ... 'úvway-ax̂-'urá-'urú   'oǫa-a   'urá-pugá...
            there-it-be-that   bones-*her*   be-REM
            '... then there remained his bones...'

A pre-verbal definite NP subject may also appear modified by a demonstrative
article, as in:[18]

(13)   ... 'ú-vwa-ax̂-unúv 'ú   yúupuci   ya'á-'uwá-xwa-pugá...
            then-it-then   that   porcupine   hard-jump-ASP-REM
            '... so right there and then Porcupine jumped real hard...'

Finally, the pre-verbal definite subject NP may also appear with the independent
pronoun functioning as 'article', as in:[19]

(14)   x̂-'urá-'urú   'uwás   yúupu-ci   'urá-pugá...
            then-be-that   *he*   Porcupine   be-REM
            'Once upon a time there was Porcupine...'

2.1.7. *Double-occurring subject (SVS word-order)*

In a small number of instances, the definite subject — either independent
pronoun or full NP — occurs twice within the clause, both before and after the
verb. While this is obviously a feature of a typically oral, loose style, I have
chosen to record it as one subject-marking device. As an example consider:[20]

(15)   ... 'umús-'urá   motóni-vaaci-mu,   'úmu piisci-u...
            they-be   scatter-BCKGR-PL   they children-PL
            'now they have scattered, the children did...'

2.1.8. *Referential-indefinite subjects*

The overwhelming majority of indefinite subjects appear in the SV word-
order. It is a bit hard to tell an indefinite-referential from a definite NP in Ute,
since in these particular texts most of the major participants are known to the

audience and, especially when unmarked by articles or pronouns, may be interpreted in the English context as either definite or indefinite. In the Ute context they are more likely to thus be definite. There is no particular marking for indefinite NP's in Ute, especially referential ones. It is safest to assume indefiniteness of subject when it is modified by a numeral, as in:[21]

(16)   ... x-'urá   wáa-máamci-u 'úm*   'urá-p*gá. ..
                  then-be   two-women-PL   they be-REM
              '. . . then there were two women there. . .'

In spite of being introduced for the first time into the discourse, 'two women' is marked by a definitizing independent pronoun. The sole occurence of a VS-ordered indefinite referential subject NP in the transcripts is:[22]

(17)   ... qováa-vay-'u p*í-av-kway   t*r*pi-ky*-p*gá, píisci-u. ..
                  front-at-his   eye-OWN-KIND throw-PL-REM   children-PL
         ⎰'. . . in front of him some children were juggling their eyes. . .' ⎱
         ⎱'. . . in front of him they were juggling their eyes, children. . .' ⎰

There are no non-referential subjects attested in the text.

2.2. *Direct-Object marking devices*

No attempt was made here to distinguish between direct objects that are semantically patients and those that are semantically datives, given that in Ute grammar the two are indistinguishable, and that there were no post-positionally marked dative objects in the text (although presumably they can be found in the language, see Givón (1981)). The topic-marking devices used with direct objects are illustrated below.

2.2.1. *Zero anaphora*

Unlike for subjects, where this is the most frequent device, for direct objects this is less infrequent. As examples consider:[23]

(18)   ... márataani-am*   'uní-p*gá-s,   máy-na-'u   'urú,
                  that-type-they   do-REM-CONJ   say-REL-his   that
              '. . . so they brought him that type, the kind that he asked for,

'u-vwáa-s   cʉkúr'*a*-pʉgá,
there-at-CONJ   cut-REM-∅
and they cut *them*,
'úr*u*-'urá-'urú 'ǫ́ǫa-pa-'u   yuná-pʉgá-s. . .
that-be-that   bone-DIR-his   put-REM-CONJ-∅
and they fitted *them* through his bones. . .'

2.2.2. *Clitic pronouns/grammatical agreement*

This is a much more frequent anaphoric device for direct objects in Ute, and as I have indicated elsewhere the normal case is that if both the subject and object NP are anaphorically absent, the subject is marked by zero and the object by a clitic pronoun (Givón, 1982b). As an example consider:[24]

(10)   . . . "'úvway"   máy-pʉgáy-aǧa-am*ʉ*. . .
             "alright"   say-REM-HAVE-*them*-∅
         '. . . "alright" he told them. . .'

2.2.3. *Independent pronouns*

There were only a total of 6 independent direct-object pronouns found in the transcript, 5 in the OV order and 1 in the VO order. As examples consider:[25]

(20)   . . . 'úway 'uní-pʉ-vwaa. . .   (OV)
             him   make-REM-SUBORD-∅
         '. . . because he (Porcupine) made *him* so. . .'

and:[26]

(21)   . . . 'ú-vway-aǧ-'urá   'uwás-'urú   'úu-pa-xw*a*   yuná-pʉgá 'urú. . . (VO)

             then-it-be ·   he-that   there-DIR-go   put-REM   that/it
         '. . . so then he put *it* through there. . .'

Example (21) is doubtful though, since the demonstrative pronoun *'urú* 'that' may either function as the inanimate pronoun 'it' or as a grammatical emphatic suffix on the verbal word, the way it is used as suffix on the independent subject pronoun in (21) above.

2.2.4. *Full definite NP's in the OV word-order*

No attempt was made here to quantify separately the behavior of the various kinds of definite full NP's, which may be noun/names as in:[27]

(22)   . . . bági   yáa'wa-rμ-'u. . .
                  bag-OBJ carry-NOM-he
            '. . . he was carrying (the/his) bag. . .'

They are most commonly definitized by a possessive pronoun, as in:[28]

(23)   .'. . pμí-av-kway   túrɑpi-kyạ-pμgá. . .
                  eye-OWN-KIND   throw-PL-REM
            '. . . they were juggling their own eyes. . .'

They may be definitized by the use of independent pronouns, as in:[29]

(24)   . . . 'umμ́-'urá   múupuvwi'aaci-u cicính-pμgá. . .
                  them-be   maggots-PL   scoop-REM-∅
            '. . . so they scooped away the maggots. . .'

Or they may be modified by a demonstrative article, as in:[30]

(25)   . . . pμμ́'ay-av   'urú   'átμ-maní-kya. . .
                  fur-GEN-OWN that-OBJ   well-do-like-ANT
            '. . . he slicked his fur up like this (gesture). . .'

2.2.5. *Full definite NP's in the VO word-order*

Here again no attempt was made to count separately the different definitizing devices. The definite object may appear as a noun/name without further marking, as in:[31]

(26)   . . . pμsáĝa-paĝáy-kwɑ-pμgá-amμ́, mμsútkwi-gyạ-tu
                  search-walk-go-REM-they   medicine-have-OBJ
            '. . . they were searching around for the doctor. . .'

Or it may be marked with a demonstrative article, as in:[32]

(27)   . . . maáy-pʉgáy-'u-amʉ, dóctor   'uwáy. . .
            find-REM-him-they   doctor   him
         '. . . so they found him, the doctor. . .'

2.2.6. *Double appearance of definite object NP* (OVO)

In only one instance in the text we find the object NP appearing both
before and after the verb, presumably again attesting to the informal/oral nature
of the material. Thus consider:[33]

(28)   . . . mára-taa-ni-amʉ   'uní-pʉgá-s,   máy-na-'u   'urú. . .
            that-KIND-OBJ-like-they do-REM-CONJ say-REL-his that-OBJ
         '. . . so they brought him that type, the one he said (he wanted). . .'

It is clear from the text that the post-verbal NP, itself a 'headless' object relative
clause, is a clarification/expansion, as afterthought, of the preverbal NP.

2.2.7. *Indefinite NP's*

Relatively few of the DO NP's in these texts are indefinite, and all of
those appear pre-verbally (OV). It is in general hard to decide whether *referential* indefinite NP's are really indefinite, because they introduce participants that
are traditionally known to the hearer, who in the Ute tradition is normally quite
familiar with the story to begin with. Being morphologically unmarked of course
does not single out an object NP in Ute as indefinite. Thus, the referential object in (29) below was counted here as indefinite-referential, but it could very
well have been translated as definite:[34]

(29)   . . . 'ú-vwaa-tʉ   sʉʉ́vʉ-pʉ   tʉvwíwi-pʉgá-s. . .
            there-at-DIR   cottonwood-OBJ   ask-REM-CONJ
         '. . . so then he asked *a/the* cottonwood tree. . .'

Non-referential direct object NP's in Ute are not always marked morphologically in any way, although often they may be incorporated into the verb without
their normal noun suffix (see Givón, 1981). The very few in these texts were
distinguished purely semantically. As an example consider:[35]

(30)   . . . 'ʉá-'napʉ   'úru-'urú   'uwás   'úu-pa
            trap-INSTR-OBJ   that-that-OBJ   he   there-DIR

yuná-na-pµga-s. . .
put-HAB-REM-CONJ. . .
'. . . he used to put traps that way. . .'

2.3. Locative Objects

All locative objects are definite in these texts, and none of them involve clitic pronouns or zero anaphora. The major categories distinguished here are:

2.3.1. Independent pronouns with locative suffix

These pronouns normally refer to the animate major participants in the story. The bulk of these appear pre-verbally(OV), some as free elements, as in:[36]

(31)   . . . 'uwá-vaa-cux   pọrọ́-pµgá. . .
            him-at-toward walk-PL-REM
            '. . . so they all walked toward him. . .'

though it may also appear (in one instance) as a free element post-verbally (VO) as in:[37]

(32)   . . . mµí-kµ-vaaci-mµ   'uwá-vaa-cux. . .
            lead-BEN-BCKGR-they him-at-toward
            '. . . so they led him toward him. . .'

With post-positions such as cux/tux 'toward', which are defective verbs and may also appear as the main verbs cugwá-/tugwá, 'move toward (animate object)'/ 'move toward (inanimate object)', respectively, the pronoun may often be incorporated into the verb at a pre-verbal (OV) position, as in:[38]

(33)   . . . 'uwá-vaa-cugwá-pµgá-amµ. . .
            him-at-go-toward-REM-they
            '. . . so they went to him. . .'

2.3.2. Deictic locative objects

Deictic locative objects in Ute involve the deictic prefixes 'i(i)- 'here/ proximate', ma(a)- 'there-visible' or 'u(u)- 'there-invisible', with a locative suffix attached to them. Unlike the object pronouns, above, whose referential properties are obvious, the reference of the deictic locatives is vague and hard to objectively define. Rather, they tend to receive their reference from the speech *situation* and face-to-face interaction, in terms of gestures, deictic pointing, mimmickry, facial expression or simply other imponderables not directly recoverable from mere transcripts. Semantically these locatives should be counted as "definite" is spite of that vagueness. Syntactically they appear mostly preverbally (OV), as in:[39]

(34)   . . . 'u-má-tugwá-ax̂   turávi-pugá. . .
              there-LOC-toward-it throw-REM
              '. . . and he threw it in there. . .'

Less commonly one may find these locative objects post-verbally (VO), as in:[40]

(35)   . . . 'ú-vway-ax̂-unúv   'ú   yúupu-ci   ya'á-'uwá'a-pugá,
              there-at-it-EXACT   that   porcupine-SUBJ hard-jump-REM
              'i-vą́ą-ta-s. . .
              here-at-OBJ-CONJ
              '. . . so right there and then Porcupine took a great leap there. . .'

2.3.3. *Full NP definite locative objects*
     The locative post-position may also mark a full definite NP, and may then appear in the OV word-order, as in:[41]

(36)   . . . tupúy-ci   'urú   kanúgaa-rux   'uní'a-pugá-amu. . .
              rock-GEN   that-OBJ   foothill-along move-REM-they
              '. . . (they were) moving along the cliffside. . .'

They may also appear post-verbally (VO), as in:[42]

(37)   . . . puí-av-kway   túrapi-kya-pugá, píisci-u,   wa'á-pu
              eye-OWN-KIND   throw-PL-REM   children-PL piñon-OBJ
              wunúru-ma-tux. . .
              stand-NOM/OBJ-in-to
              'they were throwing their eyes, the children were, into the standing piñon tree. . .'

2.3.4. *Indefinite full NP locative objects*
     Very few full-NP locative objects are referential indefinite, appearing either pre-verbally (OV), as in:[43]

(38)   . . . 'ú-vway-ax̂-'urú   sǫnía-vụ   'urú   kwasí-m-av
          there-at-it-that   cedar-bark-OBJ   that-OBJ   tail-LOC-OWN
          pacá'a-ti-pụgá   'uwás. . .
          stick-CAUS-REM   he
          '. . . so then he tied some cedar bark to his own tail. . .'

Rarely they may also appear post-verbally, as in:[44]

(39)   . . . maní-wụnụ́-pụgá-s   'iví-ci   'u-má-tux. . .
          do-like-stand-REM-CONJ   stick/branch-OBJ   there-LOC-along
          '. . . he was standing like that (gesture) next to the branch. . .'

No non-referential (indefinite) locative NP's were found in the text.

2.4.   Manner objects/adverbs

The overwhelming majority of manner adverbs in Ute are noun, adjective or verb stems incorporated into the verb at a prefixal position (see Givón, 1981). They are, by definition, non-referential. Here I counted only the free word, non-incorporated manner adverbs, which are rather few. All of them are pre-verbal (OV), as in:[45]

(40)   . . . 'ụvụ́s káatụ   tǫ́ǫvaĝa-pụgá   'uwás. . .
          end   river-rock-OBJ   rumble-REM   she
          '. . . well finally she rumbled like river-rock. . .'

Other oblique NP's appear in too insignificant numbers to warrant counting in these texts.

3. Methodology of text counting

In this study I employed four measurements for assessing topic continuity. The first two — referential distance and persistence — are applied to all case-roles, although the measure of persistence for *subject* NP's is modified slightly as compared to that used in other studies in this volume (as well as for *object* NP's in this study).

3.1.   Referential distance ('look-back')

I counted the number of clauses 'to the left' between the present appearance of a referent and its previous appearance in the register, regardless of what device (including zero anaphora) marked that previous appearance. Non-appearance inside direct-quoted portions of the narrative was *not* counted as a gap, while appearance inside such direct-quote portions *was* counted as as an instance of occurrence. The same rule also applies to relative clauses. All other clause types are treated as main clauses.

3.2. *Persistence ('decay')*

For object NP's, I followed the same procedure as in the other studies in this volume, counting the number of clauses 'to the right' in which the referent persists *at whatever case-role*, so long as it is an argument of the verb. For subjects only, this was modified to measure a narrower sense of persistence, i.e only *as subjects* of the following clauses. Since the subject is the *main topic* of clauses (Givón, 1982c), this is still a significant measure of topic continuity. As above, the absence of a referent in direct-quoted portions of the narrative or within a relative clause was *not* counted as a gap. But neither was presence in either of them counted as an added clause in the persisting chain.

3.3. *Same-subject (SS) vs. different subject (DS)*

To assess the more traditional *switch-reference* function of various subjectmarking deviced in Ute, I counted here whether a particular instance of a referent appearing as subject either continued, after a preceding clause where it also appeared as a subject (SS), or alternatively appeared following a clause in which another referent was the subject (DS), regardless of whether the original referent participated in the clause in another (non-subject) capacity or not.[46] A typical instance of SS appears in the second clause of (41) below:[47]

(41)   ... sináwa-v*i*   'urá-puڱgá; 'úu-pa-puڱgá   x-'urá. . .
            Sináwav*i*-SUBJ   be-REM   ṭhere-pass-REM-∅   then-be
            '. . . it was Sináwavi; *he* was passing through there. . .'

A typical example of DS appears in the second clause of (42) below:[48]

(42)   ... "'uڱvús-aĝa"   máy-kyạ-puڱgá; x-'urá   'uwás   puڱí-av
            "alright"   say-PL-REM   then-be   he   eye-OWN
            túpuڱna-puڱgá. . .
            pull-REM
            '. . . "alright" they said; so then *he* pulled out his own eye. . .'

3.4. *Contiguity to major thematic breaks/junctures* (Subject NP's only)

As suggested in the introduction to this volume, similar topic-marking devices may be used to impart discontinuity/continuity generated from different sources − *topic* continuity in terms of either referential distance or the potential interference from other referents in the register, or *action* or *thematic* continuity in terms of the presence of discernible breaks in the sequential action or thematic organization of the narrative. In order to assess this possibility in Ute, the entire four-story text used in this study was marked, by intuitive means, as to the presence of major action/theme breaks. Two types of breaks were recorded − and accorded equal weight in the measurements:

(i) *A major paragraph-initiation discontinuity*

This is a clear thematic, action (and often participant) discontinuity, where there is a change to a new location, time, participant, and where the sequential action is broken *without* a subsequent resumption. In our Appendix 1 such a discontinuity/break is marked by paragraph-initial indentation. As an example consider:[49]

(43)   . . . naná-nakwá-tu̱-s   'uwás-'urá   'uní-pu̱gá,
            each-one-OBJ-CONJ he-be   do-REM
            '. . . and he did the same thing to both (eyes),

            ma-váa   x-'urá   nawá-s   pacá'wa-xwa-pu̱gá,
            there-at   then-be   both-CONJ   stick-ASP-REM
            and both of them got stuck there,

            'u-vwáa-s   ka-pu̱í-'a-atu̱   tu̱gá-xwa-pu̱gá;
            there-at-CONJ   NEG-eye-NEG-HAVE-NOM-SUBJ   become-ASP-REM
            so he became blind;

            'umu̱s-'urá mo̱tó̱ni-va̱a̱ci-mu̱,   'úmu̱ píisci-u,
            they-be   scatter-BCKGR-PL   they children-PL
            now the children then hurriedly scattered,

            'uní-kya-x̱a-s-amu̱   'urú. . .
            do-PL-ANT-CONJ-they   that-OBJ
            having done that. . .'

In the three clauses in (43) preceding the paragraph break, the action, in sequence, is focused on Sináwavi and his doings. The paragraph initial break switches us to the children and their doings.

(ii) *Paragraph-medial interjections/background information*

This is an interjection — usually rather short — *temporarily* breaking the sequential action (and participant & theme continuity) *within* a thematic paragraph, after which the action is *resumed.* In our Appendix 1 such a break is marked by three consecutive slashed (///) at the beginning of the clause that starts the break. As an example consider:[50]

(44)   . . . 'umús̱-'urá mo̱to̱ni-va̱a̱ci-mu,   'úmu̱ píisci-u,
                    they-be   scatter-BCKGR-PL   they children-PL
            '. . . now the children then hurriedly scattered,

            'uní-kya-x̱a-s-amu̱   'urú,
            do-PL-ANT-CONJ-they   that-OBJ
            having done that,

            x-'urá   'uwás   'úu-pa   wáay-va̱a̱ci,   'ú Sináwavi. . .
            then-be   he   there-DIR follow-BCKGR   that Sináwavi
            and he himself continued to meander around there, Sináwavi did —

            ///núu-ci-gya̱-y. . .
            Human-be-IMM
            he was human, you know . . .

            'úu-pa   wáay-va̱a̱ci-'urá. . .
            there-DIR follow-BCKGR-be
            he just kept meandering around there. . .'

The relatively short interjection above, a reminder of Sináwavi's being a human being (in those olden days), is followed by a resumption of the line of description concerning his blind meanderings in the bush.

In performing this measurement, I simply divided the occurences of any subject-marking device into two: It either occured in the very clause *initiating a major break* of either type, or else it occured *elsewhere,* e.i. in a clause that is paragraph medial or final, or one which may directly follow the second type of discontinuity (the latter on the assumption that resumption of the action after a *short* interjection represents thematic continuity rather than break).

In addition to the four measurements described above, I also performed two other more conventional measurements on the text:
(a) The percent of *animates/humans* in the categories Subject, Direct-Object, Locative-Object and Manner-adverb;
(b) The distribution of the *major-word-order types* (SVO, SOV, OVS, OSV, VSO, VOS) in the text, with 'object' counted separately for direct and indirect

objects. The results of the various measurements are described in section 4.
below and further discussed in section 5.

4. Numerical results of measurements
4.1. Topic-continuity properties of subjects
4.1.1. Referential distance ('lookback')

The average values for referential distance for the various categories of
subject are presented in Table I. As predicted on general grounds and shown in
the other studies in this volume, we observe a continuum behavior here with a
number of predictable sub-sections, whereby the zero-anaphora and clitic pronoun ('agreement') categories have the lowest − or *most continuous* values, independent pronouns come next, then full NP's, all within the bounds of *definite*
devices. Both within the independent pronoun and full NP categories, the VS
(comment-topic) word order is shown to be the more continuous, here essentially approximating the value for clitic pronouns. The SV (or topic-comment)
order is shown consistently to be of lower continuity, used over much larger
gaps of referential distance.

In Table II an attempt is made to assess the amount of variability within
each category, with respect to referential distance, as well as the *prototype*
behavior of the categories − as compared to the average values in Table I.
This type of comparison is crucial, since when counts are low − somewhere
below 40 tokens per category in these texts − the existence of one token with
an exceptionally high referential distance is bound to affect the average enor-
mously. The problem is of course compounded by our assigning, arbitrarily,
the maximal number 20 when no coreference is found within the first twenty
clauses to the left. It may very well be that such a choice *over*-represents the
putative length of the relevant "register" within which the "presence" of a
previous mention is relevant. The average distance values are compared to the
prototype values in Table III, where for prototypicality we assume the close
bunching of at least 70-90 percent of the tokens within the category.[51] The
results are quite instructive. High-count categories show very distinct prototypical bunching, all closely supporting the hierarchy of average values in Table I.
Thus, ∅, clitic pronouns (AGR) and the VS wordorder with full NP's bunch
as the most localized referential devices, with most of the tokens showing
values of 1-2 clauses to the left. The SV-ordered independent pronoun and the
SVS category (repeated subject on both sides of the verb, either with pronouns
or full NP's) bunch at the next range, between 1-4 clauses to the left. While the
SV-ordered full NP's scatter much more pronouncedly toward the higher regions

of the 1-to-20 scale, with the values for the SV-NP category taken together ranging all across the scale, but again skewed toward the higher region of the scale.

TABLE I: *Average Referential Distance for Subjects*

category	N	Ave. Ref. Distance in no. of clauses
Ø	321	1.21
AGR	42	1.54
VS-NP	25	1.48
VS-PRO	61	1.95
SV-PRO	75	2.80
SVS	13	2.84
SV-NP:	39	10.84
With DEM	10	5.80
With PRO	10	10.50
unmodified[a]	19	13.31

a) By 'unmodified' we don't mean here modification by clitic possessor ('genitive') pronouns or their reflexive-possessor counterparts (see section 2.1.6., above for an example).

TABLE II: *Percent Distribution of Referential Distance within Subject Categories*

No. of clauses	Ø N	Ø per	AGR N	AGR per	VS-NP N	VS-NP per	VS-PRO N	VS-PRO per	SV-PRO N	SV-PRO per	SVS N	SVS per	SV-NP w/DEM N	per	w/PRO N	per	unmodified N	per
1	278	0.86	29	0.69	17	0.68	31	0.50	27	0.36	4	0.31	2	0.20	3	0.30	4	0.17
2	25	0.08	8	0.19	6	0.24	17	0.28	18	0.25	5	0.39	3	0.30	1	0.10	1	0.06
3	10	0.03	3	0.07	1	0.04	6	0.09	11	0.13	1	0.08	/		/		1	0.06
4	4	0.015	1	0.025	/		3	0.04	8	0.10	2	0.14	1	0.10	/			
5	4	0.015	/		1	0.04	2	0.03	4	0.05			/				1	0.06
6			/				1	0.015	3	0.04			1	0.10				
7			1	0.025			/		1	0.01								
8							1	0.015	3						1	0.10		
9																		
10													2	0.20				
11									1	0.01								
12									1	0.01	1	0.08			1	0.10		
13																		
14																		
15																		
16																		
17																		
18																		
19																		
20									1	0.013			1	0.10	4	0.40	12	0.64
totals	321		42		25		61		75		13		10		10		19	

TABLE III: *Comparison of average values of referential distance with prototype distribution for subject categories*

category	average ref-distance	distance range within which 70-90 percent of category is found	
∅	1.21	1 clause	(86 percent)
AGR	1.54	1-2 clauses	(88 percent)
VS-NP	1.48	1-2 clauses	(92 percent)
VS-PRO	1.95	1-3 clauses	(87 percent)
SV-PRO	2.80	1-4 clauses	(84 percent)
SVS	2.84	1-4 clauses	(92 percent)
SV-NP w/DEM	5.80	1-10 clauses	(90 percent)
SV-NP w/PRO	10.50	2-20 clauses	(70 percent)
SV-NP unmodif.	13.31	3-20 clauses	(76 percent)
Average SV-NP	10.84	2-20 clauses	(74 percent)

4.1.2. *Persistence as subject ('decay')*

The results of this measurement, which assesses the distance – in number of clauses to the right – within which subject NP's marked by various devices retain the function of clausal subject – are summarized in Tables IV, V and VI below. The categories SVS and Ref(erential)-Ind(efinite)[51] can be eliminated from consideration due to low counts. When both the average persistence values and the prototype distribution are considered, it seems that we can divide the scale into 3 sub-ranges:

(a) Devices such as *grammatical agreement/clitic pronouns* and *VS-ordered independent pronouns* tend, in Ute, to appear in high frequency at *paragraph-final* positions, where the chance of persisting as subject are lower since at the boundary of thematic paragraph both action and participants/topics tend to undergo major switches (as compared to paragraph medial or initial, see further below). The average values of these devices are lowest, and the bulk ('proto-type') – 77-79 percent – tends to distribute at the values of 0-1 clauses to the right.

(b) Devices such as *zero-anaphora* and *VS-ordered definite NP's,* which tend to distribute in *paragraph-medial* positions, where the average values are higher values.

(c) Devices such as *SV-ordered* Definite NP'S and independent pronouns, where the average values are highest, and the prototype distribution pulls further toward higher values. These devices, as we have seen earlier, tend to be highly *discontinuous* in terms of referential distance to the left. They thus tend to represent the *beginnings* of new thematic paragraphs or the beginnings of new equi-topic ('equi-subject') chains. One would thus expect the average equi-subject persistence for these devices to be the highest.

TABLE IV: *Average value of persistence as subject ('decay')*
for the various subject-marking categories

category	N	Average persistence in no. of clauses
AGR	42	0.761
VS-PRO	61	1.131
REF-INDEF-NP	12	1.250
∅	321	1.333
VS-NP	25	1.400
SV-NP (combined)	39	1.615
SV-PRO	75	1.680
SVS	13	1.692

4.1.3. *The same subject (SS) vs. different subject (DS) measurement*

The results of this measurement are given in Tables VII and VIII, below. The ranking obtained in Table VII, in terms of the percentage of SS vs. DS within each category, follows in broad outline the ranking given in the measurement of referential distance. Zero-anaphora and grammatical agreement are shown to be primarily categories which *preserve subject continuity*, with 82 and 58 percent SS values, respectively. The middle range is occupied by the VS-ordered devices, with 44 percent SS for the VS-ordered DEF-NP and 35 percent

TABLE V: *Percent Distribution of Persistence as Subject within Subject Categories*

No. Of Clauses	AGR		VS-PRO		REF-INDEF		Ø		VS-NP		SV-NP		SV-PRO		SVS	
	N	per	N	per	N	per	N	per	N	per	N	per	N	per	N	per
0	23	0.54	33	0.54	7	0.58	161	0.50	11	0.43	8	0.21	25	0.33	3	0.23
1	10	0.25	14	0.23	1	0.08	68	0.21	4	0.16	20	0.51	20	0.27	3	0.23
2	6	0.14	6	0.10	1	0.08	47	0.14	4	0.16	1	0.03	11	0.14	3	0.23
3	2	0.05	3	0.05	1	0.08	22	0.06	3	0.12	4	0.10	10	0.13	3	0.23
4	1	0.025	2	0.03	1	0.08	14	0.04	2	0.09	2	0.04	4	0.05	1	0.08
5			/		1	0.08	7	0.02	/		3	0.075	2	0.03		
6			/				4	0.01	1	0.04	1	0.025	2	0.03		
7			2	0.03			1	0.002					1	0.01		
8			/				2	0.005								
9			/				2	0.005								
10			/				2	0.005								
11			/				1	0.002								
12			1	0.02			/									
13							1	0.002								
14																
totals	42		61		12		321		25		39		75		13	

TABLE VI: *Comparison of average values of persistence as subject with prototype distribution for subject categories*

category	average no. of clauses persistance as subj.	distance range within which 75-95 percent of category is found
AGR	0.761	0-1 clauses (79 percent)
VS-PRO	1.131	0-1 clauses (77 percent)
REF-INDEF	1.250	0-3 clauses (84 percent)
∅	1.333	0-2 clauses (85 percent)
VS-NP	1.400	0-3 clauses (87 percent)
SV-NP	1.615	0-3 clauses (85 percent)
SV-PRO	1.680	0-3 clauses (87 percent)
SVS	1.692	0-3 (92 percent)

TABLE VII: *Relative distribution of DS vs. VS occurences with each subject-marking cateogry*

category	SS		DS		TOTAL	
	N	percent	N	percent	N	percent
∅	264	0.82	57	0.18	321	1.00
AGR	24	0.58	18	0.42	42	1.00
VS-NP	11	0.44	14	0.56	25	1.00
VS-PRO	21	0.34	40	0.66	61	1.00
SV-NP	7	0.18	32	0.82	39	1.00
SVS	2	0.15	11	0.85	13	1.00
SV-PRO	4	0.05	71	0.95	75	1.00
totals	333	0.58	243	0.42	576	1.00

TABLE VIII: *Prototype distribution of the SS and DS functions across the entire subject-marking category range*

category	percent of total SS in various categories		percent of total DS in various categories	
	N	percent	N	percent
∅	264	0.79	57	0.23
AGR	24	0.07	18	0.075
VS-NP	11	0.03	14	0.057
VS-PRO	21	0.063	40	0.17
SV-NP	7	0.021	32	0.13
SVS	2	0.006	11	0.045
SV-PRO	4	0.012	71	0.29
total	333	1.00	243	1.00

SS for the VS-ordered pronouns. Finally, the SV-ordered devices (including SVS) are shown as primarily *subject switching* devices, with values ranging from 82 percent DS (SV-NP) to 92 percent DS (SV-PRO).

In Table VIII each of the two functions − SS and DS − is assessed as to within which grammatical devices it distributes most typically. The results are highly prototypical for the SS (subject continuity) function, with 86 percent of its tokens distributing within only two − the most continuous − categories: Zero anaphora (79 percent of the function) and grammatical agreement (7 percent of the function). On the other hand, the DS function is distributed much more widely across the scale, with 70 percent of its total showing in the five less-continuous categories, only 29 percent showing in the top discontinuous category (SV-PRO), and 23 percent still showing in the most continuous category (∅). The latter figure is obviously influenced by the fact that ∅ is by far the most numerous subject type in the entire sample (321 our of 576 subjects in the text counted, or 55.7 percent).

In terms of the grammar of *switch reference*, our counts show that the most prototypical SS marker (i.e. continuing subject) is *zero anaphora*, and the most typical (if any) marker for switch reference or DS (i.e. switch subject) is the *independent pronoun*, where the combined VS and SV orders cover 46 percent of all the DS functioned performed in the text.[52]

4.1.4. *Contiguity to a major thematic break/juncture*

The results of this measurement are given in Tables IX and X, below. The first four categories — zero anaphora, grammatical agreement and the VS word-order with both pronouns and NP's — all show between 88 and 100 percent *paragraph-continuation* distribution. Thus, not only are these categories used typically when the subject or topic is continuous (vis. the referential distance and SS/DS measurements above), but they also tend to distribute in *paragraph medial* (or *final*, as was suggested for the AGR and VS-PRO categories, see section 4.1.2. above), i.e. *not* following a major thematic break. On the other hand, the four other categories — SV-PRO, SV-NP, SVS and referential-indefinite NP's — show a much higher percentage of *paragraph break* in them, although the absolute percentages are considerably lower, suggesting presumably less-bunched prototype behavior[53] (34, 38, 53, 67 percent, respectively).

TABLE IX: *Relative distribution of Major Break/paragraph Intial vs. continuation/paragraph medial within each subject-marking category*

category	BREAK		CONTINUATION		TOTALS	
	N	percent	N	percent	N	percent
∅	1	0.004	320	0.996	321	1.00
AGR	/	/	42	1.00	42	1.00
VS-PRO	6	0.09	55	0.91	61	1.00
VS-NP	3	0.12	22	0.88	25	1.00
SV-PRO	26	0.34	49	0.66	75	1.00
SV-NP	15	0.38	24	0.62	39	1.00
SVS	7	0.53	6	0.47	13	1.00
REF-INDEF- -NP	8	0.67	4	0.33	12	1.00
total	66	0.12	522	0.88	588	1.00

TABLE X: *Prototype distribution of the paragraph break vs. paragraph continuation functions across the entire subject-marking category range*

category	PARAGRAPH BREAK		PARAGRAPH CONTINUATION	
	N	percent	N	percent
Ø	1	0.015	320	0.61
AGR	/	/	42	0.08
VS-PRO	6	0.09	55	0.10
VS-NP	3	0.045	22	0.042
SV-PRO	26	0.39	49	0.093
SV-NP	15	0.23	24	0.045
SVS	7	0.10	6	0.011
REF-DEF-NP	8	0.12	4	0.008
total	66	1.00	522	1.00

As can be seen from Table X, above, similar facts are revealed from observing the distribution of the "break" vs. "continuation" functions across the various subject-marking categories. The four most continuous categories account for *83 percent* of the instances of paragraph-medial (or final) tokens, while the four less-continuous categories account for *84 percent* of the instances of paragraph-initial ('break') tokens. Further, within the continuous category, *61 percent* of all tokens appear in the *zero-anaphora* category, again tagging it as the most continuity-marking category in the grammar. Conversely, *62 percent* of all tokens of the discontinuous ('break') category appear in either one of the SV-ordered devices, *39 percent* for the SV-PRO and *23 percent* for the SV-NP. The contrast between zero anaphora vs. independent pronouns functions not only to signal topic/subject continuity vs. switching but also marks the thematic continuity of the text. Further, the SV word-order signals discontinuity both in terms of topics/participants as well as in terms of theme. In other words, participant continuity and thematic continuity in texts tend to go to quite an extent hand in hand, whereby major breaks disrupt both types of continuity.

4.2. *Topic continuity properties of direct objects*
4.2.1. *Referential distance ('lookback')*

The results of this measurement, for the various direct object marking categories are given in Tables XI, XII, XIII below. First, one could divide the five categories sufficiently attested in the text into three distinct ranges:

(a) *Proximate range*: Zero anaphora and grammatical agreement/clitic pronoun, with the numerical balance shifting dramatically toward the clitic pronouns, here carry essentially the bulk of the functional load carried for subject NP's by the zero anaphora category.[54] The prototype distribution in Table XII and XIII makes it clear that essentially both categories exhibit the typical referential distance of *one* clause to the left.

(b) *Intermediate range*: A fairly similar prototype distribution is observed here for the independent pronouns and the VO-ordered NP's, with the average value for the latter probably over-weighted by the presence of two tokens of 20 (i.e. not attested in the register previously) which thus biases the rather small sample.

TABLE XI: *Average Referential Distance for Direct Objects*

category	N	ave. ref. distance in no. of clauses
∅	11	1.55
AGR	71	1.36
[VO-PRO]	[1]	[1.00][a]
OV-PRO	12	2.41
Total PRO	13	2.30
VO-NP	13	4.46
OV-NP	34	9.67
[OVO]	[1]	[1.00][b]

a) Count too small to be considered.
b) Count too small to be considered.

Number of Clauses	Ø N	Ø percent	AGR N	AGR percent	PRO N	PRO percent	VO-NP N	VO-NP percent	OV-NP N	OV-NP percent
1	9	0.82	58	0.81	8	0.61	8	0.62	10	0.29
2	1	0.09	8	0.11	/		1	0.075	3	0.09
3	/		2	0.035	/		1	0.075	2	0.06
4	/		2	0.035	3	0.23	1	0.075	3	0.09
5	/				2	0.16			1	0.03
6	1	0.09								
7										
8										
9			1	0.014					1	0.03
10										
11										
12										
13										
14										
16										
17										
18										
19										
20							2	0.15	14	0.41
total	11	1.00	71	1.00	13	1.00	13	1.00	34	1.00

TABLE XII: *Percent Distribution of Referential Distance within the Direcht Object Categories*

TABLE XIII: *Comparison of average values of referential distance
for direct objects with prototype distribution*

category	average ref. distance	distance range within which 80-90 percent of the category is found
∅	1.55	1 clause (82 percent)
AGR	1.36	1 clause (81 percent)
PRO	2.30	1-4 clauses (84 percent)
VO-NP	4.46	1-4 clauses (84 percent)
OV-NP	9.67	1-10 clause (59 percent)[a]

a) The maximal value 20 clauses ref. distance is of course arbitrary, representing largely NP's that are appearing in the register for the first time. While that category is the largest for OV-NP's, it is obviously impossible to characterize it as 'distance range'.

(c) *Remote range*: The OV-NP word order, with fully 41 percent of the sample appearing in the register for the first time, although the next big chunk — 29 percent of the sample — exhibit the smallest referential distance of 1 clause only. The results, in broad outline, replicate the hierarchies shown fro subject NP's earlier, although, as shown elsewhere in this volume, the average values for direct objects (and other oblique cate-ories, see below) tend to be higher than for subjects. In other words, the subject category tends to be more continuous in discourse, which is obviously expected. Such a conclusion will be further strengthened when the percent distribution of the various grammatican devices within subject and object categories is considered, whereby the relative role of the more continuous devices within the subject sample is much larger (see section 5, below).

4.2.2. *Persistence ('decay')*

The persistence value measured here is different from the one measured for subjects (persistence *as subject* in number of clauses to the right). It involves persistence, in number of clauses to the right, at *whatever* role. Most commonly, NP's in the high persistence categories tend to turn into *subjects* in the subsequent clauses, a fact that gives them higher persistence values, given the higher continuity values for subjects in general. This measure thus assesses the *importance* of topics in discourse, and the role of various grammatical devices in introducing important ('persistent') or less-important ('fast decaying') topics into the register. As one can see from the results in Tables XIV, XV, XVI below, important object-topics in Ute tend to be marked by three grammatical devices: Grammatical agreement (clitic pronouns), independent pronouns and the VO word-order with full NP's. Of these, grammatical agreement is numerically predominant. Within the direct object category, then, this category signals topics which are both highly *continuous* in terms of referential distance, thus predictable to the hearer, but also *important* in terms of their survivability in the register. The latter corresponds closely to observations made by Haile (1970), Hetzron (1971) and Givón (1976).

TABLE XIV: *Average values of persistence ('decay') for the various direct-object categories*

category	N	average persistence in no. of clauses
∅	11	1.09
AGR	71	3.253
PRO	13	3.69
VO-NP	13	4.15
OV-NP	34	0.94
[REF-INDEF-NP	4	2.25][a]

a) The count is too low to consider this category seriously.

Number of Clauses	∅ N	∅ percent	AGR N	AGR percent	PRO N	PRO percent	VO-NP N	VO-NP percent	OV-NP N	OV-NP percent	REF-INDEF-NP N	REF-INDEF-NP percent
0	5	0.45	21	0.30	4	0.31	4	0.33	20	0.59	2	0.50
1	4	0.36	13	0.19	1	0.074	2	0.15	8	0.24	/	
2	1	0.095	8	0.12	3	0.23	2	0.15	/		/	
3	/		3	0.04	1	0.074	1	0.076	4	0.11	/	
4	/		8	0.12	/		/		1	0.03	1	0.25
5	/		3	0.04	/		/		/		1	0.25
6	1	0.095	5	0.07	1	0.074	1	0.76	/			
7			2	0.028	1	0.074	/	0.076	1	0.03		
8			/		/		/		/			
9			2	0.028	/		/		/			
10			/		/		/					
11			/		/		/					
12			1	0.014	1	0.074	/					
13			/		1	0.074	1	0.076				
14			2	0.028			/					
15			2	0.028			/					
16			/				/					
17			/				/					
18							/					
19			1	0.014			1	0.076				
total	11	1.00	71	1.00	13	1.00	13	1.00	34	1.00	4	1.00

TABLE XV: *Percent distribution of persistence within direct-object categories*

TABLE XVI: *Comparison of average values of persistence with prototype distribution for direct-object categories*

Category	average persistence in no. of clauses	distance range within which 80-90 percent of category found
∅	1.09	0-1 clauses (81 percent)
AGR	3.253	0-6 clauses (86 percent)
PRO	3.69	0-7 clauses (85 percent)
VO-NP	4.15	0-8 clauses (85 percent)
OV-NP	0.94	0-1 clauses (83 percent)
[REF-INDEF-NP	2.25	0-5 clauses (100 percent)][a]

a) Counts too low to be taken seriously.

Once again, the difference between OV and VO-ordered definite NP's is striking. The OV-NP category exhibits the lowest persistence values in the sample, while the VO-NP category — though with lower counts and thus less reliability in measurement — exhibits the highest values. These differences closely parallel the difference in referential distance, see above. The OV-ordered direct object position is thus one where arguments tend to enter into the register briefly, and disappear fast. The VO-ordered direct object position, on the other hand, tends to mark continuous, important participants, as we have already noted above.

4.3. *Topic continuity properties of indirect objects*

Of all post-positional 'indirect' objects in our text, only locative objects appear in sufficient numbers to allow the application of our measurements, though in looking at word-order we also included manner adverbs (the free-word ones).

4.3.1. *The referential distance measurement ('lookback')*

The results of this measurement, for definite locatives only, are given in Tables XVII, XVIII, XIX, below. While the absolute values for the largely inanimate categories of VO and OV ordered LOC-NP's are higher that the averages observed for subjects and direct objects, the relative hierarchy remains the same, with pronouns (the largely animate category here) at the lower end of the scale (most continuous), VO-ordered NP's in the middle, and OV-ordered

NP's at the top (i.e. least continuous). The categories of zero anaphora and grammatical agreement (clitic pronouns) do not appear here. As we shall see further below, the correlation with animacy is relevant across the entire sample, in comparing the behavior of subjects, direct objects and indirect objects.

TABLE XVII: *Average Referential Distance for Indirect Objects*

Category	N	ave. ref. distance in no. of clauses
ANIMATE-PRO-LOC		
[VO-ordered	1	1.00]a
OV-ordered (free)	13	1.61
[OV-ordered (frozen)	4	1.00]b
Total PRO	18	1.44
DEF-NP-LOC		
VO-ordered	7	10.85
OV-ordered	14	15.42
[OVO	2	7.00]c
DEICTIC-LOC		(no exact reference)
VO-ordered	5	
OV-ordered	43	
Total DEICT	48	
INDEF-NP-LOC (all OV)		(no previous reference)
Referential	2	
Non-referential	2	(no reference)
Total INDEF-LOC	4	
MANNER ADVERB (all OV)	10	(non-referential)

a) Count too low to consider independently.
b) Count too low to consider independently.
c) Count too low to consider seriously.

TABLE XVIII: *Percent Distribution of Referential Distance within the Indirect Object Categories* (definite-locatives only)

Number of clauses	AN-PRO-LOC N	AN-PRO-LOC percent	VO-NP-LOC N	VO-NP-LOC percent	OV-LOC-NP N	OV-LOC-NP percent
1	14	0.78	/		/	
2	2	0.11	1	0.144	/	
3	1	0.055	/		/	
4	/		2	0.284	1	0.07
5	1	0.055	/		2	0.14
6			/		/	
7			/		1	0.07
8			/		/	
9			/		/	
10			/		/	
11			/		/	
12			1	0.144	/	
13			/		/	
14			1	0.144	/	
15			/	0.144	/	
16			/		1	0.07
17			/		/	
18			/		/	
19			/		/	
20			2	0.284	9	0.65
total	13	1.00	7	1.00	14	1.00

TABLE XIX: *Comparison of average values of referential distance for indirect (locative) objects with prototype distributions*

category	average ref. distance	distance range within which 70-90 percent of category is found	
ANIM-PRO-LOC	1.44	1-2 clauses	(89 percent)
VO-NP-LOC	10.85	4-20 clauses	(85 percent)
OV-NP-LOC	15.42	15-20 clauses	(72 percent)

4.3.2. Persistence ('decay')

The results of this measurement are given in Tables XX, XXI, XXII, below. Essentially, only one category – animate pronoun locatives – shows a measure of topic persistence ('importance') in discourse, with the average value (3.00 clauses to the right) essentially comparable to that of direct object independent pronouns (3.69 clauses). The category Manner Adverb is not really likely to persist, since its informational properties are overwhelmingly *non-referential* (attributive, predicational). The categories of full-NP locative, while definite, show themselves to be of relative insignificance as entry points for important participants in discourse, thus contrasting sharply with direct object NP's – or at least with the more continuous and topically salient VO-ordered definite object NP.

TABLE XX: *Average values of persistence ('decay') for Indirect Objects (locatives, manner)*

category	N	average persistance in no. of clauses
ANIM-PRO-LOC	13	3.00
VO-NP-LOC	7	0.142
OV-NP-LOC	14	0.000
MANNER	10	0.000

4.4. Animacy

The stories comprising the Ute text in this study are overwhelmingly about the actions and tribulations of *animate, cognizing, communicating* participants. Essentially, those participants are stand-ins for universal human prototypes.[55] Thus, a certain measure of the topical importance of the various NP-types in the text can be derived from counting the percent of animate NP's within each category. The results of this count are given in Table XXIV, below. Only full NP's and independent pronouns were counted, so that the sample is strongly biased toward *under*-representing the more *continuous* and more *animate* categories zero anaphora and agreement/clitic pronouns in the subject and direct object case-roles. Nevertheless, the relative distribution of animacy show the expected biase for this type of animate-oriented narrative, with 88 percent animates in the subject category, 50 percent for direct objects, 22 percent for

Number of	ANIM-PRO-LOC N	percent	VO-NP-LOC N	percent	OV-NP-LOC N	percent	MANNER ADV N	percent
0	4	0.30	6	0.08	14	1.00	10	1.00
1	1	0.076	1	0.14				
2	1	0.076						
3	3	0.23						
4	1	0.076						
5	1	0.076						
6	1	0.076						
7	/							
8	/							
9	/							
10	/							
11	/							
12	1	0.076						
total	13	1.00	7	1.00	14	1.00	10	1.00

TABLE XXI: *Percent distribution of persistence of indirect objects*

locatives and none for manner adverbs. As we shall see further below, this measurement correlates directly with both the degree of topic continuity (in particular referential distance) of the various case roles, as well as with the distribution of pre-verbal vs. post-verbal word-order for both subjects and objects.

TABLE XXII: *Comparison of average values of persistence with prototype distribution of indirect objects*

category	average persistence in no. of clauses	distance range within which 85-100 percent of category found	
ANIM-PRO-LOC	3.00	0-5 clauses	(85 percent)
VO-NP-LOC	0.142	0 clauses	(86 percent)
OV-NP-LOC	0.000	0 clauses	(100 percent)
MANNER ADV	0.000	0 clauses	(100 percent)

TABLE XXIV: *Percent of animate vs. inanimate NP's in the major care-role categories* (NP *and independent PRO only*)

category	ANIMATE		INANIMATE		TOTAL	
	N	percent	N	percent	N	percent
Subject	186	0.88	26	0.12	212	1.00
Direct Object	34	0.50	35	0.50	69	1.00
Locative Object	20	0.22	71	0.78	91	1.00
Manner Adverb	/	0.00	10	1.00	10.	1.00

4.5. *Word-order distribution*

The distribution of pre vs. post-verbal word-orders for the major categories in the Ute text is given in Table XXV, below. The most continuous and most highly referential category of subject exhibits overall 41 percent of *post verbal* — VS — word-order. The less continuous, less referential direct object category exhibits 20 percent *post-verbal* — VO — word-order. The less referential, less continuous category of locative object exhibits only 14 percent *post-verbal* — VO — word-order. While the totally non-referential, attributive category of manner adverb exhibits 100 percent *pre-verbal* — OV — word order. Within the subject, direct object and locative object, further, the categories indefinite and non-referential — the least continuous — exhibit almost across the board 100 percent *pre-verbal* —SV or OV — word-order. The significance of these facts and their correlation to topic continuity, topic importance and animacy will be discussed in section 5., below.

TABLE XXV: *The distribution of word-order in tha major grammatical categories*

	VS/VO		SV/OV		TOTAL	
Category	N	percent	N	percent	N	percent
SUBJECT						
PRO	61	0.45	75	0.55	136	1.00
DEF-NP	25	0.39	39	0.61	64	1.00
REF-INDEF-NP	1	0.09	11	0.91	12	1.00
TOTAL SUBJECT	87	0.41	125	0.59	212	1.00
DIR-OBJECT						
PRO	1	0.08	12	0.92	13	1.00
DEF-NP	13	0.28	34	0.72	47	1.00
REF-INDEF-NP	/	/	4	1.00	4	1.00
NON-REF-NP	/	/	5	1.00	5	1.00
TOTAL DIR-OBJ	14	0.20	55	0.80	69	1.00
LOC-OBJECT						
ANIM-PRO	1	0.06	17	0.94	18	1.00
DEF-NP	7	0.33	14	0.67	21	1.00
DEICTIC	5	0.11	43	0.89	48	1.00
INDEF-NP	/	/	4	1.00	4	1.00
TOTAL LOC-OBJ	13	0.14	78	0.86	91	1.00
MANNER ADVERB	/	/	10	1.00	10	1.00

In Table XXVII we present the distribution of the six hypothetically possible major word-order types (cf. Greenberg, 1966) found in the text in all instances where both independent (NP, PRO) subject and object were present. Due to the large percentage of zero anaphora and clitic pronouns in the two major categories, subject and direct object, the counts are obviously much smaller than desirable, and a larger sample would be required in order to raise their reliability eventually. But even given the low counts, it is obvious that overall as well as in the major object categories two word-order types predominate: The SOV word order, which is the historical word-order of Ute (and Uto-Aztecan), and OVS. Within the more prototypical object category, direct object, further, the

two word orders are almost of equal frequency. The significance of these facts
and their relation to word-order change from SOV will be discussed in section 5.,
below.

TABLE XXVI: *The distribution of major word-order types with full
NP's or independent pronouns in the Ute narrative text*

type	DIR. OBJ. N	DIR. OBJ. percent	LOC. OBJ N	LOC. OBJ percent	MANNER N	MANNER percent	TOTAL N	TOTAL percent
SVO	3	0.13	2	0.07	/		5	0.092
VSO	2	0.09	2	0.09	/		4	0.074
OSV	3	0.13	1	0.04	/		4	0.074
VOS	/		/		/		/	
SOV	7	0.32	18	0.64	3	1.00	28	0.52
OVS	6	0.27	5	0.18	/		11	0.20
SOSV	1	0.045	/		/		1	0.018
SOVS	1	0.045	/		/		1	0.018
Total	23	1.00	28	1.00	3	1.00	54	1.00

5. Discussion

5.1. Referential distance and topic continuity

This is our most reliable measurement for the topic continuity property
in terms of distance from the last mention in the register, and thus presumably
accessibility to the hearer or even the speaker.[56] For subjects and direct objects,
a clear separation is evident between three major marking devices:

(a)   *Most continuous/localized*: Zero anaphora and clitc pronouns/agreement;
(b)   *Intermediate*: Independent pronouns;
(c)   *Least continuous*: Full NP's

The functional load of the lower range (a) in Ute is carried primarily by zero
anaphora for subjects and clitic pronouns for direct objects. The relatively low
figure for locative independent pronouns should reflect, I believe, the fact that

this device carries the functional load of the lower range as well for this case-role.

In all categories where a comparison between pre-verbal and post-verbal ordering of the NP's is possible, the post-verbal (VS, VO) order clearly shows itself to be a device coding *more continuous* topics. In the subject category, the VS-ordered NP shows even more continuous (i.e. lower) values than the independent pronouns. Since we have not assessed in this study the important factor of *potential interference*, i.e. the presence of contrasting or other NP's within the near register to the left, full discrimination of the marking devices is not possible. We shall discuss the use of word-order in Ute in a separate section below.

The results of the average referential distance measurement for the three major case-roles are summarized as a graph in Chart 1, below. Locative objects are clearly the *least continuous* topics of the three. Subjects and direct objects are not as clearly separated in this respect. If the Three full-NP subject categories are thrown together (see Table I above), for the pre-verbal word-order, the values for this least-continuous marking device for subject and direct object become essentially the same (10.84 clauses for subject, vs. 9.67 for direct object). Though the subject is clearly *more continuous* than the direct object in the post-verbal ordering (VS vs. VO). There is, however, another measure which clearly shows that overall in the text the subject is much continuous. Thus, in Table XXVII, below, we express — for subjects, direct objects and locative objects — the percent in the entire sample of categories with referential distance values 2.0 or lower. Such categories comprise *76 percent* of the total sample for subject, *56 percent* for direct object and only *19 percent* for locative object, the only oblique category with high enough counts in the text.

5.2. *Continuity, animacy and topicality*

There is a strong correlation between the average continuity values expressed as percentages of high-continuity categories for the three major case-roles (Table XXVII) and the percent of *animacy* in these categories as given in Table XXIV, above. This correlation is expressed as graph in Chart 2, below. As can be seen, the correlation is essentially direct. Our measure of referential distance thus correlates to animacy in essentially a way predicted in the topic-hierarchy literature (cf. for example Givón, 1976). Further, the three major case-roles hierarchize, in terms of their topicality, in the same way predicted elsewhere (Givón, 1982c), showing the subject as the *primary topic* in the clause and the direct object the *secondary topic*. As we shall see further below, both

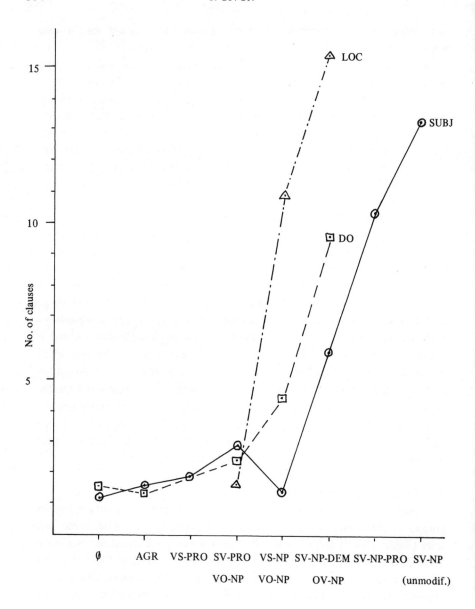

CHART 1: *Average Referential Distance for the Three Major Case-Roles*

the animacy and the referential-distance measures correlate with the distribution of pre- vs. post-verbal word order in the major case-roles in Ute.

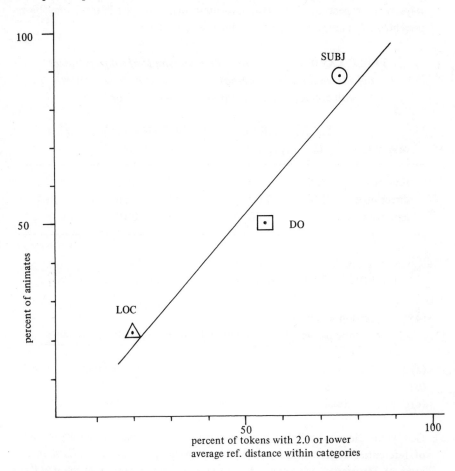

CHART 2: *Correlation between animacy and topic-continuity, as measured by referential distance for the three major case-roles*

5.3. Topic persistence ('decay')

Several provisos must be born in mind before our measure of topic persistence can be correlated to referential distance. Topic persistence clearly reflects topic importance and thus topicality. However, the reflection is not direct. Categories of *high topical importance* may in fact distribute in opposite ways with respect to these two measurements. This distribution may be represented schematically in the following predictive table:

TABLE XXVII: *Percent within the total sample of subjects, direct objects and locative objects of tokens belonging to categories with average referential distance values of 2.0 or lower*

	TOTAL SAMPLE		CATEGORIES WITH 2.0 or lower	
case role	N	percent	N	percent
subject	588	1.00	449	0.76
direct object	146	1.00	83	0.56
locative object	91	1.00	18	0.19

PREDICTIONS OF THE BEHAVIOR OF IMPORTANT TOPICS[57]

(45)	position within the thematic paragraph	referential distance	expected persistence
(a)	medial	low	medium
(b)	initial	high	high
(c)	final	low	low

One would thus expect that topic-marking devices of high continuity in terms of referential distance (low values there) would give only a *medium to low* value of persistence, since they tend to appear, on the average, in the *middle or the end* of the thematic paragraph. On the other hand, topic-marking devices of low continuty (high referential distance), if used to introduce (or re-introduce) into the register important referents, would be expected to show the *highest* persistence values, since they appear at the *initial* position of thematic paragraphs.

These predictions are indeed born out in the Ute study. Thus, for example, for *subjects*, zero-anaphora, VS-NP and VS-PRO all have the lowest referential distance (2.0 clauses or lower) in Table I, above. They also occupy the *mid range* in terms of persistence (Table V, above), with values in the range of 1.131-1.40 clauses. The category of agreement (clitic pronoun) seems to buck the trend here, being of low referential distance but equally low (lowest) persistence. (0.761). But this simply tags it as a *paragraph-final* marking device, i.e. category (45c). Finally, devices with the *highest* referential distance (lowest continuity to the left), such as the SV-ordered NP's, SV ordered independent pronouns and the SVS device, exhibit also the *highest* persistence values in Table IV all between 1.615-1.695 clauses to the right. This identifies them clearly as *paragraph-initial* topic-marking devices, i.e. category (45b), above.

As suggested above, the subject is the *primary* – most important – topic in the clause, and obviously also in the thematic paragraph. The conformance of the ref-distance and persistence values found in this study to the predictions made in (45) clearly demonstrates that. The *direct object*, on the other hand, is not the case-role marking the most important topic in the clause. However, it may serve as the *entry point* into the register of important topics, which then – if important/persistent enough – may convert into clausal subjects. In fact in Ute, with virtually no use of indefinite subject NP's to introduce new arguments into the register, the role of the direct object NP in introducing or reintroducing arguments into the register becomes crucial. In surveying the persistence figures in Table XIV and comparing them to the referential-distance figures in Table XI, above, the following division is apparent:

(a)   *Zero anaphora and grammatical agreement*: While essentially of the same high continuity in terms of ref-distance, zero anaphora marks *unimportant* topics, while *grammatical agreement* (clitic pronouns) marks topics of considerable importance (persistence values of 1.09 vs. 3.253, respectively).

(b)   *Independent pronouns*: The ref-distance value of this marking device is still relatively low (2.30 clauses), while their persistence value is next to the highest (3.69 clauses). This is thus, for direct objects, a device marking the *most continuous* topics in terms of a combined view to both left and right.

(c)   *The VO-ordered DEF-NP*: This device re-introduces a referent into the register following a medium gap of absence (4.46 ref-distance), but such reintroduced topics are of the *highest persistence* (4.15 clauses). This device is still fairly close to the independent pronoun.

(d)   *The OV-ordered DEF-NP*: This is the least-continuous topic-marking device for direct objects, with the lowest persistence value (0.94 clauses) and the highest ref-distance (9.67 clauses). It clearly marks topics that enter into the register briefly and disappear quickly. Their information value is thus likely to be *less referential* and more *attributive/predicational.* As we shall see further below, this observation correlates closely with other measures of topicality/ referentiality.

The role of *referential-indefinite* direct objects as an entry-point of topics into the register cannot be assessed here, due to low counts. The particular texts studied here tend to neutralize the distinction between definite and indefinite (referential) arguments, due to the universal familiarity of members of the culture with the major participants in the stories. This is reminiscent of Kalmár's (1979, 1980) observation for Eskimo. It contrasts sharply with Givón's (1979, Ch. 2) text-counts for English.

5.4. *Topic persistence, animacy and case-roles*

The present study does not allow direct comparison of persistence values for subjects and objects, since subject persistence was measured in a narrower way, *qua subject*, while object persistent was measured broadly, i.e. in *whatever* grammatical role, including subject. The comparison of the persistence values of the direct and locative objects is, as expected, striking. Not only are locative objects of high ref-distance (low continuity), but their bulk is also of *low persistence*, with values for the VO and OV-ordered LOC-NP's essentially at 0.00 clauses. The only category here marking more persistent — important — topics is the *animate* independent pronoun, with the persistence value of 3.00 clauses, essentially in the same range as the DO independent pronouns, above (3.69 clauses). These animates are not there to mark the location of events/states, but essentially as *dative-goal* participants, important for themselves and not only as spatial points of reference. Otherwise, the locative object role is prototypically not one either introducing or maintaining important topic in Ute discourse.

Another way of comparing the major case-roles in terms of persistence is by computing the percent of tokens in each total sample belonging to highpersistence categories. In order to make the subject somewhat comparable to the objects, its scale range of 0.761 to 1.692 average persistence values was divided roughly in half, with categories from 0.70 to 1.25 considered of low persistance, and those with values from 1.30 to 1.70 considered of high persistence. For objects, the scale from 0.00 to 4.15 was similarly divided, with categories from 0.00 to 2.00 considered of low persistence, and those from 2.00 to 4.15 of high persistence. The results are presented in Table XXVIII, below. They are again quite striking, with *79 percent* of the subject falling in the high-persistence categories, *69 percent* of direct objects, *14 percent* only of locative objects and 0.00 of manner adverbs. These results correlate directly to either the percent of *animacy* or of *low referential distance* (which themselves go hand in hand, see Chart 2.,

TABLE XXVIII: *Percent within the total sample of subjects, direct objects and locative objects of tokens belonging to categories of high persistence values (1.30 and over for subjects, 2.00 and over for objects)*

	TOTAL SAMPLE		HIGH-PERSISTENCE CATEGORIES	
case role	N	percent	N	percent
subject	588	1.00	470	0.79
direct object	146	1.00	101	0.69
locative object	91	1.00	13	0.14
[manner adverb	10	1.00	/	0.00]

a) This non-referential category may ve viewed as the base-line bottom in terms of topicality, by whatever measure. It is essentially as non-topical or as attributive as the verb.

above). This correlation (with animacy) is expressed as a graph in Chart 3, below.

5.5. *Continuity and switch-reference*

As the results recorded in Tables VII and VIII, section 4.1.3, above, clearly suggest, there is a strong correlation between topic continuity in terms of our measure of referential distance and the percent of same-subject measurement recorded. This correlation is expressed as a descending graph in Chart 4, below. One category (SV-NP) would press for strengthening the correlation even further. It is *one* of the lowest in terms of percent of SS in the sample, but the *highest* — seemingly disproportionately — in terms of referential distance (i.e. lowest in continuity). The *direction* of its deviation from the graph is thus not disturbing, although at the moment the reasons cannot be assessed.

In terms of categorial bunching, we have here essentially three separate ranges:
(a) *The most continuous devices*: Zero-anaphora and grammatical agreement (clitic pronouns), with the highest percent of SS (subject continuity);
(b) *The middle range*: VS-ordered NP's and independent pronouns, with intermediate values of SS (subject continuity);
(c) *The least continuous devices*: SV-ordered NP's and independent pronouns and the minor SVS-NP category, with the lowest (below 18) percent of SS in the sample.

In terms of the relative distribution of the two functions — SS and DS —

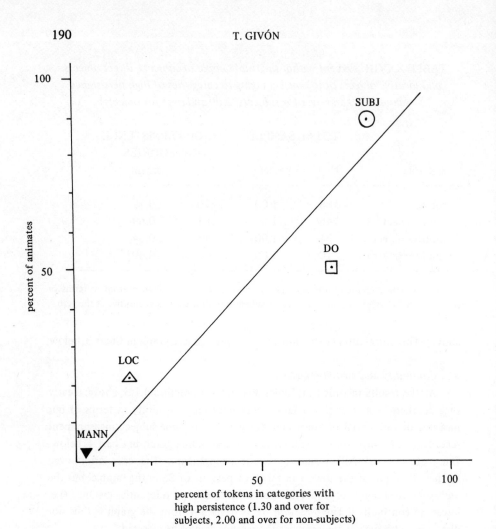

CHART 3: *Correlation between animacy and topic persistence
for the four case-roles*

across the various subject-marking devices, the combined two most continuous
categories, zero anaphora and clitic pronouns/agreement, account for *86 percent*
of the total *same-subject* function in the entire sample. And zero anaphora by
itself accounts for *79 percent*. This in essence approaches categoriality.

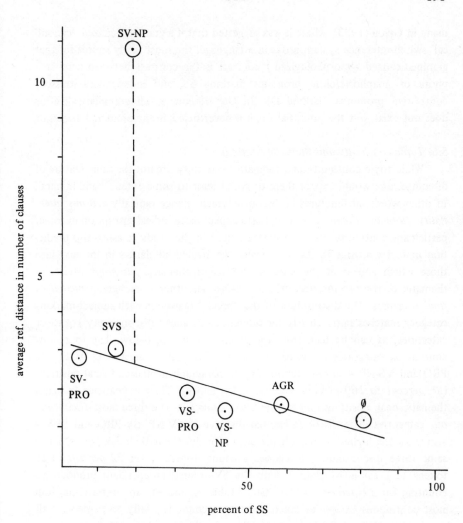

CHART 4: *Correlation between percent of same-subject (SS and referential distance for subject marking categories*

The functional load of *swith-subject* is not distributed quite as categorially. Nevertheless, the combined SV- and VS- ordered *independent pronouns* account for *46 percent* of the DS category, and SV-PRO by itself accounts for the largest chunk — *29 percent.* These results conform rather closely to predictions made in Givón (1983), where it was suggested that if a grammaticalized, 'canonical' switch-reference system arises in a language, the most likely source for that grammaticalized ('morphologized') contrast is the contrast between zero anaphora or anaphoric/clitic pronouns marking SS, and independent/stressed/contrastive pronouns markind DS. In Ute of course full grammaticalization does not exist, but the potential for it is nevertheless in the predicted direction.

5.6. *Topic continuity and thematic continuity*

While topic continuity and thematic continuity are not the same feature of discourse, one would expect them to go, at least to some extent, hand in hand. In other words, at junctures in discourse which change radically *action-sequentiality, time* and *theme*, one would also expect more radical disruption in topic/participant continuity. The one measure used in this study to assess this prediction in fact confirms it. As one recalls, we divided all clauses in the text into those which appear at the initiation of major thematic *paragraph breaks* or thematic *digressions/interjections*, as against all other − paragraph *medial* or *final* − clauses. The distribution of the "break" feature in each subject-marking category matches fairly closely the referential distance ('discontinuity') of those categories, as can be seen from the graph in Chart 5, below. The four *most* continuous categories in terms of lowest referential distance − Ø, AGR, VS-PRO and VS-NP − appear almost only in paragraph medial and final positions (*88 percent to 100 percent*, see Table IX, above). Their appearance in major thematic beak positions ranges from *0 to 12 percent.* The three most *discontinuous* categories in terms of referential distance − SV-NP, SV-PRO and SVS − also show the highest values for presence at major thematic break points. These same three discontinuous categories account, together, for *72 percent* of all tokens of break-intial clauses, with the SV-ordered independent pronoun accounting for *39 percent* all by itself (Table X, above). In contrast, the four most continuous categories taken together account for fully *83 percent* of all paragraph-medial or final clauses in the text. While such correlations are not absolute, there is clearly a rather substantial parallelism between major breaks in thematic continuity in text and corresponding breaks in topic/participant continuity. Major *junctures* in discourse should be thus expected to represent high discontinuity in the four parameters which constitute the major *threads* of the narrative:

(a)   Continuity of time   (c)   Continuity of action
(b)   Continuity of place   (d)   Continuity of participants

Parameters (a), (b) and (c) above are of course the traditional *Three Unities* of the Greek theater. While they are obviously much harder to quantify in a study of this type, they are in principle amenable to study by similar methodologies as applied here to participant continuity.

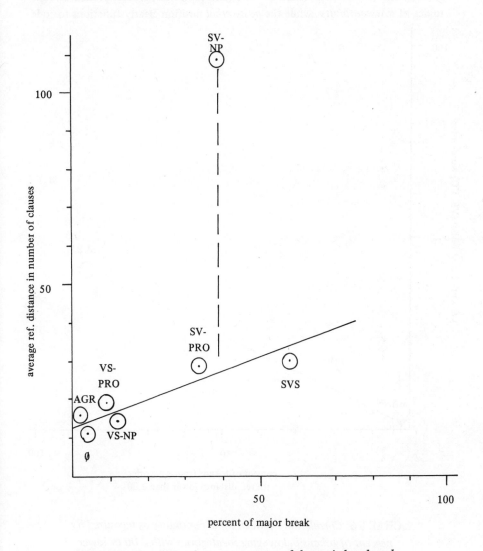

CHART 5: *Correlation between percent of thematic break and referential distance for subject marking categories*

5.7. *The discourse-pragmatics of word-order variation in Ute*

This study demonstrates clearly that both for the VS/SV and VO/OV word-order variation in Ute, the controlling factors are closely linked to topic continuity. The *pre-verbal* position of NP's (and pronouns) is clearly used to code topics of *low continuity*, while the *post-verbal* position clearly functions to code

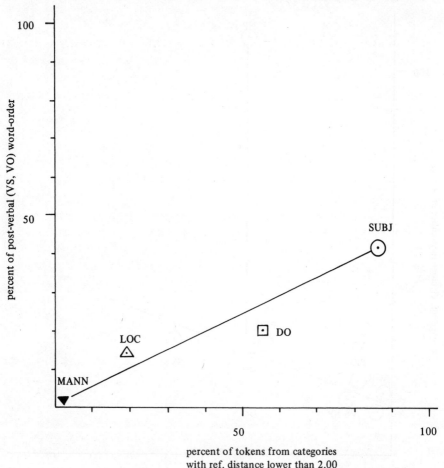

CHART 6: *Correlation between topic continuity as measured by percent of tokens belownging tocategories with 2.00 or lower referentual distance, and post-verbal (VS, VO) word-order for the major case-roles*

topics of *high continuity*. Further, as shown in section 5.3. above, for direct objects the OV word-order also contrasts sharply with the VO order with respect to *topic persistence*, with the OV order consistently coding NP's with very low persistence in the discourse, while the VO wordorder codes NP's of much higher persistence – and thus topical *importance*.

The correlation between topic continuity as expressed by referential distance figures taken from Table XXVII above, and the percent of *post-verbal* word-order (VS, VO) taken from Table XXV, is expressed – for the four major case-roles – as a graph in Chart 6, below. We are indeed dealing with a direct correlation, whereby the category subject has both the highest measure of topic continuity and the highest percent of post-verbal word-order, followed in order by direct object, locative object and manner adverb.

A similar correlation can be shown between word-order and animacy. Thus, in Chart 7, below, a graph is presented of the word-order percentages from Table XXV, above, and the animacy percentages from Table XXIV, above. The correlation is essentially as direct as that in Chart 6. While other elements of continuity, such as potential interference from other referents in the register, semantic redundancy derived from the lexical items in the clauses or various aspects of larger thematic continuity were not assessed in this study, the data clearly support a strong correlation between the degree of topic continuity for a given clause participant, and the chance that the participant would appear post-verbally.

Lastly, the results of this study lend further support to the hierarch of topic continuity shown in Givón (1982a) concerning universals of word-order and topic-NP expression, to wit:

(46)
COMMENT > COMMENT-TOPIC > TOPIC-COMMENT > (REPEATED) TOPIC
  ($\emptyset$ topic)   ($\emptyset$ comment)

According to this hierarchy, the most predictable, obvious, continuous topic simply goes *unexpressed*. At a lower level of predictability/continuity it is expressed *post-verbally*. At a lower yet level of predictability/continuity it is expressed *pre-verbally*. And at the lowest level of predictability/continuity it is expressed *alone*, with *repetition*, without any comment. A transparent psychological principle ought to account for such a hierarchy:

(47)   "Attend first to the most urgent task"

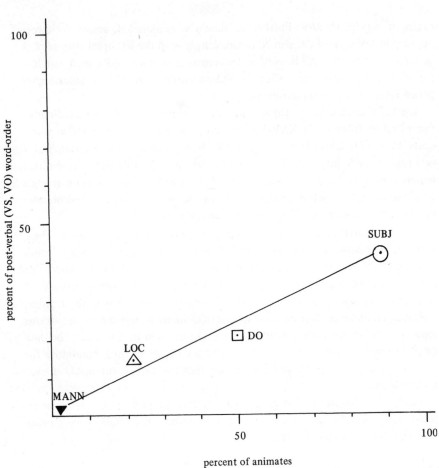

CHART 7: *Correlation between percent of animacy and the post-verbal*
word-order (VS, VO) for the major case-roles

5.8. *Topicality, topic-continuity and word-order change*

Ute, like the Uto-Aztecan family in general, is clearly a fairly recent ex-SOV
language. As our Table XXV suggests, the SV word-order is still at the level of
59 percent in our texts, and the OV word order for direct objects is still at the
level of *80 percent* in our texts. And in clauses with both subject and either
direct, locative or manner object, the overall percentage of the SOV word order

is still *52 percent*, with the closest competitor — OVS — showing at *20 percent*. As we have show above, however, the incidence of post-verbal placement of NP's in Ute is directly correlated to their degree of *topicality*, in terms of our measures of *topic continuity* and *animacy*. Our Ute data thus afford us a unique perspective about the dynamics of word-order change from SOV.

In a prophetic article, Hyman (1975) suggested that the order of change from OV to VO word-order for various object NP's should follow their degree of topicality, so that the most topical would change to VO first, given the discourse device of "afterthought topic". While Hyman's specific prediction — that indirect object would always change first, as they seem to have done in Niger-Congo (see also Givón, 1975) — is not upheld in this study, the general principle suggested by him is indeed fully confirmed by the Ute data. What it suggests, however, is that given the highest topicality of the *subject*, the word-order OVS — the one ruled out as non-existent by Greenberg (1966) but recently reported for Carib by Derbyshire and Pullum (1981) — should be the major discernible intermediate word-order when an SOV language is drifting away from its old rigidity. This suggestion has been in fact made recently by Derbyshire (1979). And this is precisely what our data, as presented in both Tables XXV and XXVI tend to suggest. In terms of text frequency, in a pragmatically-controlled word-order of a language at a fairly early stage of drifting away from SOV, the post-verbal subject clearly outpaces the post-verbal object, and the word-order OVS clearly outpaces all other word-orders except for the original SOV. Ute, of course, has not yet reached the point of word-order stabilization and *re-rigidi-fication*. Neither, one suspects, have the Carrib languages reported as "OVS" by Derbyshire and Pullum (1981). Whether the OVS order indeed becomes a rigid one in the drift away from SOV, as do SVO (Hyman, 1975, Givón, 1975, 1977) or verb-first (Givón, 1977), remains to be seen, Very clearly though, the determination of the direction of this drift by the *topicality* of the major arguments militates toward a major change toward . . . VS. . . . , as predicted in Givón (1977). Further studies, in ex-SOV languages a bit more advanced than Ute, will have to be undertaken in order to assess the relative viability of SVO, VSO or OVS as the most likely targets in the natural drift from SOV. What I have shown here, I think rather conclusively, is that such a drift is mediated by simple and quantifiable factors of discourse pragmatics.

NOTES

1) Ute is a member of the Southern Numic and Numic sub-divisions of the Uto-Aztecan family. It is still spoken on three Ute reservations in South-Western Colorado and North-Eastern Utah. This study was supported in part by a grant from the National Endowment for the Humanities for a project titled "Ute Traditional Narratives and Word-Order Change", a support that is hereby gratefully acknowledged. I also wish to acknowledge the support and encouragement of the Southern Ute Tribal Council and its long-time chairman, Mr. Leonard C. Burch, in initiating and supporting the Ute Language Program and various studies undertaken under its auspices (Givón 1980, Givón 1981), of which this is only a small part. Most of all, I am indebted to the elders of the Southern Ute Tribe and members of the Ute Language Committee for their knowledge, their generosity and their concern. The actual stories studied here were all told by Mollie B. Cloud, tribal elder, committee member and a stroy-teller extraordinaire.

2) The entire collection will be published by the Souther Ute Tribe through Ute Press, Ignacio, Colorado. A sample story is given in the appendix 1.

3) From "Sináwavi losing his eyes", as told by Mollie B. Cloud; p. 8 of transcript.

4) See discussion in Steele (1975, 1977). The "second position clitic" was probably never an abstract mechanical principle as Steele would have it, but rather a reflex of word-order pragmatics, whereby the first word in the clause represented a highly *discontinuous* ('surprising') piece of information, and pronouns – which as clitics represent a much more *continuous* ('predictable') topical element – then came as a following element after that word, eventually cliticizing to it. The order thus reflects that of COMMENT-TOPIC or SURPRISING-PREDICTABLE or the a natural pragmatic ordering, the Prague School notwithstanding (see discussion in Givón, 1982a and section 5.7., below). The table of clitic pronoun forms of Ute may be found in Appendix 2, below.

5) From "Sináwavi losing his eyes", as told by Mollie B. Cloud, p. 8 of transcript.

6) From "Sináwavi losing his eyes", as told by Mollie B. Cloud, p. 10 of transcript.

7) From "Sináwavi losing his eyes", as told by Mollie B. Cloud, p. 10 of transcript.

8) From "Sináwavi losing his eyes", as told by Mollie B. Cloud, p. 11 of transcript. The various forms of the Ute independent subject pronouns may be found in Appendix II below.

9) From "Sináwavi losing his eyes", as told by Mollie B. Cloud, p. 8 of transcript.

10) From "Sináwavi losing his eyes", as told by Mollie B. Cloud, p. 9 of transcript.

11) From "Porcupine, Buffalo-Cow and Sináwavi", as told by Mollie B. Cloud, p. 18 of transcript.

12) Since subjects in the VS word-order are most likely an 'afterthought' pragmatic device (see discussion further below), their appearance following an intonation pause – thus reminiscent of R-dislocation – is only natural.

13) From "Porcupine, Buffalo-Cow and Sináwavi", as told by Mollie B. Cloud, p. 16 of transcript. For the forms of Ute demonstratives/articles, see Appendix II, below.

14) In the sense that a pronoun is used first, then the full NP is added for 'insurance' sake, presumably as an 'escalation' of the topic-marking strategy.

15) From "Porcupine, Buffalo-Cow and Sináwavi", as told by Mollie B. Cloud, p. 23 of transcript.

16) From "Sináwaví losing his eyes", as told by Mollie B. Cloud, p. 8 8 of transcript.

17) From "Sináwaví losing his eyes", as told by Mollie B. Cloud, p. 13 of transcript.

18) From "Porcupine, Buffalo-Cow and Sináwaví", as told by Mollie B. Cloud, p. 22 of transcript.

19) From "Porcupine, Buffalo-Cow and Sináwaví", as told by Mollie B. Cloud, p. 16 of transcript.

20) From "Sinawaví losing his eyes", as told by Mollie B. Cloud, p. 8 of transcript.

21) From "Sinawaví losing his eyes", as told by Mollie B. Cloud, p. 8 of transcript.

22) From "Sinawaví losing his eyes", as told by Mollie B. Cloud, p. 8 of transcript.

23) From "Sinawaví losing his eyes", as told by Mollie B. Cloud, p. 14 of transcript.

24) From "Sinawaví losing his eyes", as told by Mollie B. Cloud, p. 13 of transcript.

25) From "Sinawaví losing his eyes", as told by Mollie B. Cloud, p. 15 of transcript.

26) From "Sinawaví losing his eyes", as told by Mollie B. Cloud, p. 14 of transcript.

27) From "Sinawaví losing his eyes", as told by Mollie B. Cloud, p. 12 of transcript.

28) From "Sinawaví losing his eyes", as told by Mollie B. Cloud, p. 8 of transcript.

29) From "Sinawaví losing his eyes", as told by Mollie B. Cloud, p. 12 of transcript.

30) From "Porcupine, Buffalo-Cow and Sináwaví", as told by Mollie B. Cloud, p. 19 of transcript.

31) From "Sinawaví losing his eyes", as told by Mollie B. Cloud, p. 12 of transcript.

32) From "Sinawaví losing his eyes", as told by Mollie B. Cloud, p. 12 of transcript.

33) From "Sinawaví losing his eyes", as told by Mollie B. Cloud, p. 13 of transcript.

34) From "Porcupine, Buffalo-Cow and Sináwaví", as told by Mollie B. Cloud, p. 17 of transcript.

35) From "Hungry Coyote, Rabbit and the White-Man's chicken", as told by Mollie B. Cloud, p. 40 of transcript.

36) From "Sinawaví losing his eyes", as told by Mollie B. Cloud, p. 12 of transcript.

37) From "Sinawaví losing his eyes", as told by Mollie B. Cloud, p. 12 of transcript.

38) From "Sinawaví losing his eyes", as told by Mollie B. Cloud, p. 10 of transcript.

39) From "Sinawaví losing his eyes", as told by Mollie B. Cloud, p. 8 of transcript.

40) From "Porcupine, Buffalo-Cow and Sináwaví", as told by Mollie B. Cloud, p. 22 of transcript.

41) From "Sinawaví losing his eyes", as told by Mollie B. Cloud, p. 10 of transcript.

42) From "Sinawaví losing his eyes", as told by Mollie B. Cloud, p. 8 of transcript.

43) From "Sinawav

43) From "Hungry Coyote and Fox", as told by Mollie B. Cloud, p. 36 of transcript.

44) From "Hungry Coyote & Fox", as told by Mollie B. Cloud, p. 31 of transcript.

45) From "Porcupine, Buffalo- Cow and Sináwaví", as told by Mollie B. Cloud, p. 19 of transcript.

46) For many details on switch reference in general, see Haiman and Munro (eds, 1983).

47) From "Sinawaví losing his eyes", as told by Mollie B. Cloud, p. 8 of transcript.

48) From "Sinawaví losing his eyes", as told by Mollie B. Cloud, p. 8 of transcript.

49) From "Sinawaví losing his eyes", as told by Mollie B. Cloud, p. 9 of transcript.

50) From "Sinawaví losing his eyes", as told by Mollie B. Cloud, p. 9 of transcript.

51) In terms of the total sample, the category referential-indefinite subject is negligible, with only 12 tokens out of the total of 588 referential subjects. Since many more new

argument enter the discourse during the span of the four stories counted, obviously new referential arguments in Ute enter the discourse register more typically either as *definite sujects* or, more likely, as *direct objects* (see below). In Table II above, only 6 tokens of definite subjects exhibit the values of 20 for referential distance, a value assigned arbitrarily to tokens with no previously attested appearance in the register.

52) This corresponds closely to general typological predictions made in Givón (1983).

53) As can be seen in other measurements above, the more continuous categories seem much more specialized in terms of prototype behavior, showing much more bunching within a relatively small portion of the measurement range, while the less continuous categories tend to scatter more.

54) See discussion in Givón (1981, Ch. 6, as well as 1982b).

55) The Ute texts studied here are essentially didactic entertainment for children and adults, where well known animal characters stand for equally well known human proto-types within Ute traditional culture. Further, in the American Indian tradition in general, animates and humans are not considered as separate as in Western culture, neither in their general behavior nor in their grammatical characterization.

56) Initially I formulated the measurements of referential distance and potential inter-ference in terms of the difficulty the *hearer* is likely to experience in assigning coreference/identity relations to NP's. In terms of the speaker's choice of grammatical devices, one may say that they are chosen according to the speaker's *anticipation* of the *hearer's* difficulty. But it may well be that the speaker also experiences a correlated psychological difficulty in either bringing a referent back into the register over a large gap of absence (referential distance), or in expressing the 'right' referent in the presence of potentially confusing other referents close by in the register.

57) One may define 'important topic' operationally as one which persists *longer* continu-ously in the discourse register. Our referential distance and persistence measurements re-present two separate aspects of this. The best measure would presumably be that of *average length of equi-topic continuous chains.*

REFERENCES

Derbyshire, D. (1979) "A diachronic explanation for the origin of OVS in some Carib languages", *SIL Working Papers* vol. XXIII, pp. 35-46

Derbyshire, D. and G. Pullum (1981) "Object-initial languages", IJAL 47.3

Givón, T. (1975) "Serial verbs and syntactic change: Niger-Congo", in C. Li (ed.), *Word Order and Word Order Change*, Austin: University of Texas Press

—————— (1976) "Topic, pronoun and grammatical agreement", in C. Li (ed.) *Subject and Topic*, NY: Academic Press

—————— (1977) "The drift from VSO in Biblical Hebrew: The pragmatics of tense-aspect", in C. Li (ed.) *Mechanisms for Syntactic Change*, Austin: University of Texas Press

—————(1979) *On Understanding Grammar*, NY: Academic Press

—————(1980) *Ute Dictionary*, Ignacio, Colorado: Ute Press

—————(1981) *Ute Reference Grammar*, Ignacio, Colorado: Ute Press

—————(1982a) "Universals of discourse structure and second language acquisition", in W. Rutherford (ed.) *Language Universals and Second Language Acquisition,* TSL vol. 5, Amsterdam: J. Benjamins.

—————(1982b) "Typology and functional domains", *Studies in Lanuage,* 6.1

—————(1982c) "Direct object and dative shifting: The semantics and pragmatics of case", in F. Plank (ed.) *Objects,* NY: Academic Press (in press)

—————(1983) "Topic continuity in discourse: The functional domain of switch-reference", in J. Haiman and P. Munro (eds) *Switch Reference, Typological Studies in Language,* vol. 2, Amsterdam: J. Benjamins

Greenberg, J. (1966) "Some universals of grammar with particular reference to the order of meaningful elements", in J. Greenberg (ed.) *Universals of Language,* Cambridge: MIT Press

Haile, G. (1970) "The suffix pronoun in Amharic", in C.-W. Kim and H. Stahlke (eds) *Papers in African Linguistics,* Edmonton: Linguistic Research, Inc.

Haiman, J. and P. Munro (eds, 1983) *Switch Reference, Typological Studies in Language,* vol. 2, Amsterdam: J. Benjamins

Hyman, L. (1975) "The change from SOV to SVO: Evidence from Niger-Congo", in C. Li (ed.) *Word Order and Word Order Change,* Austin: University of Texas

Hetzron, R. (1971) "Presentative function and presentative movement" *Studies in African Linguistics, Supplement no. 2*

Kalmár, I (1979) *Case and Context in Innkfifut (Eskimo),* Ottawa: National Museum of Man, Mercury Series 49

—————(1980) "The Anti-passive and grammatical relations in Eskimo", in F. Plank (ed.) *Ergativity: Toward a Theory of Grammatical Relations,* NY: Academic Press

Steele, S. (1977) "Clisis and diachromy", in C.Li (ed.) *Mechanisms for syntactic change,* Austin: University of Texas Press

APPENDIX 1:
"Sináwavi loses his eyes", a traditional Ute story

told by: Mollie B. Cloud
recorded by: Pat Rael
date recorded: 9-3-76
transcribed by: Neil Cloud, Sunshine Smith, T. G.

'uwás-kway 'in*h*   'urá-pu̧gá, sináwa-v*i* 'u,   Sináwa-v*i* 'urá-pu̧gá;
he-KIND WH-subj be-REM Sináwav*i* DEM-SUBJ Sináwav*i* be-REM
'There was once what's-his-name, that Sináwavi, there was Sináwav*i*;

'úu-pa-pu̧gá   x-'urá,   'i-vá̧a̧-ni   x-'urá,   qováa-va-'iná-'u   'urá. . .
there-DIR-REM then-be here-at-do then-be front-at-LOC-his be
he was passing through there, and right there, in front of him. . .

qováa-vay-'u pu̧í-av-kway   tu̧r*a*pi-kya̧-pu̧gá,   píisci-u,   wa'á-pu̧
front-at-his eye-OWN-KIND throw-PL-REM   children-PL piñon-OBJ
wu̧nú̧-ru̧-ma-tux;
stand-ADJ-LOC-to
in front of him they were juggling their eyes, those children, right into a tall-
standing piñon tree;

'uwás-'urá 'umú̧-vwaa-cugwá-xw*a*-pu̧gá,   x-'urá   'áy-pu̧gá:
he-be   them-at-approach-go-REM   then-be say-REM
so he approached them and then said:

"'ag̃á-ni-gya maní-ky*a̧*-x̂a   'atá-ci-u-n?"   máy-pu̧gá.
why-do-ING do-like-PL-ANT kin-PL-my   say-REM
"Why are you acting like that, my kinsmen?" he asked them,

"nú̧'-aa ka-mu̧ní-wa   kiyá̧-gw*a*-wa-tu̧?" máy-pu̧gá 'uwás-kway;
I-Q   NEG-you-with play-go-NEG-NOM say-REM   he-KIND
"why shouldn't I play with you too?" he said, what's-his-name;

x-'urá-s   "'u̧vú̧sa-gâ"   'áy-ky*a̧*-pu̧gá; x-'urá   'uwás pu̧í-av
then-be-CONJ end-ING   say-PL-REM   then-be he   eye-OWN
túpu̧na-pu̧gá,
pull-out-REM
so they said: "Alright"; so he pulled out his own eye,

'u-má-tugwá-ax̂ tu̧ráv*i*-pu̧gá, 'u-rúx   múkw*i*-pu̧gá,   'úu-pa-taa-s
there-LOC-to-it throw-REM there-under put-head-REM there-DIR-OBJ-CONJ

taví-pʉgá;
fall-REM
and he threw it in there, and he stuck his head under there, and right there it
dropped back into place;

sʉkwá-na-ĝa-tʉ   'uní-'wh-pʉgá-s;   x-'urá   'umʉ́-a-tʉ
other-LOC-HAVE-OBJ do-??-REM-CONJ   then-be them-PART-NOM
sotónaa-pʉ-ci-'u,
bad-wish-REM-SUB-him
so he did the same with the other eye; then one of them put a hex on him,

kɑcí-s -ax̂   ĝwá-nʉ, ma-váa ĝwá-nʉ, pacá'a-gupʉ wa'á-pʉ-máy-pʉgá;
NEG-CONJ-it go-IMP there-at go-IMP stick-MOD   piñon-OBJ say-REM
that it wouldn't fall right, that it would go there and get stuck up in the piñon
tree;

/// 'urú-s-'urá   'uní-'wh-pʉgá, pacá'a-pʉgá;
    that-CONJ-be   do-??-REM   stick-REM
    so that's what happened, it got stuck up there;

        'ú-vway 'uwás pʉí-av. . . pɑ-páax̂a-porǫ́-xwɑ-pʉgá. . . pʉí-av
        then   he   eye-OWN RED-cry-walk-go-REM   eye-OWN
        maáy-ti-ci. . .
        find-CAUS-SUB
        Well then, Sin-awavi ran around screaming about his eyes, trying to find
        them. . .

/// naná-nakwá-tʉ-s x-'uwás-'urá 'uní-'wh-pʉgá, ma-váa x-'urá   nawá-s
    each-OBJ-CONJ   then-he-be   do-??-REM   there-at then-be both-CONJ
    he did that to each one of them, so they both

pacá'a-kwa-pʉgá, 'u-vwáa-s   ka-pʉí-'a-tʉ   tʉgá-xwɑ-pʉgá;
stick-ASP-REM   there-at-CONJ NEG-eye-HAVE/NEG-NOM become-ASP-REM
got stuck, and so he became blind;

        'umʉ́s-'urá motǫ́ni-vaa-ci-m̥u, 'úmʉ píis-ci-u,   'uní-kya-x̂a-sʉ-mʉ
        they-be   scatter-BCKGR-they those children-PL do-PL-ANT-CONJ-they
        'urú,
        that-OBJ
        Now the children scattered away, having done that,

x-'urá   'uwás 'úupa   wáay-vąą-c*i*. . . 'ú   sináwa-v*i*. . . ///núu-ci-gyą-y. . .
then-be he   there-DIR follow-BCKGR that Sináwav*i*. . .   human-be-IMM
and he followed around that-a-way . . . that Sináwav*i*. . . he was human (in those
days). . .

'úu-pa   wáay-vąą-c*i*-'urá,   'u-vwáa   x-'urá   tupúy-payá-ağa-t*u*
there-DIR follow-BCKGR-be there-at   then-be rock-side-HAVE-NOM
'urá-vąą-c*i*,
be-BACKGR
so he followed that-a-way, there was a rocky cliff-side there,

tupúy-ci-aağa-tu   payá-ağa-vaac*i*,   wíî-kya-vaaci-ną,
rock-HAVE-NOM   side-HAVE-BCKGR fall-ANT-BCKGR-REL
'úraa 'unúv-'urá   'u-ná
be-EMPH EXACT-be there-LOC
a place with rocky precipice, where he had fallen, and that's right where

pawí-kwa-pugá   'uwás, ka-mááy-wa-t*u*   'urá;   x-'urá
go-toward-move-REM he   NEG-see-NEG-NOM be   then-be
pa'á-qovíc'ay-kw*a*-kwa-pugá
full-break-ASP-ANT-REM
he went (down), not being able to see; then, having completely devastated

'icátwa-'u, manúx 'qqa-ğa-pu-'u,   'u-vwá-n*a*-'urá 'aví-na-pugá 'uwás
limb-his   all-OBJ   bone-DEFUNCT-his there-at-LOC-be lie-HAB-REM he
his limbs, all his poor bones, he was just lying down there

kiyáa-'awí-tavá-p*u*;
certain-long-day-NOM
for a certain length of time;

x-'urá   wáa-máam*a*-ci-u 'úm*u* 'urá-pugá, 'inîi-sap*a*   'urá-puáy-vąąc*i*,
Then-be two-women-PL those be-REM WH-MOD be-REM-BCKGR
Then those two women, whover they may have been,

'úm*u*-'urá 'úu-pa-m   pağáy'w*a*-pugá-vaac*i*; pağáy'w*a*-kwa-m*u*-'urú,
they-be   there-DIR-LOC walk-REM-BCKGR walk-SUB-they-that
tupúy-ci 'urú
rock-that-OBJ
they were walking about there; and while walking about, moving alone the

kanúgaa-rux   'uní-'a-pųgá-amʉ,   paĝáy'wa-kwa-amʉ-'urá-'urú. . .
hill-side-along do-go-REM-they   walk-SUB-they-be-that
rocky hillside, while walking around there. . .

'i-vą́ą-ci pikí-gwaná-pųgá,   payáa-ma-tʉ   'avátʉ
there-at rotten-smell-REM side-LOC-NOM big
'aĝá-ra-tʉ-paa-tʉ-sapa
WH-like-NOM-DIR-NOM-MOD
there was a rotten smell there, at the hillside, that big what-cha-ma-callit

'urá-pųgá-váaci,   pikí-gwaná-pųgá;   'umʉ́s-urá 'ugwí-'nh-pųgá-amʉ,
be-REM-BCKGR rotten-smell-REM they-be   sniff-INTENS-REM-they
it was, a rotten smell; so they sniffed around

"'aĝáa-va-tʉ   kwaná-yh?" máy-pųgá-amʉ,;   súwii-ni   máa-pa-tʉ
WH-at-NOM   smell-IMM   say-REM-they   other-SUBJ   there-DIR-DIR
pųní-'ni-pųgá:
look-INTENS-REM
"Where is it (coming from)?" they wondered; so the other one looked around
that way:

"'uwá-na-'u   'aví"   máy-pųgá;   'uwá-vaa-cugwá-pųgá-amʉ:
there-LOC-he   lie-IMM   say-REM   him-at-approach-REM-they
"There he is, lying" she said; so they approached him:

"'úuuuu. . .niguni- 'urá!"   'uwá-vaa-cugwá-amʉ,   'uwá-n   'apáĝa-pųgá;
lo   be   him-at-toward-they   him-LOC speak-REM
"Wow!" they approached him and they talked to him;

'apáĝa-pųgá 'uwás: "'i-vą́ą-nʉ-s   'aví-mi" máy-pųgá, "navá-xwa-xwa-pʉáy,
speak-REM   he   here-at-I-CONJ   lie-HAB say-REM   just-go-ASP-REM
so he spoke to them: "Here I am, lying" he said, "it was an accident,

ka-pʉí-'ạ-y"   máy-pųgá, "nʉ́nạy pʉí-vi   ma'áyu-kwa-pųgá-tʉ"
NEG-eye-HAVE/NEG-IMM say-REM   my   eye-OBJ lose-ANT-REM-NOM
máy-pųgá 'uwás;
say-REM he
and I am blind" he said, "I had lost my eyes";

'úniguni-kwá-amʉ pʉí-gya-pʉ-náaĝa-y,   múupuvwiyaa-ci-u,
lo-KIND-they   eye-DEFUNCT-be-inside-IMM maggot-PL

ka-pa'áy-wa-s;
NEG-count-NEG-CONJ
and lo — inside his poor (blind) eyes there were countless maggots;

"'úru-'urá-'urú-'u kwaná-ĝay-vaaci,   múupuvwiyaa-ci-u" máy-pųgá;
that-be-that-he   smell-ANT-BCKGR maggot-PL   say-REM
"That's what has been giving the bad smell, the maggots" he said;

"'únųųų. . ." máy-pųgá 'umų́s, "'aĝá-ni-na-'ará?" máy-pųgá-amų,
whew   say-REM they   WH-do-??-be   say-REM-they
"Whew. . ." they said, "how could this happen?"

"qoróc'ay-kų-kwa-caa-nų-s"   máy-pųgá 'uwás;
break-BEN-ANT-SUDDEN-I-CONJ say-REM he
"I've been accidentally broken" he said;

"'úuuniguni sináwa-vi-gya-pų   'áy-vąąci!"   máy-pųgá 'umųs; x-'urá
lo   Sináwavi-DEFUNCT say-BCKGR say-REM they then-be
'áy-vaaci-mų:
say-BCKGR-PL
"Wow, poor Sináwavi!" they said; then they added:

"'ųvų́sa-nų́mų, musútkwi-gyą-tu páay-kų-'u" máy-vąąci-mų,
end-we-EXCL   doctor-OBJ   call-BEN-him say-BCKGR-PL
"musútkwi-gyą-tų
doctor-SUBJ
"Quick, we've got to call a doctor for him" they said, "the doctor

'icáy-rux   'i-vąą-ni-'urú   pagá-'ni-vąąci,   'aĝá-vaa-sapa-'u
this-DIR   here-at-??-that   walk-INTENS-BCKGR WH-at-MOD-he
musútkwi-gyą-tų?"
doctor-SUBJ
is walking around in these parts, where could he be?"

máy-vąąci-mų-'urá;   "nų́mų-'urá pícų-vaa-tų-mų-s"   máy-pųgá-'urá;
say-BCKGR-PL-be   we-EXCL-be return-FUT-NOM-PL-CONJ say-REM-be
they said then; "now, we two will return here soon" they said;

"'uvwíyaĝa" máy-pųgá   'urá-'uwás;
alright   say-REM   be-he
"Alright" he said;

'ú-vway-aх̂-'urá 'umу́s paĝá-nиkwí-pụgá-amу, 'ú-pa-pụgá-amу,
there-TOP-it-be they walk-run-REM-they there-DIR-REM-they
'umу́s.
they
So right then they took off, they went that-a-way,

pусáĝa-paĝay-kу-pụgá-amу, mиsútkwi-tụ... ///dóctor 'urá-vaací-'u-lurú
search-walk-BEN-REM-they doctor-OBJ doctor be-BCKGR-he-that
searching around for a doctor (for him)... it was a doctor...

maáy-pụgáy-'u-amу, dóctor 'uwáy; 'uwás x-'urá 'ính-kway
find-REM-him-they doctor that-OBJ he then-be WH-KIND
'urá-vaací,
be-BCKGR
they found him at last, that doctor; and he was what's-his-name,

yụу́pụ-cí, 'ú-'urú 'urá-vaací, dóctor-bági-av yáa'wa-vaací;
Porcupine he-that be-BCKGR doctor-bag-OBJ-OWN carry-BCKGR
Porcupine, it was him, and he was carrying his doctor-bag;

'umу́s maáy-vạạcí-'u, 'uwá-vaa-cugwá-paaci-amу... /// kaní-vạạ-tugwá-av
they see-BCKGR-him him-at-approach-BCKGR-they house-at-toward-OWN
so they saw him, and they went toward him... he was moving toward

'uwás 'uní-'a-vaací... ipу́-paa-tụ-kwa karу́-mí-paa-tux...
he do-??-BCKGR REL-DIR-DIR-go sit-HAB-DIR-toward
his own house... (they approached) the place where he was sitting...

/// bági-av yáa'wa-rу-'u... máy-pụgá-amу:
bag-OBJ-OWN carry-ADJ-he say-REM-they
he was carrying his bag... and they said:

"ma-váa-kụ nи́u-ci-gyạ-pụ 'aví, pụí-naaĝay-'u 'icáy
there-at-FACT person-DEFUNCT lie-IMM eye-inside-his this-OBJ
'iníih-kway
WH-KIND
"Right over there there's a damaged person lying, he's got those what's-their-
name

mи́upuvwiyaa-ci-u" 'áy-vạạcí-'urá;
maggots-PL say-BCKGR-be
maggots inside his eyes" they said;

"'aĝáa-va?"   'áy-vaací   'urá-'uwás;   "'úwa-na,   'úu-pa" máy-pұgá
WH-at   say-BCKGR   be-he   there-LOC   there-DIR   say-REM
'umụ́s;
they
"Where at?" he asked; "right there, that way" they said;

mұí-kұ-vaaci-mұ   'uwá-vaa-cux,   'uwá-vaa-cux   pọró-pұgá;
lead-BEN-BCKGR-PL   him-at-toward   him-at-toward   walk-PL-REM
so they lead him toward Sináwaví, they all walked toward him;

'i-váạ-ni   'aví-pұgá   'uwás;   'uwás   pұní-'ní-pұgáy-'u:
here-at-??   lie-REM   he   he   look-INTENS-REM-him
"'ұnụ́ұұ. . ." máy-pұgá,
wow   say-REM
and right there he was lying; so the doctor examined him: "Wow. . . ." he said,

"'aĝá-ni-gya-'urá kací-n 'u-gwáy maáy-wạ-y?   'uní-kya-pұgáy-'u"
WH-do-ING-be   NEG-I   there   see-NEG-IMM   do-ANT-REM-him
'áy-kh;
say-IMM
"And how come I can't see inside there? Something must have done it to him"
he said;

x-'urá   'umụ́-taa-s-'urú,   'umụ́-'urá   múupuvwiyaa-ci-u
then-be   them-PART-OBJ-CONJ-that   them-be maggots-PL
cicí'ní-pұgá,
scoop-REM
so then the two ladies scooped out the maggots,

tụ́ұra(ra)-vaa-amұ tací-pұká-pұgá; 'umụ́s   x-'urá   wáa-máama-ci-u
out-at-they   turn-loose-REM   they   then-be   two-women-PL
and they turned them loose outside; and then they

parụ́-xwa-pұáy-aĝá-s-uk,   'átұ-clean-up-aĝáy-kұ;
wash-ASP-REM-HAVE-CONJ-it   well-clean-up-HAVE-FACT
washed it all, and they cleaned it up well;

'umụ́-'urá   wáa-máama-ci-u   'áy-pұáy-aĝa-amұ: "'uvwí"
them-be   two-women-PL   say-REM-HAVE-them   alright

máy-pu̧áy-agá-amu̧,
say-REM-HAVE-them
and then the doctor told the two women: "Alright" he told them,

"i-vá̧a̧-ci-m-'urú   kac-'úra-ax̂   tu̧vú̧-pu̧   'urá-wa, míici
here-at-LOC-that   NEG-be-it   earth-OBJ   be-NEG little
'o̧á-siyá̧-x̂a-ru̧-ni?"
yellow-mixed-ADJ-like
"Isn't there around here some yellow clay of this kind?"

máy-pu̧gá-'urá,   "'urá-taaní-'urú   'uní-na tu̧vú̧-pu̧";
say-REM-be   that-KIND-that   do-REL earth-OBJ
he said, "that kind of earth with which we can do it";

'umú̧s-'urá   'uní-ku̧-pu̧gá-sapa-amu̧. . . /// tu̧vú̧-pu̧   'urá-pu̧gá,
they-be   do-BEN-REM-MOD-they   earth   be-REM
'o̧á-siyá-x̂a-ru̧. . .
yellow-mixed-ADJ
so they started preparing it for him. . . there was some yellow-mix clay there. . .

'uwá-vaa-cux   'uní-'a-pu̧gá; 'uwás-'urá   páa-vawí-tux   'uní-pu̧gá,
him-at-toward   do-??-REM   he-be   water-toward-to   do-REM
and they went to him (with it); so he put it into water,

máavu̧-raa-ci-paní-'urá po̧ó̧tu̧kwá-tu̧   'uní-pu̧gá,   dóctor 'u,
marble-DIM-like-be round-OBJ   do-REM   doctor that-SUBJ
and he made round marble-like balls out of it, the doctor did,

pu̧í-naaga-kwa-'u yuná-pu̧gá,   maáy-pu̧gá-s 'uwás;
eye-inside-go-his put-REM   see-REM-CONJ he
and he put those into Sináwaví's eye sockets, and then he could see again;

'ú-vway-ax̂-'urá-'urú   'o̧ó̧-a   'urá-pu̧gá-vaaci-s,   qoróc'ay-kwa
there-TOP-it-be-that   bone-his be-REM-BCKGR-CONJ break-ANT
Then right then there remained his bones, they had been smashed

'agá-ni-gya-sapa-'u,   yú'u. . . 'ú-'urá   'uní-pu̧gá-s   'uwás; pu̧í-a namú
WH-do-ING-MOD-his leg   he-be   do-REM-CONJ he   eye-his first
whichever way, his legs. . . so the doctor fixed them too; first

'uní-'ní-kµ-pµgá;   x-'urá-'urú   máy-pµgá-s: "'uvwí"
do-INTENS-BEN-REM   then-be-that   say-REM-CONJ   alright
máy-pµgá-s,
say-REM-CONJ
he fixed his eyes though; so then he said: "Alright now" he said,

"'i-vá̱a̱-ci-m-'urú   'ipµ́-kway,   'uní-'wa-n-amµ...   kµ́pµ-'urú
here-at-LOC-that   WH-KIND   do-??-me-you-PL   sunflower-that-OBJ
súnflower..."
those-OBJ
"there are those what-cha-ma-call-them here, sunflowers, bring them to me"

má-ra-taa-ní-amµ   'uní-pµgá-s,   máy-na-'u   'urú;
that-KIND-OBJ-like-they   do-REM   say-REL-his   that-OBJ
so they brought him that kind, the one he was talking about;

'u-vwáa-s   cµkµ́r'a-pµgá,   'úrµ-'urá-'urú   'o̱ó̱a-pa-'u
there-at-CONJ   cut-REM   that-be-that   bone-LOC-his
yuná-pµgá-s;
put-REM-CONJ
so he cut them right there and he fitted them through Sináwaví's bones;

píigya̱-ci-m narí'aa-pµ-tux,   'úrµ-'urá túu'a-'u   'urá-'a̱y, máy-kya̱-mi...
fiber-LOC   core-OBJ-to   that-be marrow-his   be-IMM say-PL-HAB
and he made fibers of them and put them in the core (of S's bones), and they
then became his marrow, that's what they say...

'ú-vway-ax̂-'urá   'uwás   'urú   'úu-pa-ux   yuná-pµgá-s 'urú,
there-TOP-it-be   he   that-OBJ   there-DIR-it put-REM   that-OBJ
'oó̱a-ĝa-pµ-'u,
bone-DEFUNCT-his
so then he put it all in there, (in) Sináwaví's poor broken bones,

naná-cugwí-navící-kwa-pµgá-s   'urús,   ma-mácugwa-pµgá-s-'u
RECIP-stick-PL-ASP-REM-CONJ   it-SUB   RED-press-REM-CONJ-him
x-'urá;
then-be
and they began to stick together, he pressed him back together;

qorúc'ay-kwa-kwa-tụ   cicá-wụná-pụgá-s;   'uwás-'urá
broken-ANT-ASP-NOM-OBJ   throw-away-REM-CONJ   he-be
Sináwa-vi   toĝóy-pụgá;
Sináwavi   well-REM
and he threw away the broken (bones); and thus Sináwavi became well again;

máni-na   'aví-pụgá;   "'áavụ-s-'urá   'i-váạ   'aví-vạạni,   nụ́-'ará
do-like-REL lie-REM   now-CONJ-be   here-at   lie-FUT   I-be
pụ-pụ́ni-vạạ-tụ-mụ,
RED-look-FUT-NOM-you
so Sináwavi was lying there in this manner; "now you will lie here, and I will
come to check on you periodically,

súukus   tumíiku-paa -tugwá-ni"   'áy-pụgáy-'u-'urá; "'ú-vway-ax̂-'urá
one week-DIR-toward-like   say-REM-him-be   there-TOP-it-be
nụ́ 'ụmý
I   you
throughout one week or so" he told him; "then I myself will (come and)

kụrụ́ki-ti-paa-tụ   'ará-yis"   máy-pụgá;
get-up-CAUS-FUT-NOM   be-IMM-CONJ   say-REM
make you get up" he said;

    'uwás   'u-vwáa-s   'aví-pụgá;   /// 'átụ-pa   wa-wácụ-ka-pụgá;
    he   there-as-CONJ lie-REM   well-LOC RED-put-ANT-REM
    'umụ́-ga-ni
    they-TOP-??
    So Sináwavi lay down there they had placed him at a nice spot;

pụ-pụ́ni'ni-vạạ-tụ-'u-amụ   'urá-pụgá-s,   máy-pụáy-aĝa-s-umụ;
RED-look-FUT-NOM-him-they be-REM-CONJ   say-REM-HAVE-CONJ-them
"nụ́-ga-ni"
I-TOP-??
and the two ladies were to check on him too periodically, the Porcupine had
told them (to do so); "I myself (will do likewise)"

máy-pụgá-s'u... /// dóctor,   yụ́ụpụ-ci-'urú   'urá-pụgá-'u...
say-REM-CONJ-him doctor   porcupine-that   be-REM-he
/// pọró-xwa-pụgá-'urá...
walk-go-REM-be
he had told him too the doctor, it was the porcupine... they had taken off...

togóy-kwa-'u,   'u-vwáa-s   'aví-na-pugá,   piná-xwa   manáy-'ni-pugá. . .
well-SUB-he   there-at-CONJ   lie-HAB-REM   later-go   stir-INTENS-REM
when he got well, he just lay there on and on, then finally he began to stir. . .

/// "manáy'ni-'urá,   manáy'ni-nu"   máy-pugá   'uwás. . .
    stir-INTENS-be   stir-INTENS-IMPER   say-REM   he
"You shift around, stir around" the porcupine had told him. . .

piná-xway   'áyh-tugáy-pugá;   piná-xwa   puníkyaa-miyá-pugá-s-'u,
later-go   well-become-REM   later-go   see-go-PL-REM-CONJ-him
piná-raváy;
follow-day
so later he became well; later on they all came to see him, the next day;

    'u-vwáa   'uwás   'uní-'ni-pugá,   karú-pugá;   paá-ci-s
    there-at he   do-INTENS-REM   sit-up-REM   three-SUBJ-CONJ
    tugwá-ri'i-kya-ux-pugá,
    night-CAUS-ANT-ASP-REM
    So Sináwavi was hanging around there, he sat up; three nights had passed,

'aví-gya-'urú; 'i-váa-'urá-'urú   'uwás   manáy'ni-kwa-pugá;
lie-ING-that   here-at-be-that   he   stir-INTENS-ASP-REM
with him lying there, and then he began stirring;

piná-xwa   kurúki-kya-pugá,   'u-vwáa pagá-poró-pugá;
later-go   get-up-ANT-REM   there-at walk-go-REM
/// pu-púni'ni-kya-puáy-'u,
    RED-look-ANT-REM-him
and later he got up and walked around there; they had come to check on him in
the meantime,

ma-mága-na-pugá-s-'u;   'uvús;
RED-feed-HAB-REM-CONJ-him   end
and they would come and feed him from time to time too; well;

    piná-x̂wa-'urá   'uwás   togóy-kwa-'u-pugá,   pága-kwa-pugá
    later-go-be   he   well-ASP-he-REM   walk-go-REM
    'ú-vway-ax̂. . .
    there-TOP-it
    So later on he got well and took off then. . .

/// toĝóy-p̨ugá. . .'ú-'ay-'urá   mar̨uvii-p̨ugáy-'u y̨úp̨u-*ci*   'ú. . .
   well-REM   that-??-be   press-REM-him porcupine   that-SUBJ
/// toĝó -sap*a*-'urá-'urú
   right-MOD-be-that
   He got well. . . the one who pressed him back together was Porcupine. . .
for that reason

Sináwa-*vi*   'ǫá-qa-r̨u-ni   p̨uí-gya-t*ʉ*   'urá-'ay. . .   /// má   wolf
Sináwa*vi*   yellow-ADJ-like eye-HAVE-NOM be-IMM   that   wolf
paĝá'ni-*ci*   'áav*ʉ* ;
wander-NOM   now
Sináwa*vi* has yellow-like eyes. . . that wolf, he is a vagabond nowadays;

'ú'way   'uní-p̨u-vwáą(y);
him   make-REM-???
that is because Porcupine re-made him that way;

   máy-kyą-ta-mi-a-nu-kway,   p̨usáriniyą-x̂a-mi-t̨u-m*ʉ*;   'urú-sap*a*-'urá
   say-PL-PASS-HAB-??-??-KIND story -tell-PL-HAB-NOM-PL   that-MOD-be
   'urá-'ay;
   be-IMM
   That the kind of thing they tell, the story-tellers; that's the way it was;

'ú-vwaa-tugwá-sap*a*;
there-at-go-MOD
that's as far as it goes;

APPENDIX II: *Ute Pronouns and Demonstratives*

INDEPENDENT SUBJECT PRONOUN

Person	singular		dual	plural
1st	nʉ́'	'I'	tám*i* 'we-INC'	táw*i* 'we-INC'
			nʉ́m*ʉ*	'we-EXC'
2nd	'ʉ́m*ʉ*	'you'	mʉ́n*i*	'you'
3rd – VIS	máas	'he/she'	mamʉ́s	'they'
3rd-INV	'uwás	'he/she'	'umʉ́s	'they'

INDEPENDENT OBJECT/POSSESSIVE PRONOUNS

person	singular		dual	plural
1st	núnąy 'me/my'		tamí 'us/our' (INC)	tawí 'us/our' (INC)
				nųmúy 'us/our' (EXC)
2nd	'ųmúy	'you/your'		mųní 'you/your'
3rd-VIS	máay(as)	'him/his' 'her/her'		mamúas 'them/their'
3rd-INV	'uwáy(as)	'him/his' 'her/her'		'umúas 'them/their'

SUFFIX PRONOUNS

person	singular	dual	plural
1st	-n	-ram*i* (INC)	-raw*i* (INC)
		-nųm*u* (EXC)	
2nd	-m	-am*u*	
3rd-VIS-AN	-'a	-am*u*	
3rd-INVIS-AN	-'u	-am*u*	
3rd-VIS-INAN	-ax̂	(-ax̂)	
3rd-INV-INAN	-ux	-ux	

DEMONSTRATIVES

category	near SUBJ/OBJ	remote-VIS SUBJ/OBJ	remote-INV SUBJ/OBJ
inanimate	'íc*a* / 'icą́y	már*u* / marú	'úr*u* / 'urú
animate-ŞG	'ín*a* / 'aną́y	máa / máay	'ú / 'uwáy
animate-PL	'ím*u* / 'imú	mám*u* / mamú	'úm*u* / 'umú

TOPIC CONTINUITY IN BIBLICAL HEBREW NARRATIVE

ANDREW FOX *

Linguistics Department
University of California, Los Angeles

*) *Editor's note*: This paper has been exhaustively edited and re-written by the editor of this volume, who thus assumes full responsibility for the final version and the opinions expressed in it, including the transcription used for the BH data.

TABLE OF CONTNETS

1. *Introduction***

This study deals with a number of syntactic devices which code the degree of topic-NP continuity in Biblical Hebrew discourse. As in the other studies in this volume, it is assumed here that these devices hierarchize along a continuity/ predictability *scale*. This scale, in terms of the cross-linguistically most common syntactic construction, was suggested by Givón (introduction to this volume) as:

(1)   *MOST CONTINUOUS*
        zero anaphora
        unstressed/clitic pronouns (verb agreement)
        independent/stressed pronouns
        R-dislocated DEF-NP
        DEF-NP
        L-dislocated DEF-NP
        passivized (subject) NP
        Y-movement
        indefinite NP
        cleft/focused/contrasted NP
        LEAST CONTINUOUS

Many of these devices may be used with either human or non-human topics, whose continuity properties are then studied separately here, given that human NP's tend to be more topical in human discourse (Givón, 1976a, *inter alia*). Further, many of these topic-marking devices may appear in several case-roles, whose topicality in discourse may characteristically vary, most commonly along the hierarchy (Givón, 1976a):

(2)   SUBJ/AGT > DAT/BEN > ACC > LOC > OTHERS

Whenever relevant, different case-roles will be studied here separately.

2. *Data base and measurements*

This study deals exclusively with Early Biblical Hebrew (henceforth EBH, cf. Givón, 1977a) as represented in the book of Genesis. This is done to mini-

**) This study was undertaken in a seminar on Topic Continuity in Discourse under the direction of T. Givón at UCLA in the Winter term, 1981. I would like to acknowledge helpful suggestions from Paola Bentivoglio, Miachael Gasser, Phil Jaggar, Lorraine Kumpf, Ian Maddieson, Russell Schuh, Terence Wilbur, Cheryl Brown and T. Givón.

mize dialect and strata mixing, particularly in terms of word-order and tense-aspect. Known archaisms, hyper corrections and doubtful passages were eliminate from the counted text. Direct-quoted speech was also not counted.

As in other studies in this volume, the text was subjected to three measurements:

(a)   *Look-back ('referential distance')*: The distance, in number of clauses, between the last *prior* mention of a referent in the register and the current appearance that is being counted;[1]

(b)   *Decay ('persistence')*: The length of the unbroken chain, in terms of number of clauses, through which the referent remains an argument of the clause *after* the instance being counted;

(c)   *Potential interference*: The presence vs. absence of other referents in the immediately preceding discourse environment, if they are referents that are compatible with the predicate in terms of selectional restrictions.

These three measures were applied to between 300 and 50 tokens of each category. The first 41 chapters of Genesis were counted in full. For some less-frequent categories, additional text was counted to increase the total number of tokens.

3. Topic marking constructions in EBH

3.1. Zero anaphora

Since EBH exhibits obligatory subject agreement, zero anaphora applies only to objects, as in:[2]

(3)   . . . va-yi-qaḥ leḥem vi-ḥemet mayim va-yi-ten [∅]'el Hagar . . .

                                                                    [Gen., 21:14]

             and-he-took bread and-bottle-of water and-he-gave [∅]   to Hagar

'. . . so he took bread and a bottle of water and gave *them* to Hagar. . .'

3.2. Subject-verb agreement

Within the verbal paradigms of the 'imperfect' and 'perfect', EBH has an obligatory and semantically extensive subject agreement with person, gender and number. The system is less complex for participials/adjectivals, historically a nominal-based conjugation. Thus, while independent subject pronouns used with the 'perfect' or 'imperfect' tend to be contrastive/discontinuous, their use with the nominal-based conjugations incorporates the more continuous function of unstressed pronouns/verb agreement, as will be demonstrated by our text counts. The phonological elements of subject agreement are primarily suffixal in the 'perfect' and participial and primarily prefixal in the 'imperfect' (and the related *jussive*), with stem-internal changes also common. Table I, below, presents the agreement forms of the verb *qtl* 'kill'.

TABLE I: *Subject agreement in EBH*

pers/gen	perfect sg	perfect pl	imperfect sg	imperfect pl		participial sg	participial pl
1	qatal-ti	qatal-nu	'e-qtol	ni-qtol	m	qotel	qotl-im
2m	qatal-ta	qatal-tem	ti-qtol	ti-qtil-u	f ⎰qotel-et/	⎱qotl-ot
2f	qatal-t	qatal-ten	ti-qtil-i	ti-qtol-na	⎱qotil-a ⎰	
3m	qatal	qatl-u	yi-qtol	yi-qtil-u		
3f	qatl-a	---------	ti-qtol	ti-qtol-na		

3.3. *Object and genitive suffix pronouns*

Object agreement is not obligatory in EBH, so that these suffixes may be properly termed clitic pronouns. Their forms are substantially the same as those of the possessive suffixes, with the only apparent difference in the first person singular. The forms are given in Table II, below.

TABLE II: *Suffix object and possessive pronouns in EBH*

person/gender	singular	plural
1	-ni (Poss. -i/-ay)	-nu
2m	-xa	-xem
2f	-x	-xen
3m	-o, -hu	-m
3f	-ah, -ha	-n

When verbs are nominalized, the possessive pronoun form functions as their subject agreement, as in:[3]

(4)   . . .vi-Yosef ben šlošim šana bi-ʕomd-*o* lifney Parʕo. . . [Gen. 41:46]
           and-Joseph son-of thirty year at-standing-*his* before Pharo
           '. . .and Joseph was thirty years old when *he* stood in front of
           Pharo. . .'

As an example of the use of these pronouns as object pronouns, consider:

(5)   . . .va-yiven YHWH 'elohim 'et ha-ṣelaʕ 'šer laqah min ha-'adam
           and-built-he YHWH God ACC the-rib that took-he from the-man
           '. . .and God fashioned the rib that he had removed from Adam
                                                                    [Gen., 2:22]
           li-'išah, va-yivi'e-*ha* 'el ha-'adam. . .
           to-woman and brought-he-*her* to the-man
           into a woman, and he brought *her* then to Adam. . .'

Finally, the simple possessive use of these suffix pronouns may be seen in:

(6)   . . .vi-'et kol ʕof kanaf li-mine-*hu*. . .   [Gen. 1:21]
           and-ACC all bird-of wind to-kind-*its*
           '. . .and (He made) the feathered birds of *their* various kinds. . .'

3.4. *Independent pronouns*

The independent pronouns for subject, direct object and indirect/dative
object are given in Table III, below.

TABLE III: *Independent pronouns in EBH*

pers/ gend.	subject		direct object		dative	
	sg	pl	sg	pl	sg	pl
1	'ani	'anaxnu, 'anu	'oti	'otanu	li	lanu
2m	'ata	'atem	'otxa	'etxem	lixa	laxem
2f	'at	'aten	'otax	'etxen	lax	laxen
3m	hu'	hem	'oto	'otam	lo	lahem
3f	hi'	hen	'ota	'otan	la	lahen

Since the most continuous/anaphoric pronominal function for subjects is carried out by the obligatory subject agreement, independent subject pronouns for finite verbal predicates in EBH are largely contrastive and discontinuous. Thus consider:

(7)   . . .vi-kuš yalad 'et Nimrod,
                and-Kush begat-he ACC Nimrod
            '. . . and Kush begat Nimrod,

            hu' heḥel li-hyot gibor ba-'areṣ. . .   [Gen. 10:8]
            he began-he to-be hero in-the-land
            and *he is the one who* began being a hero in the land. . .'

On the other hand, nominal, participial, or adjectival predicates tend to allow subject pronouns in a non-contrastive, largely anaphoric/continuous capacity, since their subject agreement conjugation is weaker (see above). As an example consider:

(8)   . . .va-tipataḥna ʕeney šney-hem, va-yedʕu ki ʕarumin *hem*. . .
                                                                    [Gen., 3:7]
                and-opened eyes-of two-they and-knew-they that naked *they*
            '. . .and their eyes then opened, and they knew that *they* were
                naked. . .'

Example (8) above also illustrates the use of the independent subject pronoun as a *copula.*

As our counts will demonstrate, independent object pronouns are used both contrastively and anaphorically, and they thus overlap in their anaphoric function with the suffix object pronouns. As a non-contrastive use of the pronoun, consider:

(9)   . . .va-yasem YHWH li-qayin 'ot li-bilti hakot *'oto* kol moṣ'-*o*. . .
                                                                    [Gen., 4:15]
                and-put-he YHWH to-Cain sign for-not hitting *him* all finder-*him*
            '. . .and God put a sign on Cain, to warn those who find *him* against
                hitting *him*. . .'

In (9) above, the first pronoun refering to Cain is independent, the second a suffix. Similarly:

(10)   . . .bi-yom bro' 'elohim 'adam bi-dmut 'elohim ʕasah *'oto*. . .
                                                            [Gen. 5:1]
                at-day-of creating-of God man in-image-of God made-he *him*
                '. . .the day God created man, he made *him* in His image. . .'

As an example of a contrastive use of the independent object pronoun, consider:

(11)   . . .va-yo'mer YHWH 'el noah: "Bo' 'ata vi-xol beyt-xa 'el ha-teva,
                and-said-he YHWH to Noah come you and-all house-your to the-
                ark
                '. . .and God said to Noah: "Come yourself and all your household
                into the ark,

                ki *'otxa* ra'iti ṣadiq li-fanay ba-dor ha-zeh. . .   [Gen., 7:1]
                for *you* saw-I righteous in-face-my in-the-generation the-this
                because *it is only you* that I've judged to be righteous in front of me
                of this entire generation. . .'

Finally, indirect/prepositional object pronouns have no verb-agreement counterparts, and thus fulfil both anaphoric/continuous and contrastive/discontinuous
functions in EBH. As examples of the use of these pronouns anaphorically in
different prepositional cases, consider:

(12)   . . .ha-min ha-ʕeṣ 'ašer ṣiviti-xa li-bilti 'axol *mi-meno* 'axalta?. . .
                Q-from the-tree that ordered-I-you to-not eat *from-it* ate-you
                '. . .did you eat from the tree *from which* I forbade you to eat?. . .'
                                                            [Gen., 3:11]
(13)   . . .ha-'išah 'ašer natata *'imad-i*, hi' natna *l-i*, va-'oxel. . .   [Gen., 3:12]
                the-woman that gave-you *with-me* she gave-she *to-me* and-I-ate
                '. . .the woman you gave *me*, it was she who gave (it) to me, so I ate
                (it). . .'

Example (13) also illustrates the contrastive/emphatic use of the independent
subject pronoun, essentially with a cleft-focus value.

3.5. *The VS/SV word-order variation with definite subjects*

As noted in Givón (1977a), the VS word-order in EBH coincides almost
completely with the 'imperfect' or *topic continuity* tense-aspect, while the

SV word-order (excluding here non-verbal or participial predicates) coincides almost exclusively with the 'perfect' or *topic switching/anterior* tense-aspect. As an example of the use of both devices within a single passage, consider:[4]

(14) a. ...va-tahar, va-teled 'et qayin...
    and-she-conceived and-she-bore ACC Cain
    ...and she conceived and then bore Cain...

   b. ...va-tosef la-ledet 'et 'aḥiv, 'et hevel;
    and-she-continued to-bear ACC brother-his ACC Ebel
    ...and then she went on and bore his brother, Ebel;

   c. *va-yihi hevel* roʕe so'n,
    and-he-was Ebel herder-of sheep
    and Ebel became a sheep-herder,

   d. *vi-qayin haya* ʕoved 'adamah...   [Gen., 4:1-2]
    and-Cain was-he worker-of land
    and Cain was a farmer...'

In clause (14c) above, Ebel is mentioned directly after being introduced in the preceding (14b), and the VS order is used, with the verb in the 'imperfect' (prefixal) conjugation. In clause (14d), on the other hand, Cain is re-introduced after a gap of absence during which Ebel was the dominant topic, as in clauses (14b, 14c), and the SV word order — with the suffixal 'perfect' conjugation of the verb — is used to re-introduce Cain into the discourse.

3.6. *Y-movement ('contrastive topicalization')*

Due to the obligatory nature of subject agreement in EBH, it is hard to distinguish Y-movement of subjects from the use of the SV word-order in general. The SV word-order is used to re-introduce a topic into the register after a gap of absence, *not* necessarily in order to contrast it with another topic. In this study it was decided to try and distinguish those instances that are truly contrastive and *would* have received contrastive *stress* in the spoken language, even though stress is unmarked in the text. Occasionally the Y-moved NP in such examples is fortified by the conjunction *gam* 'also' with the independent pronoun. Thus consider:

(15) ...va-teled ha-bɨxira ben...
    and-she-bore the-firstborn son
    '...and the firstborn bore a son...

vi-ha-ṣ ııra *gam hi'* yalda ben. . .   [Gen., 14:37-38]
and-the-younger *also she* bore-she son
and the younger one *too* bore a son. . .'

(16)   . . .va-yave' qayin mi-pri ha-'adamah minḥah la-YHWH,
             and-he brought Cain from-fruit-of the-earth offering to-YHWH
        '. . .and Cain brought an offering to God from the fruit of the earth,

             ve-hevel hevi' *gam hu* mi-bxorot ṣo'n-o. . . .   [Gen., 4:3-4]
             and-Ebel brought-he *also he* from-first-born-PL-of sheep-his
             and Ebel *too* brought (offerings) from the first-born of his
             sheep. . .'

While the differentiation between non-contrastive and contrastive usage of the SV word-order is admittedly difficult, it was felt worth while to attempt such a separation. As noted in Givón (1979, Ch. 2), Y-movement and the use of contrastive independent pronouns tend to be a more *localized* topic-switching device, commonly bringing back into the register a topic that was mentioned only 2-3 clauses before. On the other hand, the non-contrastive SV word-order in EBH, or its equivalent *left-dislocation* in English (see Givón, in this volume), tend to be used to re-introduce a topic back into the register over a much larger gap of absence. As we shall see further below, this earlier claim is confirmed by our text-counts here.

Unlike the SV word order for subjects, the OV word-order for objects in EBH is always a contrastive, localized referential device, and thus fully equivalent with Y-movement. As an example of this device in EBH, consider:

(17)   . . .u-bney yavan 'elišah vi-taršiš kitim vi-dodanim;
             and-sons of Yavan Elisha and-Tarshish Kitim and Dodanim
        '. . .and the sons of Yavan were Elisha and Tarshis Kitim and
             Dodanim;
             me-'eleh nifridu 'iyey haǵoyim. . .   [Gen., 10:4-5]
             from-those split-they islands-of the-gentiles
             and from those the islands of the gentiles separated. . .'

What can be seen in (17) is that the OV word-order precipitates *subject post-posing* (i.e. OVS word-order) as suggested in Givón (1977a). The discontinuous nature of the OV/Y-movement word-order is also confirmed by the use of the 'perfect' tense aspect in (17), where both the subject and the object are discontinuous topics, though for different reasons.

3.7. *Passive*

A number of grammatical verbal categories in EBH qualify for the label 'passive', some more middle-voice or adjectival in nature, some more verbal. In this study no attempt was made to separate them. Only passive constructions with definite subjects and VS word-order were considered. The SV word-order is exceedingly rare in the EBH passive, even more so than in the already less-frequent SV order in active clauses. As an example of some of the passive types that were counted, consider:

(18) . . .ha-haya ha-raʕa 'axalat-hu, ṭarof *ṭoraf* yosef. . .[5]   [Gen., 37:33]
   the-animal the-bad ate-she-him eating *was-eaten-he* Joseph
   '. . .wild animals have eaten him, Joseph *has been devoured*. . .'

(19) . . .u-li-šem *yulad* gam hu'. . .   [Gen., 10:21]
   and-to-Shem *was-born*-it also he
   '. . .and to Shem too *were born* (children). . .'

(20) . . .vɨ-nivrɨxu bɨ-xa kol mišpiḥot ha-'adamah. . .   [Gen., 12:3]
   and-*they-shall-be-blessed* in-you all families-of the-earth
   '. . .and all the species of the earth *will be blessed* on your account. . .'

It is exceedingly hard to find any agented passives in EBH. Example (20) above comes as close to that, as does:

(21) . . .bo' na' 'el šifḥat-i, 'ulay *'ibaneh* mi-mena. . .   [Gen., 16:2]
   come IMP to maid-my maybe *I-will-be-built* from-her
   '. . .come (and sleep with) my maid, perhaps my brood
   will be built from her/because of her. . .'

3.8. *Referential-indefinite NP's*

Referential (as well as non-referential) indefinite NP's are morphologically unmarked in EBH. As example of a referential indefinite object consider:

(22) . . .va-yimṣ'u *biqʕa* be'ereṣ šinʕar. . . . .   [Gen. 11:2]
   and-they-found *valley* in-land-of Shinar
   '. . .and they found a valley in the land of Shinar. . .'

As an example of referential indefinite subject, consider:

(23)   . . .vi-'ed yaˁaleh min ha-'areṣ. . .   [Gen. 2:6]
            and-*steam* it-came-out from the-ground
            '. . .and there was steam coming out of the ground. . .'

Unlike Modern Hebrew, where a presentative-existential VS word-order marks
many indefinite subject constructions (Givón, 1976b), in EBH this presentative word-order is not systematically found. Rather, one would expect indefinite
referential subjects to appear mostly *pre*-verbally (SV order), as in (23) above,
since the introduction of a wholly new topic into the register is obviously a
break in the topic continuity; and as we have seen above, the SV word-order in
EBH marks *discontinuous* topics. The text count results assessing this possibility will be discussed in section 4.6., below.

4. *Results of text counts*

In the tables summarizing the results, below, within each box the number on
top represents the *average* value per token, and the number below it in parentheses represents the number of tokens (N) counted.

4.1. *Zero anaphora*

The results of our three text counts for this category, for direct objects
only, are given in Table IV, below. The human DO count is too low to draw any
conclusions, and the bulk of zero anaphora in the text pertains to non-human
DO's. In terms of referential distance ('look-back'), zero anaphora is the *maximally continuous* category (1.0 clause to the left). It is also the most continuous in terms of potential interference, meaning essentially that only one viable
candidate for correct reference exists in the immediately preceding context of
this topic-marking device. Finally, it terms of persistence ('decay') in subsequent
discourse, this is a *rapidly decaying* category, at least for non-human DO's, with
the value (average 0.22 clauses to the right) essentially approaching zero. And
whatever counts above zero were due to only two tokens out of the total of 23.

4.2. *Clitic pronouns/verb agreement*

The results for subject, direct object and genitive clitic pronouns are given
in Table V, below. Referential distance values for all categories essentially ap-
proximate the 1.0 clause to the left as seen for zero anaphora (DO's, Table IV,
i.e. maximally continuous. The higher topicality of human topics is demonstrated primarily in the persistence ('decay') values, which are between 3-5
clauses to the right for humans and between 0.7-1.4 clauses for non-humans.

Case *per se* does not seem to affect the persistence values. However, when the genitive is split to subject genitives vs. all others, the persistence of the former exceeds even that of (human) subjects — 5.04 vs. 2.80 clauses to the right. This may have to do with the observation (Givón, 1976a) that possessors — being most commonly human — are normally more topical than possessed objects or parts (of the whole).

TABLE IV: Zero anaphora

		Direct Object
Lookback	Human	3.00 (1)
	Nonhuman	1.00 (23)
Decay	Human	3.00 (1)
	Nonhuman	0.22 (23)
Interference	Human	1.00 (1)
	Nonhuman	1.00 (23)

The potential interference values essentially approach the minimal values of 1.0, again tagging clitic pronouns/agreement as a highly predictable/continuous topic category.

TABLE V: Clitic pronouns/agreement

		Subject	Direct Object	Genitive (total)	Genitive Subject	Genitive Non-Subject
Lookback	Human	1.10 (285)	1.11 (46)	1.06 (187)	1.11 (27)	1.05 (160)
	Nonhuman	1.00 (10)	1.09 (11)	1.00 (21)	1.00 (1)	1.00 (20)
Decay	Human	2.80 (285)	3.61 (46)	3.06 (187)	5.04 (27)	2.73 (160)
	Nonhuman	0.70 (10)	1.27 (11)	1.33 (21)	0.00 (1)	1.40 (20)
Interference	Human	1.03 (285)	1.00 (46)	1.03 (187)	1.00 (27)	1.04 (160)
	Nonhuman	1.00 (10)	1.00 (11)	1.00 (21)	1.00 (1)	1.00 (20)

4.3. *Stressed/independent pronouns*

Independent pronouns in EBH, including demonstrative pronouns, occur with high frequency with non-verbal (nominal etc.) predicates, with or without the verb 'be'. The participle/adjectival verb form, much like nominal predicates, has a reduced system of grammatical agreement. For all these less-verbal conjugations, independent pronouns in EBH function both anaphorically (highly continuative) and contrastively.[6] This is evident in the referential distance ('look-back') results in Table IV, where the average value for subjects of participle approach the 1.0 minimal value of anaphoric pronouns/agreement (Table V), while the valuess for subjects of the two major verbal conjugations − 'imperfect' and 'perfect' − show much higher average values (1.76). This is also evident from the total counts for the categories: N = 285 for subject agreement (human), the topic-continuation category, as against $N = 51$ for independent/ stressed pronouns (human). The interference values confirm this suggestion, with the average for human subjects of the participle at the lowest (most predictable/ continuous) value of 1.00, characteristic of anaphoric/clitic pronouns (Table V). On the other hand, the value for human subjects of the 'perfect' and 'imperfect' verbal conjugation is 1.41, almost half way toward the maximal (most discontinuous) value of 2.0. These results thus confirm predictions made in Givón (1977a).

The relatively high persitence values for independent pronouns across the board (for humans) essentially tag them as a topic-*chain-initial* category (see Givón, Ute paper, in this volume). Finally, in terms of case-role, both the associative and direct object (human) independent pronoun seem to exhibit values more characteristic of anaphoric/clitic pronouns than of contrastive ones, in terms of low referential distance, low interference values and high persistence. These categories are historically related in EBH, with a certain amount of overlap between the ʔim-, ʕet and ʔit- prepositions. The results will be further discussed in section 5., below. On the other hand, the referential distance ('look-back') values for dative-benefactive and locative independent pronouns are higher, though not quite as high as for subject pronouns. These values may in fact represent a mixture between the lower anaphoric/continuative values (characteristically 1.0 clauses to the left, cf. Tables IV, V) and the contrastive pronouns values (approaching 2.0, cf. the 1.76 value for subject of true verbal categories, Table VI). The figures for the interference value do not support this suggestion, but one must remember that the locative − and to a lesser extent the dative/ benefactive − in EBH has no clitic-pronoun form, only an independent pronoun. So that the independent pronoun must perform both anaphoric and contrastive functions, muck like the subject pronouns of participial and nominal predicates.

4.4. *Post-verbal definite NP's (VS, VO word-order)*

The counts for these categories are presented in Table VII, below. As one can see, a dramatic rise occurs in the referential distance ('lookback') and potential interference values for all categories, as compared to the preceding pronominal categories. To some extent, obviously, the rise in the latter measurement is a *function* of the rise in the former, since during a long gap of absence from the register, other topics/referents occupy the main topic position and may create potential interference/ambiguity. Thus, to the extent that independent/contrastive pronouns are used to re-introduce topics after a gap of absence, that gap is

TABLE VI: Independent/stressed pronouns

		Subject Overall	subject of participle	subject of perfect or imperfect	Direct Object	dative-benefactive	Assoc.	Locative
Lookback	Human	1.66 (61)	1.10 (10)	1.76 (51)	1.20 (45)	1.40 (96)	1.06 (35)	1.33 (21)
	Nonhuman	5.73 (26)	—	—	1.00 (7)	1.00 (2)	—	1.21 (42)
Decay	Human	3.26 (61)	5.20 (10)	2.88 (51)	4.13 (45)	4.30 (96)	5.51 (35)	4.76 (21)
	Nonhuman	.65 (26)	—	—	0.43 (7)	2.50 (2)	—	0.74 (42)
Interference	Human	1.34 (61)	1.00 (10)	1.41 (51)	1.02 (45)	1.11 (96)	1.03 (35)	1.05 (21)
	Nonhuman	1.38 (26)	—	—	1.00 (7)	1.00 (2)	—	1.00 (42)

TABLE VII: Post-verbal (VS,VO) Definite NP's

		Subject	Direct Object	dative-benefac	Genitive	Assoc.	Locative	Temporal
Lookback	Human	4.83 (256)	12.18 (152)	6.55 (110)	6.22 (123)	6.63 (8)	6.29 (59)	—
	Nonhuman	10.79 (101)	12.58 (115)	5.88 (8)	10.32 (100)	10.50 (2)	10.74 (214)	12.78 (50)
Decay	Human	2.73 (256)	0.93 (152)	3.45 (110)	1.75 (123)	3.75 (8)	3.49 (59)	—
	Nonhuman	0.49 (101)	0.74 (115)	0.13 (8)	0.24 (100)	0.00 (2)	0.43 (214)	0.42 (50)
Interference	Human	1.51 (256)	1.69 (152)	1.40 (110)	1.44 (123)	1.13 (8)	1.41 (59)	—
	Nonhuman	(1.37 (101)	1.60 (115)	1.13 (8)	1.41 (100)	1.50 (2)	1.50 (214)	1.52 (50)

relatively short, normally around 1-2 clauses, as compared to the 5-12 clauses average values for post-verbal full definite NP's.

The persistence ('decay') figures show full definite NP's to be much less persistent in discourse than independent pronouns. Human NP's persist much longer in discourse than non-human ones. Among human NP's, subjects persist much longer than direct objects, while the less inert case-roles of dative-benefactive, associative and human-locatives seem to persist even longer — once introduced as full definite NP's — than subjects. On the other hand, among non-humans the DO shows the highest persistence, perhaps due to direct objects (patients) being characteristically/prototypically non-human.

TABLE VIII: Post-verbal genitive NP's ('possessor of object')
divided to subject vs. non-subject genitives

		Genitive Subject	Genitive Non-Subject
Lookback	human	2.11 (9)	6.54 (114)
Lookback	non-human	12.33 (3)	10.10 (97)
Decay	human	2.22 (9)	1.71 (114)
Decay	non-human	0.00 (3)	0.25 (97)
Interference	human	1.22 (9)	1.46 (114)
Interference	non-human	1.66 (3)	1.40 (97)

In TABLE VIII the counts for genitives ('possessors of the object') are
separated into subject genitives vs. non-subject genitives. For humans, subject
genitives prove to be much more continuous topics, with lower referential
distance values (2.11 vs. 6.54 clauses to the left on the average) and lower interference values (1.22 vs. 1.46). Human genitive subjects also persist longer (2.22
clauses to the right vs. 1.71 for non-humans).

4.5. Pre-verbal (SV ordered) definite subjects

As suggested earlier, pre-verbal objects will be considered here under the
heading of Y-movement, see further below. The pre-verbal SV word-order is thus
relevant here only for subjects.

TABLE IX: Definite Subjects in the SV word-order

		Subject Overall	Subject of Non-Verbal Clause	Subject of Verbal Clause
Lookback	Human	8.47 (77)	3.56 (16)	9.75 (61)
	Nonhuman	11.51 (65)	10.79 (14)	11.71 (51)
Decay	Human	2.03 (77)	3.50 (16)	1.64 (61)
	Nonhuman	1.12 (65)	0.43 (14)	1.31 (51)
Interference	Human	1.83 (77)	1.75 (16)	1.85 (61)
	Nonhuman	1.66 (65)	1.86 (14)	1.61 (51)

The results of our counts are presented in Table IX, below. In terms of referential distance ('look-back'), pre-verbal (SV-ordered) subjects are much more *discontinuous*, particularly in the crucial (prototypical, for subject) human category. The relevant comparison should be between human subject of verbal clauses (9.75 clauses to the left) and the VS-ordered human subjects in Table VII above, which are overwhelmingly subjects of the 'imperfect' verbal form (see Givón, 1977a), with the average ref. distance of 4.83 clauses to the left. A parallel difference in the interference count is also apparent, with SV-ordered human subjects of verbal clauses posting the figure 1.85 in Table IX, while the VS-ordered human subjects in Table VII show 1.51. A similar difference is observed for non-humans (1.37 VS-ordered subjects vs. 1.61 SV-ordered subjects). Here again one suspects that the referential distance counts are primary, while the interference counts are predictable from them.

The persistence counts are complex yet instructive. SV-ordered, less-continuous *human* subjects seem to decay faster (2.03 clauses to the right on the average) than their VS-ordered counterparts (2.73 clauses). But the situation is reversed for *non-humans* (0.49 clauses to the right for VS-ordered subjects, vs. 1.21 for SV-ordered subjects). This may again tag humans as more prototypical subjects (Hopper and Thompson, 1980).

4.6. *Referential indefinite NP's*

The results of our counts for this category are presented in Table X, below. Since the scores for referential distance ('lookback') and potential interference are assigned by *fiat*, they are of no great interest at this point. The persistence ('decay') figures for human subjects show no significant difference between referential indefinite human subject (2.90 clauses to the right on the average) and the VS-ordered definite NP human subjects (2.73 clauses). However, the indefinite counts may be less reliable due to a small sample (10 tokens). The counts for indefinite human subjects are still considerably higher than those for the SV-ordered definite subjects (2.03 clauses to the right for the latter), thus suggesting that an important topic enterring the register for the first time may have a higher probability of persisting longer than a re-introduced topic. A similar difference may be seen with non-human subjects, with persistence values of 1.12 clauses for the SV-ordered definite subjects and 2.38 for the (newly introduced) indefinite subjects.

As predicted elsewhere (Givón, 1979, Ch. 2), the direct object position is the one used to introduce the majority of new referential arguments into the dis-

TABLE X: Referential indefinite NP's

		Subject	Direct Object
Lookback	human	20.00 (10)	20.00 (42)
	non-human	20.00 (13)	20.00 (67)
Decay	human	2.90 (10)	0.83 (42)
	non-human	2.38 (13)	1.30 (67)
Interference	human	2.00 (10)	2.00 (42)
	non-human	2.00 (13)	2.00 (67)

course register, a fact evident from the much higher total counts in Table X. The persistence of arguments introduced for the first time as DO's, however, is strikingly low for both humans (0.83 clauses to the right) and non-humans (1.30 clauses). The higher persistence of non-humans here may again be due to their being more prototypical DO's.

In Table XI, below, a special count is presented, of the distribution of SV vs. VS word-order for referential indefinite subjects in the three major predication categories — 'imperfect', 'perfect' and participial/non-verbal. As we have seen above, for definite subjects the VS order was much more *continuous*, showing lower referential distance values and lower potential interference values, while the SV word-order was more *discontinuous*, characteristically used to re-introduce topics into the register after a considerable gap of absence. Since indefinite

TABLE XI: Word-order distribution with referential-
indefinite subjects

tense-aspect	VS		SV			
	N	percent	N	percent		
imperfect	6	0.60	3	0.14		
perfect	2	0.20	3	0.14		
participial/ non-verbal	2	0.20	15	0.72		
total	10	1.0	21	1.00	TOTAL SAMPLE N percent	
total sample	10	0.32	21	0.68	31	1.00

NP's are by definition *maximally discontinuous/surprising/unpredictable,* being introduced into the register for the first time, it was of interest to see whether the SV word-order would predominate with referential indefinite subjects. To this end, 31 chapters of the book of Genesis (Ch. 2 through 32) were counted. The results indeed corroborate the hypothesis: The SV word-order predominates overall in the total sample of 31 tokens by a factor of *better than 2 to 1* (0.68 percent SV vs. 0.32 percent VS). The exceptions in each category are also of interest. Within the VS category, 0.60 percent (6 tokens out of 10) appeared in the 'imperfect', the verb-form normally coding the *highest thematic* (and refer-ential) *continuity* (cf. Givón, 1977a). These instances probably represent a case where continuity at the thematic ('higher') level *overruled* discontinuity at the referential level. On the other hand, fully 86 percent (18 tokens out of 21) of the SV-ordered sample appear in the 'perfect' or participial/non-verbal, which are characteristically much more *discontinuous* categories in EBH (cf. Givón, 1977a). And the 0.14 percent of SV-order found, rather uncharacteristically, in the 'imperfect' may here represent the other type of *overrule*, where referen-tial discontinuity overruled thematic continuity.

Finally, the 2-to-1 ration of SV over VS in referential indefinite subjects should be compared to corresponding definite subject counts from Tables VII and IX, above. These show 142 tokens of SV-ordered definite subjects as against 357 tokens of VS-ordered definite subjects, or the reverse ratio of *2.5 to 1* of

VS over SV. These results further support the claim that the VS word-order in EBH codes more continuous/predictable topics, while the SV word-order codes less continuous, less predictable topics.

4.7. *Y-movement of definite NP's*

The results for this category are given in Table XII, below. The referential distance ('look-back') results corroborate prediction made earlier (Givón, 1979, Ch. 2) concerning the essentially *localized* nature of Y-movement. Y-moved human subjects exhibit an average of 1.71 clauses to the left referential distance. This is quite comparable to our other contrastive/localized device, independent/ stressed pronouns, where the average ref. distance for human subjects (cf. Table VI, above) is 1.66 clauses to the left. Both devices involve contrastive stress, and clearly involve the immediately preceding discourse context.

TABLE XII: Y-movement of definite NP's

		Subject Overall	Subject of Non-Verbal	Subject of Verbal	Direct Object	dative benefactive
Lookback	Human	1.71 (28)	1.29 (7)	1.86 (21)	2.50 (6)	4.77 (13)
	Nonhuman	———	———	———	1.66 (6)	2.00 (1)
Decay	Human	1.18 (28)	1.43 (7)	1.14 (21)	0.33 (6)	3.15 (13)
	Nonhuman	———	———	———	0.50 (6)	0.00 (1)
Interference	Human	2.00 (28)	2.00 (7)	2.00 (21)	2.00 (6)	2.00 (13)
	Nonhuman	———	———	———	2.00 (6)	2.00 (1)

TABLE XIII: DEF-subjects of passives (VS word-oder)

		subject of passive
Lookback	human	8.58 (24)
Lookback	non-human	10.58 (24)
Decay	human	2.83 (24)
Decay	non-human	0.71 (24)
Interference	human	1.33 (24)
Interference	non-human	1.58 (24)

In terms of their persistence ('decay'), Y-moved definite subjects exhibit lower average values (1.18) as compared to the SV-ordered definite subjects (cf. Table IX, above). This may reflect the possibility that SV-ordered definite subjects tend to be topic-chain *intial* elements, while Y-moved/contrasted NP's may be chain *medial* (see Givón's Ute paper in this volume as well as his Introduction).

4.8. *VS-ordered definite subjects of passive clauses*

The overall frequency of passive clauses in the EBH narrative is rather low, roughly corresponding to the English text counts given in Givón (1979, Ch. 2).[7] This fact by itself tags the passive as a *discontinuous* discourse device. The figures given in Table XIII, below, represent the counts for definite, VS-ordered subjects of passive clauses, and should be thus compared with those given for VS-ordered definite subjects of active clauses, Table VII, above. In terms of referential distance ('look-back'), human subjects of the passive show an average value of 8.58 clauses to the left, as against 4.83 clauses for human subjects of the active. The passive values are thus much closer to those of *non-human* active subjects (10.79, Table VII) or even human *direct objects* (12.18, Table VII). On the other hand, non-human subjects of the passive do not differ significantly from non-human subjects of the active (10.58 vs. 10.79 clauses to the left on the average, respectively).

Neither the potential interference nor the persistence ('decay') figures reveal any significant difference between the subjects of passive and actives.

5. *Discussion*
5.1. *Referential distance ('look-back') and topic continuity*
The results for subjects, direct objects and dative-benefactive objects are presented as graphs in Figures 1, 2 and 3 below, separately for humans and non-humans. Since subjects are overwhelmingly — prototypically — human (cf. Greenberg, 1974, Givón, 1976a, Hopper and Thompson, 1980), the curve for human subjects given in Figure 1 is first of interest. It seems to separate the topic-marking devices used in EBH into four groups in terms of ref. distance as a measure of topic continuity:

(a)   *Localized devices*: Clitic pronouns/agreement, independent pronouns and Y-movement, with average ref. distance values of 1-2 clauses to the left.

(b)   *Intermediate devices*: The VS-ordered definite NP subject, with an average ref. distance value of 4-5 clauses to the left.

(c)   *Long-distance devices*: The SV-ordered definite subject of active clauses, and the VS-ordered definite subject of passives, with average values of 7-8 clauses.

(d)   *Maximally discontinuous device*: Indefinite referential NP's, with the value set arbitrarily at 20, and perhaps set that way too high (cf. discussion in Givón's Introduction to this volume).

As we shall see further below, the three localized devices in category (a) separate better from each other by our potential interference measurement. The discontinuous nature of the passive is obvious from its closeness to the major discontinuous category — SV-ordered subjects. But the passive is also a member of two other functional domains (detransitivization and de-personalization; cf. Givón, 1981b), and thus draws part of its semantic and discourse-pragmatic characterization from those domains. The major function of the SV word

242 A. FOX

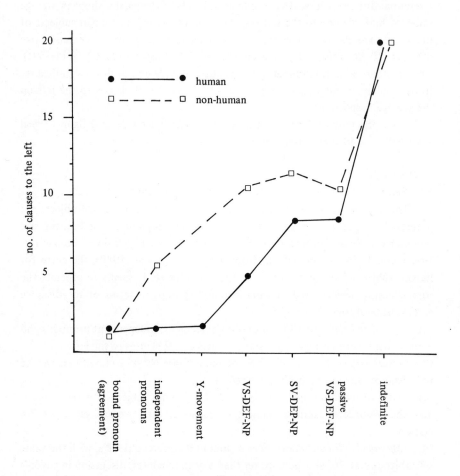

FIGURE 1.: Referential distance ('lookback') of subjects

order in EBH appears to be the re-introduction of definite topics back into the register over a considerable gap of absence. Keenan (1977) has noted that passives and L-dislocation (not counted here distinctly from the SV order) appear in English in complementary distribution, with passives appearing primarily in the written ('planned') register and L-dislocation primarily in the oral ('unplanned') register (in this connection see also Givón's paper on spoken English, in this volume). Since the SV word-order for actives in EBH is the func-

FIGURE 2.: Referential distance ('lookback') of direct objects

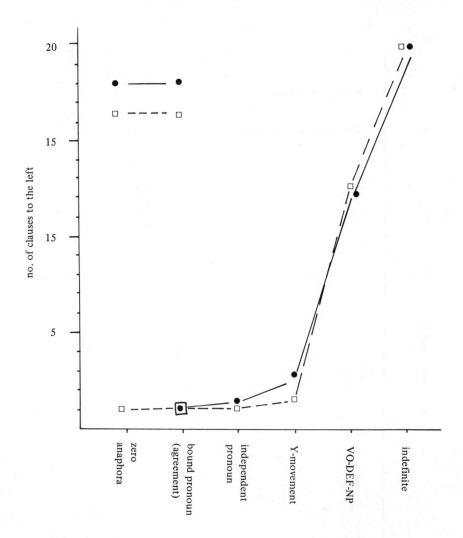

tional equivalent of L-dislocation, the rough correspondence between passives and SV-ordered actives corroborates Keenan's and Givón's observations.

The behaviour of the direct object and dative-benefactive curves in Figures 2, 3 follow roughly the same observation as for subjects above, although there are fewer coding devices involved.

FIGURE 3.: Referential distance ('lookback)
of dative-benefactive objects

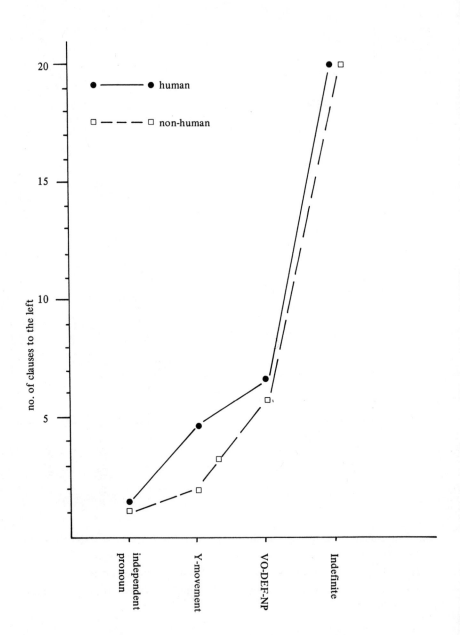

Except for the two extremes of the curve (one of them arbitrarily set), human arguments show consistently lower ref. distance values and thus prove to be more *continuous* in discourse. This is true for the prototypically human subject category, but not for the two object categories. For the dative-benefactive, also prototypically human, one suspects that the non-human counts are both low and spurious.

FIGURE 4.: Referential distance ('lookback') as correlated to the major case-arguments

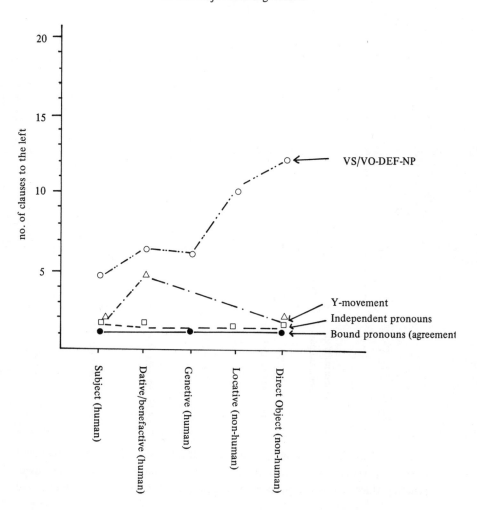

A. FOX

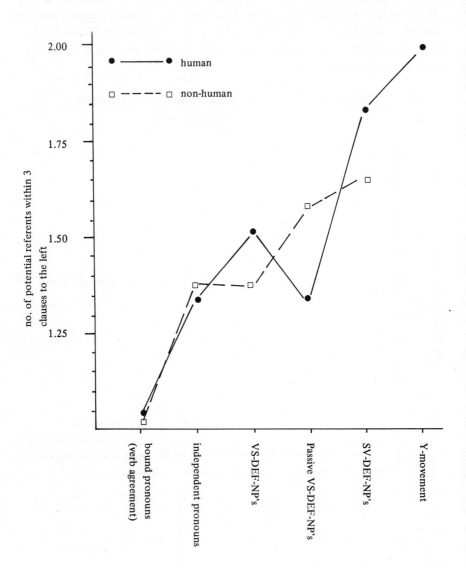

FIGURE 5.: Potential ambiguity/interference of subjects

Figure 4 displays the effect of case-role on ref. distance. For each argument type, only values from either the human or non-human category were used, pending which one is prototypical (Greenberg, 1974, Givón, 1976a, Hopper and

Thompson, 1980). The more localized coding devices − bound pronouns/agreement and independent pronouns − don't show any difference, given that their values are, to begin with, maximally continuous or very close to that. The exceedingly high value for dative-benefactives in the Y-movement category is probably a fluke, so that essentially this is also a localized category like pronouns and agreement. In the most frequent NP category − post-verbal NP's (VS, VO) − the effect of case-role is rather striking, with subjects displaying low ref-distance values, dative-benefactives and genitives higher, locative higher and direct object highest. However, to quite an extent this is predictable from the humanness of the case-roles, since the three lowest (most continuous) categories are prototypically human.

5.2. *Potential interference and topic continuity*

The results of this measurement for subjects are plotted in Figure 5, on a scale from 1.0 (no interference) to 2.0 (interference present). The major topic-marking devices hierarchize by this measurement essentially along the same relative scale as they did with the ref. distance measurement, with some significant differences. The passive and active in the VS order do not separate by this measurement (though they did by ref. distance). Y-movement, a relatively localized device in terms of ref. distance, proves to be the *most contrastive* in terms of the presence in the immediate environment of other referents. Similarly, independent pronouns, which did not separate from clitic pronouns very well by referential distance, separathe from them more clearly here and prove to be much more *contrastive*, as predicted in Givón (1977a).

The results for direct objects are plotted in Figure 6, below. Here Y-movement once again proves to be the most contrastive category. However, unlike independent subject pronouns, independent *object* pronouns exhibit essentially the same value here as do clitic object pronouns. This similarity thus recapitulates the essentially identical ref. distance values of the two categories. What we see here, one suspects, is the early beginnings of a *diachronic* process which came to full fruition later on in Mishnaic (and Modern) Hebrew, where the clitic/anaphoric pronouns were completely *displaced* by the independent pronouns, which thus lost their contrastive, topic-switching function. This obviously recapitulates a universal diachronic process (Givón, 1976a). What we see in EBH, then, are the early signs of such a process, whereby although both clitic and independent pronouns exist, the latter begin to lose their contrastive function and thus invade the anaphoric territory of clitic pronouns. Such a diachronic process is an indirect corroboration of the functional *continuum* nature of our topic-

FIGURE 6.: Potential ambiguity/interference of direct objects

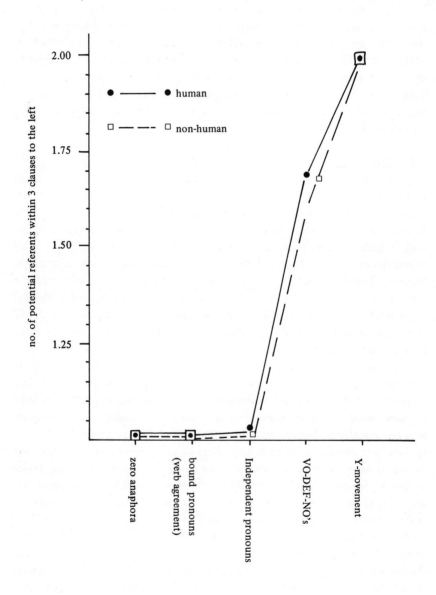

FIGURE 7.: Potential ambiguity/interference
of dative-benefactive objects

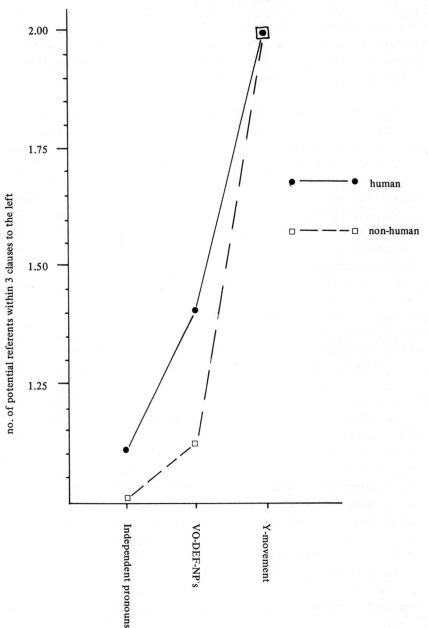

marking devices.[8]

The results for dative-benefactive objects are plotted in Figure 7. In the main, they do not deviate significantly from the general trends observed above, except that there are no clitic pronouns for this category, so that the independent pronouns presumably function both anaphorically and contrastively, which explains the relatively low values here, given that the majority of pronouns in the sample are probably anaphoric rather than contrastive.

5.3. *The persistence ('decay') measurement: Continuity in subsequent discourse*

Our first two measurements, above, assess the speaker's estimation of the two major difficulties for the *hearer* in establishing topic identification: Distance from the last previous mention in discourse, and the presence of other referents in the previous discourse. On the other hand, the persistence ('decay') measurement tries to assess the *importance* of topics in terms of likelihood of continuing to occupy center stage in the discourse register. This is thus more of a measure of the *speaker's* topical intent. There is no automatic correlation between this measurement and the other two, although there are some solid dependencies mediated by additional factors.

A summary of the results for this measurement is plotted in Figure 8, below. Two general tendencies concerning the importance − and thus *topicality* of referents are evident right away:

(a)   Human arguments consistently persist longer in subsequent discourse once they've been introduced into the register (by whatever means); and

(b)   On the whole the subject and dative-benefactive cases, prototypically human, tend to mark topics that are likely to persist longer.

Both tendencies corroborate earlier predictions (Givón, 1976a, 1979, Ch. 2).

The situation is much more complex in assessing the roles of the various topic-marking devices. Thus, the localized, contrastive Y-movement device seems to code topics of lesser overall importance, since they are least persistent in subsequent discourse. In contrast, the device of independent pronouns − a characteristic topic-switching device (see other contributions to this volume as well as Givón, 1982b), proves to be − at least for the subject and dative-benefactive category − a device used to re-introduce *highly persistent* referents back into the discourse. It is thus typical *chain-initial* topic-marking device (see Givón's Ute paper as well as his introduction to this volume).

One could also assess here the relative role of indefinite NP's in introducing important topics into the discourse. Indefinite *subjects* in EBH − commonly with the SV word-order (see above) − are indeed an important device in first

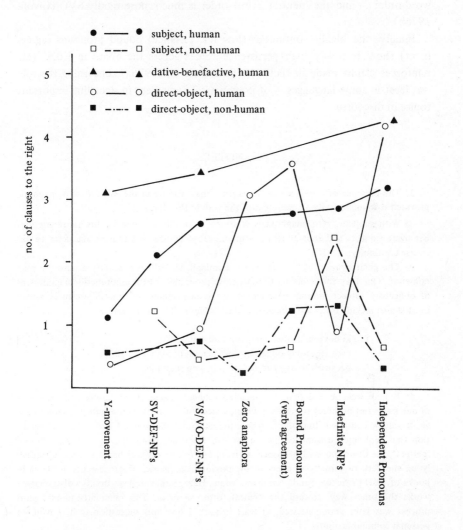

FIGURE 8.: Persistence ('decay') of topics in discourse

introduction into the register of *highly-persistent* topics. They are also by definition a *chain-initial* device. On the other hand, indefinite *objects* are of much
lower persistence here. One may thus tentatively identify the SV-ordered indefinite subject construction in EBH as a characteristic *presentative* device (Hetzron,
1971). This contrasts sharply, in typological terms, with Israeli Hebrew, where

the existential-presentative construction more characteristically employs the VS word-order – and the 'neutral' word order is much more rigidly SVO (Givón, 1976b).[9]

Finally, the highly continuous (low ref. distance) bound pronouns (agreement) show relatively high persistence values across the board in EBH. This reinforces claims made in Haile (1970) and Givón (1976a) concerning the role –at least in some languages – of grammatical agreement in signalling important topics in discourse.

NOTES

1) The presence of a referent in the register may also be in the form of zero anaphora, provided it is semantically an argument of the verb in the clause.

2) With subjects, zero anaphora is confined to infinitives, where syntactic restrictions bar overt subjects and thus allow no communicative choice, and thus no relevance to discourse continuity.

3) The genitivization of the subjects of nominalized verbs is obviously a universal phenomenon. One may thus consider these genitive pronouns in EBH as a functional equivalent of obligatory subject pronouns/agreement in the environment of non-finite clauses, which in EBH also include many adverbial-subordinate clauses. Thus consider:

> . . . ki bi-yom 'axal-*xa* mi-menu mot tamut. . .   [Gen., 2:17]
> because at-day-of eating-*your* from-it dying you-shall-die
> '. . .because the day *you* eat from it, you shall die. . .'

4) It may well be said that the so-called Biblical puzzle of the 'conversive' *waw* (*va-* in our transcription here) is merely a *phonological* function of its use with the continuative, largely VS ordered 'imperfect', where the characteristic prefixal vowels /i, i, o/ condition the 'euphonic', dissimilated /a/ in *va-*. On the other hand, the characteristically SV 'perfect', the disontinuous EBH aspect (Givón, 1977a), involves either the vowel /a/ initially on the verb or initially in many of the predominant names of participants in the early books of EBH (Yaʻakov, Sarah, 'avraham, 'adam, Hava, Rahel etc.), so that the dissimilation works the other way, toward the neutral forms *vi-* or *u-*. This inherently phonological process was later grammaticized, at least in part. I owe this suggestion to T. Givón (in personal communication).

5) The redundant infinitive preceding the main verb performs an emphatic adverbial function in EBH, in this case indicating that Joseph was eaten *up* or tore *into pieces*.

6) In non-verbal clauses in EBH. unstressed, non-contrastive independent pronouns are almost obligatory, used much like obligatory subject agreement in verbal clauses. For the contrastive/topic-switching use, see example (7), above. For the largely anaphoric, non-contrastive use, see example (8), above.

7) Givón (1979, Ch. 2) gives the overall frequency of passives in various English written texts as between 5 percent and 20 percent of all main, declerative clauses, pending on text type. Our figures here for EBH are 24/256 for human subjects – or about *8 percent*, and 24/101 for non-human subjects, or about *23 percent*. But this represents only the VS-ordered definite subjects, not including the high frequency subject pronouns/agreement.

8) For a discussion of the general principle governing such a displacement of one constuction by another, see Givón (1982c).

9) What we see here, quite possibly, is the effect of word-order typological change. EBH, like Ute (see Givón, in this volume), has pragmatically flexible word-order with the VS order being the more continuous one, and thus much more *frequent* than the discontinuous SV order. The introduction of a referential indefinite argument into the discourse obviously represents extreme *discontinuity* in topic, so that in both EBH and Ute the SV order is used. Israeli Hebrew has gravitated considerably toward a rigid SVO word-order (Givón, 1976b, 1977a), so that the more frequent *continuous* word-order there is SV. The shift toward the presentative VS word-order is thus a way of maintaning a viable *contrast* in word-order, between the more continuative (by frequency, rigidity notwithstanding) SV and the more discontinuous VS. To some extent Modern Colloquial Spanish is undergoing the same typological change right now (see Bentivoglio, in this volume).

REFERENCES

Bolinger, D. (1952) "Linear Modification", in his *Forms of English*, Cambridge: Harvard University Press (1965)

Duranti, A. and E. Ochs (1979) "Left dislocation in Italian conversation", in T. Givón (ed.) *Discourse and Syntax, Syntax and Semantics* vol. 12, NY: Academic Press

Givón T. (1974) "Verb complements and relative clauses: A diachronic case-study in Biblical Hebrew", *Afroasiatic Linguistics*, 1.4

————— (1976a) "Topic, pronoun and grammatical agreement", in C. Li (ed.) *Subject and Topic*, NY: Academic Press

————— (1976b) "On the VS word-order in Israeli Hebrew: Pragmatics and typological change", in P. Cole (ed.) *Studies in Modern Hebrew Syntax and Semantics*, Amsterdam: North Holland

————— (1977a) "The drift from VSO to SVO in Biblical Hebrew: The Pragmatics of tense-aspect", in C. Li (ed.) *Mechanisms for Syntactic Change*, Austin: University of Texas Press

————— (1977b) "Definiteness and referentiality", in J. Greenberg (ed.) *Universals of Human Language*, vol. 4, *Syntax*, Stanford: Stanford University Press

—————— (1979) *On Understanding Grammar*, NY: Academic Press

—————— (1980) *Ute Reference Grammar*, Ignacio: Ute Press

—————— (1981a) review of J. Hinds' *Anaphora in Discourse, Language*

—————— (1981b) "Typology and functional domains", *Studies in Language*, 4.3

—————— (1982a) "Tense-aspect-modality: The Creole prototype and beyond", in P. Hopper (ed.) *Tense and Aspect: Between Semantics and Pragmatics, Typological Studies in Language*, vol. 1, Amsterdam: J. Benjamins

—————— (1982b) "Topic continuity in discourse: The functional domain of switch reference", in J. Haiman and P. Munro (eds), *Switch Reference, Typological Studies in Language*, vol. 2, Amsterdam: J. Benjamins

—————— (1982c) "Function, structure and language acquisition", in D. Slobin (ed.) *The Cross-Language Study of Language Acquisition*, Hillsdale, N.J.: Ablex (in press)

Greenberg, J. (1974) "The relation of frequency to semantic feature in a case language (Russian)", *Working Papers in Language Universals*, vol. 16, Stanford University

Haile, G. (1970) "The suffix pronoun in Amharic", in C.-W. Kim and H. Stahlke (eds) *Papers in African Linguistics*, Edmonton: Linguistic Research

Hetzron, R. (1971) "Presentative function and presentative movement", *Studies in African Linguistics, Supplement no. 2*

Hopper, P. (1979) "Aspect and foregrounding in discourse", in T. Givón (ed.) *Discourse and Syntax, Syntax and Semantics* vol. 12, NY: Academic Press

Hopper, P. and S. Thompson (1980) "Transitivity in grammar and discourse", *Language*,

Keenan, Elinor (1977) "Why look at planned and unplanned discourse?", in E. Keenan and T. Bennett (eds) *Discourse Across Time and Space*, Los Angeles: University of Southern California, Linguistics Department, *SCOPIL* no. 5

TOPIC CONTINUITY AND DISCONTINUITY IN DISCOURSE:
A STUDY OF SPOKEN LATIN-AMERICAN SPANISH

PAOLA BENTIVOGLIO
Linguistics Department
University of California, Los Angeles
and
Universidad Central de Venezuela,
Caracas

TABLE OF CONTENTS

LIST OF TABLES

ABBREVIATIONS

CC . . . . .Coreferential clitic
DEF . . . . .Definite
EP . . . . .Existential-presentative
FUT . . . . .Future
GER . . . . .Gerundive
IMPF . . . . .Imperfect
IND . . . . .Indicative mood
INDF . . . . .Indefinite
INF . . . . .Infinitive
M-NP . . . . . . .Modified definite NP
NM-NP . . . . . .Non-modified definite NP
NP . . . . .Noun phrase
PART . . . . . . .Participle
PAST . . . . . . .Past tense
PERF . . . . . . .Perfect
pl. . . . . .Plural
PRES . . . . . . .Present tense
RC-NP . . . . . .Definite NP modified by a relative clause
sg. . . . . .Singular
S-DEF-EP . . . . .Subject-first Existential-presentative
SP . . . . .Stressed pronouns
SUBJ . . . . . . .Subjunctive mood
S-V . . . . .Subject-verb Existential-presentative
V-DEF-EP . . . . .Verb-first Existential-presentative
V-S . . . . .Verb-subject word-order
VAC . . . . .Verb-agreement and clitics
WO . . . . .Word-order

0. Introduction

In the present paper I intend to demonstrate that the analysis presented by Givón (1980) for Ute discourse is also valid for Spanish and can be utilized with some modifications. This analysis establishes that for any language the speaker has available a certain number of strategies in order to maintain or not maintain the continuity of a given topic-NP in the discourse:

"...The continuity/discontinuity of the *sentential topic* which serves as the 'theme' or 'subject' of the predications/verbs expressed within each clause. In more bread-and-butter terms, each sentence/clause releases *a message unit*, most commonly the verb plus its various object NP's. And that message unit, at the clause level, is about the *theme/topic.* And the theme/ topic at the clause level is usually one of the NP's, most commonly the *subject NP* . . . .

In terms of the clause-level topic continuity, we deal with the speaker's judgments as to *how easy/difficult it is for the hearer to identify uniquely the topic NP*. Pronouns, anaphora, definite markers, demonstratives and other topic-marking particles or construction/devices are, in general and also in Ute, the grammatical *means* by which the speaker attempts to make sure that the hearer can follow the clause-level topic NP, or know 'what the information in the clause is *about'* . . ."

(Givón, 1980: 302-3)

The different sections of this paper will describe each of the most common means utlized by Spanish speakers to maintain or reassess the topic-NP continuity, and to locate all these means on a scale which goes from a maximum to a minimum of continuity. For this purpose the text analyzed has been divided into clauses,[1] and each strategy found in them has been assigned a value for three different parameters: i) DISTANCE = represents the continuity/discontinuity of a topic-NP when we take into consideration the clauses which precede that containing the item under analysis; ii) DECAY = corresponds to the persistence of a given NP in the clauses which follow that containing the token under study; iii) AMBIGUITY = relates to the fact that the reference of a given topic can be either unique or non-unique, i.e., ambiguous. All the tokens have been sub-divided into two major categories: i) HUMAN, and ii) NON-HUMAN.

In order to clarify the procedures adopted for this analysis, let us consider the following example (1):

(1) a. . . . *mi abuelo*   *era*   hijo
           my grandfather   be-IND-IMPF-3sg.   son
           de ese   tipo
           of that   fellow
           [que no   quería   que   *sus*
           [who not   want-IND-IMPF sg.   that   his
           hijos   aprendieran   a   leer]
           children learn-SUBJ-PAST-3 pl. to   read-INF]

     b. y *él*   sí   *aprendió*   a   leer
          and he   yes   learn-IND-PAST-3 sg.   to   read-INF
          por *su*   propria   voluntad   y   por
          for   his   own   will   and for
          recuerdos   de *su* madre,
          recollections of his mother

     c. aunque   a *su* madre la *dejó*
          although   his mother her stop-IND-PAST-3 sg.
          de ver,
          of see-INF

     d. porque se divorció   de   *su*
          because   divorce-IND-PAST-3 sg. from   his
          papá; . . .
          daddy

'. . . my grandfather was the son of that fellow who did not want his children to learn to read, but he learned to read because of his own determination and the recollections of his mother, although he stopped seeing his mother because she divorced his father; . . .'

In (1), the items in each clause have been considered according to the above described parameters, as follows:

DISTANCE: The speaker introduced a new topic-NP into the scenario: her grandfather. *Mi abuelo* in (a) is mentioned for the first time in the discourse as a definite NP. Since this topic is not mentioned in prior clauses, the value assigned for the parameter DISTANCE is the maximum established of 20 (twenty); in (b) the stressed pronoun *él* 'he' is given for the same parameter the value of one, as *él* refers to the same topic-NP of the immediately preceding clause (a). The same value is attributed to verb-agreement in (c) (*dejó* 'left') and to the possessive *su* 'his' in (d). We can now see that all tokens will be assigned a value from 1 to 20 (no zero is allowed for this parameter), with 1 representing the maximum continuity and 20 the minimum or the maximum of discontinuity. Thus, the lower the figure the higher the degree of continuity, in the sense that the token under analysis is closer to its referent.

DECAY: The reference to a same topic-NP — namely to *mi abuelo* 'my grandfather' — is maintainted without interruptions from (a) to (d), so that the value assigned for DECAY will be 3 (three). Obviously for this parameter there are no limits, and value may go from $\emptyset$, when there is no reference to the same topic in the adjacent subsequent clause, to any number, as long as the reference is maintained. In my data the highest value assigned to an item, for DECAY, is 27 (twenty-seven), cf. example (8). It is worth noting that subordination is a powerful mechanism for interrupting the continuity, as the speaker can set up a topic in a clause, and then not refer to it in the next clause because he/she is intervening in the discourse by saying, for example, *yo creo, pienso, digo*, etc., 'I believe, think, say, etc.', as in (2), where the topic-NP — Father of the congregation of *Maristas* — has been present in the last four clauses before (2) starts. Thus, in (a) we find a normal case of verb-agreement to which is assigned the value of $\emptyset$ for DECAY, since clause (b) represents a break in the reference. Nevertheless, the reference to the same topic-NP starts again in (c) with another occurrence of verb-agreement (*lloraba* 'he was crying') and (d) with the clitic *le* 'to him' and the possessive *su* 'his'. It seems that the switching of reference from (a) to the first person of (b) and back to (c) does not impede the use of weak strategies (in the scale of continuity) such as verb-agreement and clitics. From my analysis thus far it seems clear that such interference does not break the reference of a given topic.

(2) a. Pero *le*   *entendió*   en la
         but her   understand-IND-PAST-3 sg. in the
         confesión   a-Conchita,
         confession Conchita
     b. que te   *digo*
         that to-you say-IND-PRES-1 sg.
     c. que *lloraba.*
         that cry-IND-IMPF-3 sg.
     d. Porque *le*   dijo   *su*   vida.
         because to-him say-IND-PAST-3 sg. his   life
     'But he understood Conchita in her confession, and I tell you that he was crying. Because she told him his (future) life.'

AMBIGUITY: As previously indicated this parameter has only a binary value: 1 (one) for unique reference and 2 (two) for non-unique. In (1a) *mi abuelo* receives the value 2, as it is a newly introduced topic, but *él* 'he' in (b) is assigned the value 1, because there is no doubt (be it grammatical, semantic or pragmatic) that the only one who did want to learn to read is *he*, the grandfather. Equally for verb-agreement in *dejó* 'stopped': no other NP is likely to claim the subjecthood of this verb, the only other HUMAN NP being the grandfather's father, who by our knowledge of the real world (cf. Givón, 1980: 307) cannot be in relationship with his own wife — i.e., his son's mother — that the speaker would label *su madre* 'his mother'. For the same reason — pragmatics — the only possible subject of *se divorció* 'divorced' in (d) is the grandfather's mother.

The different strategies which will be analyzed — from verb-agreement and clitics to word-order — will be assigned a value for each of the three parameters above described, and the results will be presented in separate tables, and finally compared with each other in order to establish how these devices are positioned in the scale of continuity/discontinuity in Spanish.

In the analysis all instances of a given selected item (for ex. a stressed pronoun, or a non-modified NP) have been taken into account with only the following exceptions:

    i.   - When the occurrences of a given item were more than 210 — i.e., 70 for each one of the three dialects studied — only the first 210 are present, and the rest have not been analyzed, for it is believed that such quantity is sufficient to be deemed significant;

    ii.   - In view of the fact that the sample reflects spoken narratives, where the interferences of the speaker (in first person singular and sometimes plural) and of the hearer (in this case the interviewer) are quite frequent, I have disregarded all references to first- and second-person, and I have only taken into account third-person reference. Thus, all figures reflected in the Tables, from 1 to 10, relate to third person, singular or plural, be they verb-agreements, clitics, stressed pronouns or word-order.

In section 1, after a brief presentation of the data, I will illustrate all the linguistic mechanisms analyzed in this paper; in section 2, I will present and discuss the tables containing the numeric results obtained for each of the mechanisms examplified in section 1; finally, in section 3, the findings will be compared.

1. The grammatical devices according to continuity/discontinuity: examples
1.0. The data

The text I have analyzed proceeds from the published transcriptions of tape-recorded spoken Spanish from Mexico City, Caracas and Santiago de Chile.[2] From every book I have extracted, at random, fifteen pages of narratives, a total of forty-five pages. In choosing the texts I have been more concerned with the structure, in terms of length, fluency, etc., than with the characteristics of the speakers, which are nevertheless indicated in the Appendix. This sample has not been prepared for sociolinguistic research, and in any event would be inadequate for that purpose because in the P.I.L.E.I. project the speakers are not socially stratified, as the authors of the project were only concerned that all the speakers share the characteristic of being *cultos* 'educated', within certain groups of age (I: 25-35 years, II: 36-55; III: 56 on) and equal in number of women and men. It is beyond the scope of this paper to comment upon or criticize the limitations or defects of this approach.

1.1. Verb-agreement and unstressed pronouns

In Spanish, as is well known, 'zero- appearance' of the topic-NP occurs only with verbs of modality (ex. *él quiere comer* 'he wants to eat'), participial constructions (ex. *Diciendo esto, se fue* 'Saying this he/she left'), and in a few complex sentences where the subject of the main clause and that of the subordinate are coreferential (in generative terms, sentences which allow 'Equi NP deletion'). I will not be concerned in this paper with the above mentioned constructions, which constitute the highest point in the scale of predictability and continuity.

The next point in this scale is occupied by verb-agreement, for subjects, and unstressed pronouns or clitics, for non-subjects. Verb-agreement and clitics (henceforth VAC) cover, in Spanish, areas that in other languages are covered by zero anaphora. But for Spanish whenever the verb is finite — i.e., with the exception of gerunds, participles and infinitives — the reference to the subject is always present in the verb-ending.

In coding the items for VAC I have utilized the following approach:

1. -For verb-agreement:
   a.- As already set forth in the introduction only seventy occurrences per dialect, i.e., a total of two hundred and ten, have been analyzed.
   b.- Only verbs which allow an explicit subject have been considered, so that verbs like *llover* 'rain', *hacer calor* 'be warm', etc., are not included in the

analysis, as they only occur subjectless.

c.- Verbs which appear in 3rd-person plural, without an explicit preceding referent, i.e., those which correspond to an impersonal construction as, for example, *dicen* 'they say', have also been disregarded. 3rd-person plural forms which clearly have an antecedent, hence are not impersonal, are included in the analysis.

d.- The forms *hay*, *había*, etc., 'there is, was, etc.', are not analyzed in this section, but fall into a separate class of existential/presentatives which is examined in section 1.6.

e.- In assigning a value for the parameter DISTANCE I have arbitrarily attributed a value of 1 (one) to those verbs which refer to actions narrated in more than one of the preceding clauses. These verbs are *ser* 'be', *suceder* 'happen', *pasar* 'occur', and the like. Thus, in (3e) below *fue* 'was, happened' refers to the actions expressed in (a), (c) and (d), but the total value is one and not four.

(3) a.   La   convenció,
            her   convince-IND-PAST-3 sg.

      b.   dice
            say-IND-PRES-3 sg.

      c.   que arrendó   un   auto
            that rent-IND-PAST-3 sg. a   car

      d.   y se la   llevó   a Mejillones.
            and her   take-IND-PAST-3 sg.   to Mejillones

      e.   *Fue*   el   día   sábado ...
            be-IND-PAST-3sg. the   day   saturday

'He convinced her, says that he rented a car and took her to Mejillones. It happened on a Saturday ...'

2.- For clitics:

a.- When the possessive *su* 'his/her sg.', *sus* 'his/her pl.' appears – as is often the case – in the same clause of the possessor I have assigned to this item the value 1 (one) for DISTANCE, since it has been established (cf. Introduction, p. 6) that there are no zeros insofar as this parameter is concerned. Thus, in example (4b) *su* 'his' has been attributed the value of 1 in the analysis of DISTANCE:

(4) a.   Cuando terminó   su carrera   de
           when   finish-IND-Past-3 sg. his career   of
           bachillerato
           high-school

     b.   le   dijo   a *su*   papá . . .
           to-him   sau-IND-PAST-3 sg. to his   daddy
           'When he finished his high school, he said to his daddy. . .'

   b.- The clitic *lo* has not been counted when it occurs as a predicate in a
   copulative construction, because I have not analyzed any predicate in such
   constructions, but only the copula itself. An example of the mentioned
   lo is given in (5):

(5) a.   . . . no podemos   decir
                 not can-IND-PRES-1 pl. say-INF

     b.   que sean   rusos
           that be-SUBJ—PRES-3 pl.   Russian

     c.   aunque *lo* son   de nacimiento . . .
           although   be-IND-PRES-3 pl. by birth
           'We cannot say they are Russian, although they are so by birth . . .'

Lo has, however, been taken into account when it functions as an accusative and
refers either to a nominal or pronominal antecedent or to a sentential clause.

   c.- Reflexive or pseudo-reflexive clitics – as in (6) and (7) – are not present
   in the analysis:

(6)   . . . él *se*   bañaba
               he   himself bath-IND-IMPF-3 sg.
               '. . . he was bathing himself . . .'

(7)   El *se* sentó . . .
          he   seat-IND-PAST-3 sg.
          'He sat . . .'

In Spanish, verb-agreement and clitics are in complementary distribution, as
the first only refers to subjects and the second only to non-subjects. Note that
clitics only function as accusative, dative and genitive; oblique cases require a
preposition and a stressed pronoun.

Verb-agreement and clitics can be utilized to refer both to HUMAN and

NON-HUMAN topics-NP's, as is shown in (8) and (9). (8) demonstrates how a combination of verb-agreement and clitics is utilized by a speaker in order to maintain the reference to the same HUMAN topic-NP through a chain of sixteen clauses (recalling that relative clauses are not counted as separate):

(8) a.   ... no porque *Charlie* se
             not because Charlie   himself
             hubiese   perdido ...
             have-SUBJ-PAST-3 sg. lost

     b.   sino porque justamente *hubiera*
            but   because really   have-SUBJ-PAST-3 sg.
            podido   quedarse   más   tiempo ...
            can-PART-PAST   stay-INF   more   time

     c.   porque   ya   no   *estaba*   haciendo
            because   yet   not be-IND-IMPF-3 sg. doing
            nada   especial,
            nothing   special

     d.   bueno, sí, *estaba*   aprendiendo
            well   yes be-IND-IMPF-3 sg.   learning
            idiomas,   [que eso   nunca   es tiempo perdido.]
            languages [which   never   is time   lost   ]

     e.   Bueno, *regresó,*
            well   return-IND-PAST-3 sg.

     f.   *empezó*   a trabajar   con *su*   papá
            begin-IND-PAST-3 sg.   to work-INF with his   daddy

     g.   y   *trajo*   muchas   ideas respecto
            and bring-IND-PAST-3 sg.   many   ideas in regard
            a investigar   el   sur   de   Venezuela
            to investigate-INF the   south of   Venezuela

     i.   y   allí   *empezó,*   pues, *sus*
            and there begin-IND-PAST-3 sg. then his
            aventuras ...
            adventures

     j.   *Era*   un   muchacho, para esa
            be-IND-IMPF-3sg.   a   boy   for   that
            época,   sumamente inquieto:
            time   extremely active

k.   *le*   gustaba   escalar,
      him   like-IND-IMPF-3sg.   climb-INF

l.   *le*   "   nadar,
      him   swim-INF

m. *le*   "   investigación,
      him   (the) investigation

n.   no   *podía*   quedar*se*   ni   un
      not   be able-IND-IMPF-3 sg.   remain-INF   not   a
      minuto   tranquilo.
      minute   quiet

o.   Allí   *empezó*   *sus*   actividades
      there   start-IND-PAST-3 sg.   his   activities

p.   y   *se encontró*   con   el   padre   D.B.,
      and   meet-IND-PAST-3 sg.   with the   father   D.B.
      el   vasco, [de] los   Petit Frères,
      the   basque [of] the   Petit Frères,
      [que pertenecen   a una   congregación
      [who belong-IND-PRES-3 pl. to a   congregation
      que   está   en el   sur,   unos
      that be-IND-PRES-3 sg. in the   south   some
      misioneros, pues,]
      missionaries   ]

q.   y   con él   *hizo*   *sus*   primeros
      and   with him make-IND-PAST-3 sg.   his   first
      contactos con los   indios [que   él ya
      contacts   with the   Indians, [that he already
      te   habrá   hablado.]
      to-you have-IND-FUT-3 sg. spoken   ]

'. . . not because Charlie would have been lost – he really could have stayed longer – but he wasn't doing anything special. Well, he was learning languages which is never wasted time. Well, he returned and began to work with his daddy and brought many ideas regarding the investigation of the south of Venezuela, and there his adventures began . . . At that time he was an extremely active boy: he liked to climb, he liked to swim, he liked to investigate, he could not remain quiet for a minute. There he started his activities, and met Father D.B., the basque, [of] the *Petits Frères*, some missionaries, a congregation which was in the south, and with him he made his first contacts with the Indians, about which he must have already talked to you.'

In (8) the topic-NP is only fully mentioned in the first clause (a), and then is referred to by means of verb-agreement (b - j and n - q) and the clitic *le* in (k - m). In fact, the clarity of the message is never threatened: the other two HUMAN participants — *su papá* 'his daddy' in (f), and *el padre D.B.* 'the father D.B.' in (p) — are both introduced at a very low level, in an oblique case, so that they cannot compete with the referent for subjecthood. In (k - m) equally the clitic *le* can only refer to the subject of the last verb *era* 'was' in (j); it is noteworthy that in these three clauses the topic-NP shifts from subject to dative, but the verb *gustar* 'like' does not offer alternative constructions. In this case dative is semantically very much like a subject, and in fact in these constructions (and in others similar) dative ranks higher than the grammatical subject, in terms of animacy. In (q) we find a stressed pronoun *él* 'he' in the relative clause, but its presence does not seem due to the necessity of reaffirming the topic-NP, but rather to a contrastive situation (cf. section 3) between what *he* — Charlie, the topic-NP — must already have told to the same interviewer in a preceding session and what the speaker — Charlie's mother — is presently telling the interviewer. After (q) the same topic-NP is referred to again only by means of VAC for eleven more clauses, until there is a full mention of his name, in a left-dislocated structure, because the theme changes: the mother switches from Charlie's adventures to his professional career and success. (8) and its continuation, which is omitted here for sake of brevity, is thus a demonstration of how a weak strategy like VAC can be used to maintain an uninterrupted reference to a HUMAN topic-NP along a chain of twenty-seven clauses (sixteen in (8) and eleven not presented here).

In the data there are no examples of NON-HUMAN topic-NP's comparable in length to those of HUMAN topic-NP's, but this is obviously a limitation due to the sample, as in other texts where the topics are either ANIMATE but NON-HUMAN or INANIMATE such long chains are likely to appear. In the present corpus the maximum number of clauses I have found with NON-HUMAN topic-NP is five. (9) is an example of a NON-HUMAN topic-NP — the Mexican *rebozo* 'shawl' — which is first fully mentioned in (a), and then referred to by verb-agreement (*fue* 'was') in (d) and by the Accusative clitic *lo* 'it' in (e):

(9)　a.　　Yo,　cuando　fui　　　　　　de viaje ·
　　　　　　I　　when　　go-IND-PAST-1 sg.　on (a) trip
　　　　　　al　　　Oriente,
　　　　　　to-the　East

b.   llevé   uno   [rebozo],
     take-IND-PAST-1 sg.   one   [shawl]
c.   y   no   sabes
     and   not   know-IND-PRES-2 sg.
d.   *fue*   el   gran   éxito,   así
     be-IND-PAST-1 sg.   the   big   success   thus
e.   *lo* tuve   que   regalar.
     it have-IND-PAST-1 sg.   to   donate-INF
'When I went to the East, I brought one and you don't know: it was a big
success, I had to give it away.'

The figures relative to VAC are presented in Table 1, p. 30.

1.2. Stressed pronouns

In the analysis of stressed pronouns (henceforth SP), which appear to closely follow VAC in the scale of continuity, I have taken into account:

a.- Personal pronouns as *él* 'he' and corresponding forms of the feminine
    and plural (*ella, ellos, ellas*).
b.- Demonstratives, as *éste* 'this', *aquél* 'that', *ése* 'that', and their corres-
    ponding feminine and plural forms.

Stressed pronouns can be found in any function, as Table 2 (p. 31) demonstrates, and for HUMAN and NON-HUMAN topic-NP as well, even though they
are used more frequently for HUMAN than NON-HUMAN, but again, as observed in 1.1., this may well be due to the texts analyzed. (10) is an example
of SP's which refer to a HUMAN topic-NP and (11) shows SP's referring to
NON-HUMAN topic-NP's:

(10) SP: HUMAN, Subject and Oblique/
      a.   ... y   el doctor M.L. era   un
                and   doctor M.L. be-IND-IMPF-3 sg. a
            estudiante de medicina
            student   of medicine
            [que vivía   en frente,]
            who   live-IND-IMPF-3 sg.   in front]

b. *él* y   sus   amigos venían   a
    he and his   friends come-IND-IMPF-3 pl. to
    casa de mi   mamá,
    home of my   mom

c. mi   mamá   estudiaba   *con ellos,*
    my   mom   study-IND-IMPF-3 sg. with them

d. porque *ella* les   traducía   a
    because she   them translate-IND-IMPF-3 sg.
    Testut; . . .
    Testut

'. . . and doctor M.L. was a student of medicine who lived in the front,
and he and his friends would come to my mother's house, my mother
would study with them, because she could translate Testut for them . . .'

(11) /SP: NON-HUMAN, ANIMATE, Subject/
    a. Fíjese . . . si será   listo   el
        look   if be-IND-FUT-3 sg. smart the
        animal-ito
        animal-DIMINUTIVE

    b. que   cuando me-voy   a tomar   mi
        that when   go-IND-PRES-1 sg. to drink   my
        chato,
        drink

    c. ya   sabe
        already know-IND-PRES-3 sg.

    d. que *él* tiene   que   manejar, . . .
        that he have-IND-PRES-3 sg. to   drive-INF
        'Look . . . the animal$_i$ is so smart . . . that when I'm going to get a
        drink, he$_i$ knows that he$_i$ has to 'drive', . . .'

In (12) the SP *eso* 'that' refers to the whole of the preceding clause:

(12) /SP: NON-HUMAN, NON-ANIMATE, Accusative/
    a. . . . mi prima   estudió   IBM
            my cousin-f. study-IND-PAST-3 sg. IBM

    b. estudió   una   escuela [que hay en
        study-IND-PAST-3 sg. a   school   [that is   in

la   Avenida Bulnes,   que es
the   Avenida Bulnes   which   be-IND-PRES-3 sg.
como   . . .   intérprete,]
like   interpreter]
c.   estudió   *eso*, . . .
study-IND-PAST-3 sg. that
'. . . my cousin studied IBM, she studied in a school that is located in the
Avenida Bulnes, and is like an interpreter school, she studied that. . .'

There are no examples (cf. Table 2, p. 33) of NON-HUMAN Dative and
Genitive stressed pronouns, but only of Subject, Accusative and Oblique, even
though not in great quantity. Very few of these occurrences refer to an entity of
the real world, most of them – like *eso* in (12) – refer to something mentioned
in the preceding clauses, or anticipate what is going to occur in the next
clause(s).

It is necessary to observe that in may instances the presence of SP is due to
a contrastive situation or to switch-reference, and not really to the necessity of
disambiguating the referent, as (13) and (14) exemplify:

(13) /SP: HUMAN, Subject/
a.   . . . mi abuelo   era   hijo de
. . . my grandfather   be-IND-IMPF-3 sg.   son   of
ese   tipo
that   fellow
[que no   quería   que sus
[that not   want-IND-IMPF-3 sg.   that his
hijos   aprendieran   a leer]
children   learn-SUBJ-PAST-3 pl.   to read-INF]
b.   y   *él* sí   aprendió   a leer
and he yet   learn-IND-PAST-3 sg.   to read-INF
por   su   propria voluntad   y   por recuerdos
for   his   own   will   and   for   recollections
de su   madre, . . .
of his   mother
'. . . my grandfather$_i$ was the son of that fellow who did not want his
children to learn to read, but he$_i$ learned to read because of his own determination and the recollections of his mother, . . .'

(14) /SP: HUMAN, Subject/

a. . . . y   él$_i$ vivía   allá   solo
        and he$_i$ live-IND-PAST-3 sg.   there alone

b. y   había   que   estar- le$_i$
        and   have-IND-IMPF-3 sg.   to   be-INF-him
        mandando dinero   todos los   meses
        send-GER money   every   month

c. para pagar su$_i$ departamento y   todas
        to   pay-INF his   apartment   and   all
        sus$_i$ cosas,
        his   things

d. y se cerró   la   Universidad
        and   close-IND-PAST-3 sg.   the   University

e. y   pasaron   dos   o tres   meses
        and   pass by-IND-PAST-3 pl.   two   or three   months
        que la   Universidad   estaba   cerrada,
        that the   University   be-IND-IMPF-3 sg.   closed

f. y   él estaba
        and   he be-IND-IMPF-3 sg.

g. sin   hacer   nada   allá.
        without do-INF anything   there

'. . . and he was living there alone and it was necessary to send him money
every month in order to pay for his apartment and all his expenses, and the
University closed and two or three months passed by during which the
University remained closed, and he was there without doing anything. . .'

In (13) the contrast is between what the father of the grandfather thought
– namely that his children should not learn how to read – and what to the
contrary his own son did, i.e., learned how to read in spite of his father's opin-
ion. The contrast triggers the presence of the stressed pronoun *él* 'he' in (b) and
it is reinforced by the presence of *sí* 'yes'. In this situation – as is also the case
with first-person subject pronouns (cf. Bentivoglio, 1980) – an explicit subject
– either a pronoun or a noun – is obligatory. In (14) the second stressed pronoun *él* 'he' in (f) seems to be due to the switching of the reference from the
last subject – *la Universidad* 'the University' in (e) – to the topic-NP of (a)
through (c) (*él* 'he', *le* him, *su*, *sus* 'his'). In fact, in this sequence of clauses there
are no other HUMAN NP's which can compete for the role of subject of (f)
and (g), so that apparently the only reason which justifies the presence of *él*

'he' in (f) is the change of reference. It seems to me that in a more in-depth analysis, with a more extended text, it would be necessary to separate the instances of SP due to contrast and switch-reference from those due to other reasons, or, even better, to measure the combined effect of these two factors on the presence of SP.

1.3. Stressed pronouns or NP's and coreferential clitics

In all Spanish dialects a Dative SP or NP is obligatorily preceded by a coreferential clitic, as in (15), while for Accusative there is a consistent dialectal difference (cf. Bentivoglio, 1978): all dialects show a coreferential clitic in the case of SP, whereas with NP some dialects (Argentina, for example) may have such clitics but others (Venezuela, for example) do not allow a clitic coreferential to a following NP. In order to account for this characteristic of Spanish, I have separated this construction (CC = coreferential clitic) from the unstressed pronouns on the one hand, and stressed pronouns or NP's on the other, analyzing separately all those cases in which Dative and Accusative SP's or NP's have a coreferential clitic in the same clause, as (15) - (20) exemplify:

(15) /CC: HUMAN NP, Accusative (Mexico)/
    . . . *le*   saluda   *al*   *policía* . . .
    him   greet-IND-PRES-3 sg. the policeman
    '. . . he greets the policeman . . .'

(16) /CC: HUMAN SP, Accusative/
    . . . unos lo hacían   simplemente por
    some it do-IND-IMPF-3 pl. simply   to
    complacer-*lo* *a él*, . . .
    please-him   him
    '. . . some simply did it in order to please him, . . .'

(17) /CC: NON-HUMAN NP, Accusative (Chile)/
    . . . y *una* *parte* de este aceite   *lo*
    and a   part of this oil   it
    tomó . . .
    drink-IND-PAST-3 sg.
    '. . . and she drank a portion of this oil . . .'

(18) /CC: HUMAN NP, Dative/
    . . . él *le* dijo   *a su* *papá* . . .
    he him say-IND-PAST-3 sg. to his daddy
    '. . . he said to his daddy . . .'

(19) /CC: HUMAN SP, Dative/
    . . . *le*   decía   cosas   bellas
        to-her say-IND-IMPF-3 sg. things   beautiful
        a   *ella*, . . .
        to   her
        '. . . he used to say to her beautiful things . . .'

(20) /CC: NON-HUMAN NP, Dative/
    . . . y   él no   *le*   hizo   nada
        and he not   to-it   do-IND-PAST-3 sg.   anything
        al   *caballo*; . . .
        to-the   horse
        '. . . and he didn't do anything to the horse; . . .'

In the data there are no instances of clitics coreferential to NON-HUMAN SP's, either Dative or Accusative. It is also to be noted that the four NON-HUMAN CC's found in the data (cf. Table 3b) are all cases similar to example (17), in which the NP precedes the clitics, thus making the presence of the clitic obligatory.

1.4. Definite NP's

Definite NP's (henceforth DEFNP) have been divided into three groups; i) those with only the definite article *el, la* 'the m. f. sg.' and *los, las* 'the m. f. pl.'; ii) those which are modified by a demonstrative, a possessive, a genitive or an adjective, or by any combination of the four; iii) those which are modified by a relative clause. Examples of each case are given in the corresponding sub-sections, infra. and the corresponding results are shown in Tables 4, 5, 6 and 7.

1.4.1. Non-modified definite NP's

In the analysis I have not taken into account those instances of article plus noun in lexiealized expressions such as:

     i.- *El hecho es* 'the fact is', *el caso es* 'the case is', *la verdad es* 'the truth is', and the like;
     ii.- *En, por la noche* 'at night', etc.;
     iii.- *Salir a la calle, a la playa* 'go out to the road, to the beach', *caer al suelo* 'to fall to the floor', etc.;

iv.- *Deshacer el camino* 'to go back', *pasa el tiempo* 'the time goes by',
etc.
v.- *Llegar a la conclusión* 'to get to the conclusion', etc.

All the examples given in i-v are present in the data.
(21) and (22) are examples of Non-modified NP's (henceforth NM-NP),
HUMAN and NON-HUMAN, respectively:

(21) /NM-NP: HUMAN, Subject/
> . . . entonces *el*   *señor*   le   dio
>   then   the   gentleman   him   hit-IND-PAST-3 sg.
>   por   detrás . . .
>   from   behind
> '. . . then the gentleman hit him from behind . . .'

(22) /NM-NP: NON-HUMAN, Subject/
> . . . *el* *coche*   no   estaba   en muy
>   the car   not   be-IND-IMPF-3 sg.   in very
>   buenas   condiciones . . .
>   good   conditions
> '. . . the car was not in very good conditions . . .'

For sake of brevity I will not give examples of NM-NP's in the non-subject
functions, but it is clear that they exist in the data (cf. Table 5).

1.4.2. Modified definite NP's

Modified NP's (henceforth M-NP's) may be modified by a demonstrative,
as in (22), a possessive, as in (23), a genitive, as in (24), an adjective, as in (25),
or by different combinations of demonstrative plus an adjective, etc., as in (25)
and (26).

(23) /M-NP: HUMAN, Subject, with demonstrative/
> . . . y   creyó   *esta* *señora*. . .
>   and believe-IND-PAST-3 sg. this   lady
> '. . . and this lady believed that . . .'

(24) /M-NP: HUMAN, Accusative, with possessive/
> . . . se fue   ella   a   visitar   a *su*
>   go-IND-PAST-3 sg.   she   to visit-INF   her

marido, . . .
husband
'. . . she went to visit her husband . . .'

(25) /M-NP: HUMAN, Dative, with Genitive/
    . . . le   iba   a decir   *al*
    to-him go-IND-IMPF-3 sg. to say-INF to-the
    marido   de la   señora . . .
    husband of the   lady
    '. . . she was going to say to the lady's husband . . .'

(26) /M-NP: HUMAN, Subject, with adjective/
    . . . se sentó   *la   pobre   señora,* ahí . . .
    seat-IND-PAST-3sg. the   poor   lady   there
    '. . . the poor lady sat there . . .'

(27) /M-NP: NON-HUMAN, Accusative, with adjective and demonstrative/
    . . . pero no se   mandó   a
    but   not for-himself order-IND-PAST-3 sg. to
    hacer   *el   nuevo aparato   ese*; . . .
    make-INF the new   apparatus that
    '. . . but he did not have that new apparatus made for himself . . .'

(28) /M-NP: NON-HUMAN, Oblique, with possessive and adjective/
    . . . ellas   se sienten   espléndidas *con*
    they-f.   feel-IND-PRES-3 pl. splendid   with
    sus   estudios superiores.
    their   studies superior
    '. . . they feel splendid with their superior studies . . .'

In the data (cf. Table 6, p. 38), there are NON-HUMAN occurrences equivalent to those given in (23) to (26), as well as HUMAN cases equivalent to those exemplified in (27) and (28). It is clear that in a more extended analysis it would be advisable to examine separately all types of M-NP's, as they show different degrees in regard to continuity. Because of time and space limitations the suggested analytical approach has not been undertaken in this paper.

1.4.3. Definite NP's modified by a relative clause
    There are not many instances of this type in the data, but nevertheless the division seems appropriate, in light of the results of Tables 5, 6, and 7 (pp. 37, 38, 39) which will be compared and commented upon, infra. (29) and (30) are examples of HUMAN and NON-HUMAN Definite NP's modified by a relative

clause (henceforth RC-NP):

(29) /RC-NP: HUMAN, Subject/

... *este*	*médico,*	[que	era		el	médico
this	doctor	[who	be-IND-IMPF-3 sg.		the	doctor
internista,	medico	de barrio,]			le	
internist	doctor	of neighborhood]			to-her	
había		dado a	mi	madre		
have-IND-IMPF-3 sg.		given to	my	mother		
una taza . . .						
a cup						

'. . . this doctor, who was the internist, the neighborhood doctor,
had given my mother a cup. . .'

(30) /RC-NP: NON-HUMAN, Accusative/

... él	tiene		que	hacer	...
he	have-IND-PRES-3 sg.		to	prepare-INF	
la	*ruta*	[que	va		a seguir
the	route	[that	go-IND-PRES-3 sg.		to follow
el	avión,] ...				
the	plane]				

'. . . he has to prepare the route that the plane is going to follow, . . . '

The NP modified by a relative clause also may be modified by a demonstrative, as in (29), a possessive or an adjective.

1.5. Names

All names have been analyzed collectively, regardless of their structural differences, i.e.:

a.- The name of a person, either first (*Charlie, Isabel*) or last names (*Guzmán, Freud*), or both (*Anna Freud*); of a place, from a street (*Candelaria*) to cities (*Nueva York* 'New York'), countries (*Alemania* 'Germany', *México*) and continents (*Europa* 'Europe'); of a church, a building, a school (*San Cosme*);

b.- A name preceded by the definite article: *la Universidad* 'the University' (a college), *el Mayorazgo* (a school), *el Pedregal* (a place), *la Colonia* (a historical period), *la O.P.E.P., la Internacional* (associations), *el Orinoco* (a river), etc.;

c.- A name with pre- or post-modifiers: *calcio Sandoz* 'calcium Sandoz', *la doctora von Ryman* 'doctor-f. von Ryman', *el padre F.* 'Father F.', *el gran Brasil* 'the great Brazil', etc.

Some examples are given in (31) to (36), infra:

(31) /Name: HUMAN, Subject/
  ... *Freud* tuvo   que salir   también
    Freud have-IND-PRES-3 sg. to   leave-INF also
    de   Alemania . . .
    from Germany
    '. . . also Freud had to leave Germany . . .'

(32) /Name: NON-HUMAN, Subject/
    Realmente *el*   *Brasil* está   poblado
    really   the   Brazil be-IND-PRES-3 sg. populated
    en la   costa; . . .
    in the   coast
    'Really Brazil is populated along the coast; . . .'

(33) /Name: HUMAN, Accusative/
    Conoció   *a Fromm*, . . .
    meet-IND-PAST-3 sg. Fromm
    'He met Fromm, . . .'

(34) /Name: NON-HUMAN, Accusative/
    ... cuando conquistaron   los españoles
      when   conquer-IND-PAST-3 pl. the Spaniards
    México, . . .
    Mexico
    '. . . when the Spaniards conquered Mexico, . . .'

(35) /Name: HUMAN, Oblique/
    ... porque hizo   la revolicíon
      because make-IND-PAST-3 sg. the revolution
    junto   *con Guzmán*, . . .
    together with Guzman
    '. . . because he made the revolution with Guzmán, . . .'

(36) /Name: NON-HUMAN, Oblique/
        Entonces   ella   se vino   *para   Caracas* . . .
        then   she   come-IND-PAST-3 sg. to   Caracas
        'Then she came to Caracas . . .'

The numeric results are shown in Table 8, p. 43

1.6. Existentials and presentatives
    This section examplifies those constructions characterized by:

     a.- The special forms of the verb *haber: hay, había, habrá, hubo,*
     habría, etc. 'there is, was, will be, was, could be, etc.';
     b.- Existential verbs as *ser* and *estar* 'be', *existir* 'exist', etc.
     c.- Presentative verbs as *llegar, venir,* 'arrive', 'come', *salir* 'come out',
     entrar 'enter', and the like.

It is a characteristic of Spanish (and all other subject-first languages, cf.
Givón, 1979: 72) that constructions as those characterized in a, b, and c, supra,
the unmarked word-order is V-S, and the marked S-V (for Spanish, cf. Bentivoglio and D'Introno, 1978).
    In view of the fact that existentials and presentatives (henceforth EP) occur
either with definite or indefinite NP's, this category has been subdivided as
follows: i) with a definite subject (henceforth DEF-EP), and ii) with an indefinite subject (henceforth INDF-EP). Examples for (i) are given in (37) to (42),
and for (ii) in (43) to (47), and the results are presented in Table 9, p. 44.

(37) /DEF-EP: HUMAN/
        Luego   *hay*   la   otra   chica, . . .
        then   there-is   the   other   gal
        'Then, there is the other gal, . . .'
(38) /DEF-EP: NON-HUMAN/
        . . . *hubo*   los   primeros   acuerdos y   las
            there-were   the   first   agreements and   the
        primeras   intervenciones de los   países
        first   interventions of the   countries
        productores . . .
        producing
        '. . . there were the first agreements and the first interventions of
        the producing countries . . .'

(39) /DEF-EP: HUMAN/

   . . . *estuvieron*   también las   hermanas
       be-IND-PAST-3 pl.   also   the   sisters
   del   novio, . . .
   of-the   fiancé
   '. . . there were also the fiancé's sisters, . . .'

(40) /DEF-EP: NON-HUMAN/

   . . . entonces, *está*   la   gruta . . .
       then   be-IND-PRES-3 sg. the   cave
   '. . . then there is the cave . . .'

(41) /DEF-EP: HUMAN/

   . . . en 1950 *llegó*   a México aquí
       in 1950 arrive-IND-PAST-3 sg. to Mexico here
   el   doctor Fromm . . .
   the   doctor Fromm
   '. . . in 1950 Doctor Fromm arrived in Mexico . . .'

(42) /DEF-EP: NON-HUMAN/

   . . . pero   entonces   *vino*   la
       but   then   come-IND-PAST-3 sg. the
   persecución   judía . . .
   persecution   jewish
   '. . . but then the persecution of the Jews occurred . . .'

In examining the specific examples of DEF-EP's, it is clear that these Subjects are already known to the hearer. Consider, for example, (37), supra: the speaker — a mother — is talking about her daughters and says that they are 'old', and that one of them has already graduated in Spanish Literature. Afterwards, she utters the DEF-EP examplified in (37): it is true that the speaker has not yet said anything about this daughter — *la otra chica* 'the other girl' — but it is also true that the hearer already knows that there is more than one daughter, since the speaker-mother has said previously *ya están viejas mis hijas* 'They are already old, my daughters'. It seems to me that Spanish EP's with a definite subject are not analogous to the English constructions "in which the subject is definite but constitutes a *surprise* information" (Givón, 1979: 73). There is no surprise in (37), nor in other DEF-EP constructions found in the data.

    Some support to the fact that DEF-EP's are very different from INDF-EP's is given by the types of verbs with which they co-occur, respectively: the typical verb for INDF-EP's is *hay, había*, 'there is, was', etc., whereas there are almost no occurrences of this verb with DEF-EP's, most of which appear with verbs of 'entrance into the scene' as *llegar, venir* 'come', *regresar* 'return' or *quedarse* 'remain'. Examples of INDF-EP's with verbs of 'entrance into the scene' or 're-main' are quite rare.

(43) to (47) exemplify the use of EP's with indefinite subjects, which are less numerous than those with a definite subject:

(43) /INDF-EP: HUMAN/

    ... *hay*   un   hombre con un caballo ahí.

    there-is a   man   with a horse   there

    'There is a man with a horse in that place.'

(44) /INDF-EP: NON-HUMAN/

    ... *había*   un   espejo en un   ropero grande, ...

    there-was a   mirror in a   armoir large

    '... there was a mirror in a large armoir ...'

(45) /INDF-EP: NON-HUMAN/

    ... *estaban*   unas   tablas, ...

    be-IND-IMPF-3 pl. some   lumber

    '... there was (some) lumber ...'

(46) /INDF-EP: HUMAN/

    ... *sale*   una señora por allá

    come-out-IND-PRES-3 sg. a   lady   for there

    arriba ...

    up

    '... from there a lady came out ...'

(47) /INDF-EP: NON-HUMAN/

    Vino   una ambulancia.

    arrive-IND-PAST-3 sg. an   ambulance

    'An ambulance arrived.'

In the data there are no indefinite cases with HUMAN subjects with the verbs *ser, estar* 'be' and only two cases with verbs such as *llegar, venir* 'come, arrive'. This does not mean that such constructions are impossible in Spanish, only that no examples have been found. We could infer from this observation that though possible they must nevertheless be rather infrequent, at least in spoken language.

1.7. Word-order

    Examples of S-V and V-S orders have been given already in (21) and (31),

and in (23), (26) and (34), respectively. Nevertheless let us consider additional
occurrences of both orders:

(48) /V-S and S-V: HUMAN, Definite Subject/
     a.   . . . no *son*   suficientes *los*
             not be-IND-PRES-3 pl. sufficient the
             fiscales del   Ministerio de Fomento
             inspectors of-the Ministry of Production
     b.   o *los fiscales*   no *son*   lo
             or the inspectors not be-IND-PRES-3 pl. the
             suficientemente eficientes . . .
             sufficiently   efficient
     '. . . the Ministry of Production's inspectors are not sufficient (in num-
ber) or they are not sufficiently efficient . . .'

(49) /S-V and V-S: HUMAN, Definite Subject/
     a.   . . . *el hombre andaba*   bebido
             the man   go-IND-IMPF-3 sg. drunk
     b.   — *es*   una falta andar ebrio —
             be-IND-PRES-3 sg. a   fault go-INF drunk
     c.   *se-enoja*   *el hombre,* . . .
             get angry-IND-PRES-3 sg. the man
     '. . . the man was drunk — it is a fault to go around drunk — the man gets
angry . . .'

(50) /S-V: NON-HUMAN, Definite Subject/
     a.   . . . no quiso   volver-se a Uruguay
             not want-IND-PAST-3 sg.   return-INF to Uruguay
     b.   porque *la Universidad seguía*
             because the University continue-IND-IMPF-3 sg.
             cerrada, . . .
             closed
     '. . . he did not want to return to Uruguay, because the University was still
closed . . .'

(51) /V-S: NON-HUMAN, Definite Subject/
     a.   . . . habían   problemas en la   Universidad, . . .
             there-were problems in the   University

b.   y   *se-cerró*   *la*   *Universidad, . . .*
      and   close-IND-PAST-3 sg.   the   University
'. . . there were problems in the University, and the University closed, . . .'

The figures obtained for both word-orders are presented in Table 10, p. 45.

2. Numeric results and tables

In this section I will present the numeric results, i.e., the ratios obtained by application of the methodology set forth in the Introduction, pp. 5-9. These tables are presented in the same sequence as the examples to which they relate in section 1. The discussion relevant to each linguistic device and its corresponding table(s) of results will appear in the same sub-section.

2.1. Verb-agreement and unstressed pronouns

Table 1, infra, reveals the following:

i.- DISTANCE: there is almost no difference between HUMAN and NON-HUMAN verb-agreement cases; they tend to occur very close to the previous mention of their referent, with an average distance of one and a third clauses. Dative HUMAN clitics also show a pattern very similar — predictably — to that of verb-agreement (1.43 as opposed to 1.31), whereas the few occurrences of NON-HUMAN Dative cases do not allow any inferences. The most noticeable difference (0.23) is found between HUMAN and NON-HUMAN clitics, which are both more discontinuous than all other cases, the highest point of discontinuity being attained by HUMAN clitics with an average of almost two clauses back (actually 1.79). Genitive, for which only HUMAN cases are present, shows the highest degree of continuity, with an average of 1.07.

ii.- DECAY: all HUMAN topics tend to persist in the following clauses much longer than any equivalent NON-HUMAN; the most dramatic difference of almost one and a half clauses is due to verb-agreement, followed by Accusative clitics, and finally by Dative clitics. Genitive cannot be compared as there are no such cases for NON-HUMAN. Considering the two parameters of DISTANCE and DECAY together we can affirm that the reference to a HUMAN topic-NP is expected to last almost twice as long as that of NON-HUMAN, realizing of course that the parameter which really marks this difference is DECAY and not DISTANCE.

iii.- AMBIGUITY: the only difference which is worthy of mention is that

between HUMAN and NON-HUMAN Accusative clitics, where it seems
that clitics referring to HUMAN are more ambiguous. This is easily understandable when it is recognized that the morphology of most of the
NON-HUMAN clitics − i.e., *lo* 'it' − is totally unambiguous, if there are
no HUMAN masculine referents which can claim the reference.

			NON-SUBJECT		
		SUBJECT	ACCUSAT.	DATIVE	GENITIVE
DISTANCE	HUMAN	1.31 (210)	1.79 (80)	1.43 (107)	1.07 (55)
DISTANCE	NON-HUMAN	1.29 (118)	1.56 (57)	2.8 (5)	
DECAY	HUMAN	2.18 (210)	1.44 (80)	1.1 (107)	2.4 (55)
DECAY	NON-HUMAN	0.64 (118)	0.63 (57)	0.6 (5)	
AMBIGUITY	HUMAN	1.09 (210)	1.26 (80)	1.21 (107)	1.15 (55)
AMBIGUITY	NON-HUMAN	1.03 (118)	1.07 (57)	1.4 (5)	

TABLE 1: Verb Agreement and unstressed pronouns (VAC)

2.2. Stressed pronouns

Henceforth the results will take into account word-order (hereafter WO),
as the different position of the topic-NP with respect to the verb is relevant to
the discussion of the continuity/discontinuity scale presented in 2.7.

If we consider the results of Table 2, below, in terms of each parameter, we
may observe the following:

i.- DISTANCE: there is only a small difference — less than a clause — between S-V and V-S HUMAN Subjects. Unfortunately the examples of V-S order are very few (only eleven) and thus do not allow much speculation;

| | | SUBJECT | | NON-SUBJECTS | | | | | | |
| | | S-V | V-S | ACCUSATIVE | | DATIVE | | GENITIVE | OBLQ. |
				V-ACC	ACC-V	V-DAT	DAT-V		
DISTANCE	HUMAN	2.05 (107)	1.64 (11)	—	1.0 (1)	1.0 (5)	1.0 (1)	1.3 (10)	1.5 (16)
DISTANCE	NON-HUMAN	1.38 (26)	—	1.5 (6)	—	—	—	—	1.79 (14)
DECAY	HUMAN	1.93 (107)	4.0 (11)	—	2.0 (1)	2.2 (5)	0.0 (1)	1.1 (10)	0.75 (16)
DECAY	NON HUMAN	1.15 (26)	—	1.33 (6)	—	—	—	—	1.21 (14)
AMBIGUITY	HUMAN	1.26 (107)	1.27 (11)	—	1.0 (1)	1.2 (5)	2.0 (1)	1.1 (10)	1.06 (16)
AMBIGUITY	NON-HUMAN	1.19 (26)		1.17 (6)	—	—	—	—	1.07 (14)

TABLE 2: Stressed Pronouns (SP)

nevertheless, the fact that postverbal subject pronouns show a greater degree of continuity than preverbal correlates with the findings illustrated in Table 10 (p. 45), in which postverbal DEFNP's and Names also show a greater degree of continuity. As for this parameter there is a difference (0.67) between HUMAN and NON-HUMAN Subjects, and a smaller one (only 0.29) between HUMAN and NON-HUMAN Obliques;

ii.- DECAY: postverbal HUMAN pronominal Subjects show a much smaller rate of decay than preverbal, the difference being a little more than two clauses (2.07). This result again correlates with those presented in Table 10. If we consider together the two parameters of DISTANCE and DE-CAY, we observe that there is a significant difference in terms of persist-ence between HUMAN and NON-HUMAN pronominal subjects: the for-mer may last through four and a half clauses, if we sum up the parameters DISTANCE and DECAY, whereas the latter barely reach an average of two and a half clauses. It is worth noting that pronouns following the verb tend to be closer to their referent than vice versa, but their rate of DECAY is more than twice as much when compared to that of pronouns which precede the verb.

iii.- AMBIGUITY: word-order does not seem to be relevant, nor is the dis-tinction between HUMAN and NON-HUMAN.

Occurrences of Accusative, Dative and Genitive are too few to allow any inference. The results for Oblique, however, permit some speculation: HUMAN Obliques are more continuous than HUMAN Subjects (almost a clause less), whereas the same is not true of NON-HUMAN. I suspect that this result is due to the nature of NON-HUMAN stressed pronouns, which are more abstract and can refer to the content of the preceding clause (cf. example (12), p. 17) and not only to a particular referent. In terms of DECAY the rate drops very low for both HUMAN and NON-HUMAN. No difference is noted between the two groups as for AMBIGUITY.

2.3. Stressed pronouns or NP's and coreferential clitics

Table 3, infra, reflects all the cases found in the data of clitics coreferen-tial to SP or NP, regardless of the order in which the clitics occur. However, in view of the fact that clitics are obligatory when they follow the NP (cf. 1.3., I have subdivided Table 3 into Tables 3a and 3b to highlight the different behavior of the constructions according to whether the clitics precede the NP or SP (cf. Table 3a) or follow it (cf. Table 3b).

		NON-SUBJECT			
		ACCUSATIVE		DATIVE	
		Coref. SP	Coref. NP	Coref. SP	Coref. NP
DISTANCE	HUMAN	2.0 / (3)	3.33 / (3)	6.25 / (4)	10.18 / (22)
	NON-HUMAN	—	1.5 / (4)	—	7.25 / (4)
DECAY	HUMAN	1.0 / (3)	0.67 / (3)	1.0 / (4)	1.27 / (22)
	NON-HUMAN	—	1.0 / (4)	—	0.75 / (4)
AMBIGUITY	HUMAN	1.0 / (3)	1.0 / (3)	1.0 / (4)	1.0 / (22)
	NON-HUMAN	—	1.0 / (4)	—	1.0 / (4)

TABLE 3: Clitics coreferential to SP's and NP's

As for SP's, we can only compare the results of Tables 2, 3a and 3b with regard to Dative, as there is only one HUMAN accusative SP in Table 2, and no NON-HUMAN Accusative cases in Tables 3a and 3b. As for Dative HUMAN SP's the occurrences are still too few to permit any definitive comment, but they nevertheless suggest the following tendencies:[3]

		NON-SUBJECT			
		DATIVE		ACCUSATIVE	
		Coref. NP	Coref. SP	Coref. NP	Coref. SP
DISTANCE	HUMAN	11.58 (19)	7.0 (3)	8.0 (1)	2.0 (2)
	NON-HUMAN	7.25 (4)	—	—	—
DECAY	HUMAN	1.21 (19)	1.33 (3)	1.0 (1)	0.5 (2)
	NON-HUMAN	0.75 (4)	—	—	—
AMBIGUITY	HUMAN	1.0 (22)	1.0 (3)	1.0 (1)	1.0 (2)
	NON-HUMAN	1.0 (4)	—	—	—

TABLE 3a: Clitics coreferential to following SP's and NP's

i.- With regard to DISTANCE: Dative HUMAN SP's with coreferential preceding clitic are much more discontinuous, in regard to their referent, than the equivalent bare SP's, the difference being of 6.0 clauses. We can then affirm that SP's + preceding clitic occupy, in the scale of continuity, an intermediate place between the 1.0 of bare SP's and the 11.66 of Verb-Dative NP's and Names (cf. Table 10);

| | NON-SUBJECT | | | | | | | |
| | DATIVE | | | | ACCUSATIVE | | | |
	NP	Coref.	SP	Coref.	NP	Coref.	SP	Coref.
DISTANCE HUMAN	1.33 / (3)	—	4.0 / (1)	—	1.0 / (2)	—	2.0 / (1)	—
DISTANCE NON-HUMAN					1.5 / (4)			
DECAY HUMAN	1.67 / (3)	—	0.0 / (1)	—	0.5 / (2)	—	2.0 / (1)	—
DECAY NON-HUMAN					1.0 / (4)			
AMBIGUITY HUMAN	1.0 / (3)	—	1.0 / (1)	—	1.0 / (2)	—	1.0 / (1)	—
AMBIGUITY NON-HUMAN					1.0 / (4)			

TABLE 3b: Clitics coreferential to preceding SP's and NP's

ii.- With regard to DECAY: SP's preceded by coreferential clitics (Table 3a) decay faster — half a clause— than their equivalent bare SP's. No comments are possible about the results of Table 3b, as only one occurrence has been found. Strangely enough, these constructions appear to decay even faster than definite NP's and Names (cf. Table 10);

	SUBJECT	NON-SUBJECT			
		ACCUSAT.	DATIVE	GENITIVE	OBLIQUE
DISTANCE HUMAN	8.03 / (99)	7.22 / (18)	17.0 / (3)	12.25 / (8)	11.95 / (21)
DISTANCE NON-HUMAN	8.65 / (68)	14.76 / (86)	1.0 / (1)	13.42 / (12)	16.54 / (105)
DECAY HUMAN	1.88 / (99)	1.44 / (18)	1.33 / (3)	0.63 / (8)	0.62 / (21)
DECAY NON-HUMAN	0.51 / (68)	0.33 / (86)	0.0 / (1)	0.75 / (12)	0.10 / (105)
AMBIGUITY HUMAN	1.48 / (99)	1.56 / (18)	2.0 / (3)	1.63 / (8)	1.67 / (21)
AMBIGUITY NON-HUMAN	1.72 / (68)	1.64 / (86)	1.0 / (1)	1.67 / (12)	1.75 / (105)

TABLE 4: Definite NP's (DEFNP) regardless of word-order

ii.- With regard to AMBIGUITY: SP's preceded by coreferential clitics seem to be less ambiguous than bare SP's, the average of AMBIGUITY being 1.0 for SP's plus preceding coreferential clitic, and 1.83 for bare SP's (recalling that for stressed pronouns I have collapsed the results into one, independently of word-order). This is easily understandable if we consider, for example, that *le decia* ('he said to her/him') could be ambiguous, whereas *le decia . . . a ella* – as in (19), p. 20 – cannot.

| | | SUBJECT | | NON-SUBJECTS | | | | | | |
| | | | | ACCUSATIVE | | DATIVE | | GENI-TIVE | OBLQ. |
		S-V	V-S	V-ACC	ACC-V	V-DAT	DAT-V		
DISTANCE	HUMAN	3.41 (17)	1.0 (4)	8.0 (3)	—	11.0 (1)	—	13.0 (2)	10.25 (4)
	NON-HUMAN	5.29 (17)	3.5 (6)	8.7 (17)	—		—	11.5 (2)	13.48 (25)
DECAY	HUMAN	1.0 (17)	0.5 (4)	2.0 (3)	—	3.0 (1)	—	0.0 (2)	0.0 (4)
	NON-HUMAN	0.35 (17)	0.5 (6)	0.23 (17)	—		—	0.0 (2)	0.04 (25)
AMBIGUITY	HUMAN	1.23 (17)	1.25 (4)	1.0 (3)	—	2.0 (1)	—	1.5 (2)	1.5 (4)
	NON-HUMAN	1.35 (17)	1.0 (6)	1.58 (17)	—		—	2.0 (2)	1.6 (25)

TABLE 5: Non-modified definite NP's (NM-NP)

As for NP's, the striking differences in the results of Tables 3a and 3b trans-cend, for the moment, my capacity for interpretation. I can only observe that, with regard to the parameter of DISTANCE, NPs preceded by coreferential

		SUBJECT		NON-SUBJECTS					
		S-V	V-S	ACCUSATIVE		DATIVE		GENI-TIVE	OBLQ.
				V-ACC	ACC-V	V-DAT	DAT-V		
DISTANCE	HUMAN	9.24 (58)	7.53 (13)	6.57 (14)	—		—	12.8 (5)	12.37 (16)
	NON-HUMAN	11.03 (30)	7.0 (9)	15.75 (61)	—	1.0 (1)	—	13.11 (9)	17.14 (69)
DECAY	HUMAN	2.0 (58)	2.76 (13)	1.35 (14)	—			1.0 (5)	2.16 (16)
	NON-HUMAN	0.7 (30)	0.55 (9)	0.36 (61)	—	0.0 (1)		1.0 (9)	0.10 (69)
AMBIGUITY	HUMAN	1.55 (58)	1.53 (13)	1.71 (14)	—		—	1.8 (5)	1.68 (16)
	NON-HUMAN	1.7 (30)	1.33 (9)	1.7 (61)	—	1.0 (1)	—	1.66 (9)	1.78 (69)

TABLE 6: Modified definite NP's (M-NP)

clitics (cf. Table 3a) are less continuous than NP's followed by coreferential clitics (cf. Table 3b). In view of the fact that in the data there are only three

		SUBJECT	NON-SUBJECT			
			ACCU-SATIVE	DATIVE	GENITIVE	OBLIQUE
DISTANCE	HUMAN	14.14 / (7)	14.0 / (1)	20.0 / (2)	8.0 / (1)	12.0 / (1)
	NON-HUMAN	13.83 / (6)	20.0 / (8)	—	20.0 / (1)	19.92 / (11)
DECAY	HUMAN	2.14 / (7)	1.0 / (1)	0.5 / (2)	0.0 / (1)	0.0 / (1)
	NON-HUMAN	0.0 / (6)	0.25 / (8)	—	0.0 / (1)	0.27 / (11)
AMBIGUITY	HUMAN	1.85 / (7)	1.0 / (1)	2.0 / (2)	1.0 / (1)	2.0 / (1)
	NON-HUMAN	2.0 / (6)	1.75 / (8)	—	1.0 / (1)	1.9 / (11)

TABLE 7: Definite NP's modified by a relative clause (RC-)

occurrences of the latter type, it is prudent for the present to postpone any discussion on this issue until further study.

2.4. Definite NP's

Table 4 reflects the overall results of all definite NP's, whereas Tables 5, 6 and 7 show the results obtained for the three different sub-groups of DEF-NP's, as mentioned in 1.4., p. 20-23.

In the comparison of the results reflected in Tables 4, 5, 6 and 7, I will comment only upon the S-V word-order (V-S will be discussed in 2.7) and will consider each parameter separately:[4]

i.- DISTANCE: for HUMAN subjects there is a great increase in the rate of continuity/discontinuity, from the less discontinuous 3.41 of NM-NP's to the highly discontinuous 9.24 of M-NP's and the even higher 14.14 of NP's plus relative clause. The rate of difference — 10.73— found between NM-NP's and NP's modified by a relative clause is big enough to justify the division of all definite NP's into three groups. The same increase is shown by NON-HUMAN subjects, the lower point being almost two clauses more discontinuous than for HUMAN subjects (5.29 for NON-HUMAN as opposed to 3.41 for HUMAN). In the Accusative HUMAN NM-NP's are surprisingly more discontinuous (8.0) than M-NP's (6.57), but I am afraid that three cases of the former type do not permit any serious explanation, so that it would be necessary to check this result against a greater sample. The same has to be said about NP's modified by a relative clause, with only one HUMAN Accusative. NON-HUMAN Accusative cases, on the other hand, follow the expected direction: from 8.7 for NM-NP's to 15.75 of M-NP's, and finally to 20.0 of NP's plus relative clause. No comment is made about Dative, because of the almost total lack of their presence in the data.[5] Occurrences of Genitive are also too few to allow inferences. HUMAN Obliques show the same direction of Subjects in the scale of continuity/discontinuity, with 10.25 for NM-NP's, 12.37 for M-NP's and 12.0 for NP's plus relative clause (but only one case of this type is in the data). NON-HUMAN Obliques go from 13.48 of NM-NP's to 17.14 of M.NP's, to 19.72 for NP's plus relative clause. 19.72 almost reaches the top of 20 established for this parameter. It means that there is no precedent referent, i.e., the topic is newly introduced, or that the reference is to be found almost twenty clauses back in the discourse.

ii.- DECAY: the lowest rate of decay (1.0) for HUMAN Subjects corresponds to NM-NP's, whereas the highest is practically equal (2.0 and 2.14, respectively) for M-NP's and RC-NP's. NON-HUMAN Subjects all decay very fast, and reflect no significant difference among themselves, the range being from $\emptyset$ to 0.7. In HUMAN Objects the highest value for this parameter is shown by Oblique M-NP's (2.16),[6] followed by Accusative NM-NP's (2.0), Accusative M-NP's (1.35), and finally by Genitive M-NP's (1.0). The occurrences of RC-NP's HUMAN Objects are too few (five in total) to permit any comment. The values for NON-HUMAN Objects for all three types of DEFNP's are extremely low, ranging from ∅ to 1.0 for Genitive M-NP's. If the HUMAN Obliques' value is eliminated on the basis of the observation made in footnote 6, and HUMAN Accusative NM-NP's are also disregarded because of the few (three) occurrences of this type, then the highest degree of persistence is attained by HUMAN Accusative M-NP's with an average of 1.35.

iii.- AMBIGUITY: the rates for this parameter, as far as HUMAN Subjects are concerned, follow the predictable trend from the almost nonexistent ambiguity of NM-NP's (1.23) to the middle position of M-NP's (1.55), and to the near maximum of 1.85 for RC-NP's. The same situation is true for NON-HUMAN Subjects as well. HUMAN Objects all show a ratio of AMBIGUITY greater than 1.5 from the minimum of 1.5 for Genitive and Oblique NM-NP's to a maximum of 1.8 for Genitive M-NP's.[7] It also seems that the correlation between high continuity and lesser ambiguity holds for the three types of DEFNP's.

2.5. Names

The results obtained in the analysis of Names are reflected in Table 8, below.

In light of the results presented in Table 8, the following observations can be made:

i.- DISTANCE: for HUMAN Subjects, Names present a value (8.11) which situates them — in our scale of continuity/discontinuity - between NM-NP's (3.41) and M-NP's (9.24). NON-HUMAN Subjects, however, are much more discontinuous than NM- and M-NP's, but less than RC-NP's, the value of the former being 12.25 and the latter 13.83. There is also a significant difference (4.14) between HUMAN and NON-HUMAN Subjects, NON-HUMAN being more discontinuous than HUMAN. The values for Objects are all very similar and their range is very high in discontinuity, the lowest point being 12.0 for HUMAN Dative (but again, only two cases!) and the highest 15.33 for NON-HUMAN Accusative. In the comparison of HUMAN and NON-HUMAN Subjects vs. the corresponding Objects the overall result is that Subjects are more continuous (even if they range very low in the scale of continuity) than Objects, the maximum differences being found between HUMAN Obliques (14.8) and Subjects (8.11), and between NON-HUMAN Accusative (15.33) and Subjects (12.25).

		SUBJECT		NON-SUBJECTS					
				ACCUSATIVE		DATIVE		GENI-TIVE	OBLQ.
		S - V	V - S	V-ACC	Acc-V	V-DAT	DAT-V		
DISTANCE	HUMAN	8.11 (36)	7.5 (4)	13.0 (9)	—	12.0 (2)	—	12.43 (7)	14.8 (10)
	NON-HUMAN	12.25 (12)	9.2 (5)	15.33 (9)	—	—	—	13.25 (24)	14.76 (111)
DECAY	HUMAN	1.22 (36)	0.5 (4)	0.67 (9)	—	1.0 (2)	—	0.71 (7)	0.70 (10)
	NON-HUMAN	0.75 (12)	0.4 (5)	0.22 (9)	—	—	—	0.13 (24)	0.25 (111)
AMBIGUITY	HUMAN	1.53 (36)	1.5 (4)	1.78 (9)	—	1.5 (2)	—	1.43 (7)	1.6 (10)
	NON-HUMAN	1.5 (12)	1.4 (5)	1.78 (9)	—	—	—	1.79 (24)	1.78 (111)

TABLE 8: Names

ii.- DECAY: rates of decay are extremely low for all HUMAN and NON-HUMAN, Subjects and Objects as well. The maximum of persistence is represented by HUMAN Subjects with 1.22 and NON-HUMAN Subjects with 0.75. HUMAN Objects range around 0.7 and NON-HUMAN around 0.2. The overall picture is that both HUMAN Subjects and Objects rank higher than the corresponding NON-HUMAN.

iii.- AMBIGUITY: the lower point for this parameter (1.43) belongs to HUMAN Genitives which have a lesser value than HUMAN Subjects. HUMAN Subjects and Datives, as well as NON-HUMAN Subjects have almost the very same value; all other cases of HUMAN and NON-HUMAN oscillate between 1.6 and 1.79, hence they show a great degree of AMBIGUITY.

The only surprising result of Table 8 is that HUMAN Subjects have a value (8.11) which is lower – i.e., more continuous – than that of modified NP's (cf. Table 6). It is possible that this is due in part to the fact that Table 8 does not include those Names which appear in left-dislocated structures which should occupy one of the highest levels in the scale of discontinuity/surprise.

2.6. Existentials and presentatives

Table 9 below, presents the results obtained in the examination of constructions described in 1.6.

The results of Table 9, supra, clearly demonstrate that there are at least two good reasons to separate EP's into two sub-groups: i) only DEF-EP's occur in the subject-first word-order, whereas no occurrences of this type have been found among INDF-EP's. This may suggest that true EP's are only those with indefinite subjects, whereas those with definite subjects are pseudo-EP's. In fact, the very idea of definiteness with EP's seems counterintuitive: if EP's – as Givón (1979: 66) affirms – "are uttered in contexts where the speaker does not presuppose anything about the hearer's familiarity with the referent, since he is then introducing it into discourse *for the first time*", then DEF-EP's do not fit into this description: 'definite' means that they have already been somehow introduced into discourse, hence are familiar to the hearer. ii) This intuitive difference between the two types of EP's is corroborated by the different values obtained by both, in regard to DISTANCE: DEF-EP's are more continuous than INDF-EP's, the difference for HUMAN Subjects being 6.90 and that for NON-HUMAN 3.36. The other two parameters – DECAY and AMBIGUITY – do not seem to be relevant for the distinction.

Another potentially interesting difference between DEF- and INDF-EP's is that HUMAN Subjects are more frequent than NON-HUMAN with the former and NON-HUMAN are more frequent than HUMAN with the latter.

As for subject-first DEF-EP's, we observe that: i) examples are few (ten

TABLE 9

		Definite		Indefinite	
		S - V	Subject V - S	S - V	Subject V - S
DISTANCE	HUMAN	2.37 / (8)	11.51 / (31)	—	18.41 / (12)
	NON-HUMAN	3.0 / (2)	14.8 / (20)	—	18.16 / (37)
DECAY	HUMAN	1.0 / (8)	1.32 / (31)	—	1.41 / (12)
	NON-HUMAN	1.5 / (2)	0.8 / (20)	—	0.48 / (37)
AMBIGUITY	HUMAN	1.12 / (8)	1.8 / (31)	—	1.75 / (12)
	NON-HUMAN	1.5 / (2)	1.8 / (20)	—	1.86 / (37)

TABLE 9: Existential-presentatives with definite and indefinite Subject
(DEF-EP and INDF-EP)

between HUMAN and NON-HUMAN), and ii) they show a great degree of continuity (2.5), greater than, for example, that of the stressed pronouns (2.37), cf. Tables 2 and 9. NON-HUMAN subject-first DEF-EP's are less continuous than stressed pronouns, but much more than non-modified NP's (cf. Table 5), with an average difference of 2.29 clauses.

		SUBJECT		NON-SUBJECTS			
				ACCUSATIVE		DATIVE	
		S-V	V-S	V-ACC	ACC-V	V-DAT	DAT-V
DISTANCE	HUMAN	7.98 (111)	6.28 (21)	8.96 (26)	—	11.66 (3)	—
	NON-HUMAN	9.62 (59)	6.50 (20)	14.33 (87)	—	1.0 (1)	—
DECAY	HUMAN	1.59 (111)	1.9 (21)	1.19 (26)	—	1.66 (3)	—
	NON-HUMAN	0.61 (50)	0.5 (20)	0.32 (87)	—	0.0 (1)	—
AMBIGUITY	HUMAN	1.49 (111)	1.47 (21)	1.65 (26)	—	1.66 (3)	—
	NON-HUMAN	1.55 (59)	1.25 (20)	1.68 (87)	—	1.0 (1)	—

TABLE 10: NP's and Names: S-V and V-S word-order

2.7. Word-order

Table 10, infra, is the summary of Tables 5, 6, and 8, which reflect the results of Non-modified and Modified Definite NP's and Names, excluding therefrom Genitive and Oblique cases for which word-order has not been taken into account in the present analysis. This table compares the values of S-V and V-S orders for all instances of full NP's, but obviously excludes those which occur in existential-presentative constructions (cf. 2.6.). Unfortunately, the comparison can only be established with regard to Subjects, as there are no examples in the data of preverbal Accusative or Dative.[8]

Table 10 indicates the following:

    i.- DISTANCE: both HUMAN and NON-HUMAN Subjects show a lesser degree of continuity in the S-V order than in the V-S, the difference being 1.7 for HUMAN and 3.12 for NON-HUMAN.[9] According to the present results, V-S order appears to occupy – in our scale of continuity – an intermediate position between Non-modified and Modified Definite NP's, for HUMAN and NON-HUMAN NP's as well.

    ii.- DECAY: HUMAN V-S Subjects are more persistent than S-V, even if not to a great extent (the difference is only of 0.31 in favor of V-S). There is practically no difference between S-V and V-S NON-HUMAN NP's.

    iii.- AMBIGUITY: the figures for this parameter are very similar for both HUMAN S-V and V-S, and also to the analogous results obtained for M-NP's (cf. Table 6, p. 38). NON-HUMAN show a higher degree of Ambiguity for S-V than for V-S order, which again seems to be contrary to the idea of S-V order as related to new information (cf. footnote 9).

The present findings are consistent with Givón's (1979: 38) assessments about "how difficult it is likely to be for the hearer to assign the correct reference-identification of the subject." Indeed, the greater degree of continuity of V-S Subjects correlates with a greater ease of the hearer in assigning the correct reference.[10] And in this regard Spanish is very similar to Ute, so that for both languages "pre-verbal position is [. . .] a signal of *discontinuity/surprise*, while post-verbal position signals *continuity* and *predictability*." (Givón, 1980: 332).

3. Conclusions

The present conclusions are provisional in the sense that they only refer to those points in the scale of continuity/discontinuity investigated thus far;[11] they are presented here with reference to the three parameters of DISTANCE, DECAY and AMBIGUITY according to which the grammatical devices utilized by Spanish speakers to maintain, introduce or re-assess a topic-NP have been analyzed.

DISTANCE: from the Graphs I-VI, below, it is clear that the various grammatical devices analyzed in this paper can be plotted into a cline which goes from 1.20 (NON-HUMAN VAC) to 18.41 (HUMAN INDF-EP) for Subjects; from 1.56 (NON-HUMAN VAC) to 20.0 (NON-HUMAN RC-NP) for Accusative; from

1.43 (HUMAN VAC) to 20.0 (HUMAN RC-NP) for Dative; from 1.07 (HUMAN VAC) to 20.0 (NON-HUMAN RC-NP) for Genitive; and finally from 1.5 (HUMAN SP) to 19.72 (NON-HUMAN RC-NP) for Oblique. As the differences among the various functions have been examined in the corresponding sections, I will only emphasize here that in all cases the maximum of continuity – as expected – is represented by VAC and/or SP (Oblique has no VAC), and the maximum of discontinuity by INDF-EP and/or RC-NP, which proved to be the most common devices utilized by the speakers to introduce a new topic or re-introduce a topic after a long gap.

DECAY: from Graph VII the following generalizations can be inferred: i) with only one exception (NON-HUMAN VAC Genitive) HUMAN Subjects and Objects are more persistent than NON-HUMAN (when examples of both types have been found); the highest degree of persistence is shown by HUMAN Subjects, and the maximum is represented by VAC, followed by RC-NP, SP and V-S; ii) the most and least continuous devices – according to DISTANCE – are those which demonstrate the highest degree of persistence, VAC as the most continuous and RC-NP as the most discontinuous. This correlation is worthy of further analysis.

AMBIGUITY: from Graph VIII we observe again a cline: from the very low ration for both HUMAN and NON-HUMAN VAC (1.09 and 1.03, respectively) to the very high of HUMAN and NON-HUMAN RC–NP (1.85 and 2.0, respectively). We may note the following: i) HUMAN and NON-HUMAN topics – when they both occur – have very similar values; ii) there is almost no ambiguity in VAC and SP of all functions; iii) ambiguity is also very low in Subject-first DEF-EP (S-DEF-EP), NM-NP and V-S for HUMAN Subjects; iv) the ratio starts to rise over 1.5 in M-NP Subjects and in NM-NP Non-subjects; v) the value for Subject-first DEF-EP is even lower than that of SP; vi) there is a clear correlation between the two parameters of DISTANCE and AMBIGUITY, the more continuous a topic is, the less ambiguous, and vice versa.

P. BENTIVOGLIO

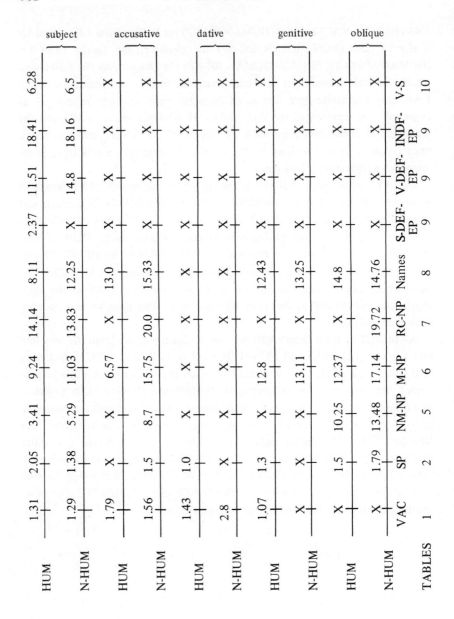

GRAPH I: Summary of Referential Distance results by case-roles and grammatical devices

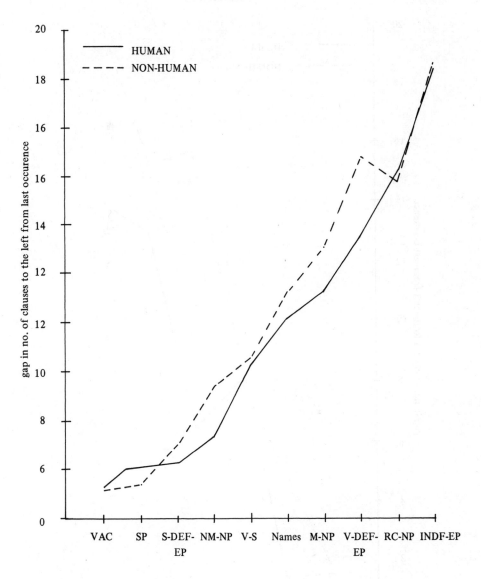

GRAPH II: Referential distance for human and non-human subject

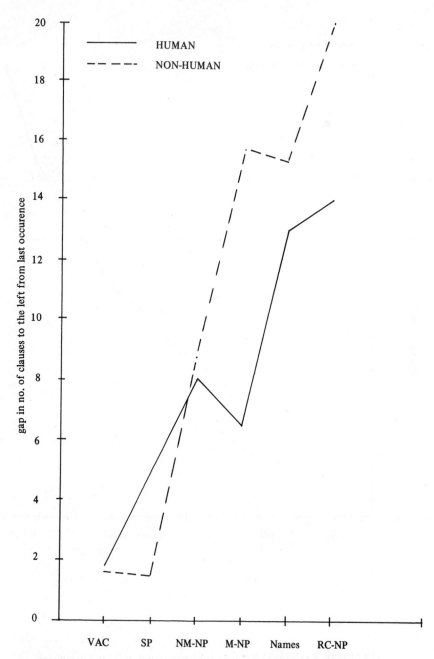

GRAPH III: Referential distance for human and non-human accusative

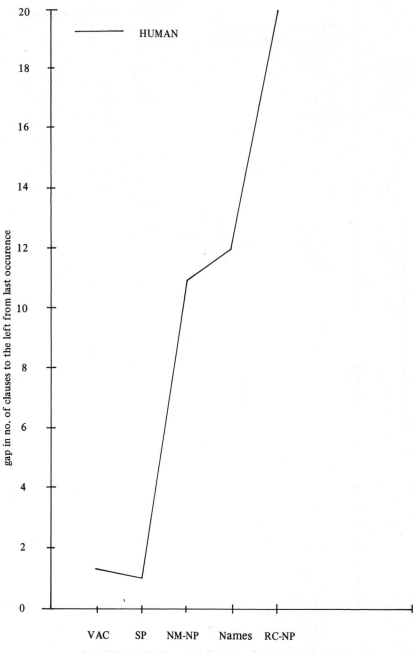

GRAPH IV: Referential distance for human dative

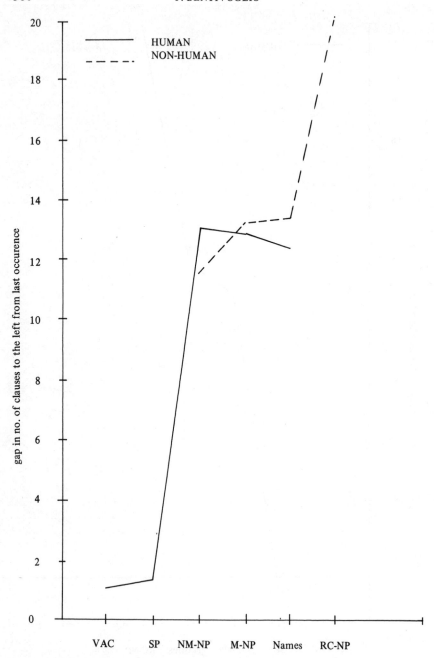

GRAPH V: Referential distance for human and non-human genitive

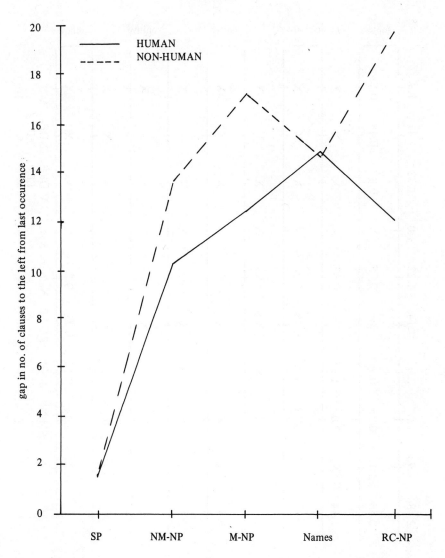

GRAPH VI: Referential distance for human and non-human oblique
case-roles

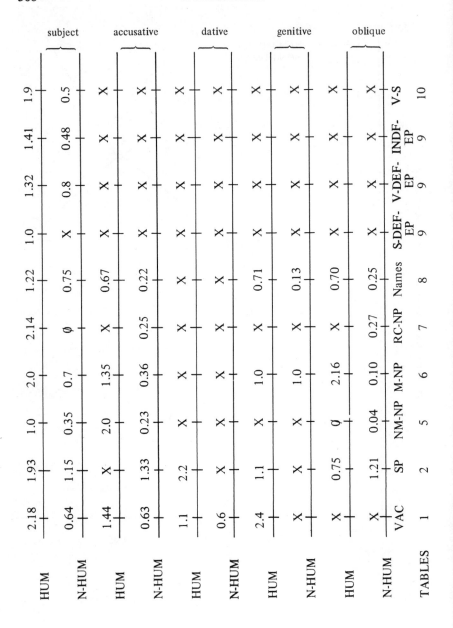

GRAPH VII: Summary of decay ('persistence') results for case-roles and
grammatical devices

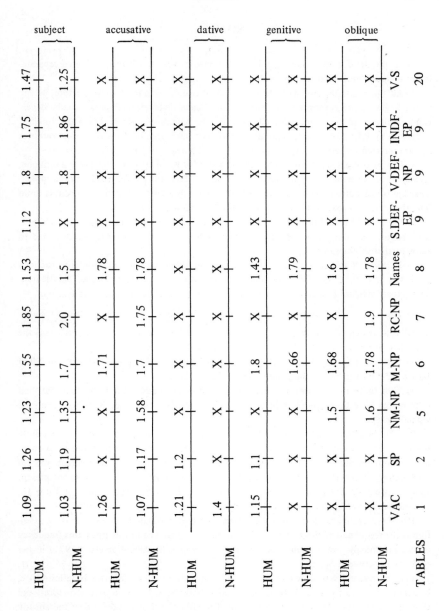

GRAPH VIII: Summary of ambiguity ('interference') results for case-roles and grammatical devices

NOTES

1) In the division into clauses, only relative clauses have not been considered separately but included in the clause they modify.

2) All the transcriptions, with the exception of two pages in the Caracas portion, belong to the linguistic project known as "Estudio coordinado de la norma lingüística culta del español hablado en las principales ciudades de Iberoamérica y de la Península Ibérica" published by P.I.L.E.I. (1967). The samples utilized have been published in three countries and are referred to, respectively, as Mexico (1971), Caracas (1979), and Santiago (1979).

3) In this comparison I have collapsed the results of HUMAN Dative in Table 2 into one, regardless of the word-order in which they occur. In fact, for clitics, word-order in spoken language is not optional but related to whether the verb with which clitics co-occur is finite (and then clitic precedes the verb) or non-finite (clitic follows the verb).

4) In Table 7 the definite NP's modified by a relative clause have not been separated into two groups, according to word-order, as there were too few occurrences of this kind to allow further subdivisions.

5) Recall that this absence may well be due to the separation of those constructions presented in Table 3, i.e., NP's preceded or followed by a coreferential clitic. This demonstrates that, in Spanish, true Datives without a coreferential clitic are almost nonexistent.

6) The value 2.16 is derived from $\frac{13}{16}$, but note that the numerator includes one instance of value 8, which obviously distorts the final result. If we discount this abnormal case the ratio then becomes 0.33, which is more consistent with the expectations.

7) I am not referring here to the values of 1.0 shown by Accusative NM-NP's or 2.0 of Dative RC-NP's because of the small number of occurrences.

8) That there are no cases of preverbal Accusative or Dative is due to the fact that their occurrences have been found in left-dislocated structures, hence they have been analyzed separately.

9) The fact that postverbal Subjects are more continuous than preverbal apparently seems to be contrary to Silva-Corvalán's (1977) general findings about the position of non-pronominal Subjects, which would constitute new information if postverbal, and old information if preverbal. This point needs to be further investigated, because in the present study existentials and presentatives are not reflected in the V-S occurrences of Table 10, whereas Silva-Corvalán has not separated EP-constructions in her general results.

10) Many problems have still to be solved; one that particularly deserves further attention is the frequency of V-S order for NP's. In the data analuzed in this study this frequency is overwhelmingly lower than that found, for example, by Silva-Corvalán (1977) in her study of Los Angeles Spanish.

11) This research has to be complemented by investigating: a) referential Indefinite NP's, b) generic NP's, c) passives, d) right-dislocated structures, e) left-dislocated structures, and f) pseudo-clefts and clefts, which results could modify the relative position of the already analyzed devices, i.e., the scale of continuity/discontinuity.

REFERENCES

Bentivoglio, P. (1978) Formación de clíticos: análisis sobre el habla culta de Caracas. In López Morales, Humberto (ed.), *Corrientes actuales en la dialectología del Caribe Hispánico.* San Juan: Editorial Universitaria.

——––. (1980) Why *canto* and not *yo canto*? The problem of first-person subject pronoun in spoken Venezuelan Spanish. M.A.thesis. Los Angeles: University of California.

——–– and F. D'Introne. (1978) Orden de palabras en el español de Caracas: un análisis sociolingüístico. Unpublished manuscript.

Givón, T. (1979) *On understanding grammar.* New York: Academic Press.

——––. (1980) *Ute reference Grammar.* Ignacio, Colorado: Ute Press.

P.I.L.E.I. (1967) *El Simposio de Bloomington. Agosto de 1964. Actas, Informes y Comunicaciones.* Bogotá: Instituto Caro y Cuervo.

Rabanales, A. and L. Contreras (eds.). (1979) *El habla culta de Santiago de Chile. Materiales para su estudio.* Santiago de Chile: Editorial Universitaria.

Silva-Corvalán, C. (1977) A discourse study of some aspects of word-order in the Spanish spoken by Mexican-Americans in West Los Angeles. M.A. thesis. Los Angeles: University of California.

Universidad Nacional Autónoma de México. (1971) *El habla de la Ciudad de México. Materiales para su estudio.* Mexico: Universidad Nacional Autónoma de México.

Universidad Central de Venezuela. (1979) *El habla culta de Caracas. Materiales para su estudio.* Caracas: Ediciones de la Facultad de Humanidades y Educación.

TOPIC CONTINUITY IN WRITTEN ENGLISH NARRATIVE

CHERYL BROWN
Linguistics Department
Brigham Young University
Provo, Utah

TABLE OF CONTENTS

1. *Introduction*

In a recent article Givón (1981) argues that ". . . functional domains in syntax are most commonly *clines,* upon which a number of more-or-less distinct points may be plotted among a functional continuum. . ." One functional domain which fits this description is that of continuity/discontinuity. How does a communicator produce language which, to his receiver, seems connected, coherent, and relevant to the subject at hand? What kinds of bridges and paths does the communicator build for his receiver to follow? What kinds of "gaps" cause the communicator to use each of the various "bridge" types at his disposal?

A partial answer to the last question was given in the same article just cited in which Givón suggests a cline showing ease of topic identification.

(1)   *Easiest topic identification* (least surprising)
              Zero anaphora
              Clitic pronouns/verb agreement
              Unstressed pronouns
              Stressed/independent pronouns
              Left dislocation
              Definite NP
              Right dislocation
              (Passivization)
              Y-movement ('topicalization')
              Cleft/focus constructions
         Most difficult topic identification (most surprising)
                                    (Givón, 1981)

Presumably, the communicator would use the structures or "points" at the top of the list when the continuity and identification gaps would be small and easy for his receiver to cross. The communicator would use the points at the bottom of the list when the gaps would be greater and more difficult for his receiver to cross and continue to follow the discourse. At least, this is what the cline implies. This paper reports on a count of actual English discourse to see if the cline is numerically verifiable.

2. *Data base*

The discourse studied for the count was taken from *Doctor No*, a James Bond thriller by Ian Fleming. It was chosen because it was narrative (a language genre not particular to only written languages) and because it was assumed that Fleming's purpose in the novel was to tell the story (produce narrative) and not to produce a literary work of art (which might distort the natural use of language for artistic purposes). Sections of conversation in the book were skipped so as to avoid the added complication of trying to determine whether a conversation is a single piece of discourse participated in by two (or more) or whether it is two pieces of intertwined discourse.

Fifty pages containing a total of 1513 main, subordinate, and other clauses were analyzed. Relative clauses, noun clauses, infinitive clauses, and gerund clauses were all counted as part of the other clauses in which they functioned. Although relative clauses were not counted as separate clauses in the measures taken, the structures appearing in them were counted separately in order to see if the type of clause in which a structure appeared had an influence on how continuous or discontinuous it was.

3. *Methodology*

Three measures were taken in the analysis. The first of these, "Lookback," is a rough measure of the size of gap that the structure on Givón's cline had to bridge. Presumably, structures at the top of the list would bridge smaller gaps than structures at the bottom of the list. The measure was figured by counting the number of clauses back from a token (an instance of the structure) to the nearest clause in which a referent for the token previously appeared. For example, in the first sentence in the following text, *Jim, Mary*, and *the typing* would all receive a lookback value of 20 because there has been no previous mention of any of them. (20 was chosen as the maximum lookback value; 1 as the minimum.) Both italicized *it*'s would have a lookback value of 1, the first being counted back to *the typing* and the second being counted back to the first. The first italicized *he* would receive a lookback value of 2, going back to *Jim* in the first clause. The second *he* would refer to the first *he* and would have a lookback value of 1. The second *Mary* would have a lookback value of 4, going back to *Mary* in the first clause and the ∅ would have a lookback value of 1.

> *Jim* insisted on helping *Mary* with *the typing*. Although *it* was a simple task, *he* managed to make *it* seem like a major ordeal. By the time *he* had finished three pages, *Mary* had finished the other ten and ∅ was ready to leave.

In the counting it was decided not to consider synonyms as the same referent if they added information that had not previously been added. This may have introduced some arbitrariness into the count. With hyponyms, also, it was decided not to accept parts for wholes or wholes for parts.

Shifting number also posed a problem in the counting of lookback. It was decided to count plurals back to the last reference to the person or item that made a plural reference possible. However, singulars were counted back to their last singular appearance. Thus, in the following passage, both *Quarrel* and *Bond* would have to be counted back to the clause where each appeared individually. *They* could be counted back to Quarrel because Bond had already been mentioned further back and the addition of Quarrel made the plural possible.

> They made haste. Quarrel took three short lengths of thick bamboo out of the boat and laid them up the flat beach. They heaved the nose of the canoe on to the first and pushed the boat up the rollers. After each yard of progress, Bond picked up the back roller and brought it to the front.
>
> (Fleming, 1958, p. 68)

The second measure given to all tokens was a measure of persistence. How many clauses after the one in which the token appeared was mention made of the same person or thing? The same problem occurred here with synonymy, hyponymy, and number. With synonymy and hyponymy, the same rules were applied as with lookback. With number, a clause was included in the count if the token in question was singular and either a singular or a plural reference occurred. If the token was plural, a clause was included only if a plural reference occurred. All counts for persistence ended when a clause was reached in which no reference was made to the token being measured. Whereas lookback measured the size of gap a structure had to span, persistence measured what kind of path into the future discourse a structure laid. Structures at the top of Givón's list would be expected to have higher persistence scores that those at the bottom of the list.

The third measure used on the tokens was one of ambiguity. It was difficult to establish a satisfactory measure of ambiguity. Only part of the tokens counted for the other measures were counted for ambiguity because of the change in counting methods part way through the analysis. The various tables list the differences in the number of tokens counted for ambiguity. The final system had three levels. A "1" was assigned to those tokens appearing in an environment (within five previous clauses) in which there was only one logically possible referent for the token. A "2" was assigned if there were two or more logically possible referents in the near context. A "3" was assigned if there were no likely referents in the near context. Indefinite referentials, for example, were always assigned a "3." Presumably, structures at the top of Givón's list should have lower ambiguity scores than those at the bottom of the list.

These three measures were taken for every token of every structure until 200 instances of each structure had been counted. After 200 instances, the tokens were included in the overall count total, but the measures were not taken. If there were not 200 instances of a structure in the discourse, all of the instances wich did occur were measured.

The averages for each measure were figured by taking the sum of each of the three measures (separately) and dividing by the total number of tokens for which the measure was taken. In addition to the averages figured for each structure, the average was also figured for those tokens referring to humans as opposed to those which referred to nonhumans. Averages were also figured for each clause type and the functions within each type (subject, direct object, etc.)

4. *Topic-marking constructions in English*

The structures counted included those given in the Givón cline with the exception of clitics/verb agreement which is not a type common to English. In addition, the area of Definite NP was expanded to five structures: (1) definite article + NP, (2) demonstrative + NP, (3) demonstrative alone (demonstrative pronoun), (4) name, and (5) NP appearing after possessives or genitives. Two types of indefinites were counted: (1) indefinite referentials and (2) existential/presentatives. A category of generics was also added.

The structures studied then were as follows:

1) *Zero anaphora*: This structure consists of deleting a NP completely. For example, the zero anaphora in the following sentences have been marked with Ø.

> John picked up his hat and Ø left.
> Ø Picking up his hat, John left.

2) *Unstressed pronouns*: This structure consists of the use of any of the personal pronouns in English without special stress. The unstressed pronouns in the following passage have been italicized:

> John picked up *his* hat and placed *it* on *his* head. Then, *he* smiled at Mary across the room and *she* waved at *him* as *he* strode out of the room.

3) *Stressed/independent pronouns*: This structure consists of the use of any of the personal pronouns with stress. These could only be detected with written narrative by reading the text aloud. In the fifty pages of text, only one such pronoun was found so this structure was eliminated from the overall presentation of data.

4) *Left dislocation*: This structure has two references to the same thing within one clause. The first referent begins the clause and the second referent is generally a pronoun. For example,

> *The cheese they made there,* they sold most of *it* to the miners.

5) *Definite article + NP*: This structure consists in English of the article *the* plus a modified or unmodified NP of some kind. For example,

> John put *the hat* on his head and strode out of *the noisy room.*

6) *Demonstrative + NP*: This structure consists of *this, that, these,* or *those* plus a NP. For example,

> John smiled at Mary as he strode out of the room. *That smile* bothered her for weeks afterwards.

7) *Demonstrative alone (demonstrative pronoun)*: This structure consists of *this, that, these,* or *those* used alone without an NP attached:

> John smiled at Mary as he strode out of the room. *That* seemed inconsistent with his previous actions.

8) *Names*: This structure consists of proper nouns. For example,

> *John* smiled at *Mary* as he strode out of the room. He had to catch a plane to *London* within the hour.

9) *NP following possessive*: This structure consists of any NP which follows either a possessive pronoun or a possessive formed in English by the use of an apostrophe. For example,

> For weeks Mary was bothered by John's *smile* and his *inconsistent manner.*

10) *Right dislocation*: Like left dislocation, this structure consists of two references within one clause to the same thing. The first referent is usually a pronoun within the regular clause and the second is usually found at the end of the clause. For example,

It bothered her for weeks, *John's smile.*

11) *Passivization*: This structure consists of bringing what would normally be an object in a clause into the subject position. For example,

The cheese was sold mostly to the miners.

In the original count, passives were not included in the total number of tokens as a separate entity. Rather, they were counted in the other categories is which they fit first. Later, they were extracted and counted as passives, but they were not subtracted from the constructions with which they were originally counted.

12) *Y-Movement*: This structure consists of moving a NP out of its normal position in English word order and placing it at the beginning of the clause. For example,

The cheese they sold mainly to the miners.

There were not enough instances of this structure in the discourse to include in the overall counts.

13) *Indefinite referentials*: This structure consists of an indefinite article (*a* or *an*) and a NP or of a plural NP with no particular referent. For example,

John picked up *a hat* which wasn't his and strode from the room.
Several *secretaries* giggled when they saw it.

14) *Existential/presentatives:* These structures consist of the *there is/ there are* type clauses such as

There were several secretaries in the room when John left.

or of other presentatives which often begin with a prepositional phrase giving place. For example,

By the hat rack stood John.

15) *Generics*: These consist of plural NPs standing for all of a type such as

Hats seem unnecessary.

Or they may consist of the English definite article and a NP standing for all of a type such as

The roseate spoonbill is a rare bird.

16) *Cleft/focus constructions*: These consist of clauses which use *it* at the beginning as a place holder only, followed by an NP which is modified by a relative clause. For example,

It was John's smile that bothered Mary for weeks afterward.

There were not enough instances of this structure in the discourse examined to include in the overall counts.

Since Right and Left Dislocations are typical of the oral rather than written register of English, an additional data-base was used for their study. The data were taken from tapes of oral narrative, approximately 4 hours of descriptions, primarily of folklore and history of a small region of Utah, told by four different speakers. The transcripts — 85 typewritten pages in all — were studied only for a three-way contrast:
(a)   R-dislocation
(b)   DEF NP's in a neutral position
(c)   L-dislocation

5. Results
5.1. *Human/non-human and topic continuity*
The influence of humanness as a continuity factor is shown on Table I.

The huge differences between the averages for human and those for nonhuman on the lookback and persistence measures is striking although not surprising. Humans are more generally the subjects of narrative and they are definitely the subjects of the particular text which was analyzed. A glance at Table IV, which is a compilation of the averages for all of the structures for all three measures, shows that for all structures except two the lookback is much less for humans

TABLE I

HUMANNESS AS A CONTINUITY/DISCONTINUITY FACTOR

	Human	Nonhuman
Average Lookback	4.45	16.22
Average Persistence	1.78	0.20
Average Ambiguity	1.38	2.02
# Tokens Counted on Lookback & Persistence	838	1337
# Tokens Counted on Ambiguity	570	972

than for nonhumans. One of the exceptions, NPs following possessives, is insignificant because of the small number of human tokens (humans are not generally possessed by other humans). The fact that the other exception, unstressed pronouns, shows a smaller lookback for nonhumans than humans is probably a result of the English pronoun system. Gender can often help us distinguish one person from another when a pronoun is used, but all nonhumans fall under the aegis of *it*. Therefore, if the referent for a nonhuman pronoun is not fairly close, confusion might result and the communicator would choose a different kind of construction to handle the situation. Consequently, unstressed pronouns are used for nonhumans only when the referent is fairly close. Gender on pronouns referring to humans makes it so the restriction for their use is not so great.

The fact that humans persist on the scene so much more than nonhumans is probably just an artefact of topicality – humans are what we talk about. The lower ambiguity score for humans than nonhumans is easily explainable through pragmatics. There are more nonhuman objects in almost any setting than there are humans, thus, a higher potential of ambiguity of reference for nonhuman tokens.

Although Table I suggests great differences between the averages for humans and for non-humans, the differences may not be solely because of humanness.

The results may be influenced by interaction with other factors such as case. Greenberg (1974) discusses the statistically high correlation of humanness with nominative case, for example.

5.2. *Clause type and topic continuity*

Table II shows the results of the count of clause type as a continuity factor. Not surprisingly, relative and noun clauses have the greatest lookback. These clauses are often not related to the story or action of the moment. They often go outside the narrative to some distant time or place in order to definitize the construction to which they are attached. Therefore, their long lookback score is not surprising; what is surprising is the fact that these clauses are so close in score to main clauses. This count may in some small way contribute to verification of Bolinger's idea that main clauses and embedded clauses may not be so different in the kinds of assertions they make (Bolinger, 1979).

TABLE II
TYPE OF CLAUSE AS A CONTINUITY/DISCONTINUITY FACTOR

	Main	Subordinate/ Participial	Relative/ Noun
Average Lookback	11.97	7.59	12.75
Average Persistence	0.81	0.95	0.62
Average Ambiguity	2.01	1.50	1.81
#Tokens Counted on Lookback & Persistence	1848	170	157
#Tokens Counted on Ambiguity	1315	129	98

The low average lookback, the relatively higher average persistence, and the lower average ambiguity of subordinate/participial clauses shows the dependence of these clauses on other clauses. Adverbial subordinate clauses and participial clauses both must be attached, either before or after, to another clause which often contains the same participants. Hence, either the lookback or the persistence is likely to be affected. Particularly with participials, the dependence is so strong that almost no ambiguity is possible. Participials which do allow ambiguity are usually classified as "dangling" modifiers and there are strong prescriptivist factors working against their use. Notice in the following passage where there is no room for ambiguity in the referent for the underlined participials.

> For minutes they darkened the skyline and then they were down on the water, *covering* several acres of it, *screeching* and *fighting* and *plunging* their heads below the surface, *cropping* at the solid field of anchovy like piranha fish feasting on a drowned horse.
>
> (Fleming, 1959, 77-78)

There may be an interaction here with clause type and construction types as well. Zero anaphora and participial phrases often occur together.

5.3. *Case-roles and topic continuity*

Table III shows the measure averages for the functions that the given tokens have within the clause.

TABLE III
CASE ROLES AS A CONTINUITY/DISCONTINUITY FACTOR

	Subject	Direct Object	Indirect Object	Genitive	Other[1]
Average Lookback	6.36	15.97	8.25	3.51	17.09
Average Persistence	1.42	.23	1.00	1.47	.22
Average Ambiguity	1.56	2.21	2.00	1.32	1.98
#Tokens Counted on Lookback & Persistence	940	244	8	116	867
#Tokens Counted on Ambiguity	678	189	4	72	599

1) *Other* includes objects of prepositions, locatives, objects of infinitives, and any other use of a nominal which would not be classified in the other four categories.

The *genitives* are easily the most continuous of the functions. This is interesting because genitives frequently occur with nouns serving as direct objects and direct objects have one of the longest lookbacks of any of the functions. The genitives serve as a particular kind of bridge to tie the generally continuous subjects to the generally discontinuous direct objects. Often the referent for the genitive will occur in the same clause and/or sentence.

Subjects are the next most continuous of the functions. This is once again a matter of topicality. We are talking about a particular topic and that topic tends to occupy the subject position and to persist.

There seems to be a great difference in the continuity of direct objects and of *indirect objects*. However, the figures should not be trusted completely because of the small number of indirect object tokens. (This small number of indirect objects is puzzling to me. I have not found an explanation for it except possibly in the style or nature of this particular text. It deserves further investigation.) The great apparent difference between direct objects and indirect objects may simply be the interaction with humanness, an interaction which is even stronger in other languages (see Givón, 1976).

The *direct object* and *other* categories seem to be similar in most of the measures. Direct objects seem slightly more continuous as measured by lookback and by persistence. However, the other category seems slightly more continuous on the basis of ambiguity. This category may have a lower score in this area because of the inclusion of locatives. Once a setting has been established, many things in that setting become unique and there is no ambiguity in reference to other things or points within the location. The other category is a grab bag for many constructions, however, so the locatives would only be one of the influencing factors here.

5.4. *Grammatical devices coding topic continuity*

Table IV gives the overall average counts and measures for all the structures with at least 20 instances in the written text. The structures are listed from left to right according to increasing average lookback total. Table V compares Givón's cline with the three clines which would be formed on the basis of the three measures for each of the structures.

5.4.1. *Zero Anaphora*: Because zero anaphora only occurs in subject position in English, the scores on Table IV are all the scores there are for the structure. While not the most common grammatical device in English discourse (unlike in Ute discourse where it is the most common device — see Givón, 1979), zero

TABLE IV

MEASUREMENTS OF TOPIC CONTINUITY/DISCONTINUITY BY CONSTRUCTION TYPE

	Ø Anaphora	Unstressed Pronouns	Demonstrative Pronouns	Passives[1]	Demonstratives + NPs	Names	Right Dislocation	Definite Articles + NPs	Existentials/ Presentatives	NPs Following Possessives	Indefinite Referentials	Generics	Overall Totals and Averages
Total # Tokens	314	1163	27	—	44	483	21	1023	102	370	514	337	4400
# Tokens Counted (Human)	234	264	0	(20)	16	226	3	39	12	7	16	22	839
# Tokens Counted (Nonhuman)	80	51	27	(17)	28	104	18	254	90	222	222	240	1336
Total # Tokens Counted	314	315	27	(37)	44	330	21	293	102	229	238	262	2175
Average Lookback (Human)	1.00	1.78	—	(6.2)	8.25	6.47	1.33	11.10	10.50	20.00	18.81	19.18	4.45
Average Lookback (Nonhuman)	1.00	1.43	2.27	(13.12)	10.75	17.63	12.83	17.51	19.18	18.28	19.19	19.23	16.22
Average Lookback Total	1.00	1.72	2.27	(9.37)	9.84	9.99	11.19	16.66	18.16	18.34	19.17	19.23	11.68
Average Persistence (Human)	2.13	1.98	—	(2.20)	.81	1.63	.33	1.03	1.75	0.00	.88	.59	1.78
Average Persistence (Nonhuman)	.78	.20	.33	(.18)	.39	.17	.44	.18	.12	.09	.13	.18	.20
Average Persistence Total	1.78	1.69	.33	(1.27)	.56	1.17	.43	.29	.31	.08	.18	.21	.81
Average Ambiguity (Human)	1.08	1.24	—	(2.08)	1.82	1.59	2.00	1.35	1.80	1.75	3.00	1.92	1.38
Average Ambiguity (Nonhuman)	1.25	1.22	1.70	(1.92)	1.87	1.85	2.89	1.38	2.32	2.10	3.00	1.50	2.02
Average Ambiguity Total	1.12	1.23	1.70	(2.00)	1.85	1.67	2.67	1.38	2.25	2.09	3.00	1.53	1.78

1) The figures for the passives are not calculated in the overall totals because all of the constructions in the passives were originally figured under one of the other constructions.

TABLE V

COMPARISON OF CLINES BASED ON AVERAGE MEASURES

Givon (1980)	Average Lookback		Average Persistence		Average Ambiguity	
Zero anaphora	Zero anaphora	1.00	Zero anaphora	1.78	Zero anaphora	1.12
Clitics/verb agree	Unstressed pronouns	1.72	Unstressed pronouns	1.69	Unstressed pronouns	1.23
Unstressed pronouns	Demonstratives alone	2.27	Passives	1.27	Def Art + NP	1.38
Stressed pronouns	Passives	9.37	Names	1.17	Generics	1.53
Left dislocation	Demonstratives + NP	9.84	Demonstrative + NP	.56	Names	1.67
Definite NP	Names	9.99	Right Dislocation	.43	Demonstratives alone	1.70
Right Dislocation	Right Dislocation	11.19	Demonstratives alone	.33	Demonstrative + NP	1.85
Passives	Def Art + NP	16.66	Existential/Pres	.31	Passives	2.00
Y-movement	Existential/Pres	18.16	Def Art + NP	.29	NPs after Poss	2.09
Cleft/focus construct	NPs after Poss	18.34	Generics	.21	Existential/Pres	2.25
	Indefinite Ref	19.17	Indefinite Ref	.18	Right Dislocation	2.67
	Generics	19.23	NPs after Poss	.08	Indefinite Ref	3.00

anaphora is decidedly the most continuous end of every cline. This position is not surprising in English. Zero anaphora is the result of Equi-NP deletion which requires identicality of NPs. Therefore, the identity of the deleted item is available in the near context of the structure. As had been discussed previously in the section about clause type, the subject of the ∅ anaphora construction is always the subject of the clause immediately before or after the construction.

In the particular text examined for this paper, in one section involving a narrative within the context of the overall story, zero anaphora is used in sentences which stand alone. Nevertheless, the subject of the preceding clauses makes the reference completely clear.

> And Strangways's friends at his club say he was perfectly normal. Left in the middle of a rubber of bridge — always did when it was getting close to his deadline. Said he'd be back in twenty minutes. Ordered drinks all round — again just as he always did — and left the club dead on six-fifteen, exactly to schedule.
>
> (Fleming, 1958, 26)

TABLE VI
UNSTRESSED PRONOUNS

		Subj	DO	IO	Gen	Oth
LOOKBACK	Human	1.73	4.60	1.00	1.39	2.13
		147	10	2	76	29
	Nonhuman	1.91	1.00	-------	1.00	1.06
		23	11		1	16
PERSISTENCE	Human	2.21	1.00	2.50	1.80	1.59
		147	10	2	76	29
	Nonhuman	0.22	0.09	-------	-------	0.25
		23	11			16
AMBIGUITY	Human	1.28	0.80	-------	1.19	1.31
		75	4		47	13
	Nonhuman	1.40	1.16	-------	-------	1.33
		10	7			9

In this particular passage, the zero anaphora serves also to signal that more of the same is coming, that everything being said is what someone else said.

5.4.2. *Unstressed pronouns*: As Table IV shows, unstressed pronouns are the most common of the devices studied in the continuity cline. While not quite as continuous as zero anaphora, unstressed pronouns are still very continuous. They allow the continuity of discourse much as zero anaphora does, but they can bridge a somewhat bigger gap because of the additional information of gender identification. Because most unstressed pronouns used are for humans (84%), gender can come into play. For nonhumans, unstressed pronouns do not supply the same gender distinction and are, therefore, not as useful as the figures in Table VI show. Numbers above the line are the averages; numbers below the line are the number of tokens.

5.4.3. *Stressed pronouns*: Only one stressed pronouns was found in the text analyzed. This pronoun is mentioned only because it exhibits the feature of contrast which is suggested for the use of stressed pronouns in other languages (Givón, 1979, 316).

TABLE VII
DEMONSTRATIVE PRONOUNS

		Subj	DO	IO	Gen	Oth
LOOKBACK	Human	-------	-------	-------	-------	-------
	Nonhuman	2.23	2.00	-------	-------	2.00
		22	1			4
PERSISTENCE	Human	-------	-------	-------	-------	-------
	Nonhuman	0.14	0.00	-------	-------	1.50
		22	1			4
AMBIGUITY	Human	-------	-------	-------	-------	-------
	Nonhuman	1.88	1.00	-------	-------	1.00
		16	1			3

They were going to have dinner together. Bond had asked Quarrel to suggest a place. After a moment of embarrassment, Quarrel had said that whenever *he* wanted to enjoy himself in Kingston he went to a waterfront nightspot called The Joy Boat.

(Fleming, 1958, 36)

5.4.4. *Demonstrative pronouns*: Although demonstrative pronouns are much more rare than unstressed pronouns, they function much like them. However, whereas pronouns refer back to a previously mentioned person or item, demonstrative pronouns refer back to entire pieces of action or to verbs rather than nouns. In fact, as Table VII shows, there were no occasions when demonstratives alone referred to humans. The following passage shows how demonstrative pronouns are used to refer to entire pieces of action or verbs rather than to nouns.

Then Bond had asked for a single room and shower at the Blue Hills Hotel, for the loan of a car and for Quarrel to meet him with the car at the airport. Most of *this* had been wrong. In particular Bond should have taken a taxi to his hotel and made contact with Quarrel later. Then he would have seen the car and had a chance to change it.

(Fleming, 1958, 34)

There is also a difference in the way THIS/THESE and THAT/THOSE are used to produce continuity. The former forms are often used to refer forward to something or an action which the receiver is not aware of yet.

'It's like *this.*' He began his antics with the pipe. "The Jamaican is a kindly lazy man with the virtues and vices of a child. He lives on a very rich island but . . . ."

(Fleming, 1958, 51)

5.4.5. *Passives*: The statistics for the passives examined are shown in Table VIII. Table V shows that passives are near the continuous end of the clines for lookback and persistence, but in the lower half of the cline for ambiguity. The higher ambiguity score is related to the impersonalization function of the passive (Givón, 1981, examines this idea). Because the agent of the passive is often suppressed (appearing, for example, in only 3 of the 34 cases in the text examined here), there is often greater ambiguity as to the performer of the action. Notice the following report from a newspaper which is part of the novel analyzed:

The *Gleaner* said that a Sunbeam Talbot, H. 2473, had been involved in a fatal accident on the Devil's Racecourse, a stretch of winding road between Spanish

TABLE VIII
PASSIVES

		Subj	DO	IO	Gen	Oth
LOOKBACK	Human	6.20 ⎯⎯ 20	-------	-------	-------	-------
	Nonhuman	12.43 ⎯⎯ 14	-------	-------	-------	16.33 ⎯⎯ 3
PERSISTENCE	Human	2.20 ⎯⎯ 20	-------	-------	-------	-------
	Nonhuman	0.21 ⎯⎯ 14	-------	-------	-------	0.00 ⎯⎯ 3
AMBIGUITY	Human	2.08 ⎯⎯ 12	-------	-------	-------	-------
	Nonhuman	1.90 ⎯⎯ 10	-------	-------	-------	2.00 ⎯⎯ 2

Town and Ocho Rios – on the Kingston-Montego route. A runaway lorry, whose driver was being traced, had crashed into the Sunbeam as it came round a bend. Both vehicles had left the road and hurtled into the ravine below. The two occupants of the Sunbeam, Ben Gibbons of Harbour Street, and Josiah Smith, no address, had been killed. A Mr. Bond, an English visitor, who had been lent the car, was asked to contact the nearest police station.

(Fleming, 1958, 63)

5.4.6.   *Demonstratives + NP*: Table IX shows the figures for demonstratives + NP. This construction is in many ways like the demonstratives alone. For example, THIS/THESE are also used with NPs to refer to items which are made more definite to the receiver in the following discourse rather than in the previous discourse.

TABLE IX
DEMONSTRATIVES + NP

		Subj	DO	IO	Gen	Oth
LOOKBACK	Human	6.77 / 9	1.00 / 1	-------	20.00 / 1	10.00 / 5
	Nonhuman	7.67 / 3	15.50 / 4	-------	-------	10.33 / 21
PERSISTENCE	Human	1.11 / 9	0.00 / 1	-------	0.00 / 1	0.60 / 5
	Nonhuman	2.67 / 3	0.00 / 4	-------	-------	0.14 / 21
AMBIGUITY	Human	1.50 / 6	-------	-------	-------	2.20 / 5
	Nonhuman	1.50 / 2	3.00 / 3	-------	-------	1.72 / 18

The affair of the roseate spoonbills and the trouble with the Audubon Society meant precisely nothing except, as M had said, that a lot of old women had got excited about some pink storks. All the same, four people had died because of these storks and, most significant of all to Bond, Quarrel was scared of Doctor No and his island. That was very odd indeed. Cayman Islanders, least of all Quarrel, did not scare easily. And why had Doctor No got *this mania* for privacy? Why did he go to such expense and trouble to keep people away from his guano island?

(Fleming, 1958, 43)

The italicized demonstrative + NP refer forward to the description of Doctor No's mania for privacy. The other demonstrative + NP (these storks) refers back to a previously mentioned item. It is possible that the author chose to use the demonstrative + NP rather than a definite article + NP to show that the narrative here refers to what Bond is thinking; it is privy to the thinker and the deictic *these* serves to somewhat exclude the intruding reader.

5.4.7. *Names*: Although Table V shows that names fall in similar positions in the clines formed by all three measures, names seem to have two distinct discontinuity situations which call for their use. The first discontinuity situation is distance. Names are used often when a previously mentioned person or thing has been out of the discourse for a while. They are also used for the first referent to a person at the beginning of a new paragraph; they assign topic for the paragraph. On the other hand, names are also used in contexts where a lot of ambiguity is possible. Often when two referents are available for any pronoun which might be used, one of the referents will be consistently referred to by name while the other is referred to by a pronoun.

> Somehow he had known that Bond had been given the job. He had wanted a picture of Bond and he had wanted to know where Bond was staying. He would be keeping an eye on Bond to see if Bond picked up any of the leads that had led to Strangways's death. If Bond did so, Bond would also have to be eliminated.
>
> (Fleming, 1958, 42)

Table X shows the breakdown of the counts on names.

TABLE X
NAMES

		Subj	DO	IO	Gen	Oth
LOOKBACK	Human	5.42	6.00	8.00	6.41	11.42
		155	6	3	29	33
	Nonhuman	10.14	19.33	-------	11.00	18.26
		7	6		2	89
PERSISTENCE	Human	1.94	1.83	0.67	0.94	0.76
		155	6	3	29	33
	Nonhuman	0.71	0.00	-------	0.00	0.13
		7	6		2	89
AMBIGUITY	Human	1.53	1.67	2.00	1.56	1.91
		112	3	2	19	22
	Nonhuman	1.67	2.00	-------	2.00	1.84
		3	5		1	51

5.4.8. *Right and Left Dislocation*

In Table XI below we compare the average values for the three measurements of R-dislocation, L-dislocation and neutral-order definite NP's. The samples combine humans/non-humans and subject/object case-roles. The measurements of persistence and ambiguity do not seem to separate the three constructions significantly. The measure of lookback does, however, showing R-dislocation to be a much more continuous device (2.22 clauses to the left) than the other two (12.24/12.42). L-dislocation and the neutral word-order do not separate in this study, but see Givón's study of colloquial English (in this volume) for clear separation of the two.

TABLE XI: RIGHT AND LEFT DISLOCATIONS
IN ORAL NARRATIVE

	L-dislocation	neutral DEF-NP	R-dislocation
N	21	33	18
LOOKBACK (average)	12.24	12.42	2.22
PERSISTENCE (average)	1.95	1.81	2.00
AMBIGUITY (average)	1.86	1.85	2.39

5.4.9. *Definite Articles + NP*: Table XII shows the use of the definite article + NP. It is interesting that the greatest use of this construction comes in functions other than subject or object. It is also interesting that definite articles are quite low on the lists of average lookback and average persistence but relatively high on the list of ambiguity. This fact indicates that the structure is used in situations where there are gaps but where the referent is very clear. In other words, definite articles are definite. Often knowledge of the way the world operates makes the referent clear. Other times previous mention (albeit at a distance) makes the referent clear. Still other times the NP is immediately followed by a relative clause or other restrictive information which makes the reference of the construction clear. Although the division could not be done in the present study, future studies should divide the definite article + NP constructions according to the three things which make them definite. The average lookback, persistence, and ambiguity scores of the three divisions might provide further clues to how this construction functions. The following passage provides some interesting

TABLE XII
DEFINITE ARTICLE + NP

		Subj	DO	IO	Gen	Oth
LOOKBACK	Human	11.10	8.33	20.00	5.75	14.00
		20	6	2	4	7
	Nonhuman	14.21	13.02	-------	14.50	19.22
		39	37		2	176
PERSISTENCE	Human	0.67	0.50	0.50	0.50	0.57
		20	6	2	4	7
	Nonhuman	0.23	0.16	0.00	0.00	0.18
		39	37		2	176
AMBIGUITY	Human	1.54	1.00	-------	1.00	2.00
		13	2		3	2
	Nonhuman	1.38	1.68	-------	1.00	1.31
		18	19		1	80

examples of the construction made definite in each of the three ways. The information in parentheses is mine.

The drinks (previous mention) came. The glasses (knowledge of world) were dripping with condensation. The small fact (previous mention) reminded Bond of other times in hot climates. A few yards away the sea (knowledge of world and previous mention) lisped on the flat sand (knowledge of world). The three-piece (previous mention) began playing 'Kitch.' Above them the palm fronds (knowledge of world) clashed softly in the night breeze (knowledge of world). A gecko chuckled somewhere in the garden (previous mention). Bond thought of the London (restriction) he had left the day (restriction) before.

(Fleming, 1958, 37)

5.4.10. *NPs following Possessives*: NPs following possessives have already been mentioned in the discussion of possessives under the continuity according to functions (see Table III). The possessives tend to tie these otherwise indefinite items to the subject at hand. Interestingly, as Table XIII shows, these constructions frequently occupy the direct object spot, the spot generally occupied by indefinites (see Givón, 1977, for a further discussion of this point.). However, these items do not seem to shift and become the topics of discourse at all. They exhibit the lowest persistence rate of any of the structures counted.

TABLE XIII:
NPs FOLLOWING POSSESSIVES

		Subj	DO	IO	Gen	Oth
LOOKBACK	Human	-------	20.00	-------	-------	20.00
			3			4
	Nonhuman	18.60	18.69	-------	-------	18.03
		30	59			133
PERSISTENCE	Human	-------	0	-------	-------	0.00
			3			4
	Nonhuman	0.23	0.14	-------	-------	0.03
		30	59			133
AMBIGUITY	Human	-------	2.00	-------	-------	1.00
			3			1
	Nonhuman	2.30	1.98			2.11
		23	47			106

5.4.11. *Generics*: As the number of tokens in the Other category on Table XIV shows, generics occurred most frequently in this text as objects of prepositions, particularly following *of* in partitives. The head noun for the prepositions was usually definite but the objects of the prepositions seemed generic. For example,

A whole flock of *birds* got up in front of it and suddenly a lot of *fire* came out of its mouth and it burned a lot of them up and all the trees they'd been roosting in.

(Fleming, 1958, 74)

In narrative, at least, generics do not become the topic of further discourse very often (hence, the low persistence score). Also, they seem to be introductions to their referents as they are on the bottom of the lookback list. Possibly because they include an entire general class, there is little ambiguity as to their referents.

TABLE XIV:
GENERICS

		Subj	DO	IO	Gen	Oth
LOOKBACK	Human	20.00	-------	-------	-------	18.20
		12				10
	Nonhuman		18.52	19.43	20.00	19.28
		23	30	1		186
PERSISTENCE	Human	1.08	-------	-------	-------	0.00
		12				10
	Nonhuman	0.13	0.17	0	-------	0.40
		23	30	1		186
AMBIGUITY	Human	2.14	-------	-------	-------	1.60
		7				5
	Nonhuman	1.84	1.78	-------	-------	1.40
		19	27			134

5.4.12. *Indefinite Referentials*: As Table XV shows, indefinite referentials are found frequently in the direct object position. They do not persist and they generally refer to something which has not been mentioned before; thus, the long lookback. Ambiguity exists only in the sense that there is generally nothing specific in the text to which the indefinite referential could refer back to so all referents are possible. The low persistence of these structures may simply be an interaction with their low ratio of humanness.

TABLE XV
INDEFINITE REFERENTIAL

		Subj	DO	IO	Gen	Oth
LOOKBACK	Human	20.00	20.00	-------	-------	16.83
		8	2			6
	Nonhuman	17.21	19.12	-------	20.00	19.41
		14	64		1	143
PERSISTENCE	Human	1.25	0.00	-------	-------	0.67
		8	2			6
	Nonhuman	0.57	0.19	-------	0	0;06
		14	64		1	143
AMBIGUITY	Human	3.00	3.00	-------	-------	3.00
		8	2			6
	Nonhuman	3.00	3.00	-------	3.00	3.00
		14	64		1	143

6. *Conclusion*

The preceding study was undertaken to determine if the cline of points along a continuum of "continuity" could be substantiated with actual figures. The results of the study suggest several things. To begin with, they *suggest* that the cline can be substantiated. Further work will have to be done before an answer can be given conclusively, however. The results also suggest that many factors enter into the matter of continuity. Topicality has a strong influence, and humanness has such a strong influence as to almost overpower any other factors. Before a definite substantiatiation can be given to the cline, the interplay of all of these factors should be examined more thoroughly. It would also be advisable to investigate the interaction of the three measures with the different structures. It is possible that we are really dealing with three different clines rather than one. Careful statistics performed and a factor analysis done based on those statistics could possibly decide that question. In conclusion, while the present study cannot be said to "prove" the reality of a continuum of continuity, it suggests that the idea of a continuum is a viable idea with many factors leaning towards its proof. It also suggests the worth of actual analysis of data to substantiate linguistic theory.

REFERENCES

Bolinger, D. (1979) "Pronouns in discourse", in T. Givón (Ed.), *Syntax and Semantics, Vol. 12, Discourse and Syntax,* New York: Academic Press.

Fleming, I. (1958) *Doctor No.* New York: Signet Books

Givón, T. (1976) "Topic, pronoun and grammatical agreement", In C. Li (Ed.), *Subject and Topic,* New York: Academic Press

—————. (1977) "Definiteness and referentiality", In J. Greenberg, C. Ferguson, and E. Moravcsik (Eds.) *Universals of Human Language* Stanford: Stanford University Press

—————. (1979) *On Understanding Grammar,* New York: Academic Press

—————. (1980) *Ute Reference Grammar.* Ignacio, Colorado: Ute Press

—————. (1981) "Typology and functional domains" *Studies in Language*

Greenberg, J. (1974) "The relation of frequency to semantic feature in a case language", *Working Papers in Language Universals, 16.* Stanford: Stanford University

TOPIC CONTINUITY IN SPOKEN ENGLISH*

T. GIVÓN
Linguistics Department
University of Oregon, Eugene

and

Ute Language Program
Southern Ute Tribe
Ignacio, Colorado

*) For the text studied here I am indebted to my good friend, fiddler, trapper, rancher, roughneck and above all story-teller extraordinaire, Harris Brown of Bloomfield, New Mexico.

TABLE OF CONTENTS

1. *Introduction*

A number of topic-marking devices, most conspicuously left and right dislocation (henceforth LD and RD, respectively), appear only in the informal, colloquial, spoken register of English. Their study is nevertheless of great interest within the context of the effect of topicality and topic continuity on word-order. English is a rigid SVO language, where pragmatic control of word order along the lines shown for the VS/SV variation in Ute, Spanish and Biblical Hebrew (see relevant chapters in this volume) or the VO/OV variation in Ute (see relevant chapter) is not attested. Nevertheless, it is possible to show that within broad limits the RD device – with the topic *following* the comment – behaves like the COMMENT-TOPIC word order of those flexible word-order languages. Similarly, the LD device – with the topic *preceding* the comment – behaves like the TOPIC-COMMENT word-order in those languages. These similarities have already been noted in a previous study using early English-based Pidgins (of Korean, Philippino and Spanish speakers) as data base (Givón, 1982). This study shows that the same is also true for spoken colloquial native American English.

The data base for this study is the typed verbatim transcript of the life story of a New Mexico man, recorded in Bloomfield, New Mexico during the winter of 1979-1980, when the narrator was about fifty-five years of age. Thirty-three pages of transcript were counted. The narrator was born in the Texas Panhandle and, like the majority of the Anglo settlers of New Mexico, speaks West Texas English. While a high school graduate, he is nevertheless a member of a primarily *oral* culture, having few occasions to express himself in writing. His narrative is thus broadly typical of the oral, colloquial genre of American English. A sample of the running transcript may be seen in the Appendix at the end of this article.

2. *Topic marking devices studied*

While my main interest was the study of the LD and RD devices, it was necessary to study a broader range of constructions in order to place those two within a proper context. Only subject NP's were studied, and within those the following topic-marking constructions:

2.1. *Zero anaphora*

Many of the zeros in the sample were *conjoined* zeros, as in:

(1)   . . . and the turkeys would come in and [∅] roost in. . .

Others were *subordinate* zeros, as in:

(2)   . . .them old cowboys had to be pretty tough [∅] to run cattle in
            that kind of stuff. . .
(3)   . . .those ol' cowboys would ride in on horseback for many miles,
            [∅] to eat with them. . .
(4)   . . .it got its name from an old cook that [∅] used to live over there. . .

No attempt was made to further differentiate between the various subtypes of
zeros in the counting.

2.2. *Pronouns*

No attempt was made initially to distinguish phonologically between
stressed and unstressed pronouns in the transcripts, although as we shall see
further below, an estimation that to some extent approximates such a distinction turns out to be essential for interpreting the behavior of pronouns in this
text. We counted only third persons, either singular or plural. As examples
consider:

(5)   . . .*He* was born in Sherman, and when *he* was about a year old *they*
            moved down to. . .Hanson. . .

2.3. *Definite NP's* [Def]

Within this category were included proper names, nouns marked by definite articles and nouns marked by demonstratives, as in:

(6)   . . .and ol' *John* told him, he said.. .
(7)   . . .Anyway, *the turkeys* would come into the river to roost. . .
(8)   . . .*that mesquite* was thick back then. . .

2.4. *Possessed definite NP's* [DEF-P]

Since the narrative is of a personal nature, many of the definite referents
are marked with the possessive pronoun, most overwhelmingly 'my', as in:

(9)   . . . Well *my dad* was born in Sherman. . .

2.5. *Definite NP's followed by a pause* [DEF-PAUSE]

As I have shown elsewhere (Givón, 1982), hesitation pauses associated with the delivery of a referent often mark it as a highly *discontinuous* topic. As a typical example of this rather infrequent category in the present text consider:

(10)   ... and of course the hunters started coming in and coyotes and *the*
       ...the predators got to take there...

2.6. *Definite NP's involving repetition [DEF-REP]*

Much like hesitation pauses, topic repetition – or substitution – has been shown elsewhere (Givón, 1982) as a mark of highly *discontinuous* topics. The same NP may be repeated, as in:

(11)   ... *ours, our homestead* was about fifty miles south of Grants...

Or else a substitution may be involved, as in:

(12)   ... *my older...three or four brothers* were born...

Admittedly, (12) may be also interpreted as an instance of hesitation/pause.

2.7. *Left dislocation* [LD]

As examples of this device consider:

(13)   ... *my dad,* all *he* ever did was farm and ranch...
(14)   ... *my great grandfather, they* came in there...

No attempt was made to further subdivide this category.

2.8. *Right dislocation* [RD]

There were only four examples of this device attested in the first sixty pages of the transcript (as compared with forty-four instances of LD in the first thirty-three pages of transcript). As examples consider:

(15)   ... *they*'d go butcher them, even *the honest ones*...
(16)   ... he wound up with fifty-nine sections of land for a ranch is what *he*
       still owns there now, *ol' John Leehugh*...

No attempt was made to further subcategorize the examples.

2.9. *Demonstrative pronouns* [DEM]

Demonstratives by themselves, most commonly 'that', are used to refer to just-concluded larger thematic units, rather than to topic-participants at the clause level. As a typical example consider:

(17)   ... the winter of thirty-one, spring of thirty-two. And ah, it was four feet [of snow] all over, that's when these ol' wild horses ate each other's tails out and ate their manes off and, and ate so many it killed a bunch of them 'cause they ate piñon needles, and dried sticks, you know, they'd ruin their stomachs and just killed them, you know. *That* was that kind of a winter. . .

In fewer instances, the referent is more nominal-topical, as in:

(18)   .. no, really it was good land Tom, it just needed a lot of development, that's the way all that country, *that*'s a. . . *that*'s a dry country up there. . .

3. *Methodology and measurements*

Two of the standard measurements employed throughout this volume were performed on the text: Referential Distance ('look-back') and Persistence ('decay'). In addition, the percent distribution of the various devices in the text was computed. As mentioned above, only *subject* topics were studied. Further, first and second pronoun subjects − including zero anaphores coreferent with them − were not counted. Only long chunks of the narrative were counted, eliminating both the contributions of the interviewer as well as short contributions of the narrator. Materials inside direct quotes were not studied, nor were they considered a gap for the purpose of computing either referential distance or persistence.

One additional measurement was performed on pronouns throughout the first sixteen pages of the text. The pronouns were divided into those with referential distance values of *one clause* as against all those with values of *two* or *more*. Each one of these two categories was then divided into two: those following a *minor juncture* vs. those following a *major juncture*. Informally, a minor junction is one where the action continues *in sequence*, without a break in the thematic continuity. Most commonly, those junctures are marked by a *comma* in the transcript, followed by 'and', 'then', 'so', 'when', 'because', or on occasion no conjunction. As typical examples consider:

(19)   . . . And ol' Juan told him, *he* said. . .

(20)   . . . he was there two or three months in the fall, you know, *and then he* had some. . .

(21)   . . . I guess he had a little something then *but he* just set him down. . .

(22)   . . . and they remembered where that ol' homestead was *'cause they*'d spend all the summer there. . .

(23)   . . . They hauled them there *so they* could go to work with them. . .

(24)   . . . a lot of them that were branded, you know, *when they* were calves, *they* wouldn't see them anymore *till they* was five or six years old. . .

In contrast, major junctures tend to be marked in this transcript by periods or pauses, quite often with a more massive introductory phrase, quite often contrastive. They tend to break action and theme continuity more severely.

As examples of various types of major junctures, consider:

(25)   . . . and that weeded them out, you know to where there are very few turkeys left. I mean, you know, that was a hundred years ago this all happened, but at one time, boy! I guess turkeys was really big in that country.
        Anyway, they lived on this river a little while. . .

(26)   . . . it was either ranches or farms, there was no mining in that country or no oil, all that came years later, you know, and a lot of that country got to be rich oil country later after they began to use oil, but back then is was just all ranchin' and farmin'. *So he ah. . .he ah* met my mother, I think in Cattle County. . .

(27)   . . . we had a sister born there too with the other three brothers and she died when she was a baby. That's the only sister we ever had, all the rest of us were boys. . . *But anyway, they* moved to McClain and. . .

In (25) above the theme prior to the major juncture is turkeys. The major juncture then reactivates the main line of the family's movements. In (26) the theme prior to the major juncture is a description of the way the country used to be in the old days. The major juncture then reactivates the doings of the main participants. In (27) the theme prior to the major juncture is the sister who died. The major juncture then moves the story back to the main line of description. As we shall see below, these examples are indeed typical of the use of pronouns at major junctures, where their referential distance is much *larger* than one clause.

4. Numerical results

4.1. Referential distance ('look-back')

The results for this measurement are given in Tables I, II and III below. Within broad bounds, they conform to what is reported elsewhere in this volume, with the zero-anaphora category once again showing itself to be the most *localized* referential device, followed by pronouns and then by full definite NP's. Unlike Spanish, where anaphoric pronouns (clitic pronouns/verb

TABLE I: Average Referential Distance
and text distribution of constructions

category	N	percent in text	ave. ref. distance in no. of clauses
Ø	117	0.16	1.01
PRO	423	0.57	1.60
RD(DEF)	4	0.005	1.00
DEM	17	0.02	1.00
DEF	69	0.09	10.15
DEF-P	44	0.06	10.29
LD (DEF)	44	0.06	15.34
DEF-REP	17	0.02	17.23
DEF-PAUSE	7	0.01	17.42
total	742	1.00	

agreement) fall into the same category with the zero and thus exhibiting essentially the lowest ref-distance values (thus contrasting with the less localized independent/stressed pronouns, see Bentivoglio, in this volume); and unlike Ute when zero, clitic pronouns and independent/stressed pronouns are clearly separable (see Givón, in this volume), in our unified pronoun category in this study a clear mixture exists between the 79 percent of all pronouns which appear at the minimal distance of one clause, and the remaining 21 percent which are used as a *less localized* referential device. The potential for such a separation is assessed by another measurement, see further below.

The referential distance for simple definite NP's and right and left dislocated DEF-NP's follows a scale already shown elsewhere (Givón, 1982) for pidgin-

TABLE II: Percent Distribution of Referential Distance within Categories

No. of Clauses	∅ N	∅ per	PRO N	PRO per	RD N	RD per	DEM N	DEM per	DEF N	DEF per	DEF-P N	DEF-P per	LD N	LD per	DEF-REP N	DEF-REP per	DEF-PAUSE N	DEF-PAUSE per
1	115	0.98	336	0.79	4	1.00	17	1.00	16	0.23	10	0.23	/		/		/	
2	2	0.02	46	0.11					4		1		1	0.02	/		1	0.14
3			12						7	0.17	4	0.22	2		1	0.06	/	
4			8	0.06					/		2		2	0.25	/		/	
5			6						1		3		1		/		/	
6			3						3	0.15	/		3		1	0.06	/	
7			1						3		1	0.16	/		/		/	
8			1						1		1		3		1	0.06	/	
9			2						2		3		/		/		/	
10			2						1		/		3	0.13	/		/	
11			2						2	0.07	2		/		/		/	
12			2	0.04					1						/		/	
13			/						/						/		/	
14			1						1				2		/		/	
15			1						1						1	0.06	/	
16			/										1		/		/	
17			/										/		/		/	
18			/										1		/		/	
19			/										/		/		/	
20			1												13	0.76	6	0.86
									26	0.38	17	0.39	26	0.60				
Total	117	1.00	423	1.00	4	1.00	17	1.00	69	1.00	44	1.00	44	1.00	17	1.00	7	1.00

TABLE III: Comparison of Average Values of Referential Distance
with Prototype Distribution of Categories

category	average ref. distance	distance range within which 70-100 percent of category is found	
∅	1.01	1 clause	(98 percent)
PRO	1.60	2 clauses	(90 percent)
RD (DEF)	1.00	1 clause	(100 percent)
DEM	1.00	1 clause	(100 percent)
DEF	10.15	2-20 clauses	(70 percent)
DEF-P	10.29	2-20 clauses	(70 percent)
LD (DEF)	15.34	11-20 clauses	(73 percent)
DEF-REP	17.23	20 clauses	(76 percent)
DEF-PAUSE	17.42	20 clauses	(86 percent)

English transcripts, with RD yielding ref-distance values essentially near the anaphoric/localized pronoun level, neutral order DEF-NP's yielding intermediate values, and LD yielding the highest values. Similarly, the devices with the highest referential distance in this study involve either hesitation pause, repetition or substitution of the DEF-NP. This again conforms to the observation made in Givón (1982). Finally, demonstrative pronouns are used in this text as a highly localized, minimal-distance referential device. However, as we shall see further below, other measurements clearly separate them from zero anaphora or anaphoric/unstressed pronouns.

4.2. *Persistence ('decay')*

As shown elsewhere (Givón, in this volume), the persistence measure does not correlate directly with referential distance, primarily because of characteristic positions of various devices at the initial, medial or final position of thematic paragraphs or 'equi-topic chains'. Our results here both conform to those obtained elsewhere as well as add some further elaborations.

With the results in the category of RD disregarded due to low counts, one can identify three devices comprising the top of the range, i.e. categories of *high persistence* and thus *high topic importance*: Pronouns, possessed definites (DEF-P) and left dislocated definites (LD). Of these, I will suggest further below that the category PRO in English is a *composite* category — purely anaphoric unstressed pronouns with referential distance values essentially the same as for zero anaphora, i.e. one clause to the left, and an average characteristic *medial*

TABLE IV: Average Values for Persistence

category	N	average persistence in no. of clauses
∅	117	1.44
PRO	423	2.04
RD (DEF)	4	2.25
DEM	17	0.24
DEF	69	1.24
DEF-P	44	2.09
LD (DEF)	44	2.16
DEF-REP	17	1.17
DEF-PAUSE	7	0.85

position within equi-topic chains; and a significant sub-category of stressed, constrastive, topic-changing pronouns, with a characteristic referential distance of 2-3 or more clauses to the left and a characteristic *initial* position, therefore, in equi-topic chains. This category, while relatively smaller (21 percent of the total sample of pronouns in the text, see Table II, above) is responsible for the unexpectedly high persistence (and referential distance) of the overall PRO category in oral English. While I did not attempt to separate the two fractions directly, an indirect corroboration of this assumption will be presented in section 4.3., below.

The high persistence of possessed DEF-NP's in this text, as compared to the category DEF itself, is due to one obvious feature of the narrative: The blood relatives (father, mother, brothers, cousins, grandparents) or to a lesser extent body part(s) of the narrator occupy the highest topical positions within this first person-based life story. For the same reason, the average (and prototypical) referential distance for the DEF-P category is relatively high: Their being in the register does not depend on proximity.Rather, much like the narrator ('I'), they are in a sense in the register continuously, by virtue of their relatedness to the narrator.

TABLE V: Percent Distribution of Persistence within Categories

no. of clauses	∅ N	∅ per	PRO N	PRO per	RD N	RD per	DEM N	DEM per	DEF N	DEF per	DEF-P N	DEF-P per	LD N	LD per	DEF-REP N	DEF-REP per	DEF-PAUSE N	DEF-PAUSE per
0	43	0.37	149	0.36	/		13	0.93	32	0.46	20	0.46	11	0.25	10	0.60	4	0.58
1	30	0.26	90	0.21	1	0.25	1	0.07	19	0.28	8	0.18	9	0.20	3	0.18	/	
2	15	0.13	62	0.15	2	0.50			7		6	0.14	10	0.23	2	0.12	3	0.42
3	17	0.14	30	0.07	/				3	0.22	1		6	0.14	1	0.05		
4	7	0.06	27	0.06	1	0.25			5		1		1	0.02	/			
5	2		19	0.04					1		2	0.18	3	0.07	/			
6	2		17	0.04					/	0.04	1		/		/			
7	/	0.04	9						/		2		3	0.07	/			
8	1		7						/		1		1	0.02	/			
9			5	0.06					1		/				1	0.05		
10			2						1		/							
11			3								1							
12			1								1	0.04						
13			1	0.01							/							
14			1								1							
15																		
total	117	1.00	423	1.00	4	1.00	14	1.00	69	1.00	45	1.00	44	1.00	17	1.00	7	1.00

TABLE VI: Comparison of average values of persistence
with prototype distribution of categories

category	average persistence	distance range within which percent of category is found	
∅	1.44	0-3 clauses	(90 percent)
PRO	2.04	0-5 clauses	(89 percent)
RD (DEF)	2.25	1-4 clauses	(100 percent)[a]
DEM	0.24	0-1 clauses	(100 percent)
DEF	1.24	0-4 clauses	(96 percent)
DEF-P	2.09	0-8 clauses	(96 percent)
LD (DEF)	2.16	0-5 clauses	(91 percent)
DEF-REP	1.17	0-2 clauses	(90 percent)
DEF-PAUSE	0.85	0-2 clauses	(100 percent)

[a] Count too low to be significant

Finally, the high persistence values of definite left-dislocation, together with the high referential distance for that category, marks it clearly at a typical *chain-initial*, new topic introducing category.

The intermediate values for persistence are shown by zero anaphora, simple definites and repeated definites (DEF-REP), with average values ranging from 1.44 clauses to the right to 1.17, respectively. Zero anaphora is prototypically a chain-medial category, so that average persistence values here are expected. The two other categories, with relatively high referential distance (in the case of DEF-REP, the highest) clearly are not as important devices for the reintroduction of important topics back into the register as are left-dislocation or stressed pronouns. Even less efficient in this capacity is pause-definite NP, with a lower yet average persistence (but obtained from a rather low count).

Closest to a typical *chain-final* category in our study is the particular usage of demonstratives (mostly *that*) observed here, with high continuity to the left (typically one clause referential distance) and virtually no continuity to the right (proto-typically zero clauses to the right, with the average of 0.24).

4.3. *Pronouns used at major and minor junctures*

As suggested earlier, there are good grounds for believing that the PRO category to which our ref. distance and persistence measurements were applied

above is a mix of two distinct grammatical devices:
(a)   Anaphoric/continuative, with low referential distance; and
(b)   Contrastive/topic changing, with higher referential distance.

In order to assess this, we divided all pronouns within 16 pages of the text into two categories: those with referential distance of one (anaphoric, continuative), and those with referential distance of two or more (contrastive or topic changing). The overall distribution was 124 or *0.78 percent* of the total in the anaphoric/ continuative category, and thirty-six or *0.22 percent* for the contrastive/topic changing category. The results, together with the division within each as to presence at a *major vs. minor discourse juncture*, are given in Table VII below. As one can see, anaphoric/continuative (and thus likely *unstressed*) pronouns in our text are overwhelmingly present − 0.93 percent − at minor discourse junctures, i.e. *in the middle* of sequential action chains, while topic-changing/contrastive pronouns (presumably *stressed*) are prototypically present − 0.75 percent − at major discourse junctures, i.e. *at the beginning* of sequential action chains. The percentages obtained in this independent measurement closely duplicate the division found in Table II, with 0.79 percent of all pronouns showing referential distance of one clause, vs. 0.21 showing two or more clauses. The figures also follow closely the percentages in Table V, where 0.79 percent of all pronouns show persistence values ranging from zero to three clauses, characteristic of *chain-medial* or *chain-final* topic-marking devices; while only 0.21 percent show higher persistence values, characteristic of *chain-initial* devices − and thus

TABLE VII: Correlation of Referential Distance of Pronouns
and their Presence at Major vs. Minor discourse Junctures

juncture	pronouns with referential distance of 1 clause		pronouns with referential distance of 2 or more clauses		all pronouns	
	N	percent	N	percent	N	percent
major	8	0.07	27	0.75	35	0.22
minor	116	0.93	9	0.25	125	0.78
totals	124	1.00	36	1.00	160	1.00
percent	0.78		0.22			

presumably of *topic-changing* categories. I shall return to discuss these results further below.

Finally, it is of interest to note that the percent distribution of minor vs. major junctures within the total pronoun sample in the counted text is identical to the percent distribution of anaphoric vs. contrastive pronouns (0.78 percent vs 0.22 percent, respectively; see Table VIII below).

5. *Discussion*
5.1. *Topic continuity/predictability and marking size*

In their broad outline, the results reported here from spoken English corroborate what is seen elsewhere in the volume concerning the correlation between the degree of continuity/predictability of topic NP's and the average size of the marking devices used to express them. This correlation may be expressed, following Givón (1982), in the implicational hierarchy:

(28)   zero > unstressed/ > stressed/   > full DEF-NP > modified DEF-NP
              clitic   independent
              pronoun   pronoun

The left-most side of the hierarchy is that of the most continuous/predictable topic, while the degree of predictability/continuity decreases to the right. In English, both spoken and written (see Brown, in this volume), the role of the *zero* device is severely limited even for subject (as compared to Japanese, see Hinds, in this volume, or Ute, see Givón, in this volume), so that complete adjacency (referential distance values around 1.00) is not the only requirement for the use of this device. Rather, the *thematic/action continuity* is an added requirement for the use of *zero*, above and beyond the already considerable thematic continuity required for the use of unstressed pronouns, see 4.3. above.

Our results strongly suggest (cf. section 4.3. and Table VII above) that English pronouns are indeed divided into two reasonably distinct categories:

(a)   Unstressed pronouns with lower ref-distance values, in essence the same as for the *zero* category; intermediate persistence/'decay' values, roughly characteristic of a chain-medial category, thus not much different from the *zero* once again;

(b)   Stressed pronouns with a higher ref-distance, probably a higher potential confusion (not measured here), and thus obviously coding topics that are less predictable, or re-introduced into the register; it is suspected (though not measured here directly) that this topic-introducing device must also exhibit higher a *persistence* measure than the intermediate value of un-

stressed pronouns, thus corresponding to other chain-initial categories
in this as well as other studies in this volume.

The various full-NP categories all exhibit lower continuity/predictability in
terms of ref-distance, with the exception of Right Dislocation, to be discussed
further below. Finally, while we did not measure the continuity properties of
modified NP's (modified by adjectives or relatives, that is), other studies in
this volume corroborate this last link in the hierarchy.

5.2. *Topic predictability and Left and Right Dislocation*

Our results fully corroborate those reported in Givón (1982) for spoken
Pidgin English. They further corroborate the results of flexible word-order
languages in this volume (Spanish, Biblical-Hebrew, Ute). In those three, pre-
verbal ordering of the topic marks it as *less* continuous/predictable, while post-
verbal ordering marks it as *more* continuous/predictable, which yield the
hierarchy:

(29)   COMMENT-TOPIC > TOPIC-COMMENT

In a rigid word-order language such as English (SVO), one finds a reflection of
this hierarchy, whereby the COMMENT-TOPIC word-order (Right Dislocation)
is much more *continuous* than the neutral order, roughly approximating the
ref-distance values of anaphoric pronouns (although our count here was too low
for total accuracy), while the TOPIC-COMMENT word-order (Left Dislocation)
is much more *discontinuous* than the neutral word-order, essentially approximating the ref-distance values recorded for the two other most discontinuous
devices, topic repetition and hesitation pause. The ordering hierarchy for
English, and presumably for other rigid-order languages, should then be:

(30)   R-Dislocation > Neutral Order > L-Dislocation

And again. the most continuous topic-marking devices are to the left, the most
discontinuous to right in the the hierarchy in (30). Our results thus also corroborate predictions made in Givón (1978, 1979 ch. 2). Further they uphold
Hyman's (1975) suggestion that R-dislocation was "an afterthought topic", thus
more akin to anaphoric/unstressed pronouns in terms of 'topicality', which is
here expressed in terms of continuity/predictability.

5.3. *Topic repetition or hesitation pause*

Our results tag these two devices, unattested in the written register but well-attested in spoken English or Pidgin English (Givón, 1982), as the most discontinuous topic-marking devices in colloquial English. This again corroborates the overall rock-bottom hierarchy suggested in Givón (1982):

(31)

COMMENT > COMMENT-TOPIC > TOPIC-COMMENT > TOPIC (REPETITION)
(zero topic)   (zero comment)

It also again recalls the psychological principle invoked there to explain this "rock bottom" universal of topic coding:

(32)   "Tend first to the most urgent task"

At the left-most extreme the topic is no problem, being totally predictable/continuous. The most urgent remaining task is thus the processing of the comment. At the right-most extreme the topic is so unpredictable/discontinuous that its identification overrides all else in the communicative process (cf. Keenan, 1975). The two word-order possibilities simply bridge the two extremes of the scale, allowing for a multi-point transition rather than a categorial binary split.

REFERENCES

Givón, T. (1978) "Definiteness and referentiality", in J. Greenberg (ed.), *Universals of Human Language*, vol. 4 (Syntax), Stanford University Press
————— (1979) *On Understanding Grammar*, NY: Academic Press
————— (1982) "Universals of discourse structure and second language acquisition", in W Rutherford (ed.) *Language Universals and Second Language Acquisition*, TSL, Vol. 5, Amsterdam: J. Benjamins (in press)
Hyman, L. (1975) "The change from SOV to SVO: Evidence from Niger-Congo", in C. Li (ed.) *Word Order and Word Order Change*, Austin: University of Texas Press
Keenan, Elinor (1975) "Making it last: Use of repetition in children's discourse", *Proc. Berkeley Linguistic Society*, vol. 1, University of California at Berkeley

APPENDIX

Sample typed transcript (pp. 14-16)

. . .That's right. . . and yeah, that's, that's still, it's about all gone now but you know when I was a kid, why boy, if you had the money you could buy worlds of railroad sections 'cause they knew they had a bunch of land they weren't ever gonna need to build railroads on. . . so you could bought, see those ol' rich ranchers that's how they wound up with lots of country. They bought that railroad land. Then after that drought down in that country, why the home-steaders starved out, you know. You just couldn't make it on a section without any water or any irrigation. It was too small amount to run cattle on. And my dad did lease some, ah, 'course BLM had land then and they had it all leased to these big ranchers. And there was a frenchman up south of Grants, ol' Juan Yarty. He had worlds of sheep. And he had all this BLM land that was around us down there. . . and he raised sheep, you know. But he'd only winter down there in the winter time and him and my dad got along good, you know, my dad had a wonderful personality, everybody liked him. And ol' Juan told him, he said: "G.B." he said, ah, "you. . help my. . . look out for my sheep and herders when I go down", he was in there about two or three months in the fall, you know, and then he had some, something further down that he wintered on. But he'd come back through there every fall, keep his sheep in there, two or three thousand head of them for about a month or so. And he told my dad, "You can use that the rest of the year", he said, "You run your cattle on it", you know, they made a deal so my dad wound up with three sections there, you know. There's how he'd run his little bunch of cows. And ol' Juan just give it to 'm 'cause, you know, back in the thirties nobody had any money. You couldn't even, it got so you, you know, you couldn't even sell cattle. We had worlds to eat up there because we raised chicken, we raised hogs, we raised ah, ah, sheep or two now and then around to eat, you know. And beef. . . why you ate all of it you could because you couldn't get rid of it, and my dad used to trade a steer to some store over there, you know, for coffee or, and sugar and things that we couldn't raise up there. But otherwise, we was there five or six years and my dad finall. . . got acquainted with old John Leehugh and he had an old well-drillin' rig, you know, an old cable-tube, and he needed some tanks built, and my dad did a lot of work with his team, ah, the little [???] and scrapers, you know, and dirt moving equipment that you had then. And old John told him, he said, "G.B., if you'll build me, a, a tank over here, I'll drill you a well". So they made that trade see. And ah, to go on with that kind of deals my dad had to have his teeth pulled, there once, you know, they got bad. And we had an old dentist lived over there on a homestead and he built teeth, and he made my dad the same trade. He said, "G.B., I'll come over to your house". I think my dad had either eighteen or twenty-eight. . . eighteen at least. And he come over there and sit my dad down in a rockin' chair in front of the. . . in front of the door. The door was in the south in that house. And he pulled all them teeth there in one evening with, you know and that's where they had all this killin' stuff. I guess he had a little something then but he just set him down there and pulled them all out. . .

SOME DIMENSIONS OF TOPIC-NP CONTINUITY
IN HAUSA NARRATIVE *)

PHILIP J. JAGGAR

Department of Linguistics, UCLA

*) In preparing this paper I have benefitted from numerous suggestions offered by Talmy Givón and by those of my colleagues/friends at UCLA who have also contributed to this volume. I would like to express additional thanks to Russell G. Schuh for exercising a healthy scepticism and questioning some of my interpretations of the Hausa facts; Sandra Thompson and Paul Schachter were also kind enough to comment on an earlier draft of the paper. Lastly, I would like to thank Sani Ahmad Sufi and Faruk Umar — both native-speakers of the Kano dialect of Hausa — who responded to my sometimes insistent queries in a patient and informed fashion. Any remaining weaknesses are my own responsibility entirely.

LIST OF TABLES

LIST OF FIGURES

ABBREVIATIONS

ADV . . . . .Adverb
ASSOC . . . . .Associative
ATM . . . . .Aspect-Tense-Modal
DEM . . . . .Demonstrative
DO . . . . .Direct object
DO-∅ . . . . .Direct object-deletion
EXIST . . . . .Existential
fem . . . . .feminine
FUT . . . . .Future
IMPERF . . . . .Imperfective
IMPERS . . . . .Impersonal (subject) pronoun
IO . . . . .Indirect object
IO-∅ . . . . .Indirect object-deletion
LOC . . . . .Locative
masc . . . . .masculine
NEG . . . . .Negative
NP . . . . .Noun phrase
plur . . . . .plural
PERF . . . . .Perfective
POSS . . . . .Possessive
PRM . . . . .Previous Reference Marker
REF-DEF . . . . .Referential-definite
REF-INDEF . . . . . .Referential-indefinite
REL . . . . .Relative
RIM . . . . .Referential Indefinite Marker
SBJV . . . . .Subjunctive
sing . . . . .singular
STR PRO . . . . .Stressed pronoun
SUBJ . . . . .Subject
SUBJ PRO-∅ . . . . . .Subject pronoun-deletion
UNSTR PRO . . . . . .Unstressed pronoun

TABLE OF CONTENTS

1. *Introduction.*

This report presents the preliminary and as yet tentative results of a quantitative investigation of a range of selected grammatical devices participating in the maintenance of clause-level NP continuity in Hausa (Chadic, Afroasiatic) narrative structure.

The last decade or so has witnessed a growing insistence, on the part of such linguists as, inter alia, Bolinger (1968, 1979), Chafe (1972, 1980), Givón (1979a, 1979b, 1981, 1982), Halliday and Hasan (1976), and Labov (1972), upon the need to look at certain syntactic phenomena from the viewpoint of their functional motivation in human communication and discourse pragmatics; in preference, that is, to concentrating on the formal, algorithmic properties of syntax, and considering often totally implausible sentences in splendid isolation.[1] In the area of studying the maintenance and identification of topic-NPs in discourse, Givón (1979a) has proposed an analytic framework that has been followed in this study.

This perspective on language hinges quite simply on the question of the degree of difficulty the speaker considers the hearer might have in assigning unique and correct reference-identification to a given topic-NP, and Givón (1981) discusses the domain of "topic-identification" in terms of a continuum easiest → most difficult assignment of topic-identity. He adds that whilst the various functional domains seem to be "reasonably universal", different languages specify, by means of various syntactic principles, disparate points within a given domain, and proceeds to suggest the following graded range of common, cross-linguistic devices:

(1)   *Easiest topic-identification* (least surprising)
            Zero anaphora
            Clitic pronouns/verb agreement
            Unstressed pronouns
            Stressed/independent pronouns
            Left dislocation
            Definite NP
            Right dislocation
            (Passivization)
            Y-movement ('topicalization')
            Cleft/focus constructions
            Most difficult topic-identification (most surprising)

2. *Methodology and measurements*

Ten construction types used in Hausa to code topic-NPs have been sub-jected here to three measurements (see Givón's introduction to this volume):

a)   the average distance — computed in terms of *the number of separate clauses* — backwards in the discourse to the previous coreferential control, overt or implied, of a given NP — the *"look-back"* parameter;
b)   the average number of clauses, to the right, in which a given NP partici-pant persists before it finally disappears in the subsequent discourse — the factor of *"decay rate"*;
c)   the number of NP arguments which are present in the five clauses pre-ceding the occurrence of a particular NP and so "potentially" competing for reference with that same NP — the value *"potential ambiguity"*.

The 'immediate environment' for counting potential interference/ambiguity from other referents was *5 clauses* to the left in this study. The integer assigned in each case represented the number of potentially-competing NPs found within that range.

3. *Topic marking constructions in Hausa*

Since it would be impossible within the confines of this paper to do justice to all facets of the domain of maintaining (and tracing) NP-continuity in Hausa narrative, I have selected for discussion what are arguably some of the more salient coding points. These are, in order of presentation:

i)   zero-anaphora of subject-agreement morphemes and objects (5.1)
ii)   pronominal anaphoric reference (5.2)
iii)   stressed independent pronouns (5.3)
iv)   referential-definite NPs (5.4.1.)
v)   proper names (5.4.2)
vi)   topic-shifting of NPs (5.5)
vii)   passivisation (5.6)
viii) clefting constructions (5.7)
ix)   referential-indéfinite NPs (5.8)

With the exception of the passive construction — cf. section 5.6. — the above coding devices have been listed, in anticipation of the data and analysis, accor-ding to their locations on the Hausa continuity scale, with (i) — zero-anaphora —

representing the most continuous/easy topic-identification, and (ix) — referential-indefinite NPs — the least cohesive, continuous topic-NP device in connected mainline discourse. These various strategies thus tend to cluster at those points predicted by Givón's graded continuum (1).

4. Data base

The Hausa text studied here was taken from a string of consecutive stories in the late Alhaji Abubakar Imam's short fiction volume *Magana Jari Ce* (1970, pp. 6-65). Occasionally, extra pages of the same work were scoured for more tokens of less common coding devices.

5. Numerical results and discussion of the topic-coding devices

In the tabulated results presented throughout this study, figures are to be interpreted as follows: The lower numerical value represents the total number of tokens of a particular syntactic type attested in the sample, and the upper value denotes the average number of separate clauses counted leftwards/backwards to the previous referential control of a given NP, overt or zero (= 'lookback"); and in the case of the "decay-rate" variable, the upper figure is the average number of distinct clauses to the right before the NP reference perishes.

5.1. Zero-anaphora

The results for zero anaphora are given in Table I below. This device is constrained in its application to certain subjectconcord markers (5.1.1) and topic-NPs which function as the direct object (5.1.2) of the clause.[2] As we shall see shortly, it is a device that can be used only in simple discourse contexts, where the identity of the topic/referent is wholly predictable.

5.1.1. Zero-anaphora of subject-agreement marker

Hausa posesses a preverbal auxiliary which functions to encode both the person-gender-number features of the grammatical subject and the aspect-tense-mode (*ATM*) of the verb.[3] In certain specifiable environments, deletion of the pronominal element which copies the features of the subject — henceforth *SUBJECT PRONOUN-∅* — may take place. The conditions on the appropriateness of this principle are as follows:[4]

(i)   the following verb must be either affirmative imperfective (neutral or relative) or iterative-habitual — cf. Table 10 (b, d) in the Appendix. In all remaining ATMs, verb-agreement is compulsory;[5]

Table 1: zero-anaphora

		SUBJECT-AGREEMENT MARKER	NON-SUBJECT (DIRECT-OBJECT)
LOOK-BACK	HUMAN	$\dfrac{0.1}{48}$	$\dfrac{1.2}{24}$
	NON-HUMAN	$\dfrac{0.0}{23}$	$\dfrac{1.3}{73}$
RATE OF DECAY	HUMAN	$\dfrac{2.8}{48}$	$\dfrac{2.2}{24}$
	NON-HUMAN	$\dfrac{1.7}{23}$	$\dfrac{1.0}{73}$
POTENTIAL AMBIGUITY	HUMAN	$\dfrac{1.4}{48}$	$\dfrac{1.0}{24}$
	NON-HUMAN	$\dfrac{1.3}{23}$	$\dfrac{1.1}{73}$

(ii)   if a given verb meets condition (i) above, then the grammatical subject must, in the general case, be overtly present in position before the person-aspect auxiliary, either as a full NP or independent pronoun, before SUBJECT PRONOUN-Ø can apply.[6] This restriction explains the low average look-back values for SUBJECT PRONOUN-Ø, both [+human] and [-human], indicated in Table 1.

As exemplification of the phenomenon, consider the following narrative fragment:

(2)　a.　　. . .Kalala *na* can[7]　　　　　　　　　　　　　　(SUBJ PRO-∅)
　　　　　Kalala-SUBJ SUBJ PRO-∅ IMPERF there-LOC
　　　　　'. . .Kalala was there
　　　b.　*na* ta fama da washi-n wuƙa,　　　　　　　　(SUBJ PRO-∅)
　　　　　SUBJ PRO-∅ IMPERF continually struggle with sharpening-of knife-
　　　　　ASSOC
　　　　　struggling with sharpening the knife,
　　　c.　sai Kalalatu ta ji a-na sallama.
　　　　　then Kalalatu-SUBJ she-PERF hear one-IMPERF announce presence
　　　　　when Kalalatu heard someone announcing their presence.'
　　　　　　　　　　　　　　　　　　　　　　　　　　　　(Imam 1970:18)

In clause (2a), "Kalala", the husband of "Kalalatu", is a reintroduced subject of the imperfective locative construction, having appeared intermittently as a subject in the preceding context, along with several other subject arguments; since, moreover, the provisions of (i) and (ii) above are satisfied, SUBJECT PRONOUN-∅ applies in (2a), with the identity of the optionally ellipted SUBJECT PRONOUN being instantly recoverable. It may be noted additionally that sentence (2a) in fact marks the beginning of a new paragraph within the story, and also that a number of other subject topic-NPs are present in the immediately preceding discourse, including the wife "Kalalatu", the same "knife", and an impersonal pronoun. I would content, therefore, that it is the conjunction of a major thematic juncture *and* the prior topic shifting which serves to require the overt reappearance of the full nominal "Kalala". The presence of this subject NP then creates the environment for SUBJECT PRO-∅ to take place, with no possibility of gender-person-number confusion of any kind.

Turning now to clause (2b), we see the repetition of the same strategy of ellipsis, the outcome of which is an equisubject, imperfective two-clause chain of zero-anaphoric reference.[8] Given the rules of his/her language, a Hausa-speaker would have no difficulty assigning unique identity to the subject argument of the composite verb "continually struggle with" in (2b), for in such circumstances it must be coreferential with the immediately preceding control — in this instance the SUBJECT PRONOUN-∅ control in (2a), itself coreferential with the subject NP "Kalala".

Consider now the complex sentence (3) which occurs later on in the same story:

(3) a. Baɗo tsammani ya-ke
         stranger-SUBJ thinking-CLEFT he-IMPERF
         'The stranger was under the impression

     b. Kalala *na* nufi-n   (SUBJ PRO-∅)
         Kalala-SUBJ SUBJ PRO-∅ IMPERF intending-of
         Kalala meant

     c. kunne-n-sa ɗaya kaɗai *ya-ke* so ya yanka.   (DO-CLEFT)
         ear-of-his one-DO-CLEFT only he-SUBJ-IMPERF want
         he-SUBJ-SBJV cut off
         that he (Kalala) wanted to cut off *only one of his* (the stranger's)
         ears.'

                                                          (Imam 1970:19)

In clause (3a), "stranger" is the subject of the matrix verb "think",[9] and
"Kalala" is, in turn, the subject argument of the embedded verb "mean" in (3b);
the structural environment for optional SUBJECT PRONOUN-∅ is thus present
in (3b) and the rule is applied, with the recoverability of the coreferential NP
guaranteed.

Turning now to the subsequent embedded clause (3c), even though it is strictly speaking "potentially" ambiguous, we in fact know from the prior linguistic
context that the subject argument of both "want" and "cut off" in (3c) is identical with that of the verb "mean" in (3b), i.e. "Kalala".[10] SUBJECT PRO-
NOUN-∅ has, however, not applied in (3c), nor indeed could it, presumably
because the left-dislocation of the cleft direct object phrase "one of his ears"
to clause-initial position (see 5.7.) is sufficiently disruptive to render use of the
strategy inappropriate here.[11]

Moving on now to the relative survival rates of the various participants,
Table 1 shows that the subject argument is more persistent than are those NPs
occupying the direct object slot — (human/non-human) averages of 2.8/1.7
versus 2.2/1.0 clauses respectively.[12] In other words, the subject position tends
to be the more continuous one, a feature which thus accords with Givón's
(1980:332) observation that ". . .the organization of discourse in general. . .is
such that while object-continuity is relatively low, subject-continuity is relatively
high." In addition, notice that human participants evince a slower decay rate than
do their less persistent non-human counterparts — an average clause number of
2.8/2.2 as against 1.7/1.0. This suggests that [+human] NPs are relatively high on
the scale of topicality and are likely to be discussed over longer stretches of
narrative, an impression which is more than borne out by the data in Figures

(1-9), presented in the concluding section 6.

Finally with regard to the strategy of SUBJECT PRONOUN-∅, it is characterised by a potential ambiguity rate − 1.4/1.3 − a relatively high average if compared with the 1.0/1.1 figures for the direct object category. This fact may be wholly trivial or it may be related to the tight restrictions of criterial condition (ii) above, which act to obviate any confusion of identity-assignment, thus guaranteeing recoverability and permitting the presence of other non-coreferential topic-NPs in the preceding 5-clause vicinity.

5.1.2. *Zero anaphora of direct objects*

As Table 1 illustrates, DIRECT OBJECT-∅ is, given the right environment of course, a relatively common phenomenon in Hausa − a total count of 97 tokens in 60 or so pages, compared with 263 instances of direct object pronominalisation (see Table 2) and 71 cases of SUBJECT PRONOUN-∅. Passage (5) below, whilst instantiating a somewhat extreme example of a zero-anaphora direct object reference with a look-back of some 16 clauses to the previous control, nonetheless illustrates the relative anaphoric freedom enjoyed by the direct object function in contrast to its subject counterpart. An emir (king) has set three young men the task of singling out one individual heron from the whole flock, and one of the young men − "Halilu-the-Crafty" − smears some kolanut spittle on the bird's wing as a means of facilitating later identification:

(5)   a.   Sarki ya ce, "Na sa fam biyar,
             emir-SUBJ he-PERF say I-SUBJ-PERF place pound five-DO
             'The emir said, "I bet five pounds,

      b.   duk wanda ya gane *ta*   (UNSTRESSED PRO)
             all REL he-SUBJ-PERF recognise her-DO
             whoever recognises *her* (the heron)

      c.   zam ba shi   (DO-∅)
             I-SUBJ-FUT give him-DO DO-∅[13]
             I will give him (the five pounds).

      d.   Baya-n haka kuma in gina masa gida,
             After-of this too I-SUBJ-SBJV build for him-IO house-DO
             And in addition I will build a house for him,

      e.   in naɗa shi Sarki-n Fada-na."
             I-SUBJ-SBJV appoint him-DO Chief-of Palace-my
             and appoint him Chief of my Palace."

f. Samari-n suka ce, "To, mun ji,
    young men-PRM-SUBJ they-PERF say good we-SUBJ-PERF hear[14]
    And the young men said, "Fine, we hear,

g. mun ko gode   (IO-∅)[15]
    we-SUBJ-PERF also thank IO-∅
    and we thank (you),

h. Allah ya kai mu gobe
    Allah-SUBJ he-SBJV bring us-DO tomorrow
    may Allah bring us to tomorrow."

i. Gari na wayewa,   (SUBJ PRO-∅)
    dawn-SUBJ SUBJ PRO-∅ IMPERF break
    Dawn was breaking,

j. balbelu suka taru. . .
    herons-SUBJ they-PERF collect
    the herons collected. . .
    intervening clauses (k. . .q)

r. Ya nema,   (DO-∅)
    he-SUBJ-PERF look for DO-∅
    He looked for (*her*), i.e. the heron

s. bai gane *ta* ba   (UNSTRESSED PRO)
    NEG he-SUBJ-PERF recognise her-DO
    but didn't recognise *her*.'

                                              (Imam 1970:8-9)

The prementioned individual "heron" is reintroduced into the discourse by means of a simple direct object pronoun in clause (5b), and when she finally resurfaces some 16 clauses later in (5r), she is specified with the zero-device, despite the fact too that several other accusative arguments have participated in the intervening context. Notice also that this self same zero-appearance then controls a pronominal reflex in (5s). Once again, the speaker/writer has made a number of subjective judgements regarding the hearer/reader's ability to correctly assign reference-identification to the NP.

It is important to observe immediately, however, that a number of additional, variables appear to influence the conditions on the acceptability of zero- and/or pronominal anaphora of non-subject NPs, and I can do no more than provide a rudimentary characterisation of what is an extremely subtle area of the grammar; one, moreover, which merits, and would reward, more serious investigation.

In reportative narrative structures of the type investigated in this study, and in the context of a chain of clauses encoded by a measured, unidirectional sequence of perfective verbs,[16] the following options appear to prevail, both for "referential-definite" *and* "referential-indefinite" arguments as specified in sections 5.4 and 5.8 respectively. Subsequent to full first mention, a given NP referent may then admit of either zero or pronominal anaphoric recall in all clauses excepting the sequence-final one, where ellipsis is preferred; at the same time, however, there is a marked predilection for picking up [+human] referents with a pronominal device, again in all but the final clause where a zero strategy is most commonly encountered. As illustration, consider the following examples, in which the first-mention NP is properly referential-definite, and all coreferential arguments are italicised: (1) Jiya 'yan sanda suka kama *wannan barawon*, (2) suka daka (*shi*), (3) suka daure $\emptyset$ '(1) Yesterday the police caught *that thief*, (2) beat *him*, (3) and imprisoned *him*', with the inclusion of the direct object pronoun *shi* in clause (2) preferable to ellipsis, though zero-anaphoric reference is certainly possible; (1) Jiya suka sayi *wannan ragon/naman*, (2) suka yanka (*shi*), (3) suka dafa $\emptyset$ '(1) Yesterday they bought *that ram/meat*, (2) slaughtered/cut *it* up, (3) and cooked *it*', with the respective [–human] and [–animate] referents in clause (1) allowing either $\emptyset$- or pronominal anaphora in (2), the referential option being simply a matter of personal preference, i.e. selection of either option does not reflect any specific intention on the part of the speaker. Exactly the same anaphoric choices, moreover, characterise recall of referential-indefinite NPs, i.e. referents which are not assumed to be uniquely identifiable to the addressee.

The facts documented above for referential-definite (and -indefinite) NPs also apply to referentially definite arguments in the context of direct, question-answer type, conversational exchanges. Thus, an initial inquiry on the lines of Ka sami *kukunka/ragonka/agogonka?* 'Did you find *your cook/ram/watch?*' would elicit either (1) I, na same *shi* 'Yes, I found *him/it*', or (2) I, na samu $\emptyset$ 'Yes, I found *him/it*', with the pronominal recall principle in (1) again the preferred option for a [+human] referent like kukunka 'your cook'. It is noteworthy, however, that face-to-face, "direct speech" discourse-genre differs from reportative, "indirect speech" in that, in the former mode, referential-indefinite arguments can only be picked up with the zero-strategy, whatever their value for the feature [human]. Hence, in answer to the direct question Ka sami *wani kuku/ rago/agogo?* 'Did you find *a cook/ram/watch?*', the only possible (affirmative) response would be I, na samu $\emptyset$ 'Yes, I found *one*', i.e. without any overt resumptive element.

The reasons for the differential anaphoric behaviour which characterises referential-indefinite arguments in the two discourse contexts are not immediately obvious. Pragmatic considerations may exert some influence, pertaining, somewhat grossly, to the fact that in direct bilateral conversations, the interactants are perhaps more involved, sharing a sense of identification within the exchange, and so are more capable of assigning correct reference. In listening to the narration of temporally-ordered experiences of some time depth, on the other hand, the addressee may be less able, in the communicator's judgement, to assign unique and proper identity to a given referent — hence the option of employing a stronger anaphoric device in this context.[17]

These observations aside, DO-∅ represents, in the general and most simple case, a highly continuous, unsurprising coding device, as the average clause lookbacks — 1.2/1.3 — show. Fragment (7) below instantiates a more typical usage of the principle, typical in that the look-back to the last control is one clause only, and the thematic continuity is characterised by a tightly-knit sequence of "relative perfective" verbs — the aspectual variant employed in sequential, unidirectional, past-action narrative flow, cf. Table 10, footnote (a) in Appendix.

(7)   a.   Ran nan, ko'ina Kalala ya sami kuɗi
           day-DEM wherever Kalala-SUBJ he-PERF get money-DO
           'One day, wherever it was Kalala got the money

      b.   sai ya tafi kasuwa
           then he-SUBJ-PERF go market-LOC
           he went to market

      c.   ya nemo *daƙwale-n kaji guda biyu*
           he-SUBJ-SBJV look for large-of chickens two-DO
           to look for *two plump chickens*

      d.   ya sawo.   (DO-∅)
           he-SUBJ-SBJV buy DO-∅
           and buy (*them*).

      e.   Ya yiwo cefane
           he-SUBJ-PERF do buying stew ingredients-DO
           He bought ingredients for the stew

      f.   ya kawo gida,   (DO-∅)
           he-SUBJ-PERF bring DO-∅ home-LOC
           brought (*them*) home,

g. ya ce wa Kalalatu ta soye kaji-n nan gaba ɗaya.
    he-SUBJ-PERF say to Kalalatu-IO she-SUBJ-SBJV fry
    chickens-PRM DEM-DO all at once
    and told Kalalatu to fry those chickens all at once.

h. Ta tashi,
    she-SUBJ-PERF get up
    She (Kalalatu) got up,

i. baya-n ya fige   (DO-∅)
    after-of he-SUBJ-PERF pluck DO-∅[18]
    and after he had plucked (*them*)

j. ya gyara mata,   (DO-∅)
    he-SUBJ-PERF clean for her-IO DO-∅
    and had cleaned (*them*) for her,

k. ta sa tukunya
    she-SUBJ-PERF put cooking pot-DO
    she put the cooking pot on (the fire)

l. ta shiga suya.   (DO-∅)
    she-SUBJ-PERF start frying
    and started frying (*them*).'

                                                        (Imam 1970:16)

In (7), the direct object phrase "two plump chickens" is first introduced as
a referential-indefinite argument — see remarks above and section 5.8. — in
clause (c) and is referred to with ∅-anaphora in the immediately following clause.
In clause (7e) of the next sentence, a fresh accusative NP argument "buying stew
ingredients" appears, and this in turn controls zero-reference in (7f). Because of
the "potential" now for confusion of direct object topic-NPs, the NP "two
plump chickens" is reintroduced in (7g) via an escalated strategy — full NP +
PRM + DEM (see section 5.4.1.) — but is thereafter specified once again by zero
in clauses (7i-l), excepting (7k). Furthermore, all but two of the zero-anaphoric
references have a characteristic single clause look-back — the DO-∅ coreferent in
(7i) has a two clause look-back which traverses the intervening intransitive clause
(7h), and the zero-reference in (7l) also looks back two clauses to its previous
(zero) control. Observe too the in-sequence string of narrative (relative) perfective verbs used throughout the piece, excepting, that is, the two neutral perfective (anterior perfective) forms mentioned in footnote (18).

Turning now to consideration of the average decay-rates of the two categories
of ∅-anaphora in question, it is noticeable that discourse-participants in the

direct object slot disappear at a faster average rate — 2.2/1.0 clauses — than do their subject counterparts — 2.8/1.7. This feature is thus consonant with Givón's (1980:306) predictive claim that ". . .the maintenance of *the same NP onward in the subject role*, . . . is taken to be the most predictable, most expected, least-surprising and least-disruptive strategy in topic-NP identification", in contrast, that is, to object-continuity — cf. too the function-specific figures in section 6 for further substantiation of this claim.

Finally, regarding the matter of ambiguity, Table 1 reveals that there are, on average, a greater number of "potentially competing" nominal antecedents lurking in the linguistic context preceding the application of SUBJECT PRO-NOUN-∅ — 1.4/1.3 — than are present when the DIRECT OBJECT-∅ device is utilised — 1.0/1.1. I am not sure of the precise significance, if any, of this difference, though it is somewhat unusual in that one would expect a correlation between a greater average look-back and a larger number of entities "competing" for reference.

To sum up, comparison of the facts outlined in this section with the counts and analysis now provided for the remaining devices serves to support the empirically falsifiable claim that zero-anaphora is the "least marked", least pragmatically-complex strategy of topic-identification, used only when the speaker feels he will pay no communicative penalty at all. At the same time, we have seen that the factors determining the acceptability of zero-anaphora — particularly of the direct object — are not exclusively discourse-related: other Hausa-specific considerations, including the feature [±human], the lexical semantics of the verb, and even personal style, are at times clearly germane to the choice.

5.2. *Pronominal anaphora: verb (pronominal subject) -agreement and unstressed (non-subject) pronouns.*

At one notch higher on the cline of discourse (dis)continuity outlined in the introduction we find anaphoric pronominalisation — either overtly-expressed, pre-verbal subject-concord markers in the imperfective or iterative-habitual, or unstressed, post-verbal non-subject pronouns. A glance at Table 2 below illustrates how the [+human] subject-topic NP, in this case together with [+human] and highly definite dative arguments, again represent the continuity-topicality point in discourse, with look-backs and decay-rates of 1.3/2.9 and 1.3/2.5 respectively; this is in contrast to [+human] participants occupying the direct object slot which are less continuous in that they have longer average look-

Table 2: verb-agreement and unstressed pronouns.[a]

| | | SUBJECT-AGREEMENT MARKER[b] | NON-SUBJECT | | |
			DO[c]	IO[d]	[POSS[e]
LOOK-BACK	HUMAN	$\frac{1.3}{145}$	$\frac{1.6}{103}$	$\frac{1.3}{57}$	$\frac{1.1}{90}$
	NON-HUMAN	$\frac{1.1}{10}$	$\frac{1.5}{160}$	$\frac{1.6}{9}$	$\frac{1.0}{24}$
RATE OF DECAY	HUMAN	$\frac{2.9}{145}$	$\frac{2.3}{103}$	$\frac{2.5}{57}$	$\frac{2.6}{113}$
	NON-HUMAN	$\frac{0.6}{10}$	$\frac{0.9}{160}$	$\frac{0.5}{9}$	$\frac{1.1}{24}$
POTENTIAL AMBIGUITY	HUMAN	$\frac{1.5}{145}$	$\frac{1.2}{103}$	$\frac{1.0}{57}$	$\frac{1.2}{113}$
	NON-HUMAN	$\frac{1.4}{10}$	$\frac{1.1}{160}$	$\frac{0.8}{9}$	$\frac{1.2}{24}$

a) Although the pronominal elements investigated here are transcribed as discrete units in Hausa orthography, there are a number of reasons for considering themn "clitic", or at least "clitic-like" in their behaviour. Firstly, no material, with the exception of modal particles in the case of the subject pronoun-verb nexus, may intervene between them and the verbal constituent; secondly, the position of these pronouns is fixed with respect to the verb; and finally, they may not occur in isolation.

b) The subject count does not include impersonal-indefinite subject pronouns which have vacuous generic reference – see Table 10 in the Appendix.

c) Includes those patient-objects which take the form of a possessive NP or possessive pronoun when following certain deverbal nouns in imperfective constructions.

d) Non-human indirect object arguments proved hard to come by, and the total of 9 attested tokens includes several [–human, +animate] NPs. This relative paucity is not wholly surprising, however, given the fact that dative-indirect objects tend to be largely [+human] – cf. footnote (2).

e) Again, the non-human count includes several references to animals.

backs to their previous control – 1.6 – and perish at a marginally faster rate, surviving an average of 2.3. clauses to the right. It is noteworthy too, as comparison of Tables 1 and 2 will show, that the formal devices of verb agreement and unstressed pronouns are, with the possible exception of possessive pronouns, more disruptive than zero-anaphora of both the subject-concord morpheme and direct object argument (5.1), at least in terms of the look-back variable. Observe too the generally disruptive consequences which result from a non-human NP occupying either the subject or non-subject position.

One further observation on Table 2, concerning the low look-back – an average 1.1. clauses – for [+human] possessor NPs. In view of the fact that possessor arguments tend, like dative participants, to be overwhelmingly [+human] and so high in continuity, this figure is perhaps not so surprising; however, use of the device illustrated in (8) below will quite clearly act to reduce any look-back for nominals participating in genitive constructions:

(8) a.   Akwai wani mutum wai shi Kalala,
           there is-EXIST RIM-man alleged he-STR PRO Kalala[19]
           'There was once a man called Kalala,
     b.   ya-na da mata-r-sa. . .
           he-SUBJ-IMPERF with wife-of-his-POSS
           he had a (*his*) wife. . .'

                                                            (Imam 1970:15)

In (8b), the semantically redundant possessive pronoun suffix has a zero clause look-back to its last coreferential control – the subject-concord marker *ya* "he" on the imperfective auxiliary at the beginning of the same clause.

To summarise the above remarks, utilisation of the coding device of simple, non-emphatic, anaphoric pronominalisation reflects an assumption on the part of the speaker that the hearer will have little or no difficulty establishing the correct topic reference. As predicted in Givón's (1) scale, moreover, this relatively gentle device falls, in terms of the degree of continuity and presuppositionality, somewhere between the zero principles discussed in section 5.1 and the more jarring usage of the full, stressed pronouns now examined.

5.3. *Stressed independent pronouns.*

As a comparison of Tables 2 and 3 will indicate, fully stressed pronouns constitute, relative to their non-emphatic confrères of section 5.2, a clear escalation in the direction of the surprise/unpredictability end of the continuum schematised in (1). Thus, taking once again the vital measure of average number of clauses leftwards to the immediately preceding control, the difference is marked − 1.3/1.1. for subject-agreement pronouns, and 1.6/2.2 for stressed subject pronouns.

Table 3: stressed pronouns.[a]

	SUBJECT [b]	
	HUMAN	NON-HUMAN
LOOK-BACK	1.6 <hr> 36	2.2 <hr> 9
DECAY-RATE	2.6 <hr> 36	1.8 <hr> 9
POTENTIAL AMBIGUITY	1.4 <hr> 36	1.4 <hr> 9

a) The grammar of Hausa possesses a number of syntactically-determined processes which automatically convert a (non-subject) pronoun into the stressed form in pragmatically neutral environments, e.g. following the negative existential predicator *babu* − babu ita "there isn't one (fem. sing.)" − and the sociative-instrumental particle *da* − na zo da ita "I brought it (fem. sing.)". However, since these particular morphosyntactic operations are in no way discourse-related, surface occurrences of stressed independent pronouns triggered by these rules are not considered here.

b) Although a number of additional pages were scanned, I came across only a negligible and so statistically irrelevant number of non-subject stressed pronouns, hence the absence of this category in Table 3.

From a distributional point of view, the emphatic-stressed pronouns occur typically in topic-shift and cleft constructions — cf. sections 5.5 and 5.7 below. Passage (9) exemplifies some of the discourse factors which regularly influence the selection of an independent pronoun as a means of identifying a given topic-NP in a non-contrastive environment. A grandfather is about to construct an effigy with which to frighten his allegedly fearless grandson:

(9) a.   Da *kaka-n nan nasa* ya ji haka
     when grandfather-PRM DEM-SUBJ of his-POSS he-PERF
     hear this-DO
     'When *that grandfather* of his heard this

   b.   sai ya tashi,
     then he-SUBJ-PERF get up
     he got up,

   c.   ya sami karare,
     he-SUBJ-PERF get cornstalks-DO
     got some cornstalks,[20]

   d.   ya ɗaura wani mutum-mutumi dogo,
     he-SUBJ-PERF tie together RIM-effigy tall-DO
     tied together a tall effigy,

   e.   ya sa masa fara-r riga,
     he-SUBJ-PERF put to him-IO white-of gown-DO
     put a white gown on him,

   f.   *shi* kuma ya sa wa ka-n-sa fara. (STR PRO/TOPICALISA/TION)
     he-STR PRO also he-SUBJ-PERF put to head-of-his-IO white-DO
     and *he* put white (earth) on his head.'

                                 (Imam 1970:20)

In clause (9a), the NP "grandfather" is reintroduced as a subject following a discourse absence of 7 clauses and some shifting around of topic nominals — hence the appearance here of the highly escalated strategy of full NP + PRM +

DEM + POSS. The same NP, moreover, persists in that role throughout the re-
mainder of the passage. The occurrence in (9f) of an upgraded device — a full
stressed pronoun — is explicable, I would suggest, in the following terms. The
introduction in (9d) of a fresh participant which is destined to assume some importance in the ensuing story — the "effigy" — represents a thematic juncture,
though the extent to which this new argument might itself be a "potential
candidate" for the subject-topic role in (9f) is debatable, given the real-world
knowledge that an inanimate object cannot cover its own head with white earth;
the hearer thus has no alternative but to assign "grandfather" as the only
possible subject of the verb "put" in (9f). The writer uses a discourse-determined
escalated device, therefore, in order to call the attention of his audience to the
fact that the NP "grandfather" is not yet to be ousted as the clause-level topic,
hence the use too of the conjoining particle kuma "also" in (9f) as an additional
means of signalling the continuity of the topic, maintenance of the same NP onward in subject role tending to be the least marked discourse strategy.

The occurrence of a full independent pronoun is, moreover, a categorial feature of contrastive sentences in which some pronominal element has been
clefted, as illustrated in example (10). "Nomau the Farmer" has set his heart
upon a certain young girl and attempts to win over his father "Chief Farmer":

(10) a.   Sai ya ce wa Sarkin-n Noma
          then he-SUBJ-PERF say to Chief-of Farming-IO
          'Then he (Nomau) said to Chief Farmer
     b.   lalle shi ma *ita* za a nema masa. (STR PRO/DO-CLEFT)[21]
          surely he-STR PRO also she-STR PRO-CLEFT FUT-IMPERSONAL
          seek for him-IO
          surely as far as he (Nomau) was concerned *she* (the girl) would be
          sought for him (Nomau).'

                                                            (Imam 1970:74)

In (10b) the NP "girl" reappears after a gap of 5 clauses, and the writer presumably feels obliged to supply information over and above a mere unstressed (or
∅) pronoun in order to facilitate topic-recall and also, of course, to emphasise
the discourse-unrelated fact that "Nomau" wants this girl and no other — hence
the use of the stressed pronoun. It is this type of function, moreover, which
contributes to the above-mentioned high average look-back of these pronouns,
relative, that is, to their unstressed counterparts.

Table 4: referential-definite NPs [±PRM].[a]

| | | SUBJECT | | NON-SUBJECT | | | | | |
| | | | | DO | | IO | | POSS | |
		−PRM	+PRM	−PRM	+PRM	−PRM	+PRM	−PRM	+PRM
LOOK-BACK	HUMAN	6.2 / 43	12.5 / 21	4.9 / 20	9.9 / 18	7.0 / 17	10.0 / 11	8.1 / 20	12.7 / 18
	NON-HUMAN	9.0 / 19	14.6 / 13	8.0 / 41	15.8 / 39	6.4 / 4	—	8.3 / 6	11.4 / 9
RATE OF DECAY	HUMAN	1.9 / 43	2.0 / 31	1.4 / 20	1.5 / 18	2.0 / 17	2.1 / 11	0.8 / 20	0.9 / 18
	NON-HUMAN	1.5 / 19	0.9 / 13	1.1 / 41	1.1 / 39	2.0 / 4	—	1.2 / 6	1.4 / 9
POTENTIAL AMBIGUITY	HUMAN	2.0 / 43	2.0 / 31	1.2 / 20	2.0 / 18	2.0 / 17	1.9 / 11	1.2 / 20	1.2 / 18
	NON-HUMAN	1.6 / 19	1.9 / 13	1.3 / 41	1.4 / 39	1.8 / 4	—	1.6 / 6	1.4 / 9

a) In the [+ PRM] case, with or without an additional demonstrative.

5.4. *Referential-definite NPs.*[22]

Hausa possesses two categories of REF-DEF NP:

a)   zero-coded REF-DEF NPs, i.e. full NPs which are not modified by any deictic formative and which represent the "lower", less surprising device;

b)   REF-DEF NPs specified by a following cliticised deictic determiner — here dubbed the "P(revious) R(eference) M(arker) (*PRM*) — with or without an additional demonstrative, cf. Table 11(a) in Appendix. This is the "higher", more surprising device.

5.4.1. *REF-DEF NPs [-proper name].*

In this section we shall take a contrastive look at the above two categories and their participation in the grammar of Hausa discourse. The text-counts point to a striking degree of interpredictability between the use or not of the PRM on the one hand, and the dimension of (dis)continuity on the other.[23]

As the designation itself suggests, the appearance of the PRM on a noun serves to refer back to the occurrence of that same nominal at some point earlier in the discourse[24] — to a "previously opened file", using Du Bois' (1980:209) insightful phrase, cf. remarks on "referential-indefinite" NPs in 5.8. Historically, the PRM itself must have been either a deictic element in its own right, freely combinable with a demonstrative, or simply a reduced version of the combined NP + PRM noun-modifier + remote DEM, which is a frequently occurring construction in Hausa — cf. (9a), (11c), and (11e) for instance.[25]

Turning our attention first of all to the sub-category REF-DEF NP [-PRM], comparison of Tables 3 and 4 reveals that, in accordance with the hierarchical claims given in (1), they rank much higher than stressed pronouns on the scale-range of continuity → discontinuity — total average look-backs (subject position) of 6.2/9.0 versus 1.6/2.2 respectively. These findings also support Givón's (1980:316-317) observation that, in contrast to full independent pronouns, ". . .most commonly definite NP's are used when a topic-NP is reintroduced into the discourse over a larger gap of absence."

Just as significant for the analysis, however, is the fact that those REF-DEF topic-NPs which do bear the cliticised PRM represent a demonstrably stronger strategy of topic-recall, signalling a substantial degree of discourse disruption. Compare, for example, the relative look-backs for the respective subject arguments — 12.5/14.6 [+PRM] versus 6.2/9.0 [-PRM].[26]

By way of illustration, consider the following narrative fragment. "Nomau" has stolen a bag of money from a man who immediately suspects his own wife of the theft. "Nomau" later returns to the scene of the crime:

(11) a.   Daga nan sai Nomau ya ɗauki jaka
            from there then Nomau-SUBJ he-PERF take bag-DO
            'Then Nomau took the bag (of money)

      b.   ya koma.
            he-SUBJ-PERF return
            and returned.

      c.   Ya tafi har ƙofa-r zaure-n *mutumi-n nan* (PRM+DEM)
            he-SUBJ-PERF go right doorway-of entrance
            hut-LOC-of man-PRM-DEM
            He went right to the doorway of the entrance
            hut of *that/the man*

      d.   ya shiga. . .
            he-SUBJ-PERF go in
            went in. . .

      e.   sai ya ji *mutumi-n nan* na ta zagi-n *mata-r*. . .(PRM+DEM, PRM)
            then he-SUBJ-PERF hear man-DO-PRM-DEM SUBJ/PRO-∅
            IMPERF continually abusing-of wife-PRM
            and he heard *that/the man* abusing *the wife*. . .'

                                                    (Imam 1970:39)

A relatively large gap of some 9 clauses separates the NP "man" in (11c) from its last overt mention, and a number of other NP arguments have been bandied around, hence the use of the upgraded strategy NP + PRM + DEM. Observe too that the same strong device is employed again in (11e), even though the identical NP has, in this case, "disappeared" for only a single clause. This particular decision cannot, therefore, be influenced by discourse considerations, i.e. relative ease/difficulty of topic-identification, as such, but is presumably motivated by the fact that if the speaker/writer had used a simple unstressed pronoun "him" in place of the full strategy "that/the man", then either of the two masculine singular arguments — "Nomau" or "man" — could potentially at least have been interpreted as the subject of the verb "hear" in (11e).[27] Such examples underline, in my judgement, the importance of making an analytical separation between such functionally distinct cause-and-effect factors.

Finally, the recalled NP "wife" in (11e) is marked with the PRM after an absence of 10 clauses.

5.4.2. REF-DEF NPs [+proper name].

Table 5 provides the data on this particular category. If we compare the average

Table 5: proper names.[a]

	SUBJECT[b]	NON-SUBJECT[c]		
		DO	IO	[POSS
LOOK-BACK	13.6 / 100	11.6 / 53	14.9 / 28	13.0 / 30
DECAY-RATE	2.2 / 100	0.7 / 53	1.9 / 28	1.1 / 30
POTENTIAL AMBIGUITY	1.7 / 100	1.6 / 53	1.6 / 28	1.5 / 30

a) Since only an insignificant number of non-human proper names were encountered – mainly names of locations, months, and 2 references to the book "A Thousand and One Nights" – only [+human] proper names are considered in the Table 5 counts.

b) The "SUBJECT" category does not include the numerous references to "Allah", or the occasional mention of his adversary.

c) Because [+human] proper names occupy, in the general case, the slot of clausal subject, a number of extra pages were combed to secure examples of proper names with these other, non-subject, functions.

look-back and decay-rate in Tables 4 and 5, it becomes apparent that the [+proper name] referential device represents a coding principle somewhat higher than REF-DEF NPs [–PRM] on the cline of (discontinuity); it is also marginally more disruptive than are REF-DEF NPs [+PRM]. In terms of the principles outlined in section 1, the exact implications of these differences are unclear; and the extent to which this category localises at a comparable point on the hierarchy in other languages is also an open question.

5.5. *Topic-shifting/left-dislocation.*

The statistical text-counts furnished in Table 6 suggest that topic-shift construction-types are used when the hearer's assignment of coreferential identity is adjudged by the speaker to be more difficult than is the case, for example,

Table 6: topic-shifted NPs.

	SUBJECT [+human] [a]
LOOK-BACK	$\dfrac{12.9}{39}$
DECAY-RATE	$\dfrac{2.1}{39}$
POTENTIAL AMBIGUITY	$\dfrac{1.7}{39}$

a) Left-dislocation of main clause subjects is the most frequently encountered option. Instances of non-human topic-shifted subjects and topicalised non-subjects have a relatively low text frequency, at least in Imam (1970), hence their non-inclusion in Table 6.

with definite full NPs [–PRM] (cf. Table 4) – average look-backs for [+human]
topic-shifted NPs of 12.9 clauses compared with an average 6.2 clauses for REF-
DEF NPs [–PRM]. In fact, left-dislocated NPs cluster, predictably, at about the
same point on the scale as REF-DEF NPs [+PRM] and proper names in terms
of their discourse-markedness/presuppositionality; and topicalised nominals, in
so far as they are normally [+definite] arguments, also naturally take the PRM.[28]
Passage (12) exemplifies the phenomenon nicely:

(12) a. To, *Sarkin-n nan kuwa* na kiwo-n balbelu (TOPIC-SHIFT-SUBJECT)
          kama-r ɗari. . .
          well, Emir-PRM-DEM-SUBJ and SUBJ/PRO-Ø IMPERF
          tend-of herons like-of hundred
          'Well, *as for that/the Emir* he tended about one hundred herons. . .
      b. . . .*a ciki-n balbelu-n nan* akwai (TOPIC SHIFT-ADV)
          wata wadda Sarki ya-ke so.
          at inside-of herons-PRM-DEM there are RIM-one which-REL Emir-
          SUBJ he-IMPERF like
          . . .*amongst those herons* there was one which the Emir liked.
      c. Ba don kome ba kuwa,
          NEG because of anything NEG and
          For no other reason,
      d. sai don *ita* ta fi amincewa da mutane. (TOPIC-SHIFT-SUBJECT)
          except because she-STR PRO-SUBJ she-PERF
          exceed trusting with people-ASSOC
          than that *she* was more trustful of people.'
          (Imam 1970:7)]

Notice, first of all, the highly-marked, definitised nature of the various topicalised constituents in (12). Taking (12a) as illustration, the reason the writer considers use of topic-shift to be felicitous cannot be ascribed, in this case at least,
to any substantial discourse absence on the part of the NP "Emir", for this same
argument was also the subject of the clause immediately before (12a). Rather, it
is motivated by the fact that another [+human] NP has been vying for the theme
position in the prior context; consequently the writer, assuming that the hearer/
reader will have difficulty in identifying the coreferent if he merely provides a
pronoun of some kind, supplies more explicit information in the form of a
topicalised NP + PRM + DEM strategy. Observe too the presence of the modal
particle kuwa "as for, and" in position following the topic-nominal in (12a) –

one of a number of common topic-marking conjunctions in the language. In such environments, therefore, it is the shunting back and forth of various nominal themes which acts to precipitate use of the left-dislocation device in Hausa.

Narrative fragments (13) and (14) instantiate a slightly different topic-shift construction-type, termed "contrastive topic-shifting" by Givón (1977:317). Following the theft of some money, a group of Fulani men are brought before a judge who says:

(13) a.   "To, Sarki-n Dogarai, tafi da su.
             good, Chief-of Bodyguards, go-IMPERATIVE with them
             ' "Good, Chief Bodyguard, away with them!

      b.   *Kai kuwa*, Sarki-n Fawa, tafi da wannan (CONTRASTIVE TOPIC—
                                                                    SHIFT)

             mai kuɗi-n.
             you-STR PRO and, Chief-of Butchering, go-IMPERATIVE with this
             one-DEM with money-PRM
             And you, Chief Butcher, take away this one with the money!" '
                                                        (Imam 1970:28)

And in a later story, a compound-head invites a villager to put down his load and come and eat with him:

(14) a.   Baƙauye ya ajiye kaya-n ice-n
             villager-SUBJ he-PERF put down load-of wood-PRM-DO
             'The villager put down the load of wood,

      b.   ya zo
             he-SUBJ-PERF come
             came

      c.   ya zauna,
             he-SUBJ-PERF sit down
             and sat down

      d.   suka fara ci-n abinci,
             they-SUBJ-PERF start eating-of food-DO
             they started to eat,

      e.   kafin mai gida ya kai loma guda,
             before compound-head-SUBJ he-SBJV take mouthful one-DO
             before the compound-head could take a single mouthful,

f.   *shi* ya kai uku.[29]   (CONTRASTIVE TOPIC-SHIFT)
      he-STR PRO-SUBJ he-PERF take three-DO
      he (the villager) had taken three.'

                                              (Imam 1970:30)

In (14), both participants — "compound-head" and "villager" — have been mentioned as prior topic-themes in the story, and because reference in clause (14f) to the NP "villager" is in contrast to the preceding argument-topic "compound-head" in (14e) in terms of the verbal action "take", "villager" is recalled contrastively by means of a full independent pronoun.

5.6. *Passive constructions.*

The statistics in Table 7 permit the following generalisation, which may or may not be of cross-linguistic relevance: the attested passive subject NPs, whilst all [+REF-DEF] in keeping with the global pragmatic-semantic typology of passives, are nonetheless characterised by a markedly low average clause look-back — 1.5/1.8. Compare the figures in Table 7 with those for topic-shifted NPs [+human] — 12.9 (Table 6) — and clefted subjects NPs — 15.1 (Table 8 below).

Table 7: passive subjects.[a]

	HUMAN	NON-HUMAN
LOOK-BACK	1.5	1.8
	——	——
	2	12
DECAY-RATE	1.0	0.4
	——	——
	2	12
POTENTIAL	1.5	1.1
AMBIGUITY	2	12

a) The Hausa passive rule is highly constrained, in contrast that is, to languages such as English. Thus, the 14 tokens listed in Table 7 represent the total culled from Imam's (1970) entire volume — some 234 pages in all. Furthermore, the relative topicality of the agent argument is extremely low, so low, in fact, that the absence of any agent-of-passive borders on being categorial. See Jaggar (1981a, 1981b) for more extensive accounts of this particular passive-type in Hausa.

Furthermore, the survival rate of these same passive subjects is also relatively
low — an average 1.0/0.4 clauses to the right; this is again in stark contrast to
the other left-dislocation processes considered in this report — topic-shifting
(section 5.5) and clefting (section 5.7.).[30] It would appear, therefore, that
according to the quantitative measures utilised here at least, the formal device
of passivisation does not fall within the same functional domain as these other
"foregrounding" operations. In this regard, it may be noted that whilst passive
must be considered as an integral point somewhere on the continuum, Givón
himself is clearly unsure about its precise location for the parenthesises the function in (1) and later writes, ". . .the exact position of passivization along this
continuum is not fully clear, and may depend in part on he particular passive-
type in a language. . ." (1981). I have nothing cogent to say about why a device
whose function seems to be universally one of "promoting" a non-agent argument to the status of clause subject-topic might differ from language to language with regard to its point of integration on the (dis)continuity dimension.

Consider, as exemplification, passage (15) which illustrates an archetypical
transitive-based passive construction. Kalalatu, the wife of **Kalala**, in hungrily
frying two chickens he, i.e. Kalala (to use a stronger, more explicit strategy!),
has brought home [cf. (7)]:

(15) a.   Ta ci gaba da suya
           she-SUBJ-PERF continue with frying
           'She continued with the frying

     b.   k̃anshi na jifa-r-ta. . .   SUBJ PRO-∅)
           sweet smell-SUBJ SUBJ PRO-∅ IMPERF throwing-of-her-DO
           the sweet smell knocking her over. . .

     c.   . . .sai ta fara tsame
           then she-SUBJ-PERF begin taking out bits
           . . .then she began picking out bits

     d.   ta-na ci. . .   (DO-∅)
           she-SUBJ IMPERF eat DO-∅
           and eating (*them*, i.e. *the chickens*). . .

     e.   . . .kafin *su soyu*   (PASSIVE)
           before they-SUBJ-SBJV fry-PASSIVE
           . . .before *they were completely fried*

     f.   ta kusa cinye rabi-n kaza.
           she-SUBJ-PERF near eat up half-of chicken-DO
           she had eaten up almost half a chicken.'

                                                              (Imam 1970:16)

Notice that the "foregrounded" passive subject "they", i.e. the "chickens" in (15e) has a look-back of a single clause only to its last control — the zero-anaphoric appearance of the same NP as the direct object of the transitive verb "eat" in (15d).

5.7. *Clefting constructions.*

Table 8 below reveals that focus constructions in Hausa evince a marked degree of presuppositional complexity within the discourse, i.e. they approach, more than any other device so far considered, the upper reaches of the continuum relative ease → difficulty of topic-identification. We see, for example, that [+human] NP clefts display an average look-back of 15.1/12.5/13.9 for subjects, direct objects and indirect objects respectively, and that [-human] subject/ direct objects clefts enjoy an even greater average leftwards look — 17.2/16.2 clauses. Compare the above 15.1 clefted subject figure, for instance, with that of the corresponding topic-shifted NPs given in Table 6 — 12.9. Notice, at the same time, that [+human] participants, whatever their sentence function, continue to represent a more stable discourse factor than their [-human] counterparts, with lower average look-backs, in the main, and a longer survival rate.

Returning the the immediate issue, these lofty look-back averages are a direct reflection of the fact that clefted, focussed NPs are either indefinite, i.e. introduced for the first time, or are known arguments which re-emerge in the discourse, usually following a lengthy absence. Consider discourse fragment (16) below. "Yusha'u" has boasted that nothing can frighten him, so the Emir's daughter slips into his room in the middle of the night and pours cold water upon him, whereupon he jumps up in fright:

(16) a.   Da Yusha'u ya buɗe ido-n-sa,
          when Yusha'u-SUBJ he-PERF open eye-of-his-DO
          'When Yusha'u opened his eyes,

     b.   ya gane *makirci* ne aka yi masa. . .   (DO-CLEFT)
          he-SUBJ-PERF realise trick-DO-CLEFT COPULAR
          IMPERS-SUBJ-PERF do to him-IO
          he realised that *a trick* had been played on him. . .'
                                                (Imam 1970:25)

In (16b), the clefted direct object NP "trick" is introduced for the first time as a properly indefinite argument. The same NP decays immediately — cf. the relative fast decay-rates of clefted nominals, 0.6/0.9 for subject NPs as against 1.9/

Table 8: clefted NPs.[a]

		SUBJECT[b]	NON-SUBJECT DO	NON-SUBJECT IO	NON-SUBJECT POSS
LOOK-BACK[c]	HUMAN	15.1/20	12.5/7	13.9/3	—
	NON-HUMAN	17.2/9	16.2/23	—	—
RATE OF DECAY	HUMAN	0.6/20	0.3/7	1.0/3	—
	NON-HUMAN	0.9/9	0.2/23	—	—
POTENTIAL AMBIGUITY	HUMAN	1.9/20	1.5/7	1.6/3	—
	NON-HUMAN	1.8/9	1.7/23	—	—

a) Approximately 100 pages were scanned in order to collect a statistically significant number of tokens of this phenomenon.

b) Again, references to "Allah" are not included; also excluded from consideration here are instances of clefting in non-verbal equational constructions.

c) In accordance with the methodological guidelines suggested by Givón, a 20-clause maximum look-back is specified for indefinite clefted nominals. See also footnote (b) to Table 9.

1.5 for REF-DEF NPs [-PRM] — another function of their generally disruptive nature.

It is noteworthy too that counter-expectational contrastive focussing in Hausa is more destructive of the neutral syntax than any of the other operations involving left-dislocation of an element — topic-shift and passivisation. Thus, left-attraction of the emphatic-focus constituent under clefting is accompanied by an obligatory shift to the relative (perfective/imperfective) aspects, the (optional) insertion of the copular following the cleft, and zero-appearance of the focussed element in the "out-of focus" clause.[31] This structural-pragmatic correlation serves to support Givón's (1979a:78, 217-218) claim that more presuppositional variants exhibit greater syntactic complexity than the corresponding neutral patterns.[32]

Consider a further example. In (17), a Fulani man has awoken to find that some of his money has been stolen during the night:

(17) a.   Ya fa tashi da zage-zage,
          he-SUBJ-PERF indeed get up with abusing
          'He got up ranting and raving,

   b.   ya ce *'yan'uwa-n-sa* suka sace   (SUBJ-CLEFT, DO-∅)
        don baƙi-n ciki.
        he-SUBJ-PERF say brothers-of-his-SUBJ-CLEFT they-PERF steal
        DO-∅ because of blackness-of stomach and said that *his brothers* stole
        (it) because they were sad.'

                                                            (Imam 1970:27)

In (17b) the REF-DEF NP "his brothers" is contrastively focussed, having resurfaced after a discourse absence of some 21 clauses.

5.8. *Referential-indefinite NPs.*

In this final section we examine the lowest level of discourse presuppositionality — the interesting case of referential-indefinite NPs which are overtly specified with the "R(eferential) I(ndefinite) M(arker)" (RIM) already noted above, the variant forms of which are listed in Table 11 (b) of the Appendix.[33] For the purposes of this exposition, I consider a given NP to be "referential-indefinite" in a semantic-pragmatic sense if it is "referential" in the sense specified in footnote (22), and is additionally "indefinite" in that the addressee is presumed unable to assign unique identity to the referent, i.e. to unambiguously link the NP to the idea it represents.[34] A word, first of all though, regarding the Hausa-specific conditions which seem to determine the appearance or otherwise of this particular deictic device.

Table 9: referential-indefinite NPs [+RIM].

		SUBJECT	NON-SUBJECT	
			DO	LOCATIVE[a]
LOOK-BACK	HUMAN[b]	20.0 ⎯ 41	20.0 ⎯ 20	⎯
LOOK-BACK	NON-HUMAN[b]	20.0 ⎯ 9	20.0 ⎯ 37	20.0 ⎯ 15
RATE OF DECAY	HUMAN	3.7 ⎯ 41	2.9 ⎯ 20	⎯
RATE OF DECAY	NON-HUMAN	0.3 ⎯ 9	0.2 ⎯ 37	0.2 ⎯ 15
POTENTIAL AMBIGUITY	HUMAN[b]	2.0 ⎯ 41	2.0 ⎯ 20	⎯
POTENTIAL AMBIGUITY	NON-HUMAN[b]	2.0 ⎯ 9	2.0 ⎯ 37	2.0 ⎯ 15

a) The locative function is included in Table 9 to catch the locative cases – much more frequent in this count than either dativaI or genitival NPs.

b) All REF-INDEF NPs are arbitrarily assigned an average look-back of 20 clauses, and an average potential ambiguity rate of 2 NP arguments – cf. footnote (c) in Table 8. ments – cf. footnote (c) in Table 8.

[+human] arguments, whatever their grammatical function within the clause, which are REF-INDEF according to the above criteria are, almost without exception, modified by a pre-positional RIM.[35] Thus, all 41 REF-INDEF subjects in Table 9 are instances of [+ human] participants freshly introduced via the conduit of existential-presentative constructions, example (18) being typical. An almost equally common means of introducing the [+human] leitmotif of a story, and one which accounts for several of the 20 [+human] direct object tokens in Table 9, is to make it the object of an impersonal perfective construction, a literal gloss of which would be on the lines of "Once upon a time, one did X. . .", where X is a REF-INDEF NP; this particular strategy is evidenced in (19). The use of the RIM in passages (18) and (19), both of which signal the beginning of a new story, is archetypical:

(18) a. Akwai *wani Sarki* wanda ya-ke da (RIM + SUBJ, RIM + ASSOC OB-
         wata jakadiya. . .   JECT)
         there is-EXIST RIM-Emir REL-SUBJ he-IMPERF
         with RIM-housekeeper-ASSOC
         'There was once *a (certain/specific) Emir* who had *a (certain/
         specific) housekeeper*. . .'
                                                                  (Imam 1970:42)

(19) a. *A wata ƙasa* an yi *wadànsu madìnka* (RIM + ADV, RIM + DO)
         guda uku. . .
         in RIM-country-ADV IMPERS-SUBJ-PERF do
         RIM-tailors-DO unit three
         '*In a (certain/specific) country* there were once three *(certain/
         specific) tailors*. . .'
                                                                  (Imam 1970:89)

Since the NPs underlined in examples (18) and (19) meet the definitional conditions specified above, they are automatically modified by the RIM; indeed, they would be unacceptable without this operator. The RIM thus functions to "activate a new mental file" on the freshly-introduced [+human] referents – cf. Du Bois (1980:209). Thereafter in the plot, these same participants, now semantically REF-DEF of course, appear with or without the PRM as the case may be, with use of the PRM simply referring back to a previously opened file – see section 5.4.1 and remarks in footnote (23).

Regarding first mention of inanimate, non-locative entities, perusal of any Hausa text will indicate that the decision to employ an RIM or not can go either way basically – see also Jaggar (1982). That is, such NPs, whatever their function in the sentence, do not necessarily appear with the modifying RIM, even if they are in fact destined to persist as themes into the discourse, and I suspect that factors akin to those outlined in footnote (23) for use of the PRM may be at work. In the following passage, the NP "dream" occurs as a brand-new participant and survives as an important item of communication in the rest of the story, yet no RIM is utilised:

(20) a.   Ran goma-sha-biyu ga wannan wata, watau dare-n Mauludi,
        day ten-and-two to DEM-month, that is eve-of Maulud
        'On the twelfth day of that month, that is on the eve of Maulud,[36]

    b.   ya-na barci
        he-SUBJ-IMPERF sleep
        he was sleeping

    c.   sai ya yi *mafarki*. . .
        then he-SUBJ-PERF do dream-DO
        when he had *a (certain/specific)* dream. . .'

                                                (Imam 1970:11)

An additional noteworthy feature is that, given an appropriate context, a single NP may be modified by both a pre-positional RIM *and* a post-positional PRM, with or without a following restrictive relative clause. Consider, in this regard, sentence (21). The Emir is discussing the most convenient time for his housekeeper to give him some money and suggests the late afternoon since:

(21) a.   "Ga shi kuma lokaci-n ba *wadânsu mutane-n*   (RIM + SUBJ + PRM)
        da za su fitine ni."
        look at it too time-PRM NEG EXIST RIM-men-PRM-SUBJ
        REL FUT they bother me-DO
        ' "And look, at that time there are no *people* who will bother me." '

                                              (Imam 1970:43)

Finally, observe the strong rightwards persistence of the [+human] REF-INDEF NPs in Table 9 — clause-averages of 3.7 and 2.9 for subject and object positions respectively. This is in stark contrast to the extremely rapid decay-rate of the corresponding non-human arguments — 0.3 (subject), 0.2 (direct object), and 0.2 (locative object). These facts merely serve to confirm the observation, made at several points in the foregoing analysis, that there would seem to be a natural communicative tendency in discourse for human referents to be discussed over relatively long stretches of narrative.

6. Concluding remarks and summaries

It seems to me difficult to argue, with any real conviction, against Givón's (1979a:31) statement to the effect that "If a language is an instrument of communication, then it is bizarre to try and understand its structure without reference to communicative setting and communicative function". The theoretical and methodological underpinnings of the foregoing analysis stem from a desire to break out of the transformational-generative straitjacket and look instead at the various ways in which one Hausa-speaker/writer at least utilises, within flesh-and-blood narrative discourse, the various coding devices at his disposal.

It is hoped this report has demonstrated that a number of central syntactic phenomena in Hausa are at least partly explicable by reference to certain features of the communicative system, and that statistical properties of real live discourse crucially participate in such an analysis. At the same time, we have noted that such an approach must make allowance for a residue of non-discourse-determined factors which may act to contrain a speaker-writer's referential choices, over and above, that is, general cognitive restrictions deriving from short-term memory capacity. These constraints include: language-particular properties, e.g. the fact that Hausa enjoys greater freedom for inexplicit direct object reference than English for instance, also allowing the feature [±human] and the lexical semantics of certain verbs to influence referential options; and considerations of individual stylistic preference no doubt play some part in shaping the final choice. An additional dimension, moreover, and one not addressed in this report, relates to how differing discourse-genres, e.g. written vs. oral, tightly-edited vs. spontaneous texts, straight narrative vs. bilateral conversation (briefly explored in 5.1.2), affect the devices employed to establish and then track entities.

At the level of (discourse) grammar investigated, i.e. that of topic-NP (dis)-continuity, a number of guiding principles have emerged, and it is worth recalling some of the more salient. It is apparent, in the first place, that the continuum we have been working with is a finely graded one. Secondly, a systematic disparity characterises the discourse behaviour of subject as opposed to direct object NPs, with the subject-topic role clearly representing the continuity marker in the narrative tracts considered. Finally, [+human] participants, whatever their syntactic function, have been shown to have a more continuous function, displaying a larger average look-back value and surviving over longer average stretches than do their [-human] counterparts. These and other principles are now summarised, according to grammatical role, in Figures (1-9).

FIGURE 1: Subject function, values for "look-back" parameter

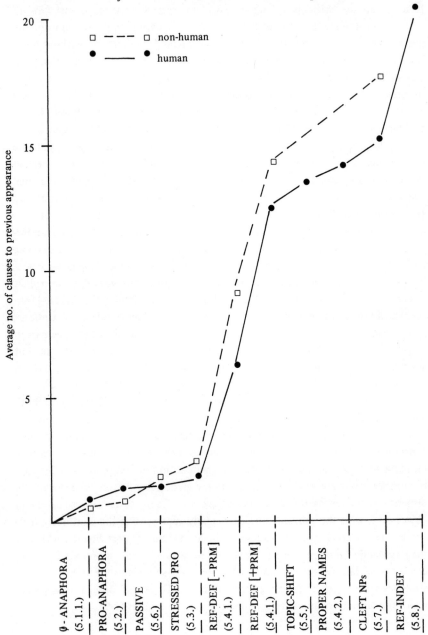

FIGURE 2: Direct object function, values for "look-back" parameter

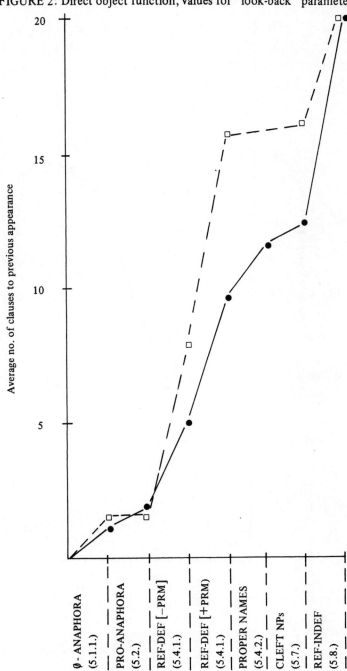

FIGURE 3: Indirect object function, values for "look-back" parameter

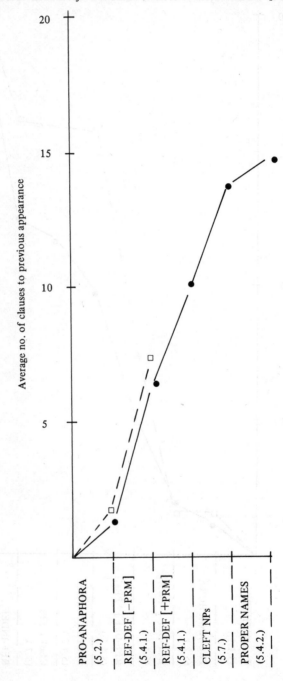

FIGURE 4: Subject function, values for "decay-rate" parameter
Note different scale for Figures (4-9)

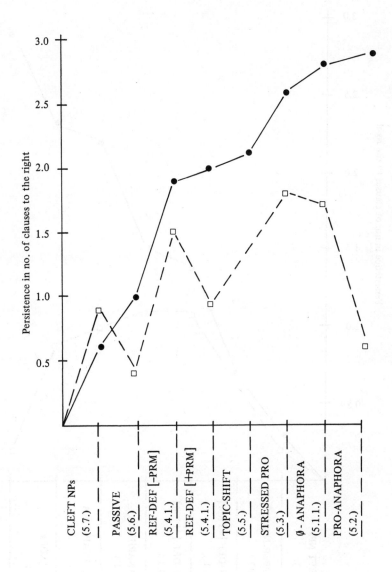

FIGURE 5: Direct object function, values for "decay-rate" parameter

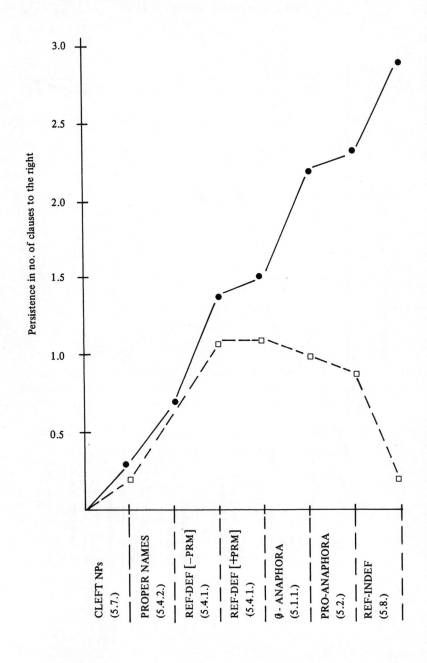

FIGURE 6: Indirect object function, values for "decay-rate" parameter

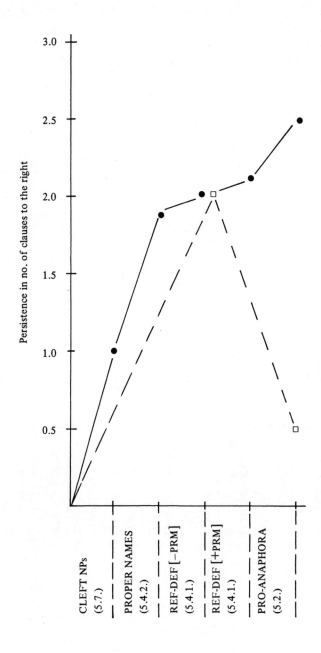

FIGURE 7: Subject function, values for "potential ambiguity" parameter

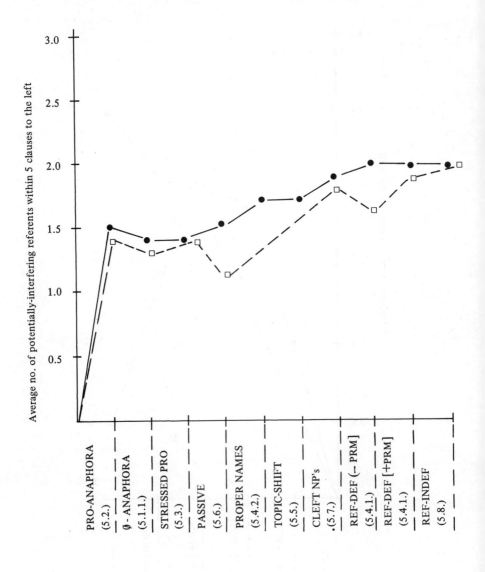

FIGURE 8: Direct object function, values for "potential ambiguity" parameter

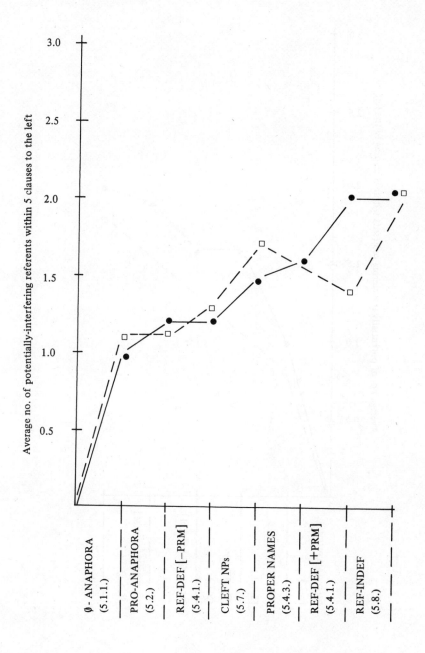

FIGURE 9: Indirect object function, values for "potential ambiguity" parameter

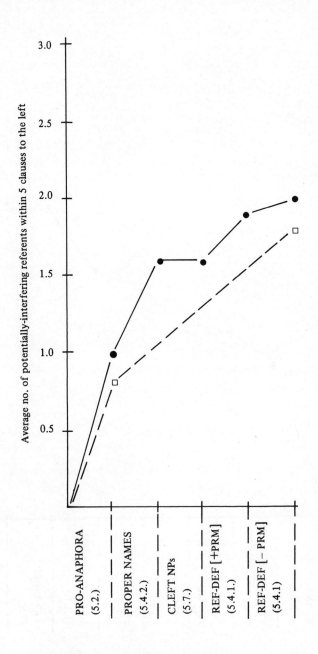

NOTES

1) García's (1979) paper represents perhaps the most extreme statement of this position. Mention should also be made of studies by such as Duranti and Ochs (1979), who furnish data on the gradation of relative ease → difficulty of topic-identification in Italian, and Sankoff and Brown (1976) who examine relativisation in New Guinea Tok Pisin within the wider context of discourse functions.

2) Given the right conditions, ellipsis of both the subject-concord morpheme and direct object NP within a single clause is possible, e.g. Wa ∅ ke neman abinci? 'Who's looking for food?' – Audu ne ∅ ke nema ∅ 'It's .Audu who's looking for it', though I happened upon no instances of this in the whole of Imam (1970). Zero-anaphoric reference to indirect object arguments is rare in pragmatically neutral clauses, with (5g) below a possible instantiation (cf. too fn. [15]) – hence the absence of any such category in Table 1. This formal feature undoubtedly correlates with the cross-language generalisation that datival-indirect objects tend, as Givón (1979a:53, fn. 26) has observed, to be overwhelmingly [+human], and the Hausa-specific fact that [+human] referents, regardless of their grammatical function, are usually picked up with a resumptive pronoun of some kind – cf. my remarks on the interface between anaphora and the semantic features [±human] and [±referential] in section 5.1.2.

3) I use the label "aspect-tense(-mode)", instead of the more commonly encountered cover-term "tense-aspect", in order to capture the fact that the Hausa verbal system is more accurately characterised as an aspect-dominated one.

4) The constraints on referential choice considered here are of the following types: listener- and speaker-related cognitive constraints, e.g. short term memory, allied to various Hausa-specific syntactic conditions, in addition to discourse-determined factors pertaining to such phenomena as "episode boundaries" and "thematic junctures". See Clancy (1980) and Hinds (1977, 1978, 1979) for extensive discussions of similar referential options in English and Japanese.

The precise distribution of the SUBJECT PRONOUN-∅ rule remains to be worked out. My own impression is that the situation tilts towards free individual variation, with no fixed pattern of preference. At the same time, a thorough search of Imam (1970) and other texts appears to indicate that whereas in neutral, non-relative constructions the decision to employ the device or not can go either way, it is applied with much greater frequency in syntactic environments which require a relative imperfective construction, and especially in the context of relative clause formation. There is probably a correlation too between ellipsis and fast speech tempo. Newman and Schuh (1974:27-29), it is worth noting, hypothesise that although use of a copy third person pronoun following an overtly expressed subject NP is an accomplished feature of modern Hausa, the reverse, i.e. zero-marking, was true historically, the innovative use of a copy pronominal clitic having developed under analogical pressure from other, non-third person, subject pronouns.

5) Excepting, that is, second person singular imperative forms, where obligatory addressee-deletion takes place – cf. examples (13a) and (13b); in addition, stylistic deletion of the third person singular masculine subject pronoun, referring to "Allah", optionally takes place in certain fixed formulae expressed in the subjunctive mood, e.g. Allah ∅ ji ƙansa

'may Allah have mercy on his soul!', again especially in the context of fast tempo speech.

6) Newman's (1976:177) observation that "In the context of a noun (or non-personal pronoun) subject, the third person aspect pronouns can optionally be deleted. . .", along with McConvell's (1977:2) comment that "In some tenses the agreement marker on the Auxiliary may be optionally omitted. . .This only happens where there is an overt subject NP present in surface structure. . ." merit some elaboration therefore. Deletion may occur following the interrogative, relative and universal pronouns [±human], and also the referential-indefinite marker — see section 5.8. Zero-appearance of the subject-concord marker may also apply in the second and third persons, in which case the presence of a full, independent pronoun is required. It may be noted too that the grammatical subject controlling the subsequent zero-occurrence is not constrained to appearance, whether as a full nominal or independent pronoun, *immediately* to the left of the person-aspect auxiliary — as (2) indicates, the rule can follow — (2b) — upon its prior application — (2a). In addition, postnominal demonstratives and/or the copular morpheme may all intervene between the NP control and ∅-strategy, as may modal particles and even full relative clauses, the antecedent head of which can be the subject or object of the relative clause.

7) The relatively rigid neutral word order in Hausa is: S V (IO) (DO) (ADV). Standard (Kano, Hausa orthography is used throughout (b, d, k, ts and 'y indicating glottalised consonants), with the addition of hyphens to mark morpheme-boundaries; and constituents pertinent to the discussion in hand are *italicized*.

8) This was the only instance of such a chain I encountered in a search of more than 80 pages, though I do recall isolated examples of the same phenomenon in other works; and iterative-habitual chains never occur, regardless of the zero strategy, because of an ATM-sequence rule in Hausa which converts all but the sequence-initial iterative-habitual auxiliary into the subjunctive. The said chain must, furthermore, involve identical (imperfective) aspects and rarely, if ever, exceeds the two-verb sequence illustrated in (2a-b). This restriction may relate to the fact that a sequence of imperfective verbs denotes overlapping simultaneity of the respective verbal actions and that there is a pragmatic limit to the number of such verbs which may participate in simultaneous action.

9) As indicated in the morphological gloss for (3a), the verb "think" has been formally clefted, but this is no more than a stylistic decive often employed with non-factive perceptual verbs like "think" and "hear", and also with intensional verbs, e.g. "want". It does not have any contrastive-emphatic force, therefore, unlike the cleft construction in (3c) for instance — cf. section 5.7.

10) If sentence (3) were taken in communicative isolation, then either "stranger" (3a) or "Kalala" (3b) could be interpreted as controlling coreference of the subject pronoun of the main verb "want" in (3c) — both arguments are maximally similar in that they share the features [+human, +3rd person, +masc. sing.]. It is interesting to note too in this regard that in the environment of certain relative formations, use of the SUBJECT PRONOUN-∅ device serves to disambiguate an expression which would be potentially ambiguous with the subject-agreement marker. Thus compare:

(4)   a.   mutumi-n da *ke* magana da shi   (SUBJ PRO-∅)
            man$_i$-PRM-SUBJ REL SUBJ$_i$ PRO-∅ IMPERF
            speak with him$_j$-ASSOC
            'the man who is speaking with him'

with:

      b.   mutumi-n da *ya-ke* magana da shi
            man$_i$ -PRM-SUBJ REL he$_i$-SUBJ-IMPERF (interpretation a., subject relative,
                                                                                    as (4a))
            SPEAK with him$_j$-ASSOC
            'the man who is speaking with him'

or: man$_i$-PRM-ASSOC REL he$_j$-SUBJ-IMPERF (interpretation b., associative ob-
                                                                            ject relative)
            speak with him$_i$-ASSOC
            'the man whom he is speaking with'

11) Compare McConvell's (1977:15ff.) somewhat tortuous attempt to explain the in-
ability of the device to apply in such contexts in terms of a complex array of crucially
ordered syntactic rules.

12) Henceforth, unless otherwise indicated, [+human] statistical values appear before,
and [−human] values after, the slash.

13) With this particular variant of the Hausa verb "give", the element which is semantically the datival-recipient argument bears the grammatical case of direct object in relation
to the verb. Furthermore, whereas a prementioned, and normally [−human], direct object
"gift" is often erased in the ensuing linguistic context, as in (5c), a known, usually [+hu-
man], recipient NP is always picked up with a pronominal reflex, again as in (5c).

14) *PRM* = "P(revious) R(eference) M(arker)", discussed in section 5.4.

15) At least we have on our hands an example of INDIRECT OBJECT-∅ if we analyse
the verb gode 'thank' as being subcategorised for a following indirect object argument −
excluding, that is, the case of Allah, who appears, quite exceptionally, as a direct object in
the fixed phrase Mun gode Allah 'We thank Allah'. Alternatively of course, one could simply
treat it as a lexically intransitive verb, governing an optional datival object, in which case
(5g) would not be the outcome of any deletion rule.

16) As attested in clause (5r), however, the narrative sequence does not have to be a
tightly-knit one to allow the application of NP ellipsis.

17) These remarks reflect, at least, the stated intuitions of those of may Hausa-speaking
friends I consulted on the matter, and they might go some way to explicating the phenomenon. If these claims are on the right track, they imply, of course, that there exist, for Hausa-
speakers, "psychologically real" degrees of "referent identifiability" correlating with the
two discourse genres. Russell Schuh [p.c] has, moreover, correctly reminded me that the
lexical semantics of a given verb may sometimes exert an influence upon the choice of anaphoric device. At the same time, the claim in Cowan and Schuh (1976:135) that "When the
object [of verbs like *sani* 'know' and *gani* 'see'] is a specific concrete person or thing, they
must be followed by the direct object pronouns" cannot be sustained in such a powerful
form. As formulated, it probably accounts for the presence of the direct object pronoun
following the sensory-perceptual verb gane "recognise" in (5s), but pronominalisation is by
no means categorial with [−human] referents. In Bagari et al. (1979:36), for example, the

following clause occurs:

(6)   . . .bai *gani* ba.   (DO-∅)
          NEG he-SUBJ-PERF see D∅-∅ NEG
          '. . .he didn't see (*it*).'

where the zero-mentioned direct object argument refers back some 5 clauses to a referential-definite inanimate NP "ring". Notice that according to the criterial conditions suggested above, it would have been equally appropriate for this same NP to have been anaphorically specified by means of a direct object pronoun shi 'it'. Cowan and Schuh *are* correct, however, in maintaining that perceptual nonfactive verbs in Hausa control only pronominal-anaphora of [+human] object NPs — if the referent in (6) had been [+human], a postverbal pronominal reflex would have been compulsory.

18) The verbs in clauses (7i) and (7j) are in the "neutral perfective" aspectual form, use of which signals "anterior perfective" actions in Hausa narrative tracts — cf. the pluperfects of the English glosses. For an account of the function and distribution, within narrative discourse, of the neutral perfective, see Jaggar (1982).

19) *RIM* is the shorthand I use to denote the "R(eferential) I(ndefinite) M(arker)" — a coding device used categorially with certain nominal categories at the beginning of a new story as in (8a). And *STR PRO* = "STR(essed) PRO(noun)". See discussions in sections 5.3 and 5.8.

20) Notice the string of subject pronoun-deletions in the English versions of (9c-e) — a strategy permissible only in tight-knit, clause-chaining sequences.

21) Clause (10b) also contains a non-contrastive, topic-shifted indirect object — the stressed pronoun shi 'he', cf. section 5.5.

22) I take a given nominal argument to be "referential" from a discourse-pragmatic viewpoint if, following Du Bois' (1980) characterisation, it is ". . .used to speak about an objet as an object, with continuous identity over time" (1980:208), and additionally "definite" or "specific" if the same referent is assumed, by the speaker, to be uniquely identifiable to the hearer. By "continuity of identity", Du Bois (1980) understands that a referential concept ". . .may serve as a focus for future references" (1980:209), though the opportunity is not always taken of course. He later (1980:269) introduces the term "prop" to specify ". . .an object whose continuity of identity is ignored. . .", and "participant" to denote ". . .a human, animal, or object whose continuity of identity is salient enough to be maintained". Apropos of these claims, Skinner (1974) has rightly observed that the parameter of [+importance to the unfolding plot] is, in contrast to such notions as specificity, previous reference etc., ". . .rather more subjective and extremely sensitive to the speaker's individual emotions or sense of style" (1974:253). Cf. too my comments on the use of the PRM in footnote (23).

23) The exact conditions on the felicitous use of the deictic PRM are extremely difficult, if not impossible, to pin down with any real precision. Quite apart from discourse-pragmatic variables, considerations of personal style, idiolect, "planned" versus "unplanned" speech, and even, as I have suggested elsewhere (1980:77), exposure on the part of bilingual speakers to the use of the English definite article, may all impinge upon the decision. Interestingly, comparison of Imam (1970) with earlier editions of Magana Jari Ce reveals a

growing fondness for the PRM.

24) The same clitic is also suffixed to the antecedent head NPs of restrictive relative clauses in Hausa —cf. (4b). It may also be employed to encode NPs which are definitised via their "uniqueness", i.e. they exist as unique single members of a given category, subject, of course, to various pragmatic and/or culture-dependent conventions, e.g. "*the* wife", and sublocales like "*the* kitchen" etc. Related to this function, the same deictic is also used to map implied reference, the precise conditioning of which is once again clearly culturally-determined to some degree. For instance, in anticipation of a reward for services rendered, a Hausa-speaker might enquire ina goro-*n*? 'Where is *the* kolanut?', i.e. the "kolanut/reward" expected in the circumstances. None of the foregoing functions have been included in the Table 4 counts.

Finally in this regard, nominal references to entities of which there exists a single, unique instance in the ordinary consciousness of people, e.g. 'the sun', 'the moon', and, amongst the Islam-embracing Hausa, 'the Prophet', are never accompanied by an accessory PRM — cf. too my remarks in footnote (35) below. Halliday and Hasan (1976:71) term such referential mentions "homophoric", in the sense that ". . .the referent is identifiable on extra-linguistic grounds no matter whan the situation".

25) The two devices are, at least for the purposes of this exposition, treated as conveying essentially the same degree of semantic stress, discourse-presuppositionality etc., hence the decision to collapse the two for the purposes of Table 4. Whether this is the case in reality, i.e. whether my assumption that they belong to the same basic mapping area, is correct, remains an open question. Hausa also permits the maximal conjunction of STR PRO + NP + PRM + DEM, and I would suspect that this particular strategy *does* constitute an escalation — the number of attested examples was insufficient to quantify this impression however.

26) Subject, as well as indirect object nominals, are overwhelmingly definite in Hausa. At the same time, referential-indefinite arguments do occur as the newly-introduced subjects of existential-presentative constructions — see Givón (1977, 1979a) for an extensive discussion of cross-language constraints on indefinite subject nominals, and section 5.8 for examples from Hausa.

27) Either that, or we have on our hands an illustration of what Givón (1979a:39) terms "overkill" strategy — the overuse by the speaker of a particular device for the purpose of communicative insurance.

28) For a detailed description of these and other salient features of the operation, see Jaggar (1978).

29) Another case of the neutral perfective encoding an out-of-sequence, anterior event — cf. footnote (18).

30) For arguments in favour of considering these various operations as belonging to the same functional domain, see Givón (1979a, 1981) and Keenan (to appear).

31) Schachter's (1973) term. See also Jaggar (1978:73-75) for a contrastive analysis of the mechanisms of topicalisation and clefting in Hausa.

32) They are also subject to more stringent distributional restrictions than are the neutral forms — cf. remarks in footnote (a) of Table 8.

33) As indicated in footnote (a) of Table (11b), a typologically interesting feature of the RIM in Hausa is that it is also used to encode the meanings 'another, others etc.', and a remarkable parallel to this has been noted by John Du Bois [p.c.] in Sacapultec, a language

of the Mayan family. Adopting a suggestion mooted by Du Bois [p.c.], the unitary semantic principle underlying these seemingly disparate functions – 'a certain' and 'another' – may be a discourse-related one, entailing the notion of "theme-switching". This approach involves the assumption that an initial-mention NP bearing an RIM encodes a switch from a zero linguistic environment as it were, i.e. where no preceding "theme" in fact exists. Seen in this light, the problem of accounting for the two interpretations of the RIM is possibly resolved. See Skinner (1974) for a more comprehensive analysis of the discourse-determined functions of this particular grammatical operator.

34) See Chafe (1976:30-31), Du Bois (1980:220ff.), and Givón (1977) for illuminating discussions of the notions "definite" and "indefinite".

35) In addition, newly-introduced locatives important to the unfolding story are normally modified in a similar fashion – cf. (19) – as are animals, though the rule is by no means categorial in this case, as (7c) illustrates. Exceptions to the rule are not without interest. Thus, nouns like "emir" which tend to be "unique" to a given, culture-bound, universe – cf. observations in footnote (24) – will only be marked with the RIM if introduced, as fresh participants, right at the beginning of a new story, as in (18); once, however, a proper frame has been evoked for "emir" to be assigned "uniqueness", e.g. prior mention of his domain, then first appearance will almost always be zero-coded, i.e. definite reference with only partial identifiability is permissible. Finally, Neil Skinner [p.c.] has reminded me of the additional fact that initial reference to such specific kinship terms as "older brother" and "younger brother", e.g. "There was once a (certain) older brother and a (certain) younger brother. . .", are not obliged to carry an RIM, even though this first reference may be in the opening clause of the story.

36) One of the few cases of "afterthought right-dislocation" I encountered.

REFERENCES

Bagari, Dauda M., William R. Leben, and Faye McNair Knox. 1979. *Manual of Hausa Idioms.* Bloomington, Indiana: Indiana University Linguistics Club.

Bolinger, Dwight. 1968. "Judgements of grammaticality." *Lingua* 21:34-40.

–––––. 1979. "Pronouns in discourse." In Talmy Givón (Ed.), *Syntax and Semantics, Vol. 12, Discourse and Syntax*, pp. 289-309. New York: Academic Press.

Chafe, Wallace L. 1972. "Discourse structure and human knowledge." In Roy O. Freedle and J.B. Carrol (Eds.) *Language Comprehension and the Acquisition of Knowledge.* New York: Halsted Press.

–––––. 1976. "Givenness, contrastiveness, definiteness, subjects, and point of view." In Charles N. Li (ed.), *Subject and Topic*, pp. 25-55. New York: Academic Press.

–––––, (Ed.) 1980. *The Pear Stories: Cognitive, Cultural, and Linguistic Aspects of Narrative Production.* Norwood, N.J.: Ablex.

Clancy, Patricia M. 1980. "Referential choice in English and Japanese narrative discourse." In Wallace L. Chafe (Ed.), *The Pear Stories: Cognitive, Cultural, and Linguistic Aspects of Narrative Production*, pp. 127-202. Norwood, N.J.: Ablex.

Cowan, J. Ronayne, and Russell G. Schuh. 1976. *Spoken Hausa.* Ithaca, New York: Spoken Language Series.

Duranti, A., and Elinor Ochs. 1979. "Left dislocation in spoken Italian." In Talmy Givón (Ed.), *Syntax and Semantics, Vol. 12, Discourse and Syntax*, pp. 377-416. New York: Academic Press.

Du Bois, John W. 1980. "Beyond definiteness: The trace of identity in discourse." In Wallace L. Chafe (Ed.), *The Pear Stories: Cognitive, Cultural, and Linguistic Aspects of Narrative Production*, pp. 203-274. Norwood, N.J.: Ablex.

García, Erica C. 1979. "Discourse without syntax." In Talmy Givón (Ed.), *Syntax and Semantics, Vol. 12, Discourse and Syntax*, pp. 23-49. New York: Academic Press.

Givón, Talmy. 1977. "Definiteness and referentiality." In Joseph Greenberg, C. Ferguson, and E. Moravcsik (Eds.), *Universals of Human Language,* pp. 291-330. Stanford: Stanford University Press.

—————. 1979a. *On Understanding Grammar.* New York: Academic Press.

—————, (Ed.) 1979b. *Syntax and Semantics, Vol. 12, Discourse and Syntax.* New York: Academic Press.

—————. 1980. *Ute Reference Grammar.* Ignacio, Colorado: Ute Press,

—————. 1981. "Typology and functional domains." *Studies in Language* (in press).

—————. 1983. *Syntax: A Functional-Typological Introduction.* Amsterdam, J. Benjamins.

Halliday, Michael A.K., and Ruqaiya Hasan. 1976. *Cohesion in English.* London: Longman.

Hinds, John. 1977. "Paragraph structure and pronominalization." *Papers in Linguistics* 10:77-99.

—————. 1978. "Anaphora in Japanese conversation." In John Hinds (Ed.), *Anaphora in Discourse.* Alberta: Linguistic Research, Inc.

—————. 1979. "Ellipsis and prior mention in Japanese conversation." In A. Makkai and V. Makkai (Eds.), *The Fifth LACUS Forum 1978.* Columbia, S.C.: Hornbeam Press, Inc.

Imam, Abubakar. 1970 [1939]. *Magana Jari Ce, Vol. 2.* Zaria, Nigeria: Northern Nigerian Publishing Company.

Jaggar, Philip J. 1978. "And what about. . . ? – Topicalisation in Hausa." *Studies in African Linguistics* 9(1):69-81.

––––––. 1980. Review of H. Jungraithmayr and W.J.G. Möhlig, *Einführung in die Hausa-Sprache. Journal of African Languages and Linguistics* 2(1):75-78.

––––––. 1981a. "Some unusual lexical passives in Hausa." MS. Los Angeles: University of California.

––––––. 1981b. "Varieties of passive in Hausa." In William R. Leben (Ed.), *Papers from the Twelfth Annual Conference on African Linguistics. Studies in African Linguistics*, Supp. 8:73-77.

––––––. 1982. "The two perfective aspects of Hausa and their roles in the flow-control of narrative structures." MS. Los Angeles: University of California.

Keenan, Edward L. (to appear). "Passive in universal grammar." In Tim Shopen et al. (Eds.), *A Field Guide to Syntactic Typology.*

Labov, William. 1972. "The transformation of experience in narrative syntax." *Language in the Inner City*, pp. 354-396. Philadelphia: University of Pennesylvania Press.

Ma Newman, Roxana. 1976. "The two relative continuous markers in Hausa." *Studies in African Linguistics*, Supp. 6:177-190.

McConvell, Patrick. 1977. "Relativisation and the ordering of cross-reference rules in Hausa." *Studies in African Linguistics* 8(1):1-31.

Newman, Paul, and Russell G. Schuh. 1974. "The Hausa aspect system." *Afroasiatic Linguistics* 1(1):1-39.

Sankoff, Gillian, and Penelope Brown. 1976. "The origins of syntax in discourse: A case study of Tok Pisin Relatives." *Language* 52:631-666.

Schachter, Paul M. 1973. "Focus and relativization." *Language* 49:19-46.

Skinner, Neil. 1974. "Hausa wani/wata/wa'dansu and its semantic features." In Erhard Voeltz (Ed.), *Third Annual Conference on African Linguistics. Indiana University Publications, African Series, Vol. 7*, pp. 251-257.

a) So-called because of the appearance of these auxiliary subject pronouns in environments involving relativisation/subordination – a non-categorial rule in the case of the imperfective. The "relative perfective" is also the aspectual form employed to encode verbal actions occurring within sequential past action narrative; the "neutral perfective" fulfills the anterior look-back function in background fragments of narrative structures – for details, see Jaggar (1982).

APPENDIX

Table 10: Hausa aspect-tense-modal system (affirmative Kano Hausa forms).

a) PERFECTIVE

	NEUTRAL	RELATIVE[a]	
Sing. 1	naa zoo[b]	na zoo	'I came, have/had come' etc.
2m	kaa zoo	ka zoo	'you (masc.) " " ' etc.
2f	kin zoo	kikà zoo	'you (fem.) " " ' etc.
3m	yaa zoo	ya zoo	'he came, has/had come' etc.
3f	taa zoo	ta zoo	'she " " " ' etc.
Plur. 1	mun zoo	mukà zoo	'we came, have/had come' etc.
2	kun zoo	kukà zoo	'you (plur.) " " ' etc.
3	sun zoo	sukà zoo	'they " " ' etc.
Impers.	an zoo	akà zoo	'one came, has/had come' etc.

b) IMPERFECTIVE

	NEUTRAL	RELATIVE[a]	
Sing. 1	i-nàa zuwàa[c]	na-kèe zuwàa	'I am/was/will be coming'[d]
2m	ka-nàa zuwàa	ka-kèe zuwàa	'you (masc.) are/were/will be coming'
2f	ki-nàa zuwàa	ki-kèe zuwàa	'you (fem.) " " " '
3m	ya-nàa zuwàa	ya-kèe zuwàa	'he is/was/will be coming'
3f	ta-nàa zuwàa	ta-kèe zuwàa	'she " " " '
Plur. 1	mu-nàa zuwàa	mu-kèe zuwàa	'we are/were/will be coming'
2	ku-nàa zuwàa	ku-kèe zuwàa	'you (plur.) " " '
3	su-nàa zuwàa	su-kèe zuwàa	'they " " '
Impers.	a-nàa zuwàa	a-kèe zuwàa	'one is/was/will be coming'

b) For the purpose of these and other paradigms in Tables (10-12), double letters are used to indicate long vowels, and grave and circumflex accents signal low and falling tones respectively. high tones being unmarked.

c) The deverbal nominal form which this particular verb assumes in the imperfective.

d) The imperfective also possesses a context-sensitive iterative-habitual reading.

c) SUBJUNCTIVE

Sing. 1	ìn	zoo	'I should/may etc. come'
2m	kà	zoo	'you (masc.) " " '
2f	kì	zoo	'you (fem.) " " '
3m	yà	zoo	'he " " '
3f	tà	zoo	-'she " " '
Plur. 1	mù	zoo	'we " " '
2	kù	zoo	'you (plur.) " " '
3	sù	zoo	'they " " '
Impers.	à	zoo	'one " " '

d) ITERATIVE-HABITUAL

na-kàn	zoo	'I (habitually come'
ka-kàn	zoo	'you (masc.) " " '
ki-kàn	zoo	'you (fem.) " " '
ya-kàn	zoo	'he " " comes'
ta-kàn	zoo	'she [" " comes'
mu-kàn	zoo	'we " " come'
ku-kàn	zoo	'you (plur.) " " '
su-kàn	zoo	'they " " '
a-kàn	zoo	'one " " comes'

e) FUTURE ("DEFINITE")

Sing. 1	zâ-n	zoo	'I will/was going to come'
2m	zaa-kà	zoo	'you (masc.) will/were " '
2f	zaa-kì	zoo	'you (fem.) " " '
3m	zâ-i	zoo	'he will/was " " '
3f	zaa-tà	zoo	'she " " '
1	zaa-mù	zoo	'we will/were " '
2	zaa-kù	zoo	'you (plur.) " " '
3	zaa-sù	zoo	'they " " '
Impers.	zaa-à	zoo	'one will/was " '

f) FUTURE ("POTENTIAL")

nâa	zoo	'I (probably) will/was going to come'
kâa	zoo	'you (masc.) will/were " " '
kyâa	zoo	'you (fem.) " " '
yâa	zoo	'he will/was " " '
tâa	zoo	'she " " '
mâa	zoo	'we will/were " " '
kwâa	zoo	'you (plur.) " " '
sâa	zoo	'they " " '
âa	zoo	'one will/was " " '

Table 11: deictic elements (Kano Hausa).

a) "PREVIOUS REFERENCE MARKER" (post-clitic)		b) "REFERENTIAL-INDEFINITE MARKER" (pre-nominal)[a]	
Masc. sing. noun (X)	X-ǹ 'the/that X'	wani (X)	'a *certain/specific* X'
Fem. sing noun (Y)	Y-r̃ 'the/that Y'	wata (Y)	'a *certain/specific* Y'
Plural noun (Z)	Z-ǹ 'the/those Z'	waɗansu (Z)	'some *certain/specific* Z'
		wasu (Z)	

c) DEMONSTRATIVES
pre-nominal[b]   post-nominal

	pre-nominal	post-nominal
Masc. sing NP (X)	wànnan/wàncan X	X-ǹ nan/can 'that X (non-visible) / *that* X (remote non-visible)'
Fem. sing NP (Y)	wànnan/wàccan Y	Y-r̃ nan/can 'that Y (" ") / *that* Y (" ")'
Plural NP (Z)	waɗannan/waɗàncan Z	Z-ǹ nan/can 'those Z (" ") / *those* Z (" ")'

a) Is free to occur in isolation, and may also be used to indicate 'another X/Y, other Z'.

b) May also occur in isolation as an anaphoric pronoun and, less frequently, in post-nominal position. Both the *nan*- and *can*-marked demonstrative elements – listed to the left and right respectively of the slashes in Table 11(c) – encode entities which are non-visible, with the *can*-signalled variants additionally mapping objects which are more remote-distal in a temporal or spatial sense. Hausa also possesses two *nan*- and *can*-marked demonstrative sets, tonally distinct from the above, which serve, in the general case, to encode referents which are visible, with a partial overlapping in the mappings of the visible and non-visible deictic fields.

Table 12: the Hausa pronominal system.[a]

STRESSED		UNSTRESSED			
		DOb	IO	POSSESSIVE	(masc. sing. or plural/fem. sing. noun possessed)
Sing.	1	nii	ni	minì	-naa/-taa	
	2m	kai	ka	makà	-n/-r-kà	,,
	2f	ke	ki	mikì	-n/-r-kì	,,
	3m	shii	shi	masà	-n/-r-sà	,,
	3f	ita	ta	matà	-n/-r-tà	,,
Plural	1	muu	mu	manà	-n/-r-mù	,,
	2	kuu	ku	mukù	-n/-r-kù	,,
	3	suu	su	musù	-n/-r-sù	,,

a) This is not the entire array of Hausa pronouns — Table 12 simply includes those pronominal paradigms relevant to this study. As ever, the forms listed are the current Standard (Kano) Hausa ones.

b) The tone of the direct object pronoun is, in the general case, polar to the tone on the immediately preceding syllable.

TOPIC CONTINUITY AND THE VOICING SYSTEM
OF AN ERGATIVE LANGUAGE: CHAMORRO *

ANN COOREMAN
Linguistics Department
University of Oregon, Eugene

*) Many thanks to my informant Vicky Manibussan, a native speaker from the island of Guam, who provided and helped transcribe the narratives on which this pilot study is based. The reader should be aware of the limitations of the data itself. The pilot study should not be seen as a final end product but needs to be enlarged by incorporating narratives from different speakers and by looking at conversations as well to check whether the same pragmatic principles hold. Many thanks are also due to Talmy Givón who was my advisor throughout this research project.

TABLE OF CONTENTS

0. Introduction.

In this paper I will discuss two aspects of morphology linked to the hierarchy of topicality in the ergative Austronesian language Chamorro, spoken on the Northern Marianas. The first aspect involves different syntactic coding devices for noun phrases in Chamorro which allow the native speaker to indicate whether a topic NP in the sentence is continued or not, i.e when a new topic is introduced for the first time a different coding device will be employed than when the same topic has been continually mentioned over a series of sentences in the immediately preceding discourse or when the topic is reintroduced in the conversation. Below I will present the results of Givón's quantitative method applied to the most common NP coding devices in Chamorro. The results will confirm Givón's (1980, 1981a and 1982) earlier hypothesis based on data from Ute that the syntactic coding devices of the NP's can be ordered hierarchically, where at the top are syntactic devices involving higher topicality or continuity and thus presumably ones for which the referential identification is easier. Closer to the bottom are syntactic devices involving less continuity, higher surprise and therefore difficulty in assigning referentiality of the topic. Givón proposes the following hierarchy which is in part attested by my own Chamorro data and by the languages studied in other papers in this volume:

(1)   zero anaphora > unstressed/bound pronouns or grammatical agreement > stressed/independent pronouns > right dislocated NP's > simple definite NP's > left dislocated NP's > indefinite NP's > Y-movement > cleft/focus constructions.

The second part of this paper is more interesting than the first since it demonstrates how the quantitative analysis can be used to differentiate between five different syntactic coding devices for semantically transitve sentences in Chamorro according to the degree of topicality/continuity of the two main participants in the clause. Semantically transitive sentences are those sentences which have both an Agent and an Affected Participant (Patient or Dative) in the underlying proposition.

The appearance of five such devices in one particular language is striking and invites the linguist to look for an explanation for their existence. Since languages tend to be economical systems of communication one may at least assume that these five construction types have different functions, i.e. certain restrictions are imposed which may be syntactic or pragmatic in nature.

There are three active and two passive constructions in Chamorro which code semantically transitive sentences. The question arises why a language would need three different ways of coding a clause in which the main participant is the Agent and two distinct ways in which the Affected Participant seems to be highlighted. The fact that the five constructions appear in overlapping environments (see also Chung 1979) suggests that their distribution cannot be predicted on the basis of syntactic considerations alone. One is thus obliged to look for an explanation for their existence elsewhere.

In the past decade more and more linguists have become interested in finding pragmatic functional grounds for syntactic and morphosyntactic coding devices and a large body of literature has arisen on that topic. (Bolinger 1979; Creider 1979; Duranti and Ochs 1979; Erteschik-Shir 1979; García 1979; Givón 1979, 1980; Hopper 1979; Hopper and Thompson 1980, among others).

There are many indications in recent literature that the syntactic coding of semantically transitive sentences, i.e. those with both an Agent and an Affected Participant, is not entirely independent of discourse context, e.g. the topic status of both arguments in the clause.

There are at least two aspects involved in measuring the topic status of any referent in the discourse:

  i) *the nature of the NP* through which reference is made,
  ii) the status of this referent as *given* or *new* information in the discourse register as established between the interlocutors.

In connection with the first aspect, linguists have observed that certain NP's (e.g.pronouns) tend to appear as topics in the discourse more often than others (e.g. indefinite NP's) and thus they have ranked these NP's on a hierarchy of natural topics (cf. Hawkinson and Hyman 1974, Givón 1976, inter alia). The first part of this paper will provide some evidence for this particular hierarchy and its importance with respect to syntax.

Hopper and Thompson (1980) have related the way transitive clauses are coded syntactically to the properties of both the Agent and the Affected Participant. Two of the parameters involved in their analysis, viz. the degree of "individuation" and "agency", can clearly be correlated to the hierarchy of natural topics. Furthermore, they noted that the way transitivity gets marked in the sentence is dependent on the function of the sentence as a whole in the discourse, which they ultimately related back to the distinction between backgrounded and foregrounded information.

In some ergative languages the choice between the ergative and non-ergative markers in a semantically transitive sentence is also dependent on the topic status of the two major arguments. To cite one example: Chung (1981) claimed that in Chamorro a *semantic parameter* filters out the sentences in which the Affected Participant is of higher "*individuation*" than the Agent/Subject. This constraint seems to be rather a *discourse pragmatic* restriction as it operates along the same hierarchy of topicality. Chamorro seems to rule out sentences in which the Agent NP's rank lower than the Affected Participants on the hierarchy. According to Chung antipassives and passives will be used instead of the ergative construction in such cases.

The same hierarchy of natural topics seems to be involved in the explanation of split ergativity systems.

Based on the theory of markedness Silverstein (1976) set up a hierarchy of NP's which he called "the hierarchy of features". He observed that in many languages with split ergativity, those NP's which are the most marked in his system tend to be involved in a nominative-accusative coding system for transitive clauses. The least marked NP's on the other hand, are syntactically coded along ergative-absolutive lines. Since Silverstein's hierarchy matches the hierarchy of topicality, one is led to conclude that the different syntactic coding systems, ergative vs. accusative, are dependent on the discourse context, related to the degree of topicality of the major arguments in the transitive clause. The items which are likely to be marked on a nominative-accusative basis are also more likely to appear as topics in natural discourse.

Similarly, Scott De Lancey's explanation (1981) of split ergativity systems in terms of "attention flow" and "viewpoint" can be brought to terms with the same hierarchy of topicality.

There are two clear examples of languages in which the distinction between given and new information provides a pragmatic discourse based constraint on the syntactic coding of semantically transitive clauses.

Dixon (1972) observes that Dyirbal has a specific construction in which the verb is marked with *ŋay-* and which is used in a certain type of sentence coordination. This particular construction has been identified as an antipassive by Michael Silverstein (1976) and indicates that the second sentence in the co-ordinated pair has a transitive Agent/Subject which is coreferential with either the absolutive intransitive Agent or the absolutive transitive direct object of the previous clause. This particular antipassive construction is involved in creating *topic chains* (Dixon 1972:79-81) and will never be the first clause at the onset of a new discourse.

According to Kalmár (1979, 1980) the converse of this principle holds in Inuktituk (Eskimo). The direct object in antipassive clauses may be definite or indefinite but is always a new item in the discourse register as established between the interlocutors. Text frequency counts result in the observation that the antipassive clause is constrained to the first few clauses in discourse. Ergative sentences make up the bulk of the stories.

Already Chung's analysis of the choice between the ergative and the non-ergative passive or antipassive construction in certain cases can be ultimately traced back to the discourse notion of topicality. Below in part two of this paper, I will present further evidence that the five syntactic devices we find in Chamorro differ at least in one important pragmatic aspect, i.e. different relative degrees of topic continuity of the Agent and the Affected Participant in the clause correspond to the choice of one construction over the others. We could conclude then that the five constructions code different segments of the functional domain of topicality in semantically transitive clauses.

1. Morphological Preliminaries.

Before presenting the functional analysis of the syntactic coding devices of the NP's and semantically transitive sentences in Chamorro discourse it seems useful to outline briefly some of the characteristics of Chamorro morphology (see also Chung 1981). A short sample text has been added to the paper as an appendix.

1.1. Case markers.

Indefinite NP's in Chamorro are not marked for case. Within the definite NP's three categories should be distinguished: pronouns, proper names, and common nouns. The class of the proper names also include nouns which are used to name specific individuals such as father, mother, priest, etc. The case markers for definite NP's are:

	Unmarked	Oblique	Locative
pronouns	∅	nu	gidza
common nouns	∅	ni	gi
proper names	si	as	giãs

The unmarked definite common nouns can be preceded by the definite article *i*. The unmarked case is used for subjects, direct objects, and prepositional objects. The oblique case is used for the so-called "demoted" NP's like Patients in the antipassive construction or in the active ergative construction after dative movement has applied. It is also used for instruments and passive agents. Sometimes the locative marker is used to indicate such a passive Agent.

Examples:

(2) *Si   Maria   ha-   'adios.*
     p.n.-unm. Mary   E.3s.   goodbye
     'Mary says goodbye.'

(3) *Hu- na'i   si   Maria   ni   lepblu.*
     E.1s. give p.n.-unm. Mary   c.n.-obl. book
     'I gave Mary the book.'

(4) S_1-*in*$_2$- *anani*$_i$ *giäs   /as   nana- ña   u- hanao.*
     PASS$_2$ -tell$_1$ p.n.-LOC/p.n.-obl.   mother-POSS-3s. IRR.3s.-go
     'She was told by her mother to go./Her mother told her to go.'

(5) *I   tsäkä p_1-in$_2$- inu'$_1$ ni   kátu.*
     the   mouse PASS$_2$ -kill$_1$ c.n.-obl. cat
     'The mouse was killed by the cat.'

(6) *Gwaha   serena   gi   papa   tasi.*
     Be/have mermaid   c.n.-LOC below   sea
     'The mermaid is under the sea./There is a mermaid under the sea.'

1.2. Pronouns.

Since Chamorro is an ergative language it employs basically two sets of pronouns, absolutive and ergative ones. The absolutive pronouns are used as subjects of intransitive sentences and direct objects of transitive ones. The ergative pronouns can be used as subjects of transitive clauses but since in transitive sentences agreement with the subject in person and number is marked on the verb, these ergative pronouns are superfluous and do not generally occur in narrative discourse. When they are used at all they carry a sense of marked emphasis. Both sets of pronouns show number and person but no gender.

	Ergative Pronouns	
	singular	plural
first person	gwahu	hita (incl.)/hami (excl.)
second person	hagu	hamdzu
third person	gwidza	siha

	Absolutive Pronouns	
	singular	plural
first person	dzu'	hit (incl.)/ham (excl.)
second person	hao	hamdzu
third person	gwi'	siha

Examples:

(7)   *Ha- gwaidzǎ dzu'.*
        E. 3s.-love   Abs.1s.
        'He/she loves me.'
(8)   *Hu- gwaidzǎ gwi'.*
        E.1s.- love   Abs.3s.
        'I love him/her.'
(9)   *Mu- nǎŋu dzu'.*
        Sing.- swim Abs.1s.
        'I swim/swam.'

1.3. Verb-subject agreement.

Chamorro distinguishes between irrealis and realis. The realis is used to mark events which occurred in the past or in the present; the irrealis refers to future events and is used also for certain types of modality, e.g. in verb complements after verbs of manipulation. The distinction between realis and irrealis runs through the paradigms of subject agreement markers and constitutes an ergative split: the ergative-absolutive distinction is upheld only in realis clauses. Compare (10) with (7), (8), and (9):

(10)   *Pǎra bai-hu- nǎŋu.*
        FUT IRR.1s.- swim
        'I will swim.'

In realis clauses transitive verbs agree in both person and number with the subject. Chung (1981) has called this conveniently *ergative agreement* since the agreement is *only* with the transitive subject.

	Ergative Agreement		
	singular	plural	
first person	hu-	ta-	(incl.)/in- (excl.)
second person	un-	in-	
third person	ha-	ma-	

Examples:

(11)   *Hu- sakke i   gwihan.*
        E.1s.-steal the   fish
        'I steal/stole the fish.'
(12)   *si   tata- hu   ha- toksa hulu' i   lemmai.*
        p.n.-unm. father-POSS.1s. E.3s.- poke up the breadfruit
        'My father poked up at the breadfruit.'

The intransitive clauses exhibit *number agreement* with the subject.

	Number Agreement	
	singular	plural
realis	-um-/$\emptyset$	man-
irrealis	$\emptyset$	fan-

Examples:

(13) H_1-um_2-$anao_1$ *dzu'.*
        $sing_2$-go_1 Abs.1s.
        'I go/went away.'
(14)   *I   serena   man-gaigi gi   tasi.*
        the   mermaid   PL- be   c.n.-obl. sea
        'The mermaids are in the sea./There are mermaids in the sea.'

The infix -*um*- has an allomorph *mu*- when the stem of the verb has an initial nasal (cf. (9)).

In the irrealis both transitive and intransitive verbs show agreement in person and number with the subject. The same verbal prefixes are used for both. Chung (1981) called this type *subject agreement* as it is distinct from the *ergative agreement* in form and domain of application. The prefixes indicate agreement with either the transitive or the intransitive subject.

	Subject Agreement	
	singular	plural
first person	(bai)-(h)u-	ta- (incl.)/in-(excl.)
second person	un-	in-
third person	(h)u-	(h)u-(intransitive)/(h)uma-(trans.)

Subject agreement is limited to irrealis clauses and will never cooccur with *ergative agreement.* However, it will combine with the plural *number agreement* prefix *fan-* in intransitive sentences.

Examples:

(15)　　*I　serena　u-　　fan- gaigi gi　　　　tasi.*
　　　　the　mermaid IRR.3pl.-PL.- be　c.n.-LOC　sea
　　　　'The mermaids will be in the sea.'

(16)　　*Ha- tagu' dzu'　si　　　Pedro　na　　bai-hu- hanao.*
　　　　E.3s.-tell　Abs.1s.　p.n.-unm.　Peter　Compl.　IRR.1s.-go
　　　　'Peter told me to go.'

(17)　　*Antisdi un-　　hanao　păra un-　　tso'gwi.*
　　　　before　IRR.2s.-go　　　　FUT　IRR.2s.- do
　　　　'Before you go to do something.'

(18)　　*I　amerikano ma- disidi na　　păra huma- tsuli tatti*
　　　　the　Americans E.3Pl.- decide compl.　FUT　IRR.3pl.-take back
　　　　ta'lu idză Guam.
　　　　again class. Guam
　　　　'The Americans decided to take Guam back again.'

2. Part I: Topic continuity and the syntactic coding of NP's

2.1. Grammatical devices investigated.

2.1.1. Grammatical agreement and zero-anaphora.

As I will show below these grammatical devices mark those referents with the highest degree of topic continuity in discourse. Givón lists the zero-anaphora device as marking the highest topical referents with grammatical agreement next in line (cf. (1)). I have lumped the two categories together for the following reasons: these two devices both mark highly topical referents. They cannot be compared in order to decide which one ranks highest on the hierarchy of grammatical devices for the simple reason that the highest topical subjects are most often marked by verb agreement and much less frequently by zero anaphora (e.g. with auxiliaries such as *siña* "can", *sigi* "keep on, continue", verbs like *kulan* 'look like", and sometimes in fast speech, verbs which regularly agree with the subject). All other grammatical roles such as direct objects, indirect objects etc. never agree with the verb and can only be coded as highly topical/continuous referents through zero anaphora.

Examples:

(19) ...ha- unu' i palao'an na maseha tai manu
      E.3s.-know the woman compl. regardless how much
      malago'- ña si tata- ña ti siña
      want- POSS-3s.p.n.-unm. father-POSS.3s.not can
      ha- asagwa esti otru na taotao. (Subject grammatical
      E.3s.-marry this other link. man agreement)
      '. . . the woman knew that regardless of how much her father wanted
      her to, she could not marry this other man.'

(20) ...anai ha- tsuli' i gaoli dzä ha- toksa hulu' i lemmai
      when E.3s.- take the stick and E.3s.- poke up the breadfruit
      anai potduŋ ha- bira gwi'. . . (subject ∅-anaphora)
      when ∅-fall E.3s.- turn Abs.3s.
      '. . .when he took a stick and poked up at the breadfruit he turned
      around when it fell. . .'

(21) Ha- saŋan-i i taotao na ti malellifa maseha
      E3s.- tell-DAT the people compl. not forget-RED regardless
      hafa bida-ñiha. (accusative ∅-anaphora)
      what do- POSS-3pl.
      'He told the people he was not forgetting *them* regardless of what
      they did.'

(22) Ha- tsuli' si pali' i santus dzä ma- laksi-dzi
      E.3s.-take p.n.-unm. priest the saint and PASS-sew-DAT
      magagu(∅) dzä ma- na'- minagagu si Santa Maria.
      clothes and PASS-CAUS- dress p.n.-unm. saint Mary
      (dative ∅-an.)
      'The priest took the saint and clothes were sewn *for her* and the
      Virgin Mary was dressed up.'

The markers -dzi/-i in (22) and (21) are allomorphs which indicate the presence of a dative or beneficiary participant in the sentence. This marker is attached to the verb only when the participant has been promoted to the grammatical case role of direct object. It is not an agreement marker since it does not agree in person, number, or gender with the dative or beneficiary. It would be interesting to compare those datives which have been promoted to direct object with those that have not (as in (26)). As of yet the small number of datives in general and non-promoted datives in particular in my data base do not permit such a comparison.

There are no ∅-anaphora genitives in my data. Such constructions occur in some expressions in languages such as French. Compare:

(23)   Il   a   cassé   la   jambe.
             he   has broken the   leg
             'He broke his leg.'

(24)   Il   a   cassé   la   jambe   de   Marie.
             he   has broken the   leg   of   Mary
             'He broke Mary's leg.'

In general a possessor in such sentences is overtly expressed only when the genitive is not coreferential with the subject.

2.1.2. Independent pronouns.

The use of full pronouns as a coding device for highly topical referents is not nearly as frequent as ∅-anaphora or subject agreement for subjects. It is also fairly rare for direct objects, be it accusatives or datives. However, this coding device is the only one attested in the data for highly continuous topic possessors.

Examples:

(25)   . . .*saŋan-i*   *i*   *taotao na   matai i ma'gas-ñiha*   *as*
        ∅- tell- DAT the people compl. ∅-die the chief- POSS.3pl.p.n.-obl
        Alu dză gwidză păra u-   famaolik todu i taotao.
        Alu   and E.3s.   FUT IRR.3s.- take care   all   the people
                                      (subject pronoun)
        'He told the people that their chief had died, namely Alu, and that he would take care of all the people.'

(26)   *Pues ma-   bira siha   tatti gwatu gidza   Hagatña păra*
        then E.3PL- turn Abs.3PL back there c.n.-LOC Agaña FUT
        i   palasdzu dză ma-   bomba ădzu lokwi'.
        the   palace   and E.3pl.- bomb   that also
                                   (accusative demonstrative pron.)
        'Then they returned to Agaña again to the Governor's house and bombed that also.'

(27)   *Ma- saŋan-i   si   pali'   dză ilek-ña*
        E.3pl.-tell- DAT p.n.-unm. priest   and say- POSS.3s.

si pali' gidza siha na. . . (dative pronoun)
p.n.-unm. priest c.n.-LOC Abs.3pl. compl.
'They told the priest and the priest said to them. . .'

(28) *Ma- gotdi i gaputulu-ñiha dzä g_1-um_2-aloppi*
E.3pl.-tie the hair- POSS.3pl. and UM_2-jump$_1$
hudzum esta papa gi tasi dzä a- punu siha.
out DIR down c.n.-LOC sea and REC-kill Abs.3pl.
(genitive pronoun)
'They tied their hair together and jumped down into the sea and killed each other.'

As is the case in Ute (cf. Givón 1983, this volume) and Spanish (cf. Bentivoglio 1983, this volume) deviation from the basic V.S. word order pattern in Chamorro is partly controlled by pragmatic principles which are themselves not independent of the hierarchy of topicality. Even though the counts are low for pronouns in subject position in my data, the numeric results which will be given below (table 5) suggests that there is a correlation between the type of word order selected and its function as a device indicating the degree of topic continuity of the subject referent. Examples:

(29) *Konfotmi gwi' na påra u- asagwa.* (V.S.)
confirm Abs.3s. compl. FUT IRR.3s. -marry
'He confirmed he would get married.'

(30) *Gwidza påra u- famaolik todu i taotao.* (S.V.)
E.3s. FUT IRR.3s. -take care all the people
'He would take care of all the people.'

2.1.3. Full definite NP's.

Full definite NP's can be common or proper nouns. The definite common nouns in the unmarked case are always preceded by the definite article *i*. The proper nouns are always preceded by a case marker (cf. 1.1.). Full definite NP's can be modified by demonstratives, adjectives, possessive pronouns and even by relative clauses. As Bentivoglio (1983) shows for Spanish, a distinction can be made between those NP's which are and those which are not modified. These distinct types of definite NP's have slightly different functions as devices marking the degree of topic continuity of the referents they encode. E.g. NP's modified by relative clauses tend to mark referents which are less continuous in the discourse than NP's which are only preceded by a definite article. The former need to be identified more explicitly to enable the hearer to pick out the intended referent in the disourse. In this paper I have not upheld the distinction between different categories of definite NP's. However, my own numeric results confirm Bentivoglio's findings for Spanish.

(31)   Ma- pripara siha   i   dzapanis.
         E.3pl.-prepare Abs.3pl. the   Japanese
                                        (non-modified common noun/subj)
         'The Japanese prepared themselves.'

(32)   Ilek-ña   i   asawga-ña   si   Păn.
         say- POSS.3s. the   wife- POSS.3s. p.n.-unm. Păn
                                              (modified common noun/subject)
         'Păn's wife said:. . .'

(33)   I   famagu'un ni   unsi   añus dză   mas   ma- na'-
         the children REL eleven years and   more   PASS-CAUS-
         fan-   matso'tsu' gi   gwalu'.
         IRR.pl.-work   c.n.-LOC   fields
                                        (common noun modified by rel. clause/subject)
         'The children who were eleven years old or more were put to work
         in the fields.'

(34)   Ma   tsuli' i   tano' păra Hapon.
         E.3pl. -take the   land for   Japan
                                        (non-modified common noun/acc.)
         'They captured the land for Japan.'

(35)   Man-mattu ta'lu dzăn ma-   bomba ta'lu Guam.
         PL.-come again and E.3pl. -bomb again Guam
                                        (proper noun/accus.)
         'They cane again and bombed Guam again.'

(36)   Guam ha-   sililibra   i   giput SantaMaria.
         Guam E.3s.   -celbrate-RED the   feast Saint Mary
                                        (modified common noun/acc.)
         'Guam was celebrating the feast of the Virgin Mary.'

(37)   Ma- bomba i   batku-siha ni   man-histaba gi   tasi.
         E.3pl.-bomb the   boat-PL   REL PL- -stay   c.n.-LOC sea
                                        (common noun with rel. cl./acc.
         They bombed the boats which were in the ocean.'

(38)   Ha- konni' esti i s_1-in_2-$idda_1$-ña   gi   tasi
         E.3s. take   this the NOM_2-find$_1$-POSS.3s. c.n.-LOC sea

dzä *ha-* *na'i* *si* *pali'*. (modified common noun/dative)
and E.3s. -give c.n.-unm. priest
'He took this discovery of his from the sea and gave it to the priest.'

(39) *I* *asagwa-ña* *si* *Mata'paŋ* *malagu'-ña* *ma-*

the wife- POSS.3s. p.n.-unm. M. want- POSS.3s. PAS.
tatpani. (genitive proper noun)
-baptize
'Mata'pang's wife wanted to be baptized.'

(40) *Esti* *na* *istoria* *istoria-n* *dos* *na* *taotao* *ni* *gos*

this link.story story-link two 1.p. people REL INT
um-a *gwaidza.* (common noun modified by rel.cl./genitive)
UM-REC-love
'This story is the story of two people who loved each other very much.'

As with pronouns a comparison will be made between full definite NP's in S.V. and in V.S. word order.

(41) *Ha-* *bira* *gwi'* *si* *Santa Maria dzän ha-* *fana* *i*
E.3s.-turn Abs.3s. p.n.-unm. Saint Mary and E.3s.-face the
liga. (V.S.)
wall
'The Virgin Mary turned around and faced the wall.'

(42) *I* *familia-ña* *esti* *as* *Mrs. Johnston* *mu-na'-*
the family-POSS.3s. this p.n.-obl. Mrs. Johnston UM-CAUS-
atuk *dzä* *mu-na'-* *boka* *si* *George Tweed.* (S.V.)
hide and UM-CAUS- feed p.n.-unm. George Tweed

'The family of this Mrs. Johnston hid and fed George Tweed.'

2.1.4. Indefinite NP's.

Only referential indefinite NP's are included in the analysis. Since indefinite NP's are in general used to introduce *new* topics in the discourse, they are the least topical, least continuous of all the grammatical devices investigated in this paper. Indefinite NP's in the singular can be unmarked or preceded by the numeral *un* (one) borrowed from Spanish which seems to have taken over the function of indefinite article as well. Examples:

(43)   *Dankulu   na   lunao dz_1-um_2-$endzun_1$ Guam.*   (subject)
        big   link.   earthquake UM_2-$shake_1$ Guam
        'A big earthquake shook up Guam.

(44)   *Ha-   li'i' un patgun na   ha-   go'fo'ti i   lemmai.*

        E.3s   -see   a   child   REL E.3s.-hold-RED the   breadfruit
        'He saw a child who was holding the breadfruit.'   (accusative)

(45)   *Mamahan un atumobit dzǎ ha- na'i   un familia gi*
        buy   a   car   and E.3s. -give a family c.n.-LOC
        idza Guam.   (dative)
        class. G.
        'He bought a car and gave it to a family in Guam.'

The indefinite NP coding device is unattested in my data for the genitive.

2.2. Methodology.

The quantitative method was suggested by Givón (1979, 1980). It is used in this volume for a cross-linguistic study including such languages as colloquial and written English, Biblical Hebrew, Spanish, Ute, Hausa, Japanese, Amharic, and Chamorro. The quantitative analysis assumes that each NP in the discourse has some *degree of topicality* and provides an adequate, empirical method to measure this degree of topicality for any NP in the discourse. Topicality here does not refer to what has been called the *subject* or *theme* of the paragraph or discourse, rather it refers to the degree of referential continuity of a given NP on the clausal level. Thus each NP has a degree of topicality even when introduced for the first time in the discourse and possibly functioning as the "comment' or 'focus' of the sentence in the sense of the traditional correlation of 'topic-comment' or 'topic-focus'. Presumably, a newly introduced element is more likely to have a very low degree of topicality.

In a pilot study on roughly fifty pages of transcribed Chamorro narratives each of the grammatical coding devices for third person referents as described above were subjected to three different measurements:

   i) referential distance
  ii) persistence (decay)
 iii) potential interference/ambiguity.

The parameter of *referential distance* measures the degree of *continuity* of the topic NP in terms of how many clauses to the left intervene between the last mention of the topic NP and the new mention in the clause under study. The maximum value is rather arbitrarily set at 20 since there is reason to believe that a hearer will not normally be able to retrieve referential information prior to roughly 20 clauses to the left of a new clause. Thus all indefinite NP's automaticaly get the value 20 assigned for referential distance. The parameter of *persistence* involves the persistence of the NP as topic, i.e. how many clauses to the right of the clause containing the NP will persist in having the same topic as argument of the verb. Relative clauses and direct quotes are not considered as a gap in the counts when the NP referent is not found in them, but they do count as an instance of occurrence when the NP referent appears in them. The value zero for referential distance is only assigned to genitives appearing in the same clause with a coreferential NP. Theoretically there is no upper limit to the value of persistence. In my data the highest value for this parameter of any given NP was 13. However, averages of the values for persistence within a given category of NP's never exceeded 4.25 in the data (cf. tables 1-5).

One would expect typically that a highly topical NP in the discourse has a low value for referential distance and a high one for persistence and that a non-topical NP is characterized by the opposite relation. The inverse relationship which seems to exist between the two measurements should not lead one to believe that the parameters measure essentially the same thing. *Referential distance* roughly measures the ease with which a *hearer* can identify the referent of a particular argument in the clause. Presumably in speech perception the reference of an entity is most easily identified when there is only a small gap between the previous and the new mention of that entity. The parameter of *persistence* on the other hand is related to the *speaker*'s speech production, i.e. the way he/she plans ahead which entities should be topical in the next piece of discourse. A NP which has a high value for referential distance does not necessarily have a low value for persistence. Indefinite NP's may introduce new elements in the discourse which are highly continuous and keep being mentioned in the rest of the narrative, thus causing a high value for persistence.

Finally, the measurement of *potential interference/ambiguity* assesses the existence of other arguments in the immediately preceding discourse environment that may potentially interfere with assigning correct reference to the NP. The values for this measurement are either 1 for non-interference or 2 for interference. All NP's which are introduced for the first time in the discourse (primarily as indefinite or definite full NP's) are necessarily of maximally

Table 1. Zero Anaphora and Verb Agreement

| | | SUBJECT | | NON-SUBJECTS | |
			ACCUSATIVE	DATIVE	GENETIVE
REFEREN-TIAL DISTANCE	ANIMATE	N = 444　1.21	N = 28　1.60	N = 9　1.22	——
	INANIMATE	N = 21　1.10	N = 12　1.08	——	——
PERSIS-TENCE (DECAY)	ANIMATE	1.84	1.70	1.78	——
	INANIMATE	0.43	0.17	——	——
POTENTIAL INTER-FERENCE	ANIMATE	1.14	1.1	1.44	——
	INANIMATE	1.62	1.17	——	——

Table 2. Independent Pronouns

| | SUBJECT | NON-SUBJECTS | | |
		ACCUSATIVE	DATIVE	GENETIVE
	N = 19	N = 4	N = 3	N = 49 / N = 4
REFERENTIAL DISTANCE — ANIMATE	1.15	1.50	1.00	1.06
REFERENTIAL DISTANCE — INANIMATE	—	—	—	0.25
PERSISTENCE (DECAY) — ANIMATE	1.36	1.75	5.00	1.67
PERSISTENCE (DECAY) — INANIMATE	—	—	—	4.25
POTENTIAL INTERFERENCE — ANIMATE	1.21	1.00	1.00	1.12
POTENTIAL INTERFERENCE — INANIMATE	—	—	—	1.00

Table 3. Full Definite NP's

		SUBJECT	NON-SUBJECTS		
			ACCUSATIVE	DATIVE	GENETIVE
REFEREN-TIAL DISTANCE	ANIMATE	N = 239 6.53	N = 53 6.42	N = 13 7.46	N = 26 4.50
	INANIMATE	N = 40 13.53	N = 62 7.45	—	—
PERSIS-TENCE (DECAY)	ANIMATE	1.77	1.06	1.77	1.54
	INANIMATE	0.25	0.45	—	—
POTENTIAL INTER-FERENCE	ANIMATE	1.62	1.64	1.69	1.46
	INANIMATE	1.85	1.50	—	—

Table 4. Indefinite NP's

	SUBJECT		NON-SUBJECTS			
			ACCUSATIVE		DATIVE	GENITIVE
	N = 17	N = 17	N = 10	N = 13	N = 1	
REFERENTIAL DISTANCE — ANIMATE	14.24		18.6		20.00	—
REFERENTIAL DISTANCE — INANIMATE		19.29		20.00	—	—
PERSISTENCE (DECAY) — ANIMATE	1.71		2.10		0.00	—
PERSISTENCE (DECAY) — INANIMATE		0.06		0.08	—	—
POTENTIAL INTERFERENCE — ANIMATE	2.00		2.00		2.00	—
POTENTIAL INTERFERENCE — INANIMATE		2.00		2.00	—	—

Table 5. Topic continuity of independent pronoun subjects, Full definite NP subjects, and indefinite NP subjects in different word order patterns.

	INDEPENDENT PRONOUNS		FULL DEFINITE NP'S		INDEFINITE NP'S	
	S.V.	V.S.	S.V.	V.S.	S.V.	V.S.
	N = 3	N = 15	N = 80	N = 170	N = 13	N = 15
REFERENTIAL DISTANCE	1.66	1.07	9.76	7.08	20.00	17.93
PERSISTANCE (DECAY)	0.66	1.53	1.67	1.63	0.92	0.73
POTENTIAL INTERFERENCE	1.33	1.20	1.90	1.79	2.00	2.00

ambiguous reference and are assigned value 2. The interference value of NP's already mentioned in the previous discourse takes into account their selectional restrictions (semantic, syntactic, and pragmatic) vis à vis the verb. Theoretically any NP mentioned within five previous clauses to the left of the new clause could exert interference in referential identification, provided that it can satisfy the selectional restrictions test.

In addition to the three measurements described above I have tried to assess the distribution and behavior of animate and inanimate referents in the texts in terms of topic continuity by applying the three measurements separately to the NP devices coding animate and inanimate entities in the different case roles.

2.3. Numerical results.

The above five tables give the average values for the three measurements applied to the different NP coding devices as they encode different case roles. The value for N in the tables indicates the total number of instances found. This value is given only once in the table next to the measurement for referential distance, but it applies equally well to the measurements for persistence and potential interference.

2.4. Discussion.
2.4.1. The degree of topicality and grammatical coding devices for NP referents.

Tables 1-4 show − as predicted by Givón (cf. (1)) − that the different coding devices analyzed in this paper can be ranked according to the degree of topicality of the NP referents they encode in the narrative. As graph 1 below shows for animate referents, the average value for referential distance is consistently lower for verb agreement/∅-anaphora and independent pronouns than it is for definite full NP's and indefinite NP's in all case roles investigated. This particular measurement seems to indicate that verb agreement/ ∅-anaphora and independent pronouns mark equally highly continuous topics. We can only compare the measures for animate subjects as the instances for the other NP categories are either too scarce to be taken seriously are simply non-existent.

The difference in value for referential distance for verb agreement/∅-anaphora and independent pronouns is unimportant. On a scale going from 0 to 20 a difference in value of 0.06 is negligible. However, the measurement of potential ambiguity can help us to grade the two grammatical coding devices on the topical hierarchy. The value for potential interference increases as one moves from the most topical/continuous referents to the least topical ones as exemplified

Graph 1. Distance for all animate referents

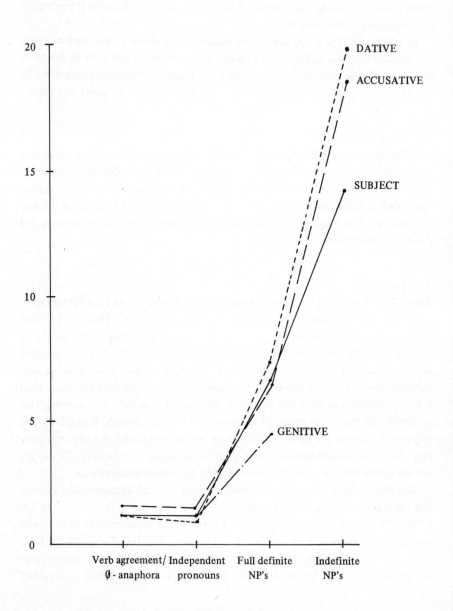

Graph 2. Potential Interference for all animate subjects

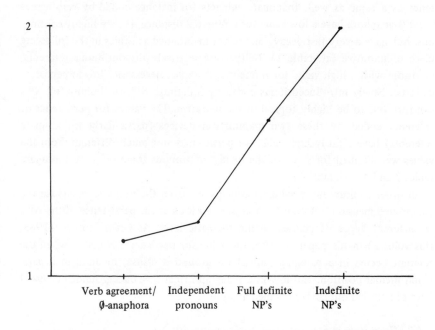

in graph 2 where for animate subjects coded by verb agreement/∅-anaphora the value is 1.14 and for animate subjects coded by indefinite NP's we obtain the maximum value of 2. A difference of 0.06 in the value for potential interference between the referents coded by verb agreement/∅-anaphora and independent pronouns is however significant. Compared to the measurement of referential distance, the same difference in average value on the scale of 1 to 2 for potential interference is 20 times greater and should be considered an important indication. It makes only sense that when the referent cannot be identified easily a stronger, more explicit device should be used. Thus one can reasonably conclude that verb agreement/∅-anaphora on the one hand is used for more topical, more easily identifiable referents, independent pronouns on the other hand for slightly less continuous topics.

The average values for persistence do not allow us to draw conclusions in connection with the degree of topicality of referents and the corresponding grammatical coding devices. What we can conclude is that the measurements of referential distance and persistence do not exactly represent two sides of the same coin. It is not the case that highly continuous referents, i.e. referents with a low value for referential distance, will necessarily have a high value for persistence as a topic as well. Inanimate subjects for instance coded by verb agreement $\emptyset$-anaphora have a low value for referential distance, i.e. are highly continuous, but have a very fast decay, i.e. are not maintained as topics in the following piece of narrative (cf. table 1). Neither are relatively discontinuous referents, i.e. those with a high value for referential distance, necessarily low in persistence value. Newly introduced items coded by indefinite NP's or definite full NP's can turn out to be highly topical in the narrative. The values for persistence of referents coded by these two grammatical devices (particularly for animate referents) have a fairly high value for persistence, not much different from the values we obtained for some of the highly continuous topic referents (compare tables 3 and 4 with table 1).

In order to draw more valuable conclusions from the numeric results for the persistence measure it would be necessary to look at the persistence of the NP's in different types of clauses on the thematic level. As Givón shows (1983, this volume) in his paper on Ute, the value for persistence is higher when the referent occurs in a paragraph initial foregrounded clause, medium in a paragraph medial position, and low in a paragraph final or a backgrounded clause. I have not carried out such a detailed analysis.

2.4.2. Grammatical case roles and topic-continuity.

Several linguists in the past have established a hierarchy of grammatical case roles according to their importance in the sentence as topics (cf. Givón 1976 among others). According to this hierarchy subjects rank higher than direct objects which in turn rank higher than indirect objects and oblique NP's. Due to the extremely low amount of clauses with both a direct and indirect object I will have to pass on a comparison between these two grammatical case roles in Chamorro narratives.

From the raw average values in tables 1 through 4 it is not immediately clear that the subject is more topical than the direct object. However, a comparison between the subject and the accusative (the prototypical direct object) according to the frequency with which both categories are coded by different grammatical devices reveals some interesting results which confirm the earlier hypothesis.

Table 6 below shows that over 60 % of the subjects in the narratives are represented by grammatical devices which code highly topical referents as we established in the previous section (cf. 2.4.1) Over 70 % of the accusatives are coded by grammatical devices which rank considerably lower on the hierarchy of topicality/continuity.

The genitive, although not a major case role in the sentence, is a fairly strong device by which topical reference can be maintained. The average value for referential distance is low compared to the other case roles and the value for

	SUBJECTS		ACCUSATIVES	
Verb Agreement/Ø-anaphora	465	58.35 %	40	21.98 %
Independent Pronouns	19	2.38 %	4	2.19 %
Full Definite NP's	279	35.00 %	115	63.18 %
Indefinite NP's	34	4.27 %	23	12.65 %
Total	797	100.00 %	182	100.00 %

Table 6. Distribution of subjects and accusatives
over grammatical devices.

persistence indicates a medium to high degree of topic continuity into the following part of the narrative. The high value 4.25 for persistence of inanimate genitives coded by the possessive pronoun represents an improbably high value. This is due to the small amount of instances and a value 10 for one of the four cases attested, which made the average value jump higher than one would probably expect with a larger amount of instances.

2.4.3. Animacy and the hierarchy of topicality.

The tables 1-4 confirm yet another hypothesis previously made by linguists that animate referents tend to be more topical than others. A comparison between the values for the three measurements for animate and inanimate referents reveals the following generalized facts (summarized for subjects in graphs 3-4-5):

    i)   in practically all the cases the average referential distance is lower for the animate referents than for the inanimate ones (exception: direct object accusatives coded by Ø-anaphora)

    ii)   the average persistence is higher for animates than for inanimates

    iii)   the potential interference is lower for animates than for inanimates (exception: direct object accusatives coded by definite full NP's)

These facts lead us to conclude that on the whole animate referents are more topical than inanimates in Chamorro narratives. They are talked about more often and tend to be maintained as topics of the conversation longer than in-

Graph 3. Referential distance for all subjects

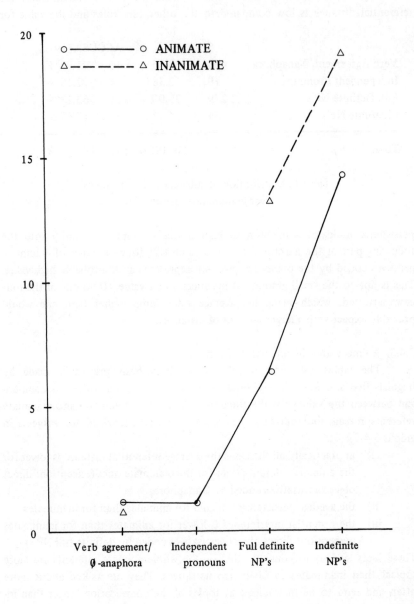

Graph 4. Persistence (decay) for all subjects.

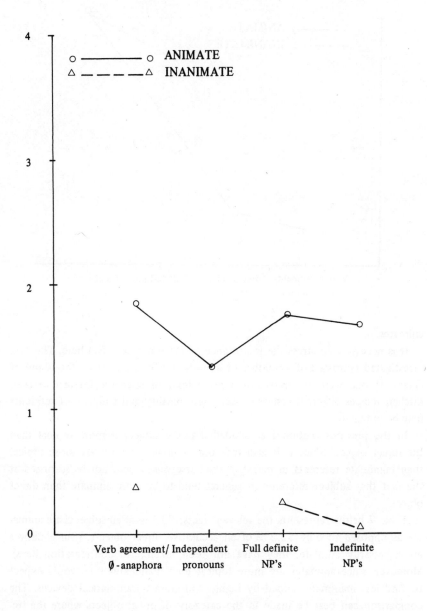

Graph 5. Potential interference (ambiguity) for all subjects.

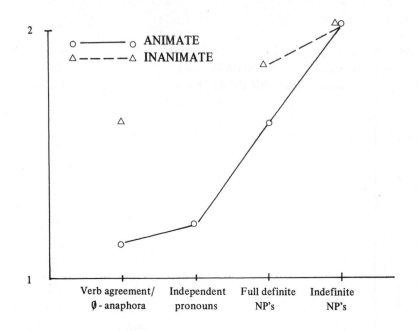

animates.

It is necessary to stress the importance of the term narratives here. The data investigated consisted of a number of legends and folk tales from the island of Guam. If one were to investigate written texts of scientific interest or even kitchen recipes different results concerning topicality and animacy of referents may be obtained.

In the previous section I concluded that the subject is more topical than the direct object. Since it is also true that animate referents are more topical than inanimate referents in narrative discourse one should not be surprised at the fact that subject referents in general tend to be more animate than direct object.

Table 7 below represents the relevant facts: 90.2 % of all subjects are animates as opposed to only 52.2 % of all accusative direct objects. (Since datives are necessarily animate, they have not been taken into consideration here). Moreover, since animates are more topical than inanimates one would expect to find less inanimates coded by highly continuous grammatical devices. The comparison can best be made in the category of direct objects where the frequency of animates and inanimates is roughly 50/50. The amount of inanimates coded by highly topical grammatical NP devices, such as $\emptyset$-anaphora and independent pronouns is considerably less than those coded by devices of lower topic continuity status. For subjects a similar situation holds: the number of inanimate subjects increases considerably moving from the top of the hierarchy of grammatical devices to the bottom.

The device of indefinite NP's makes no distinction between subjects and direct objects. It is used to introduce new animate and inanimate topics with the same frequency for subjects and direct objects.

2.4.4. Word order and topic continuity.

The basic Chamorro word order is V.S.O. Even though the majority of the clauses adhere to this basic word order, there are some that follow a deviant S.V. word order pattern. I have tried to assess at least part of the function of this deviant word order pattern by applying the quantitative method to the subject referents coded as full definite NP's, independent pronouns, and indefinite NP's in both possible word orders. The results (cf. table 5) run parallel to those obtained for Ute (cf. Givón 1983, this volume) and for Spanish (cf. Bentivoglio 1983, this volume). The deviant S.V. pattern corresponds to a higher value for referential distance and a higher value for potential interference. The tendency towards a lower value for persistence also in two out of three cases is not terribly convincing and needs to be investigated in more detail on the basis of a more extensive data base which would allow us to obtain a higher number of instances (needed especially in the category of independent pronouns).

What the values for referential distance and potential interference reveal is that the S.V. word order is used for less continuous, more surprising topics. As table 8 below shows, the frequency with which the S.V. word order is used to introduce less continuous topics into the conversation is lower for subjects coded by grammatical devices which are more continuous by nature than for those coded by highly discontinuous devices. Approximately 1/5 of the independent pronouns occur in S.V. order increasing to 1/3 for definite full NP's to almost 1/2 of the clauses with indefinite NP's. These results reveal a natural correlation between word order and the grammatical coding devices of NP's as to the topic continuity of the subject referent. Subjects which are coded by highly continuous grammatical devices are less likely to be found in the S.V. word order which is used for less topical, more surprising subjects; evidence is found in the higher values for referential distance and potential ambiguity of subjects in this particular word order pattern.

Table 7. Distribution of animates and inanimates as subject and accusative direct object coded by various grammatical devices.

	SUBJECTS			ACCUSATIVES (Direct Objects)		
	Total	Animate	Inanimate	Total	Animate	Inanimate
Verb agreement/ Ø - anaphora	465	444 95.5%	21 4.5 %	40	28 70%	12 30%
Independent pronouns	19	19 100%	—	4	4 100%	—
Full definite NP's	279	239 85.66%	40 14.34%	115	53 46.08%	62 53.92%
Indefinite NP's	34	17 50%	17 50%	23	10 43.5 %	13 56.5 %
TOTAL	797	719 90.2 %	78 9.8 %	182	95 52.2 %	87 47.8 %

Table. 8 Frequency of word order patterns for subjects
coded by different grammatical devices

	Total	S.V.		V.S.	
Independent Pronouns	18	3	17 %	15	83 %
Full definite NP's	250	80	32 %	170	68 %
Indefinite NP's	28	13	46 %	15	54 %

3. Part II: Topicality, ergativity, and transitivity

3.1. Constructions coding semantically transitive sentences.

I will not concern myself with semantically intransitive sentences which
have been exemplified above (cf. 1.3.), rather only semantically transitive
clauses, of which the ergative is one major type, will be investigated in more
detail. The ergative clause type has been amply exemplified above in section 1.3.,
the other four types will be introduced presently.

3.1.1. Passives.

There are two different kinds of passives in Chamorro: one is marked
with an -in- infix (henceforth the -IN-passive), the other is marked with a ma-
prefix (henceforth the MA-passive). Both background the Agent and foreground
the Affected Participant of the sentence in discourse. They will be discussed as
distinct constructions in this paper as they function in a slightly different way
pragmatically and differ also in one important semantic aspect. The -IN-passive
is used when the Agent of the sentence is singular, the MA-passive is used when
the Agent is plural or not known. As will be shown later on in the paper the
MA-passive occupies a different position on the hierarchy of topicality than the
-IN-passive. Moreover, the -IN-passive usually occurs with an overt Agent
whereas this is not the case with the majority of the MA-passives which are
often used as impersonal constructions. It is therefore necessary that the two
constructions be kept separate.

Since both passives are syntactically intransitive as they do have a subject
but not a direct object, they behave like ordinary intransitive verbs and agree

with the subject, i.e. the Affected Participant, in number regardless of the
number of the Agent. The singular is unmarked, the plural is indicated by the
prefix *man-* in the realis, the prefix *fan-* in the irrealis. Examples:

(46)   *Si*   *nana- hu*   *ts$_1$- in$_2$-   atgi$_1$ giäs*
         p.n.-unm.   mother-POSS.1s.   PASS$_2$-smile$_1$ p.n.-LOC
         tata- hu.
         father-POSS.1s.
         'My mother was smiled at by my father./ My father smiled at my
         mother.'

(47)   *Gwaha un   Amerikanu si   George   Tweed taotao Oregon*
         be   one   American p.n.-unm.   man
         ma- na'- atuk ni   tsamorro, ma- adzuda ni
         PASS-CAUS-hide c.n.-OBL Chamorro PASS-help   c.n.-OBL
         tsamorro.
         Chamorro
         'There was an American George Tweed, a man from Oregon, who
         was hidden and helped by the Chamorros.'

(48)   *Man-h$_1$-in$_2$- eŋaŋ$_1$ i   taotao.*
         PL-   PASS$_2$-startle$_1$ the   people
         'The people were startled.'

(49)   *Todu i   taotao   ni   man-gaigi   Guam   gwihi na   tiempu*
         all   the   people REL PL- be   there link. time
         man-ma-   tatpaŋi.
         PL- PASS- baptize
         'All the people that were in Guam at that time were baptized.'

Since both passives are semantically transitive as they have an Agent and an
Affected Participant in the underlying proposition they will be considered in
more detail in this paper. In particular, those passives with *overt Agents* will be
compared with other semantically transitive clauses according to the degree of
topicality of both the Agent and the Affected Participant. (cf. infra).

3.1.2. Antipassive.

Chamorro also has an antipassive construction which backgrounds the
direct object so that it becomes an Oblique NP or disappears altogether resulting
in a syntactically intransitive clause. The antipassive is formed by prefixing the
morpheme *man-* to the stem of the verb. Since the construction is syntactically

intransitive the antipassive verb exhibits the same kind of number agreement as the ordinary intransitive verb and the passives. In the singular the antipassive verb is unmarked but in the plural it is preceded by the prefix *man-* or *fan-* in the realis or irrealis respectively. Examples:

(50)   *I   peskadot   maŋonni'   (man+konni')   gwihan.*
        the   fisherman   A.P.-catch   fish
        'The fisherman catches/caught fish/a fish.'

(51)   *Man-man-nanaitai   lisadzu   kadda   pueŋi.*
        PL- A.P.-pray   rosary   every   night.'
        'They pray the rosary every night.'

The antipassive is an active construction in which the subject is most often agentive. Even though I will not be concerned directly with clauses which have no overt Affected Participant, antipassives of this sort appear as well in narrative discourse. The relationship between the antipassives with and without the overt Affected Participant needs to be investigated in more detail in the future.

3.1.3. The transitive -*UM*- contruction.

So far I have presented four types of semantically transitive constructions i.e. the ergative, two passives, and the antipassive. There is one other syntactic device which codes a proposition with both an Agent and an Affected Participant as subject and direct object respectively. This construction involves the infix -*um*-. It appears less frequently than the ergative construction but seems to refer to active events just as much as the ergative exemplified in 1.3. The verb in this particular transitive sentence type does not seem to exhibit any kind of agreement with the subject in my data. -*UM*- is used for both singular and plural transitive subjects. Examples:

(52)   *Si   Santa   Maria h_1-um_2-a'atan$_1$ i   tano dzän i*
        p.n.-unm. saint   Mary UM_2-protect$_1$ the   land and the
        tsamorro.
        chamorro
        'The Virgin Mary protects/protected the land and the Chamorros.'

(53)   *T_1-um_2 -atpaŋi$_1$ lahi-n   Mata'paŋ.*
        UM_2-baptize$_1$ son-link.   Mata'pang
        'He baptized Mata'pang's son.'

The infix -*um*- in the transitive sentence, used for both singular and plural sub-

jects in my data, has the same form as the singular agreement marker one finds
on ordinary intransitive verbs. The plural agreement marker in intransitive
clauses is *man-*. As of yet I have not seen the latter morpheme in transitive sentences. The relation between the transitive *-um-* and the intransitive singular
agreement marker is not clear to me yet and needs to be studied in more detail.

3.1.4. Ergative Construction.

The ergative is a realis clause type in which the verb agrees with the subject in person and number (cf. section 1.3. for an overview of the agreement
markers).

The direct object of the ergative has to refer to a specific entity which is not
necessarily definite. It has to be accompanied by a definite article *i* (unless
accompanied by certain case markers which presuppose the referential definiteness of the referent, e.g. case markers for proper names and pronouns) or the
indefinite article *un.* Whenever the direct object is non-referential, non-definite
not accompanied by an article the antipassive must be used. The matter is more
complex than presented here and the distribution and function of the article
system deserves a far more detailed study.
Examples:

(46)   *Ha- li'i'   un   patgun.*
         E.3s.-see   one   child
         'He saw a child.'

(47)   *Ha- dalallak esti i   taotao.*
         E.3s.-follow this the man
         'She followed this man.'

(48)   *Ma- gotdi   i   gaputuli-ñiha.*
         E.3pl.-tie   the hair-   POS3pl.

3.2. Methodology.

In this part of the paper the same quantitative method explained in section
2.2. above is used. In a pilot study on the same fifty pages of transcribed
Chamorro narratives, which provided the data base for the first part of this
paper, each Agent and Affected Participant of a semantically transitive clause
was subjected to only two of the measurements, viz. referential distance and
persistence. Below I will present the averages for both measurements for the two
main participants in each of the five semantically transitive constructions. In
part one we concluded tthat the syntactic coding devices of the NP's can be

ordered hierarchically. The measures for referential distance and persistence vary for each of these NP devices on the scale. For this reason I have computed the measures for Agents and Affected NP's in the five syntactic clause types according to the syntactic device used to code the NP's. Since other types of syntactic devices are underrepresented in my data or simply absent in some clause types, I will present only the results of the comparison between the Agents and the Affected Participants which are coded as definite full NP's or as ∅-anaphora or coded by verb-agreement. The overall measures will be given first. They include all types of syntactically coded Affected Participants and Agents and provide a good presentation of the overall average values for Agent and Affected Participant in all five constructions. These overall values are obviously skewed in favor of the most common syntactic device used to encode the Agent and Affected Participant in the different constructions under study but they provide a valid and important distributional schema for the five syntactic clause types in terms of the average degree of topicality of the two main participants in the proposition.

3.3. Numerical results and graphs.

The average value of the two measurements for both major participants in the five Chamorro constructions are presented below. The value for N denotes the amount of instances attested in the data. No values are given for the Affected Participant in the two last columns of the antipassive (table 9) since all Affected Participants in this construction are indefinite and non-referential NP's.

3.4. Discussion.

The results of this pilot study on a limited amount of data, viz. fifty pages of transcribed Chamorro narratives, are naturally somewhat tentative. However, as the curves show (graphs 6-11) there seems to be a fairly consistent correlation between the values for referential distance and persistence of at least the Affected Participant and the syntactic construction chosen by the Chamorro speaker. With the exception of the *MA*-passive we get a consistent rising cline for the measurement of referential distance for the Affected Participant moving from the *IN*-passive to the antipassive. The curves for the measurement of persistence show the inverse relation where the Affected Participant NP's have high persistence in the passive constructions, moving to no persistence in the Antipassive. The two clines suggest that the Affected Participants are highly continuous in passive constructions and become less continuous/less topical as one approaches the antipassive on the scale where one finds the in-

Table 9. Antipassive Construction

| | A. OVERALL RESULTS | | B. DEFINITE FULL NP'S | | C. VERB AGREEMENT/ ∅ - ANAPHORA | |
	AGENT	AFFECTED PART	AGENT	AFFECTED PART.	AGENT	AFFECTED PART.
REFEREN-TITAL DISTANCE	N = 7 1.86	N = 7 20.00	N = 1 7.00	—	N = 6 1.00	—
PERSIS-TENCE (DECAY)	1.29	0.00	0.00	—	1.50	—

Table 10. Ergative construction.

	A. OVERALL RESULTS		B. DEFINITE FULL NP'S		C. VERB AGREEMENT/ ∅- ANAPHORA	
	AGENT	AFFECTED PART	AGENT	AFFECTED PART.	AGENT	AFFECTED PART.
REFEREN-TIAL DISTANCE	N = 150 1.49	N = 150 4.35	N = 7 7.6	N = 95 8.56	N = 134 1.10	N = 32 1.38
PERSIS-TENCE (DECAY)	2.45	0.81	1.29	0.66	2.44	1.09

Table. 11. -*UM*- Construction.

	A. OVERALL RESULTS		B. DEFINITE FULL NP'S		C. VERB AGREEMENT/ Ø - ANAPHORA	
	AGENT	AFFECTED PART	AGENT	AFFECTED PART.	AGENT	AFFECTED PART.
REFEREN-TIAL DISTANCE	N = 16 2.88	N = 16 3.00	N = 4 7.50	N = 8 4.25	N = 10 1.00	N = 4 1.25
PERSIS-TENCE (DECAY)	0.63	0.81	0.25	0.50	0.70	0.50

Table 12. *-IN-* Passive

| | A. OVERALL RESULTS | | B. DEFINITE FULL NP'S | | C. VERB AGREEMENT/ ∅- ANAPHORA | |
	AGENT	AFFECTED PART.	AGENT	AFFECTED PART.	AGENT	AFFECTED PART.
	N = 16	N = 16	N = 7	N = 3	N = 7	N = 12
REFERENTIAL DISTANCE	4.06	1.38	7.00	1.67	1.14	1.42
PERSISTENCE (DECAY)	1.31	2.00	0.57	2.33	2.29	2.08

Table 13. *MA*- Passive.

	A. OVERALL RESULTS		B. DEFINITE FULL NP'S		C. VERB AGREEMENT/ ∅ - ANAPHORA	
	AGENT	AFFECTED PART	AGENT	AFFECTED PART.	AGENT	AFFECTED PART.
	N = 9	N = 9	N = 6	N = 5	N = 2	N = 4
REFERENTIAL DISTANCE	6.33	3.55	5.30	5.60	2.50	1.00
PERSISTENCE (DECAY)	0.56	1.44	0.50	1.00	0.50	2.00

Graph 6. Distance of Affected Participant and Agent:
Overall Results.

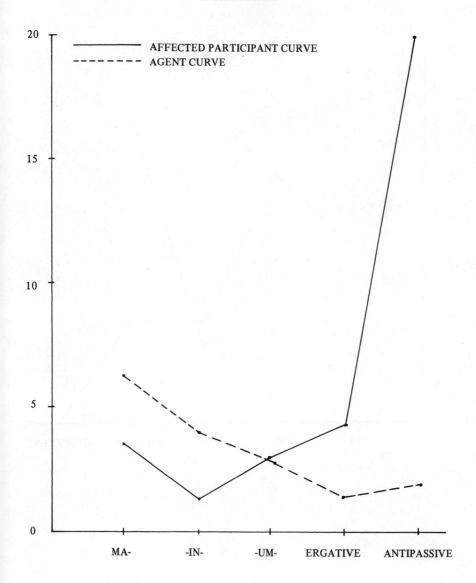

Graph 7. Persistence of Affected Participant and Agent:
Overall Results.

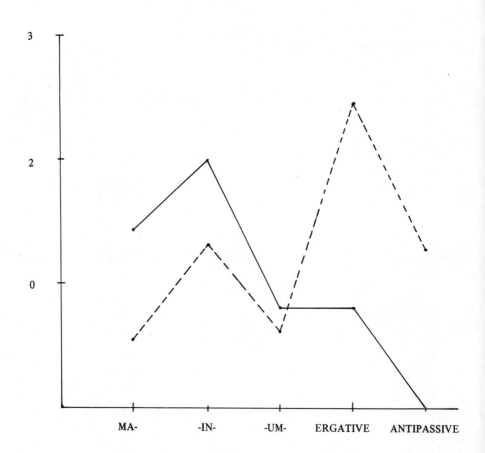

Graph 8. Distance of Affected Participant and Agent:
Definite Full NP's.

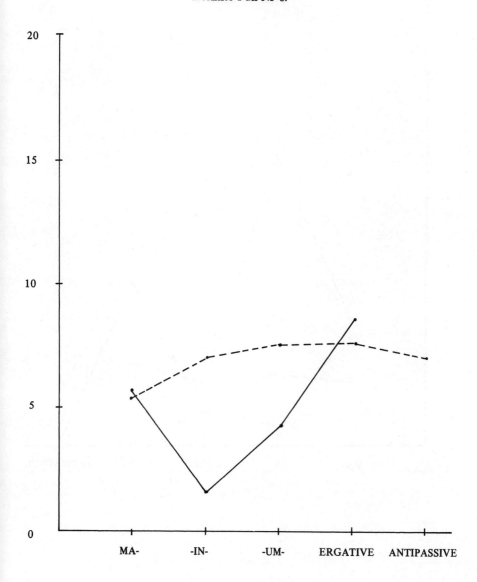

Graph 9. Persistence of Affected Participant and Agent:
Definite Full NP's.

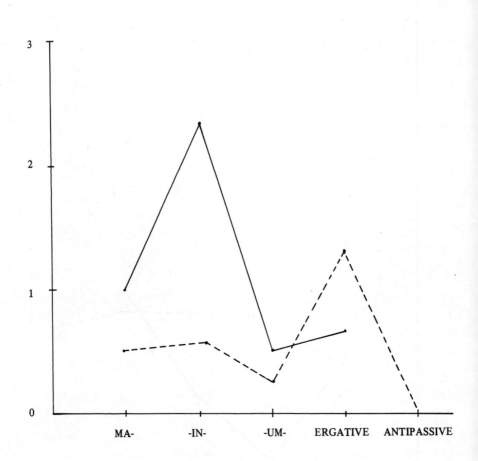

Graph 10. Distance of Affected Participant and Agent:
Verb Agreement/∅-Anaphora.

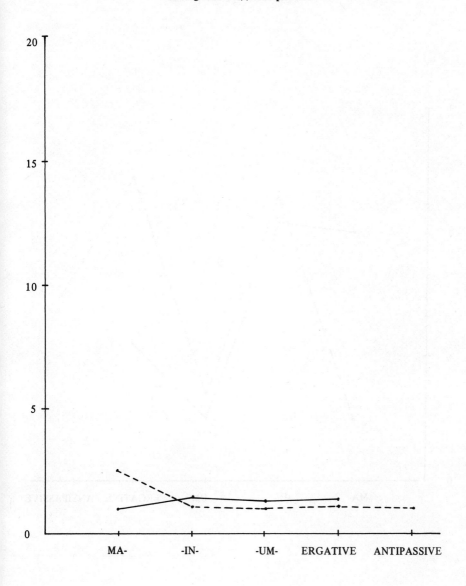

Graph 11. Persistence of Affected Participant and Agent:
Verb Agreement/∅-Anaphora.

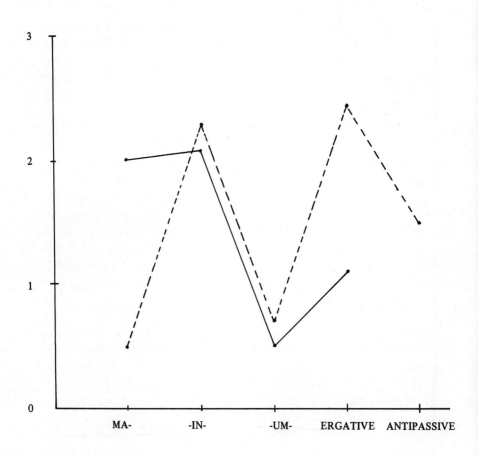

MA-   -IN-   -UM-   ERGATIVE   ANTIPASSIVE

definite/non-referential Affected Participant NP's. The overall measurements show that those constructions with highly topical Affected Participants have Agent NP's which are less continuous/less topical.

As is the case in most languages (cf. Givón 1979, 1983 (ed.) this volume, among others) we may observe that in Chamorro the most continuous/most topical argument in the sentence will tend to be selected as the syntactic subject. (cf. also part I of this paper).

As I shall discuss in more detail below, the -UM- construction seems to provide some sort of middle ground where the Agent and the Affected Participant NP's have a fairly equal degree of topicality Because of the limited data some of the values presented in tables 9-13 are not very representative as I will explain below. However, one may expect that the upgrading of the counts by extending the data base will iron out these difficulties and still support the tentative findings presented in this paper.

3.4.1. The Ergative.

On the basis of frequency — 150 ergative clauses as opposed to 48 instances of the four other syntactic types combined — we may conclude that the active ergative is the most basic construction in Chamorro narratives, i.e. the most common way in which the Chamorro speaker presents his information about actions and events. The Chamorro speaker is thus more inclined to present the Agent as the NP with the highest referential continuity/highest topicality. The measure of referential distance for the Agent is relatively low, the measure of persistence relatively high and the reverse is the case for the Affected Participant in this construction.

From a universal point of view it is not surprising that the construction which assigns highest topicality to the Agent is the most frequent in narrative discourse in a particular language since it has been established that such discourse on the whole is universally Agent oriented.

One would equally expect that a speaker uses the most basic construction to convey foreground information (cf. Hopper and Thompson 1980). This prediction is borne out by the facts presented in table 14 below. The ergative construction being the most frequent one, is used in a significant majority of the foregrounded clauses in the narratives, viz. 76.47 % of the cases.

To decide whether a clause is foregrounded or not I relied on two basic principles outlined and exemplified in more detail in Hopper and Thompson (1980):

FOREGROUNDED CLAUSES

ERGATIVE	78	76.47 %
ANTIPASSIVE	1	.99 %
-IN-PASSIVE	9	8.82%
MA-PASSIVE	6	5.88%
-UM- CONSTRUCTION	8	7.84 %
TOTAL	102	100.00 %

Table 14. Distribution of syntactic constructions
over foregrounded clauses in
Chamorro narratives.

a) the clause has to give information about main events in the narrative, thus contributing to the "backbone" or "skeleton" of the text.
b) the informational content of the clause has to be presented in sequential order.

It has been established that background clauses are not ordered relative to one another and may be moved with respect to the foregrounded clauses in the narrative (Hopper and Thompson 1980, inter alia).

We can make the additional observation (cf. table 7) that the highest topical element in the ergative construction, viz. the Agent, tends to be coded syntactically by verb agreement/$\emptyset$-anaphora alone (83 % of the instances). The less topical element, viz. the Affected Participant, is most often coded as a full definite NP (63.3 % of the cases). With the exception of the *-UM-* construction (cf.3.4.3. below) subjects in all other constructions are higher in topicality/ continuity than the second argument in the clause. Thus we find that the Agent is more topical in the antipassive and the ergative constructions whereas the Affected Participant is more topical than the Agent in both passive constructions.

3.4.2. The Antipassive.

The antipassive serves a specific pragmatic function in Chamorro when it is used as a semantically transitive sentence. This can be read off of graphs 6 and 7 streightforwardly. The Affected Participant has the maximum value of 20 for referential distance indicating that it is *new* in the discourse. The additional fact that the Affected Participant has zero persistence reflects its *non-referential-*

ity, non-specificity. The antipassive in Chamorro goes one step further than the antipassive in Inuktituk (Eskimo) as described by Kalmár (1979, 1980) (see introduction). There the antipassive indicated pragmatically that a new, not necessarily indefinite item was being introduced into the discourse. Antipassives in Eskimo introduce new possibly topical referents in oblique object position whereas the oblique object of the Chamorro antipassive has the lowest possible degree of topicality. One would thus expect the informational value of these sentences to the rest of the narrative to be fairly low. This expectation is borne out by the fact that antipassives have a high tendency to occur in backgrounded clauses, i.e. in general they are not involved in the main line of the thematic development of the narrative. Compare the following:

	Ergative		Antipassive with Affected Participant	
foregrounded clauses	78	52 %	1	14 %
backgrounded clauses	72	48 %	6	86 %
Total	150	100 %	7	100 %

table 15. Distribution of Ergative and Antipassive
in foregrounded and backgrounded clauses

The sharp contrast in distribution between the ergative and antipassive in backgrounded and foregrounded clauses may provide an explanation for the relatively lower topicality of Agents in antipassives as opposed to the ergative. Even though this needs to be checked out more carefully, one suspects that the topicality of elements in foregrounded clauses will be higher than that of elements in backgrounded clauses.

The pragmatic function of the antipassive in Chamorro then is to mark those Affected Participants in narrative discourse which are non-referential have the lowest degree of topicality. This function of antipassives with Affected Participants is in fact compatible with the function of those without. The objectless antipassives provide the extreme case of introducing non-topical elements. At the same time they provide the majority of antipassives in my data:

objectless antipassives	16	69.57 %
antipassives with objects	7	30.43 %
Total	23	100.00 %

table 16. Distribution of antipassives with and without
objects in discourse.

As we shall see below, there is a converse situation with the *MA*-passive at the
other end of the scale of syntactic constructions, where the prototypical, most
frequent *MA*-passive is agentless.

3.4.3. The *-UM-* construction.

The *-UM-* construction is the third active clause type I found in the data.
According to my informant in all these sentences — when taken in isolation —
the *-UM*-infix can be replaced by the appropriate ergative agreement marker.
This construction, like the ergative one, occurs with equal frequency in backgrounded and in foregrounded clauses (50 % in both cases).

Topping (1973: 243-244) attempted to explain this construction as an "actor
focus construction" similar to the focus constructions one finds in some Philippene languages which have also been called topicalization constructions:

> "The *actor focus* construction in Chamorro is used when the focus (or emphasis)
> is on the actor. (The actor is the one that performs the action, and is usually the sub-
> ject of the sentence). The actor focus involves the use of emphatic pronouns and the
> actor infixes -UM- and MAN-. (. . .) If the actor of the sentence is expressed by a
> proper name, the emphatic pronoun may be omitted. (. . .) The prefix MAN- is used
> instead of the -UM- when the object is indefinite."

The *MAN-* prefix Topping refers to here is the antipassive marker which I discussed earlier. Of the 16 examples of *-UM-* constructions in my data, none of
them were accompanied by an emphatic pronoun and only two had a proper
name referent. These inaccuracies on Topping's part most likely stem from
looking at example sentences obtained through direct elicitation or looking at
sentences in isolation without their proper discourse context.

If the *-UM-* construction really were a Philippene type actor topic construction, one would expect the Agent to be of markedly higher topicality/continuity
than the Affected Participant and obviously this is not borne out by the facts
(cf. table 11 and graphs 6-11). Rather, it seems to be the case that the Agent and

Affected Participant in this construction have roughly the same degree of topicality. Compared to the ergative and the two passive constructions (tables 10, 12, and 13) where there is a significant difference in the values for referential distance and persistence of Agent vs. Affected Participant, we do not find such a gap between the values of Agent and Affected Participant in the -*UM*-construction. The differences are insignificant and could go either direction, slightly in favor of the Agent or slightly in favor of a more topical Affected Participant. The seemingly large difference in values for referential distance between the two major participants when coded as definite full NP's is due to the fact that one of the Agents in four instances has a referential distance of 20, is introduced as a new element in the narrative. This high value for one of very few instances is likely to boost the average value up. One may expect that one such infrequent high value will be less signficant for the average outcome in a larger data base. Without this value 20 for referential distance for one of the Agents the average value for the three remaining instances comes out to be 3.33.

One may observe that this active construction is markedly less frequent than the ergative in narrative discourse (16 instances as against 150). This is not surprising since Agents on the whole tend to be more topical than any other argument in the clause in narratives. The instances where this is not the case are rare and are specially marked in Chamorro.

The observation that the -*UM*- construction tends to mark pragmatically Agents and Affected Participants which have roughly the same degree of topicality has a semantic correlate in Chamorro. The same construction is used for reciprocals where both arguments in the clause have equally important semantic roles in the event. Example:

(54)   *Esti i   palao'an um-a- sodda' dzăn   un pobli na*
         this   the   woman UM-REC-meet with/and a   poor link.
         hobbin taotao.
         young   man
         'This woman met (with) a poor young man.'

The -*UM*- construction marks the third step down on a cline of relative topicality of both Agent and Affected Participant. In the antipassive the Agent is the only topical argument, the Affected Participant being non-specific/non-referential, hence non-topical. The ergative pragmatically codes highly topical Agents and Affected Participants which are relatively low in continuity or topicality. The -*UM*- construction in turn presents Agents and Affected Partici-

pants with equal degree of topicality. As the next step on the cline one expects a
construction in which the Affected Participant is the most topical argument
in the clause.

3.4.4. The passive constructions.

Both passives code information units in which the Affected Participant
is more topical than the Agent. A discussion of both will necessarily involve a
comparison in order to find the function in which they differ.

Both constructions appear with equal frequency in backgrounded and foregrounded clauses (-*IN*-passive 55 % and 45 % respectively; *MA*-passives 57 % and
43 % respectively) so that on the thematic level of the narrative there seems to
be no marked difference between the two.

The limited amount of data again are responsible for the skewed outcome of
the numerical results. For the -*IN*-passive in column C, table 12, it seems that
on the whole the Agent is more topical than the Affected Participant since the
average values of referential distance and persistence are slightly lower and
higher respectively than those of the Affected Participant. The close match in
low values for distance is expected since both are syntactically coded by verb
agreement/∅-anaphora. A similar close match for persistence is against our expectations. Again, one out of seven instances of Agents has an exceptionally
high value of 8 for the measurement of persistence, which increased the average
value of the remaining 6 instances by about 70%, Without this one instance the
the average of the remaining 6 instances would have been remarkable lower,
viz. 1.33. The high value for persistence for this particular instance indicates
a switch reference in the narrative. The speaker abandoned the Affected Participant referent of the -*IN*- passive and continued talking about the Agent referent
for the next 8 clauses. Again, one may expect that increasing the data base will
level out the exceptionally high average values.

The graphs and columns with numeric results do not present all the facts.
They give the counts of those passive clauses alone where both an Agent and an
Affected Participant are present. The overall distribution of passives with and
without an Agent in the data is as follows:

	with Agent		without Agent*		total
-*IN*- passives	16	80 %	4	20 %	20
MA- passives	9	15 %	53	85 %	61

table 17. Distribution of passives with and without Agents.

Moreover, the Agents in the *-IN*-passives are all singular, previously identified referents. Three out of four 'unexpressed Agents' in this construction referred to particular events which were presented in the discourse immediately preceding the clause with the *-IN*-passive, stating the effect of the event on the Affected Participant. All of the Agents expressed in the *MA*-passive were plural Agents and often, when the Agent was not expressed it could be interpreted as referring to a group of people mentioned earlier in the narrative such as the Japanese, the Spaniards, the Americans or the Chamorro people in general. The distribution of the *-IN*- passives and the *MA*-passives according to whether the Agent is singular or plural respectively may provide an explanation for the fact that the overall results seem to suggest that the Agent in the *MA*-passive, even though consistently less topical than the Affected Participant in the same clause, is also on the whole less topical than the Agent of the *-IN*-passive, since singular referents tend to be more topical than plural referents in narratives (cf. Givón 1976, among others).

The *-IN*-passive has been called a Goal focus construction by Topping (1972: 245) where Goal refers to the direct object of a verb. Unlike the wrongful comparison of the *-UM-* construction with the Agent topic constructions, the *-IN*-passive is very similar to the Patient topic or focus constructions one finds in the Philippene languages.

Givón (1981) identified three universal features of passives:

i) a non-agent argument assumes clausal topic function instead of the subject/agent,

ii) the identity of the agent is supressed, creating an impersonal construction,

iii) the clause is detransitivized, becomes more stative, less transitive.

It seems clear that both the *-IN*-passive and the *MA*-passive share the first and in part the third function. They both take the plural subject agreement marker MAN- which is the intransitive plural agreement marker in Chamorro. In addition, the *MA*-passive codes function ii) as well, so that presumably the *MA*-passive is the more passive construction of the two.

The prefix *MA-* of the passive may very well be related historically to the third person plural agreement marker *MA-* of the ergative, so that in fact we have a historical remnant which indicates that the event was or is controlled by a plural Agent, not necessarily, in fact most unlikely present in the discourse. The fact that the passive with plural Agents, rather than the one with a singular Agent, should give rise to an impersonal construction is not surprising since — as already mentioned above — singular referents are more topical than plural referents.

3.5. Conclusion.

The five different constructions in Chamorro for semantically transitive sentences code different points along a continuum which marks the functional domain of relative topicality of both the Agent and Affected Participant in clauses. The measure for distance in grahp 6 for the overall results suggest almost a complete reverse relationship between the topicality of the Agent in relation to the Affected Participant as one moves down from the antipassive to the *MA-passive*. The term antipassive seems most appropriate in this context as its function is exactly the opposite of the function of the "most" passive *MA*-construction: the antipassive totally suppresses the Affected Participant which is non-referential or not mentioned at all. The *MA*-passive prototypically suppresses the Agent, which is less topical than in the *-IN*-passive or not mentioned at all. The antipassive in addition is syntactically marked as an intransitive sentence, evident from the fact that it takes the prefix *MAN-* to indicate plural agreement as do both passives. Syntactic transitivity involves a cline with two possible extremes, the antipassive and the *MA*-passive on opposite ends. There are two separable semantic characteristics involved in syntactic transitivity:

   i) the presence of an Agent who initiates the event,

   ii) the presence of an identifiable object that registers the bulk of the impact,
      i.e. an Affected Participant.

There seems to be an additional pragmatic condition for syntactically transitive sentences:

   iii) the Agent NP has to be more referentially continuous/more topical than
      the Affected NP in the clause.

The ergative construction in Chamorro is the best candidate to be syntactically transitive as all the characteristics apply. The antipassive is a very active construction but either involves a non-referential, hence non-identifiable Affected Participant, or no object at all. The *-IN*-passive involves both an Agent and an Affected Participant but the latter surpasses the former in degree of topicality. Both passives foreground an Affected Participant referent over the Agent, thus concentrating more on the resulting *state* than on the action itself. The *MA*-passive prototypically includes only the Affected Participant and is thus the more stative of the two. All three constructions then, the antipassive and both passives, do not abide by the three conditions stated above and are thus marked as syntactically intransitive constructions.

The *-UM-* construction violates the third condition but whether it is syntactically transitive or intransitive needs to be investigated in full detail. There is probably a historical relationship between the *-UM-* infix of the semantically transitive clause and the -*UM*- singular agreement marker for intransitive subjects. In the semantically transitive constructions in my data -*UM*- is used for both singular and plural subjects.

Even though one can observe some overlap in the functions of these five different syntactic constructions — especially in individual instances — the tendencies unearthed in this study through the quantitative analysis are important and may be schematically presented as follows:

Construction type	Degree of Topicality
antipassive	Agent >> Affected Participant (the Affected Participant gets suppressed completely)
ergative	Agent > Affected Participant
-*UM*- construction	Agent = Affected Participant
-*IN*- passive	Agent < Affected Participant
MA- passive	Agent << Affected Participant (the Agent prototypically is suppressed)

BIBLIOGRAPHY

Bentivoglio, P. (1983) — "Continuity and Discontinuity in Discourse: A Study on Latin-American Spoken Spanish." In this volume.

Bolinger, D. (1979) — "Pronouns in Discourse." In: T. Givón (ed.).

Chafe, W.L. (1979) — "The Flow of Thought and the Flow of Language." In: T. Givón (ed.).

Chung, S. (1978) — "Transderivational Relationships in Chamorro Phonology." Ms, University of California, San Diego.

————— (1979) NSF Proposal: Chamorro Syntax.

————— (1980) — "Transitivity and Surface Filters in Chamorro." In: Hollyman and Pawley (eds) — Studies in Pacific Languages and Cultures. Auckland Linguistic Society of New Zealand.

Costenoble, H. (1940) — Die Chamorro Sprache. The Hague, M. Nijhoff.

Creider, L.A. (1979) — "On the Explanation of Transformations." In: T. Givón (ed.).

De Lancey, S. (1981) — "An Interpretation of Split Ergativity and Related Patterns." *Language*, vol. 57, nr. 3.

Dixon, R.M.W. (1972) – The Dyirbal Language of Northern Queensland. Cambridge University Press, Cambridge.

––––– (1979) – "Ergativity". *Language*, vol. 55.

Duranti, A. and E. Ochs (1979) – "Left-Dislocation in Italian Conversation." In: T. Givón (ed.).

Erteschik-Shir, N. (1979) – "Discourse Constraints and Dative Movement." In: T. Givón (ed.).

Fox, A. (1983) – "Topic-Continuity and Discontinuity in Early Biblical Hebrew." In this volume.

García, E.C. (1979) – "Discourse without Syntax." In: T. Givón (ed.).

Gibson, J. (1977) – "Reflexivization in Chamorro." Ms., U.C.S.D.

––––– (1981) – Clause Union in Chamorro and in Universal Grammar. Ph.D. Dissertation, University of California, San Diego.

Givón, T. (1976) – "Topic, Pronoun and Grammatical Agreement." In: C. Li (ed.) – Subject and Topic. Academic Press, New York.

––––– (1979) – "From Discourse to Syntax: Grammar as a Processing Strategy." In: T. Givón (ed.) (1979)

––––– (ed.) (1979) – Discourse and Syntax. Syntax and Semantics, Vol. 12, Academic Press, New York.

––––– (1980) – Ute Reference Grammar. Ute Press, Ignacio, Colorado.

––––– (1981a) – "Typology and Functional Domains." *Studies in Language,* 6:2.

––––– (1982b) – "Direct Object and Dative Shifting: Semantic and Pragmatic Case." In: F. Plant (ed.) – Objects. Academic Press, New York.

––––– (1982) – "Topic-Continuity in Discourse: The Functional Domain of Switch Reference." In: Haiman, J. (ed.) – Switch Reference. Typological Studies in Language, Vol. 2, Amsterdam, J. Benjamins. (This volume)

Hawkinson, A, and Hyman, L. (1974) – "Natural Topic Hierarchies in Shona." Studies in African Linguistics, nr.4.

Hopper, P.J. (1979) – "Aspect and Foregrounding in Discourse." In: T. Givón (ed.).

Hopper, P.J. and Thompson, S.A. (1980) – "Transitivity in Grammar and Discourse." *Language*, vol. 56, nr. 2.

Horne, M. (1977) – Possessive Pronouns in Chamorro. Ms, University of California, San Diego.

Jaggar, P. (1983) – "Topic-Continuity in Hausa Narrative." In this volume.

Kalmár, I. (1979) – Case and Context in Inuktitut (Eskimo). Canadian Ethnology Service, Paper nr. 49. National Museums of Canada, Ottawa.

—————— (1980) – "The Antipassive and Grammatical Relations in Eskimo." In: F. Plank (ed.) – Ergativity. Towards a theory of grammatical relations. Academic Press, New York.

Latta, F. (1972) – "On Stress and Vowel Harmony in Chamorro." *Oceanic Linguistics*, 11, 140-151.

Newman, J. (1977) – Chamorro Vowels. Ms, University of California, San Diego.

Ochs, E. (1979) – "Planned and Unplanned Discourse." In: T. Givón (ed.)

—————— (1980) – Ergativity in Samoan Child Language. Ms, University of Southern California.

Safford, W. (1903-1905) – The Chamorro Language of Guam. *American Anthropologist*, 5:289-311, 6:95-117, 7:305-319.

Silverstein, M. (1976) – "Hierarchy of Features and Ergativity." In: R.M.W. Dixon (ed.) – Grammatical Categories in Australian Languages. Canberra, Australian Institute of Aboriginal Studies.

Topping, D. (1968) – "Chamorro Vowel Harmony." *Oceanic Linguistics*, 7.

—————— (1973) with the assitance of B. Dungca. – Chamorro Reference Grammar. University of Hawaii Press, Honolulu.

Topping, D., Ogo, P. and Dungca, B. (1975) – Chamorro – English Dictionary. University of Hawaii Press, Honolulu.

APPENDIX: Sample Text

Abbreviations used:

ABS: absolutive
COMP: complimentizer
DAT: dative
E: ergative subj.-verb agreement
FUT: future marker
INT: intensifier
Irr: irrealis subj.-verb agreement
link.: linking particle
LOC: locative
NEG: negative particle
OBL: oblique
PAS: passive

pl.: plural
PL: plural subj.-verb agreement
p.n.: proper name
POS: possessive
Q: question indicator
REC: reciprocal
RED: reduplication (progressive)
REL: relativizer
SING: singular subj.-verb agreement
s.: singular
unm.: unmarked

Two Lovers' Point

Esti   na   istoria   istoria-n   dos   taotao   ni   gos   um- a-   gwaidză
this   link.   story   story- link.   two   people   REL   INT   SING-REC-love
'This story is the story about two people who loved each other very'

lao   puedi   unu   pobli   i   otru   riku   ti   siña   man-a'asagwa.
but   because   one   poor   the   other   rich   NEG   can   PL- marry-RED
'much but because one was poor and the other rich they could not get married.'

Anai   didikiki   esti   i   palao'an   si   nana-   ña   dzăn   si
when   small-RED   this   the   woman   p.n.-unm.   mother-POS3s.   and   p.n.-unm
'when this woman was still a small girl her mother and father'

tata-   ña   gwaha   hatuŋu-ñiha   na   riku   lokwi'   dzăn   man-gai   lahi.
father-POS3s.   have   friend-POS3pl.   REL   rich   also   and   PL- have son
'had friends who were rich also and they had a son.'

Pues   ma- arekla   ginin   i   dos   saina   na   dzangien   dankulu   i
then   PAS-arrange   from the   two   parents   COMP   when   big   the
'Then it was arranged between the two sets of parents that when'

dos   păra   u-   man-a'asagwa.   Pues   anai   suttettera   hulu'   esti
two   FUT   IRR3pl-PL- marry-RED   then   when   single-RED   up   this
'two grew up they would get married. Then when the girl was still growing up'

palao'an   um-   a- sudda'   dzăn   un   pobli   na   hobin   taotao   dză
woman   SING-   REC-meet   with   one   poor   link.   young   man   and
'she met a poor young man and the two fell very much in love'

gos   um-   a- gwaidză   i   dos   gigun um- a- li'i.   Lao   anai   ha-
INT   SING-   REC-love   the   two   when SING-REC-see   but   when E3s-
'when they saw each other.   But when she'

saŋan-i   si   tata-   ña   na   malagu'   gwi'   na
tell- DAT   pn.unm.   father-POS3s.   COMP   want   ABS3s.   COMP
'told her father that she wanted to marry with this man,'

u-   asagwa   dzăn   esti   na   taotao,   man-lalalu'i   nana   dzăn
IRR3s-marry   and   this   link.   man   PL- mad   the mother   and
'her mother and father were mad'

i	tata	dzăn	ma-	saŋan-i	na	ilek-ñiha:	"Ti	siña	hao
the	father	and	E3pl-	tell-	DAT	COMP say-	POS3pl	NEG can	ABS2s.

'and told her: "You cannot marry this man'

un-	asagwa	esti	na	taotao	sa'	esta	gwaha	un	taotao
E2s.	-marry	this	link.	man	because	already	be	one	man

'because there is already a man of our choice'

in- adzik-	mami	păra	asagwa-	mu."	Anai sigi	mo'na	i
NOM-choose-POS1pl		for	husband."	-POS2s.	when keep	far	the

'for your husband." As time went on the

tiempu	ti	siña	ma-	tsapak	i	dos	dzăn mas	um-	a-
time	NEG	can	PAS-	detach	the	two	and more	SING-REC-	

'two could not be separated and the two loved each other'

gwaidză	i	dos	dzăn esti	i	pobli na	taotao.	Dzăn anai	um-	a-
love	the	two	and this	the	poor link.	man	and	when	SING-REC-

'even more, she and this poor man. And when she met with '

li'i'	dzăn esti	i	păra dipotsi-	hi	asagwa-	ña,	ha-	tuŋu'
see	and this	the	for supposed-	INT	husband-	POS3s.	E3s.-	know

'the husband which was intended for her, the woman'

i	palao'an na	maseha	tai	manu	malago'-ña	si
the	woman COMP	regardless	how	much	want-	POS3s. p.n.-unm.

'knew that regardless of how much her father wanted'

tata- ña	ti	siña ha-	asagwa	esti	otru na	taotao	sa'
father-POS3s.	NEG	can E3s.-	marry	this	other link.	man	because

'her to, she could not marry this man because she did not like him'

ti	dză- ña	dză	ti	ha-	sodda'	gi	korason-ña	na
NEG	like- POS3s.	and	NEG	E3s.	find	LOC	heart-	POS3s. COMP

'and she could not find it (the love) in her heart and'

maseha	tai	manu	na	tempu	ti	siña	u-	gwaidză. Tai
regardless	how	much	link	time	NEG	can	IRR3s.-	love none

'regardless of how much time elapsed she would not be able to love him. There'

gwihi   i   agwaidză   esti   i   otru   na   taotao.
there   the   love   this   the   other   link.   man
'was no love for this other man.'

Anai ma- arerekla   păra i   fandaŋgu   k-um-   untrata i   dos
when PAS- arrange-RED   for   the   wedding   SING- promise the   two
'When the wedding was being arranged the two promised that'

na   po   u-   a-   sudda' taftataf   gi   egga'an antisdi   u-
COMP   FUT IRR3s.- REC- meet   early-RED   LOC morning before   IRR3s.
'they would meet each other very early in the morning'

hanao   păra i   gima'dzu'us   dză   păra u-   kwentus i dos.
-go   to   the   church   and   FUT IRR3s.- talk   the two.
'before she would go to the church and the two would talk.'

Pues anai k-um-   untrata na   antisdi u-   hanao   păra i
then   when SING-promise COMP   before   IRR3s.- go   to   the
'Then they promised that — before she would go to the church — '

gimadzu'us păra u   hanao   i   dos gwătu   gi   kantu-n   tasi
church   FUT IRR3s. -go   the   two   there   LOC edge-link.   sea
'the two would go to the edge of the sea'

dză   păra u-   spia kao siña   u-matai   i   dos antisdi
and   FUT IRR3s.- look Q   can   IRR3s.-die the   two   before
'and figure out whether they could both die before she would'

u-   asagwa esti i   otru   na   taotao. Pues anai ma- arerekla
IRR3s.-marry this the   other   link. man   then when PAS- arrange-
'marry this other guy. Then when the church was being'

*   i   gima'dzu'us   gi   egga'an um-   ekakkat hudzum gi*
RED the   church   LOC morning SING-slow-RED out   LOC
'arranged in the morning she sneaked out of the'

gima' dză   h-um-   anao hulu' ha- dalallak   esti i   taotao   ni
house and   SING-go up   E3s-follow-RED this   the   man   REL
'house and climbed up and followed this poor man and'

'i   pobli dzã h-um- anao hulu' i   dos gi   kantu-n   tasi dzã
the   poor and   SING-go up   the two LOC edge- link. sea and
'the two climbed up together to the edge of the sea and'

ma- gotdi i   gaputulu-niha   dzã g-um- aloppi hudzum esta papa
E3PL-tie the hair-   POS3pl and SING- jump   out   ?   down
'they tied their hair together and jumped out down into the ocean'

gi   tasi dzã a-   punu siha.
LOC sea   and REC-kill   ABS3pl
'and they killed each other.'

Pues esta   pa'gu na   tiempu esti   na   lugat ma- fa'na'an   dos
then already now link. time   this   link. place PAS-name-RED two
'Up to this time this place has been called the two lovers'

um- a-   gwaidzã pat "Two   Lovers' Point".
? - REC-lover   or   "Two   Lovers' Point"
'or "Two Lovers' Point".'

INDEX OF NAMES

n the TYPOLOGICAL STUDIES IN LANGUAGE (TSL) series the following volumes have been published thus far, and will be published during 1984:

1. HOPPER, Paul (ed.): *TENSE-ASPECT: BETWEEN SEMANTICS & PRAGMA-TICS.* Amsterdam, 1982.

2. HAIMAN, John & Pam MUNRO (eds.): *PROCEEDINGS OF A SYMPOSIUM ON SWITCH REFERENCE, Winnipeg, May 1981.* Amsterdam, 1983.

3. GIVÓN, T. (ed.): *TOPIC CONTINUITY IN DISCOURSE: A QUANTITATIVE CROSS-LANGUAGE STUDY.* Amsterdam, 1983.

4. CHISHOLM, William, Louis T. MILIC & John GREPPIN (eds.): *INTER-ROGATIVITY: A COLLOQUIUM ON THE GRAMMAR, TYPOLOGY AND PRAGMATICS OF QUESTIONS IN SEVEN DIVERSE LANGUAGE, Cleveland, Ohio, October 5th 1981 - May 3rd 1982.* Amsterdam, 1984.

5. RUTHERFORD, William E. (ed.): *LANGUAGE UNIVERSALS AND SECOND LANGUAGE ACQUISITION.* Amsterdam, 1984.

6. HAIMAN, John (ed.): *ICONICITY IN SYNTAX. Proceedings of a Symposium on Iconicity in Syntax, Stanford, June 24-6, 1983.* Amsterdam, 1984.

7. CRAIG, Colette (ed.): *NOUN CLASSES AND CATEGORIZATION. Proceedings of a Symposium on Categorization and Noun Classification, Eugene, Ore. October 1983.* Amsterdam, 1984.

8. SLOBIN, Dan I. (ed.): *ASPECTS OF SYNTAX, SEMANTICS, AND DISCOURSE STRUCTURE IN TURKISH* (working title). *Proceedings of a Conference on Turkish Linguistics, held at Berkeley, May 1982.* Amsterdam, 1984.